AF474003

REMARKABLE SNEAKERS

Ammo Dong

SHOTS, STORIES AND DETAILS

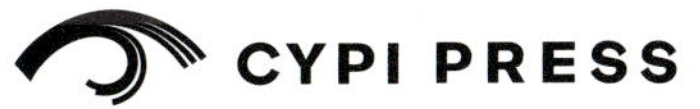

CYPI PRESS

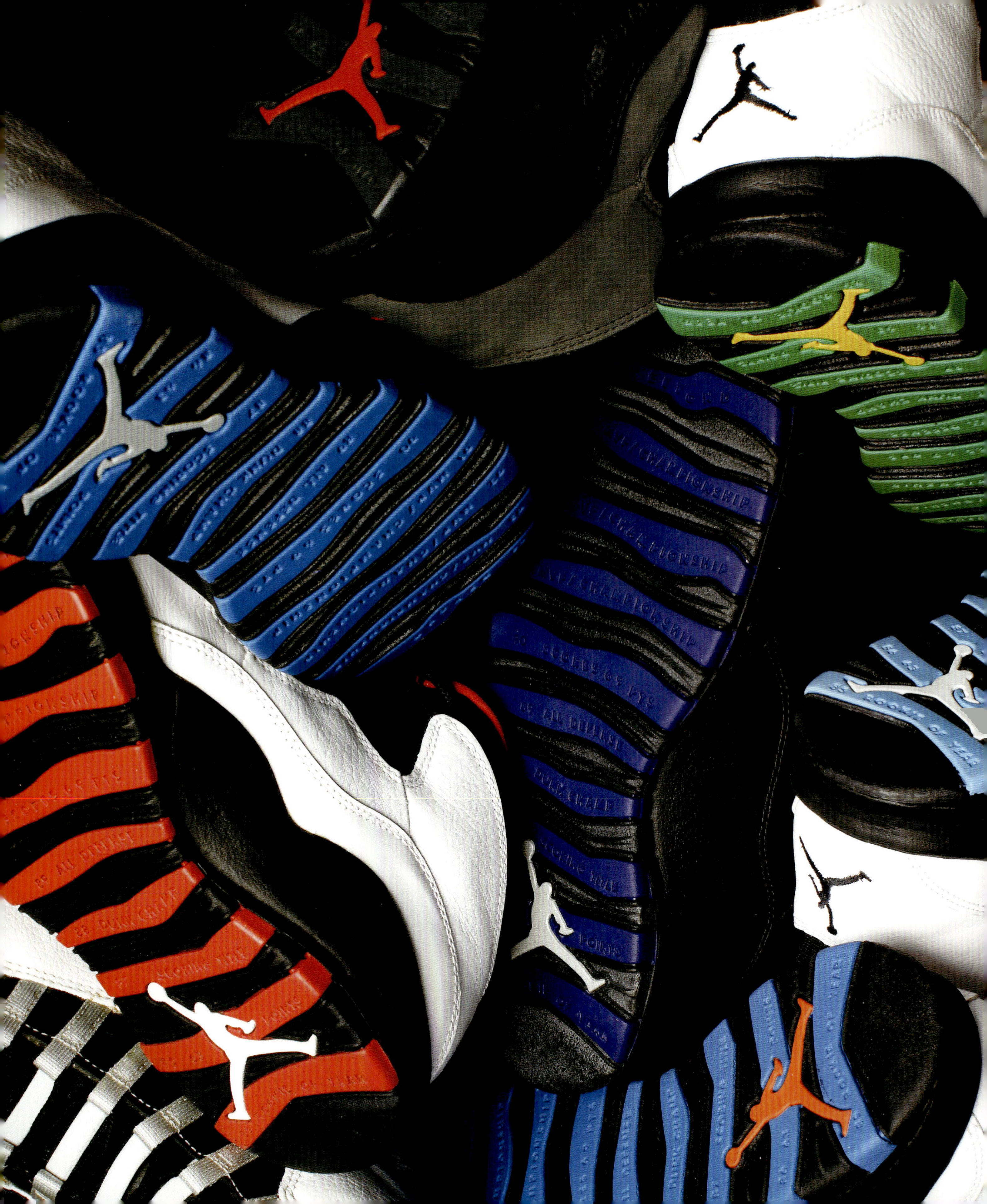

ROOKIE OF YEAR
SCORING TITLE

I have captured several thousand pairs of sneakers in my camera,
and collected several hundred pairs in my closet,
but I dare not say,
I know everything about the sneaker culture.
This book offers an intimate look into a wide variety of sneakers,
with each chapter dedicated to a specific topic,
intending to offer some insights into the culture behind the shoes.

CONTENTS

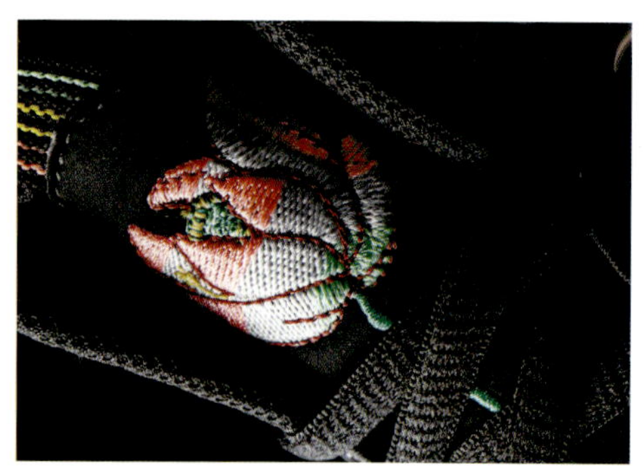

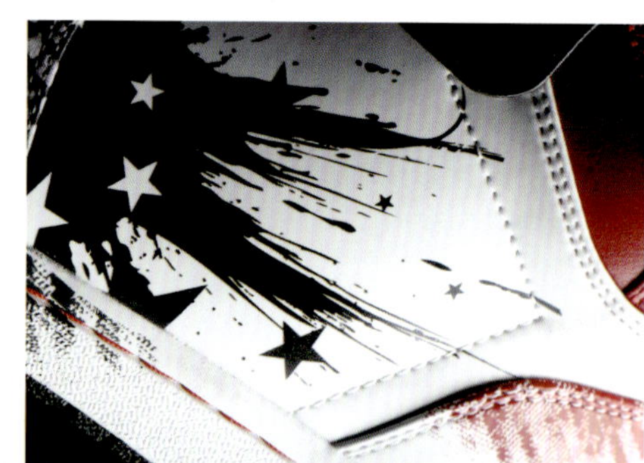

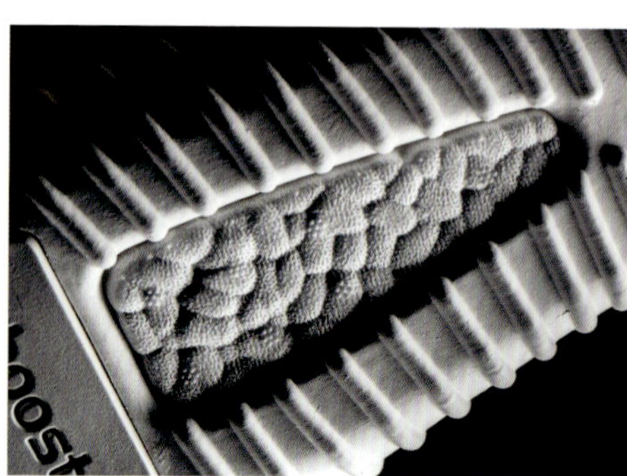

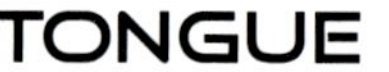

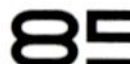

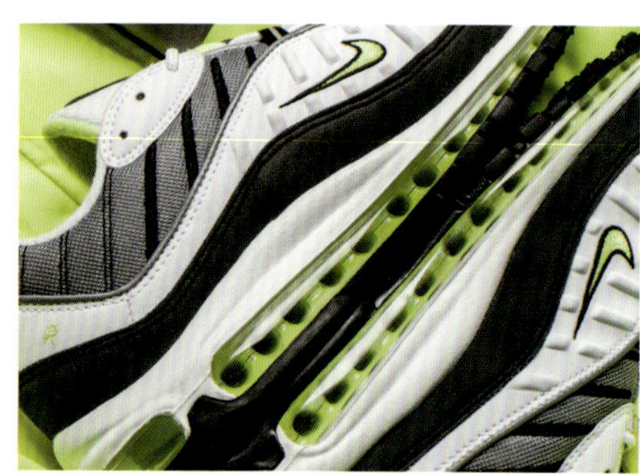

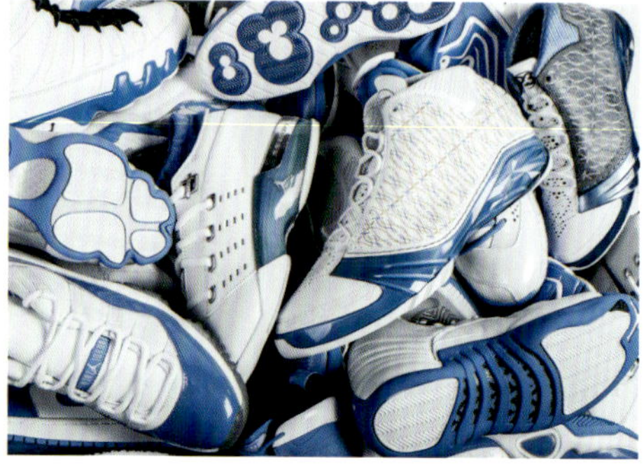

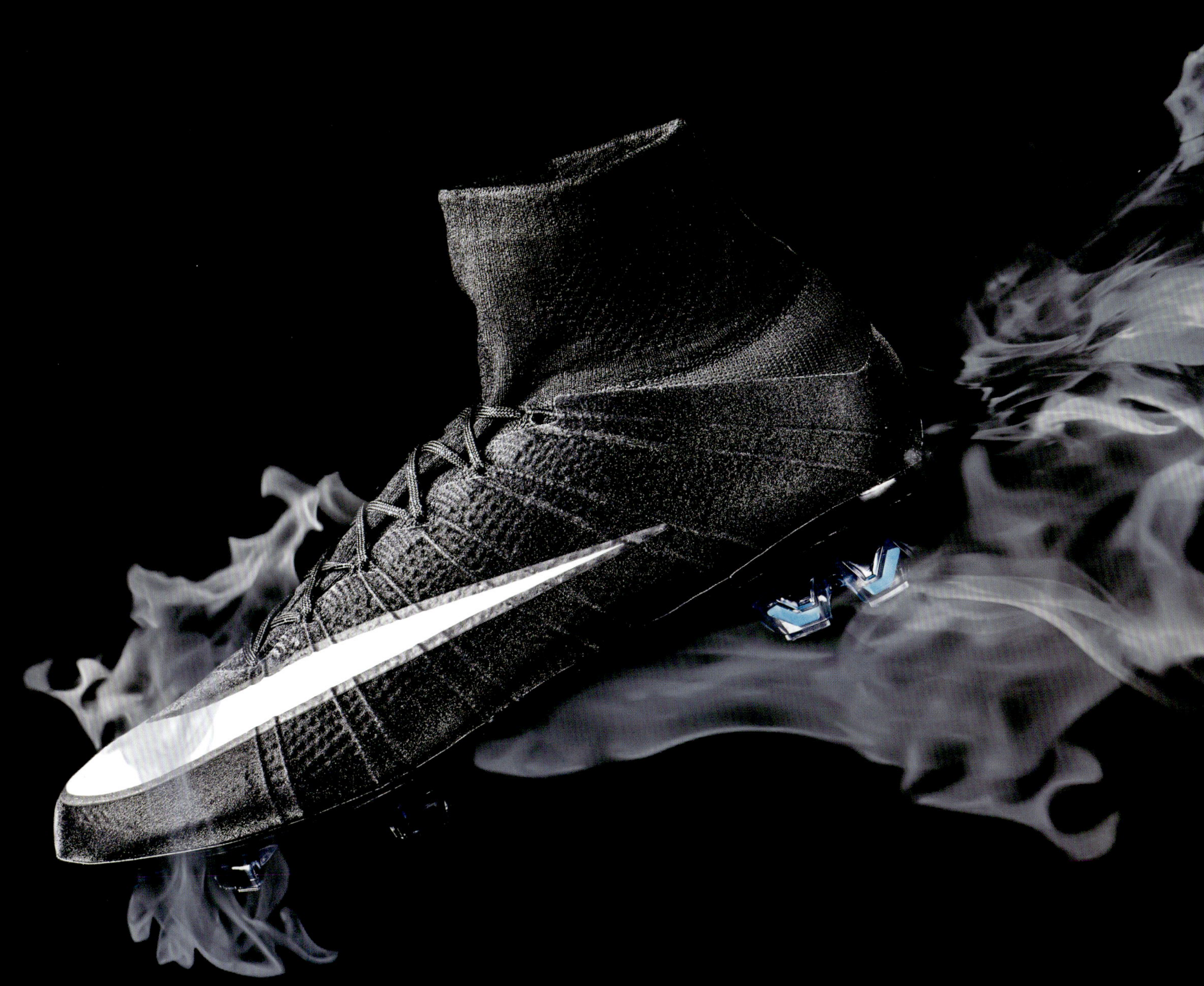

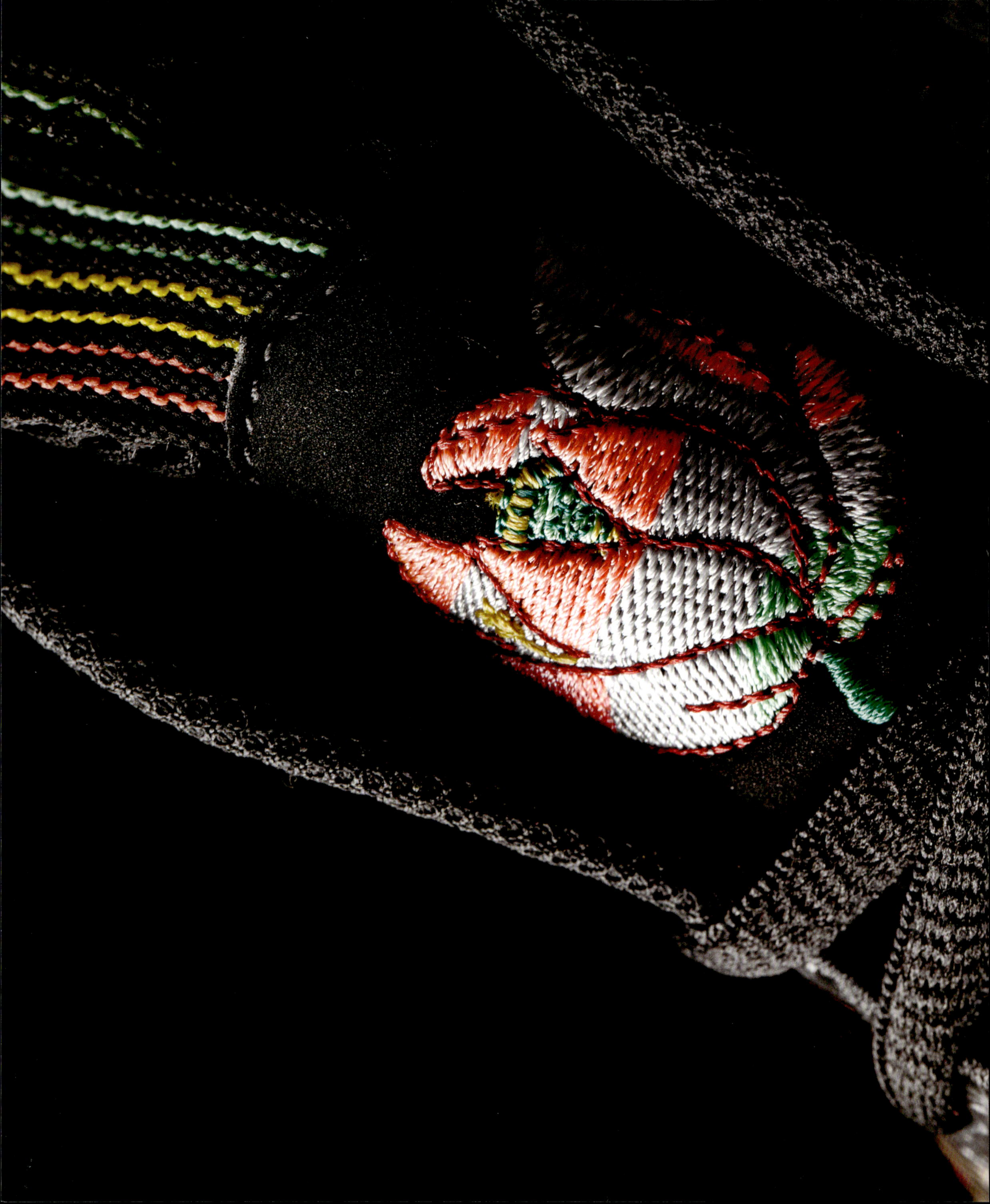

In recent years there has been a diversified trend in appearances and functions of shoe tongues, a key part of our running shoes.

TONGUE

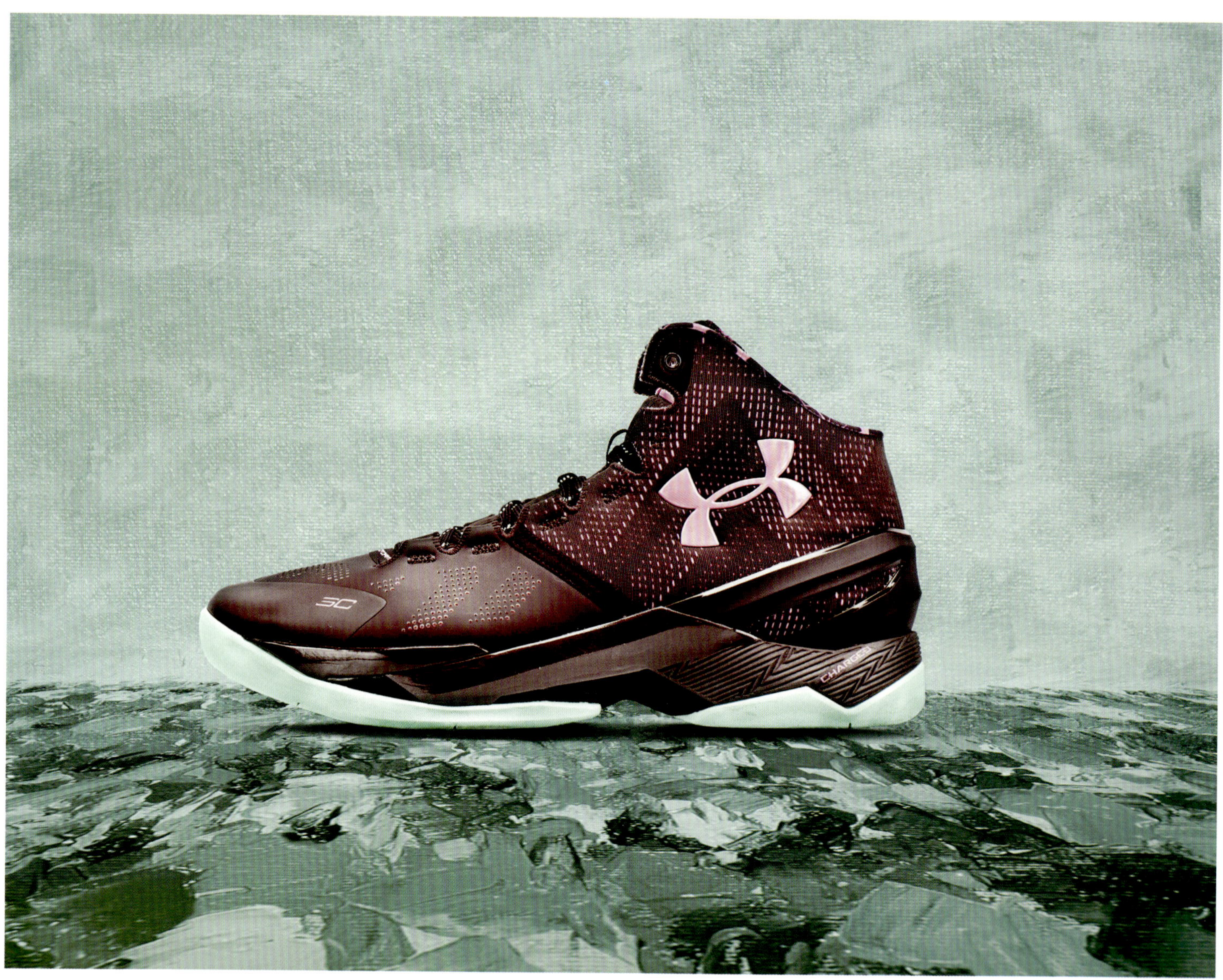

UNDER ARMOUR CURRY TWO [BHM]

Launched in early 2016 and designed by Dave Dombrow, UNDER ARMOUR CURRY TWO [BHM] uses a major color to commemorate the Black History Month. It's the first time that Curry Two has used maroon as the main color, symbolizing exiled black slaves. Its green outsole symbolizes "storming out of the shackles and showing bravery in a new world."

Details

The tongue has the initials of Stephen Curry and a "30" on it.

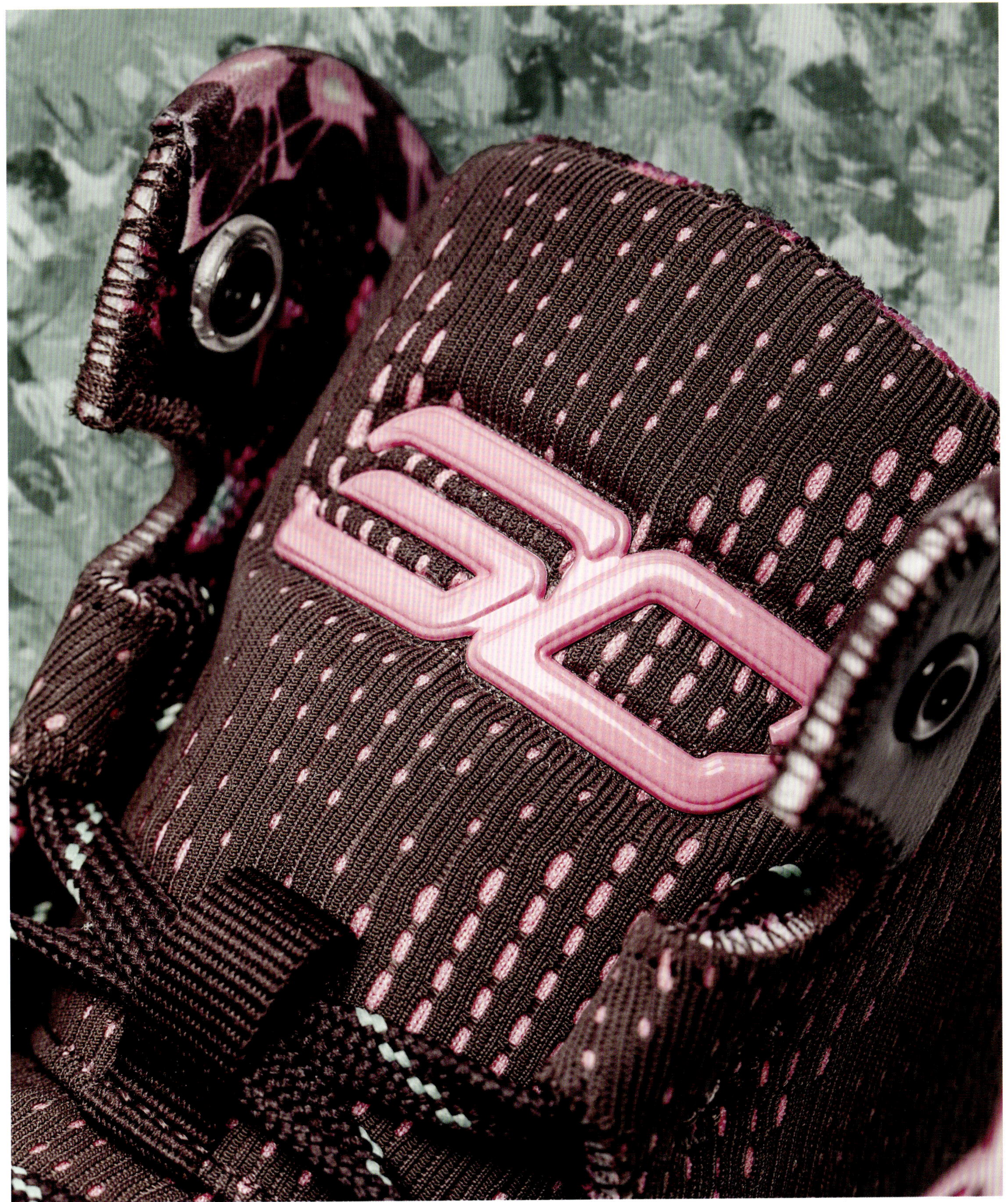

Details

The towel-material tongue is a distinctive feature of the Air Jordan 8. The Jumpman logo cuts the round zone into three parts, a classic and well-received tongue design.

AIR JORDAN 8 RETRO [AQUA]

Designed by Tinker Hatfield and released in 1993, it is the eighth signature shoe of Michael Jordan. MJ wore it during the 1993 All-Star Game. The signature picture below shows the 2007 replica, which differs from the original one in color choices (including the tongue, upper, outsole and insole).

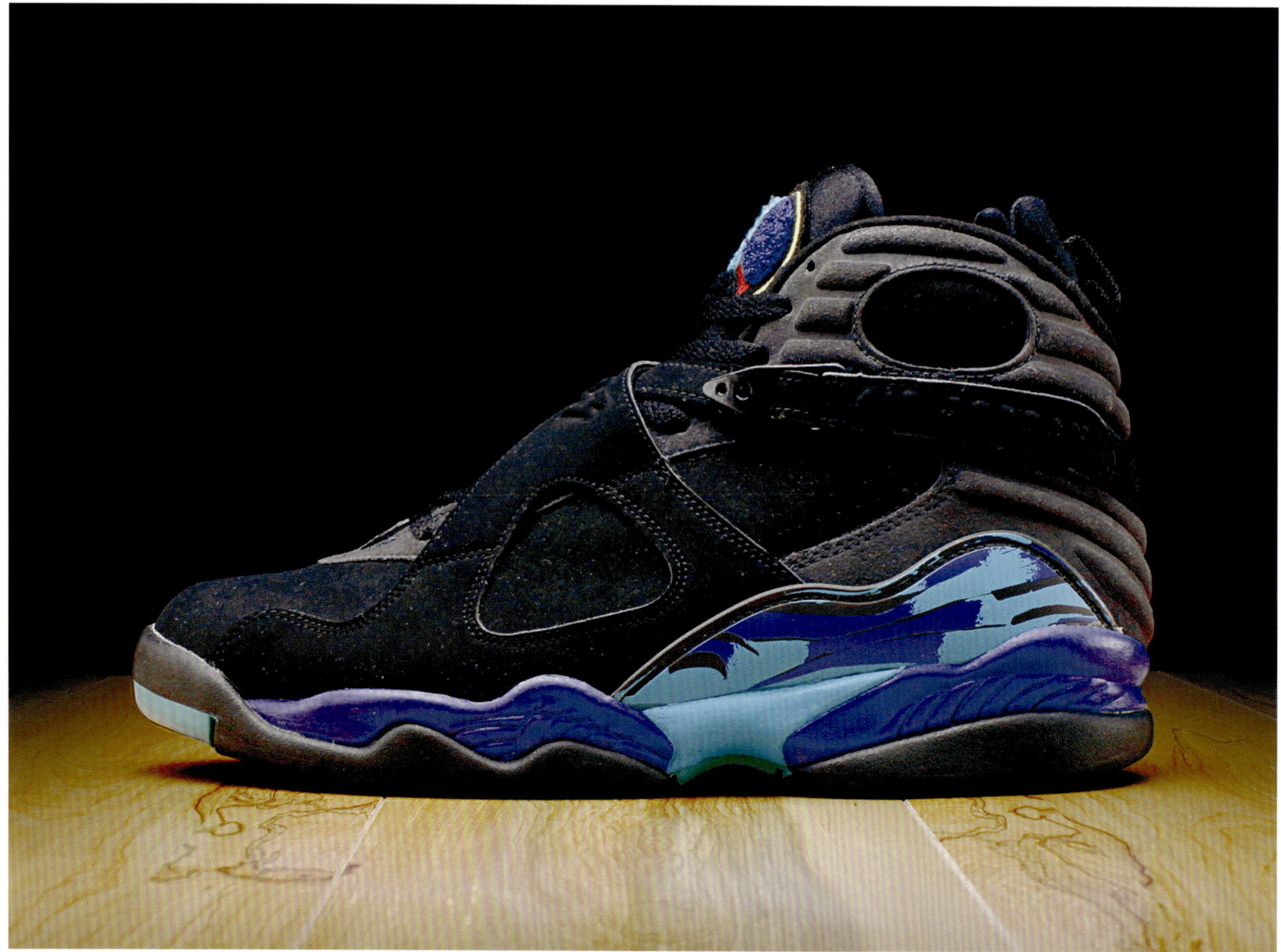

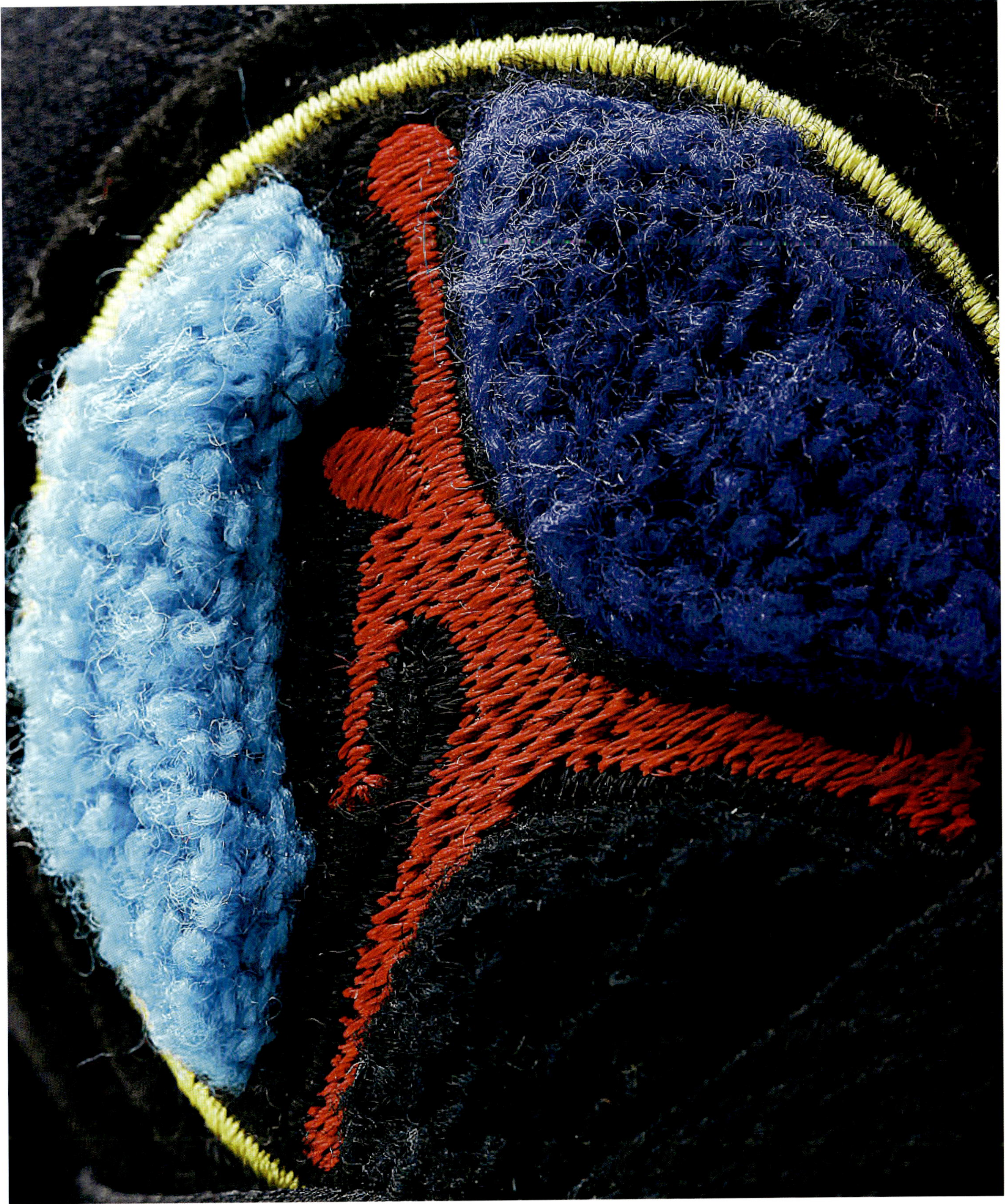

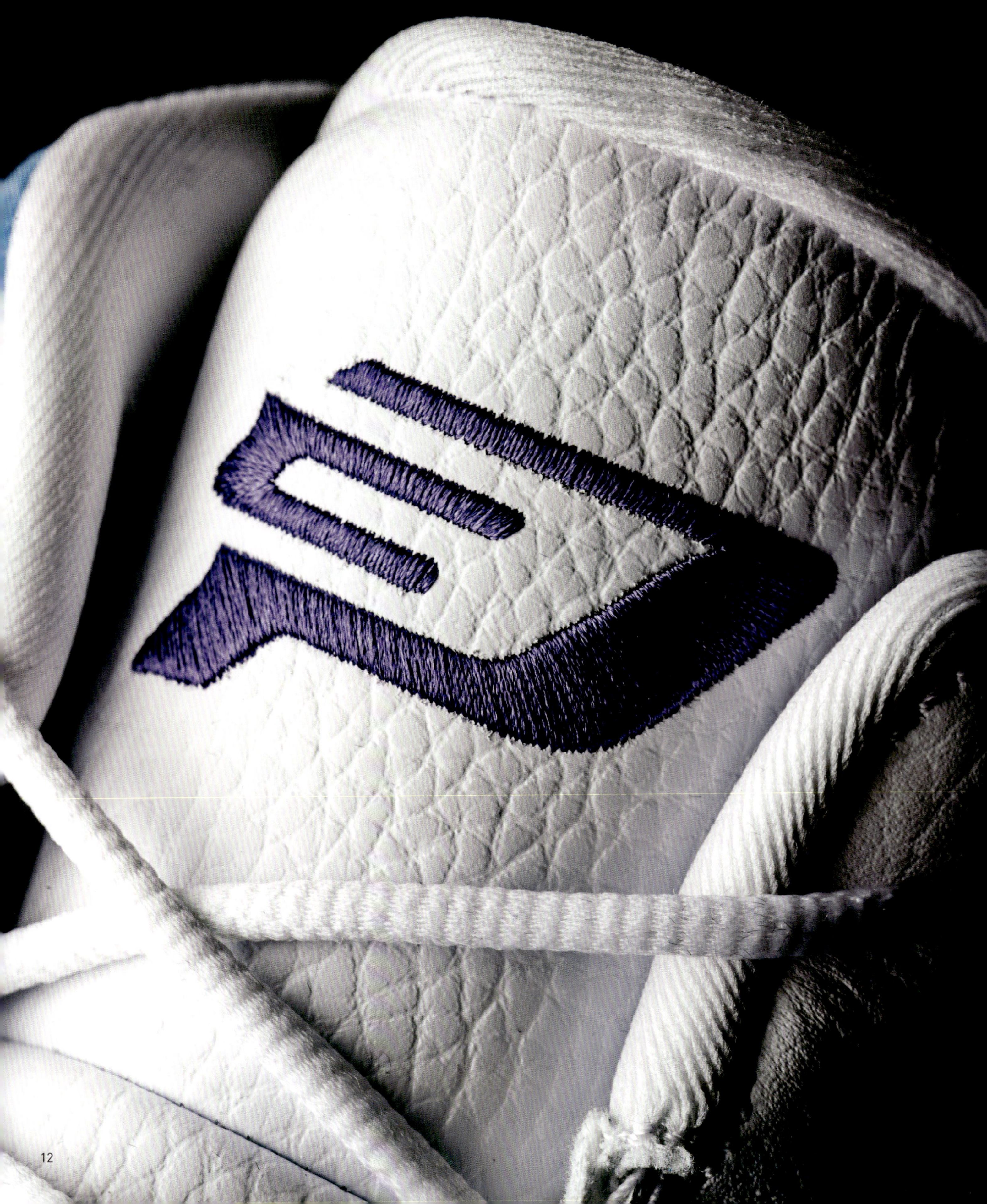

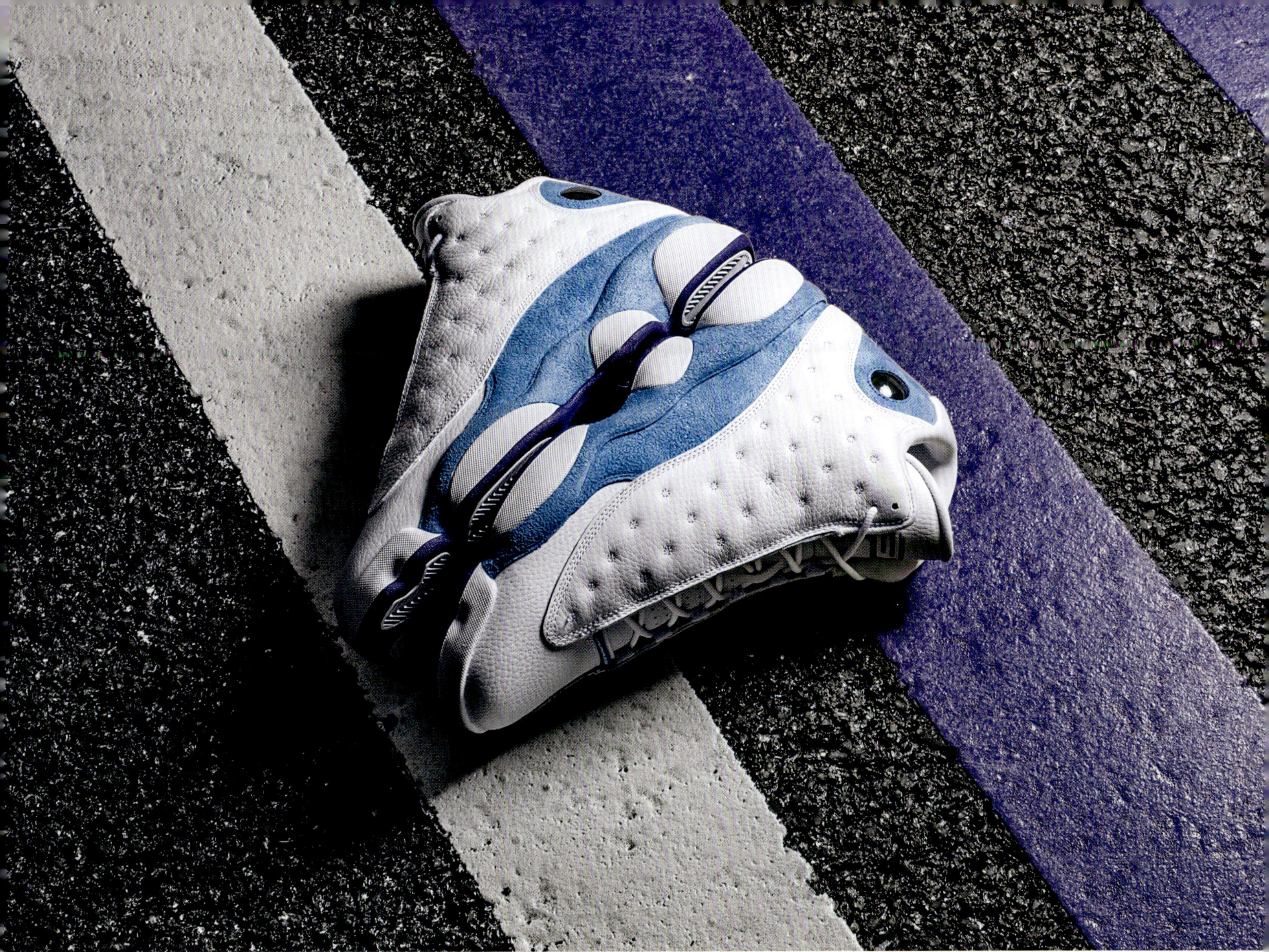

AIR JORDAN 13 RETRO CP PE [HOME]

Released exclusively in China and designed by Tinker Hatfield, it chose teal, the primary color of Charlotte Hornets — a team largely owned by Micheal Jordan.

Details

The initials of Chris Paul and the number of 3 are embroidered in the tongue.

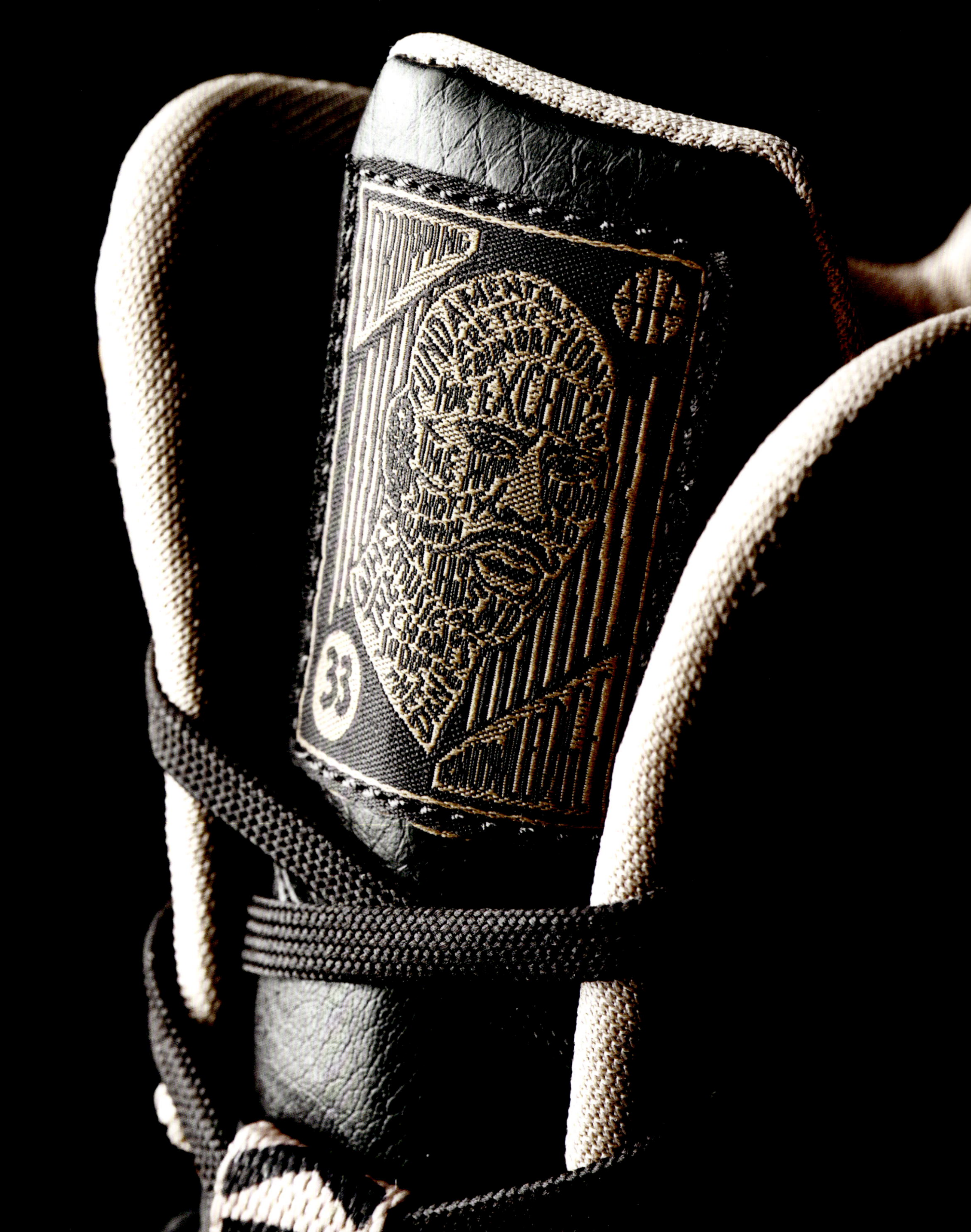

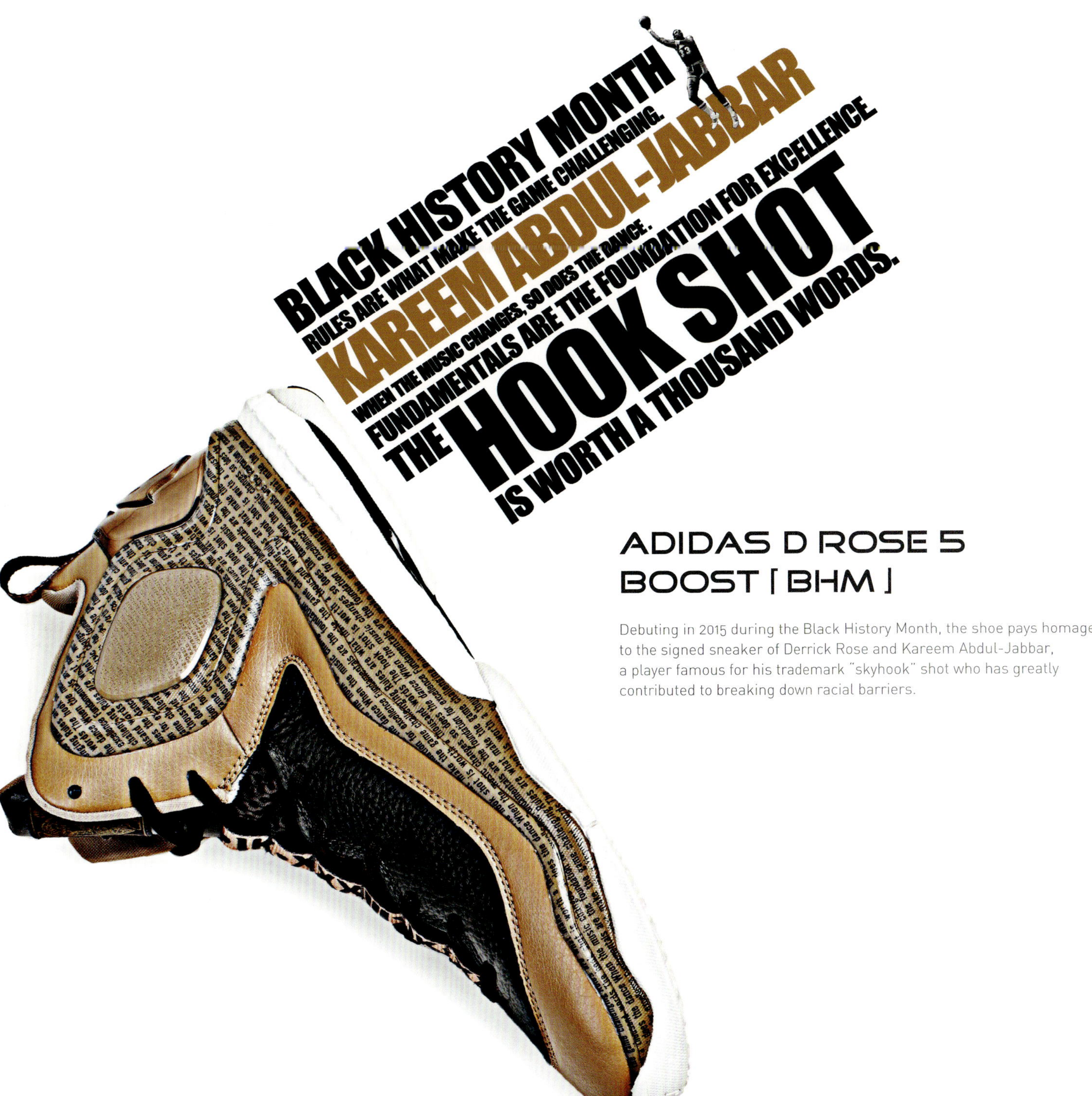

ADIDAS D ROSE 5 BOOST [BHM]

Debuting in 2015 during the Black History Month, the shoe pays homage to the signed sneaker of Derrick Rose and Kareem Abdul-Jabbar, a player famous for his trademark "skyhook" shot who has greatly contributed to breaking down racial barriers.

Details

With the avatar of Kareem Abdul-Jabbar in the tongue, the theme of the shoe is "The Hook Shot Is Worth a Thousand Words." The number "69/75" on the inside of the tongue refers to the six seasons in a row when he was with Milwaukee Bucks as a rookie player.

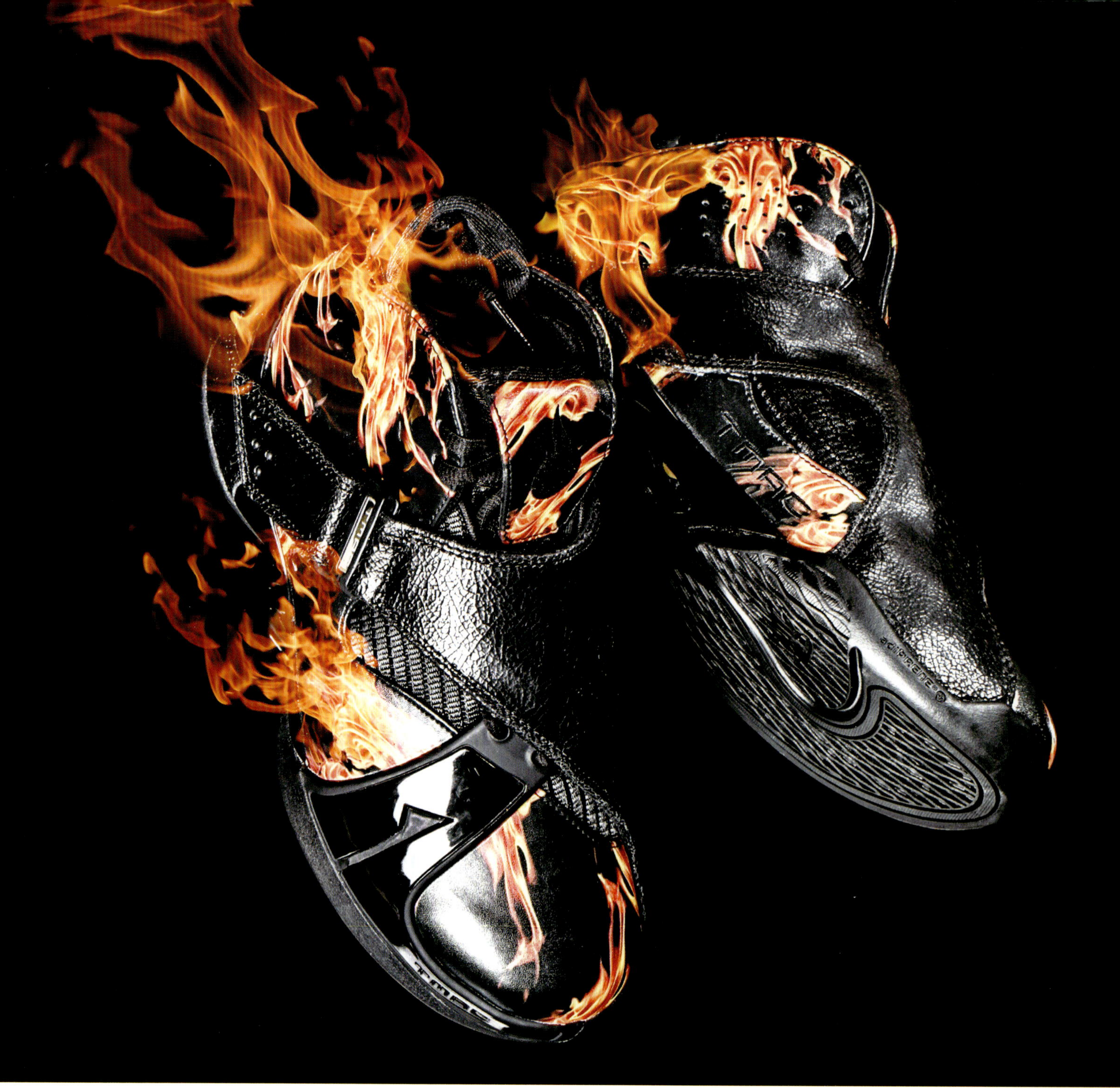

ADIDAS T-MAC 5 [FIRE]

This limited edition release of 1,172 pairs of shoes on the Chinese mainland was inspired by the tear-jerker adidas T-Mac 5 commercial. Besides this "He's on Fire" pair, there is also a "It Starts Raining" pair.

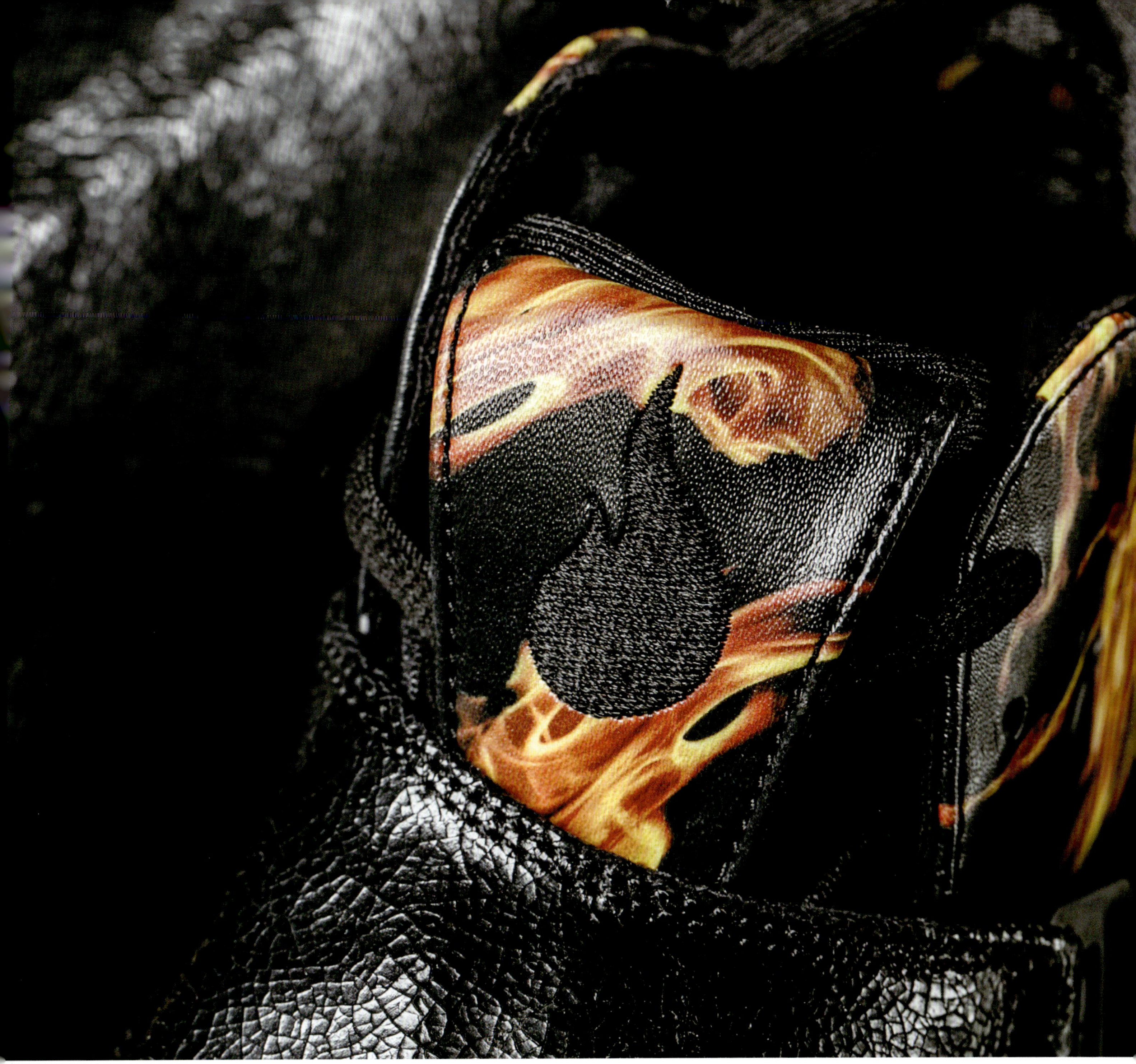

Details

A flame logo on the tongue highlights the theme – He's on Fire.

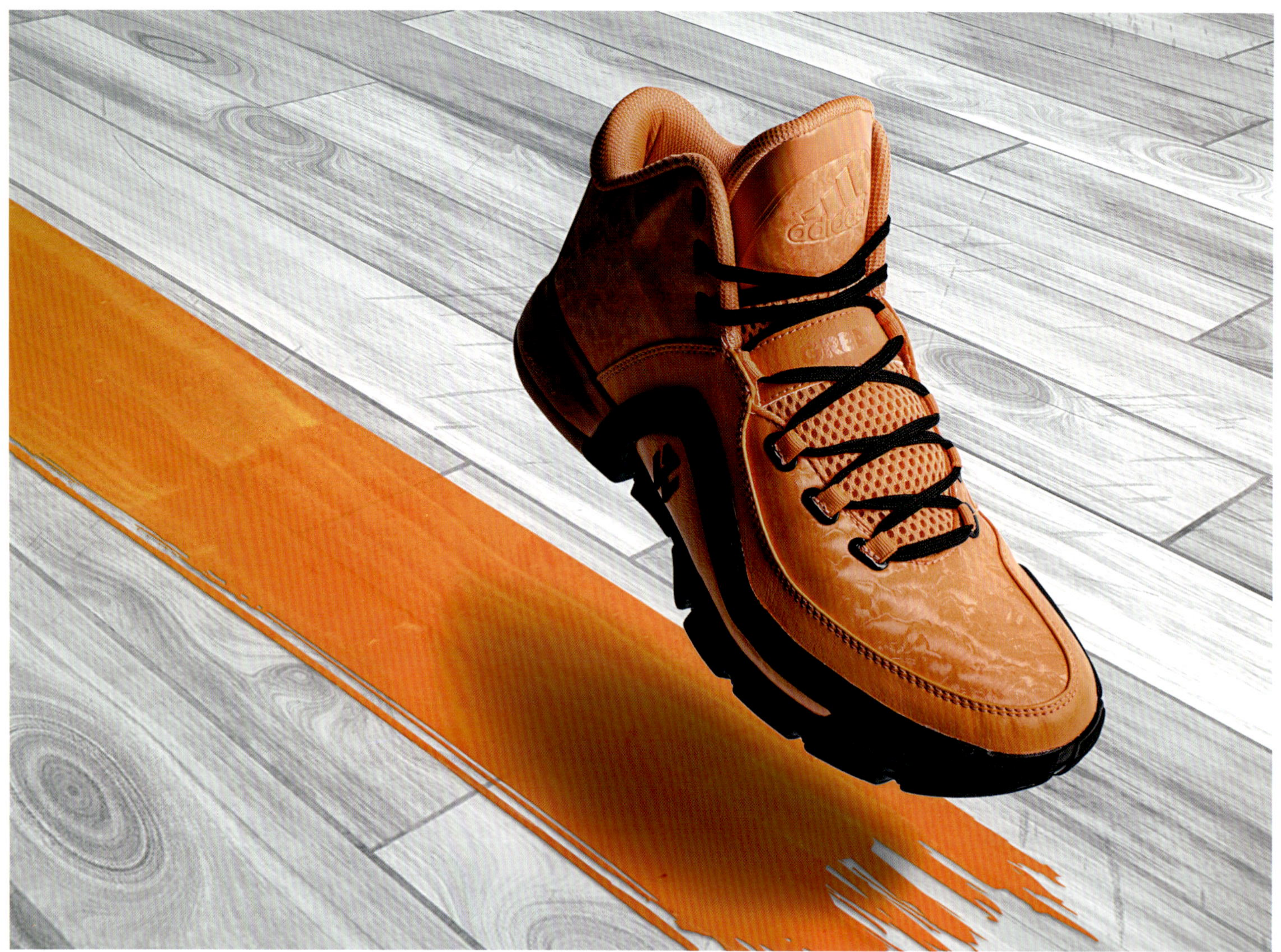

ADIDAS J WALL 2 [TAKE ON SUMMER]

Released in 2015, this is the second signature shoe of John Wall, who was signed by adidas. It features a mixture of vibrant solar orange colors, the special color combo of "Take on Summer." TOS, which integrates drafting and training, is a highly popular annual summer game for young basketball aficionados.

Details

"GREATWALL," a nickname of John Wall, is inscribed on the tongue. Coincidentally, Wall also has a tattoo of the Chinese Great Wall on his back, reminding himself to push himself to the limit and set new records.

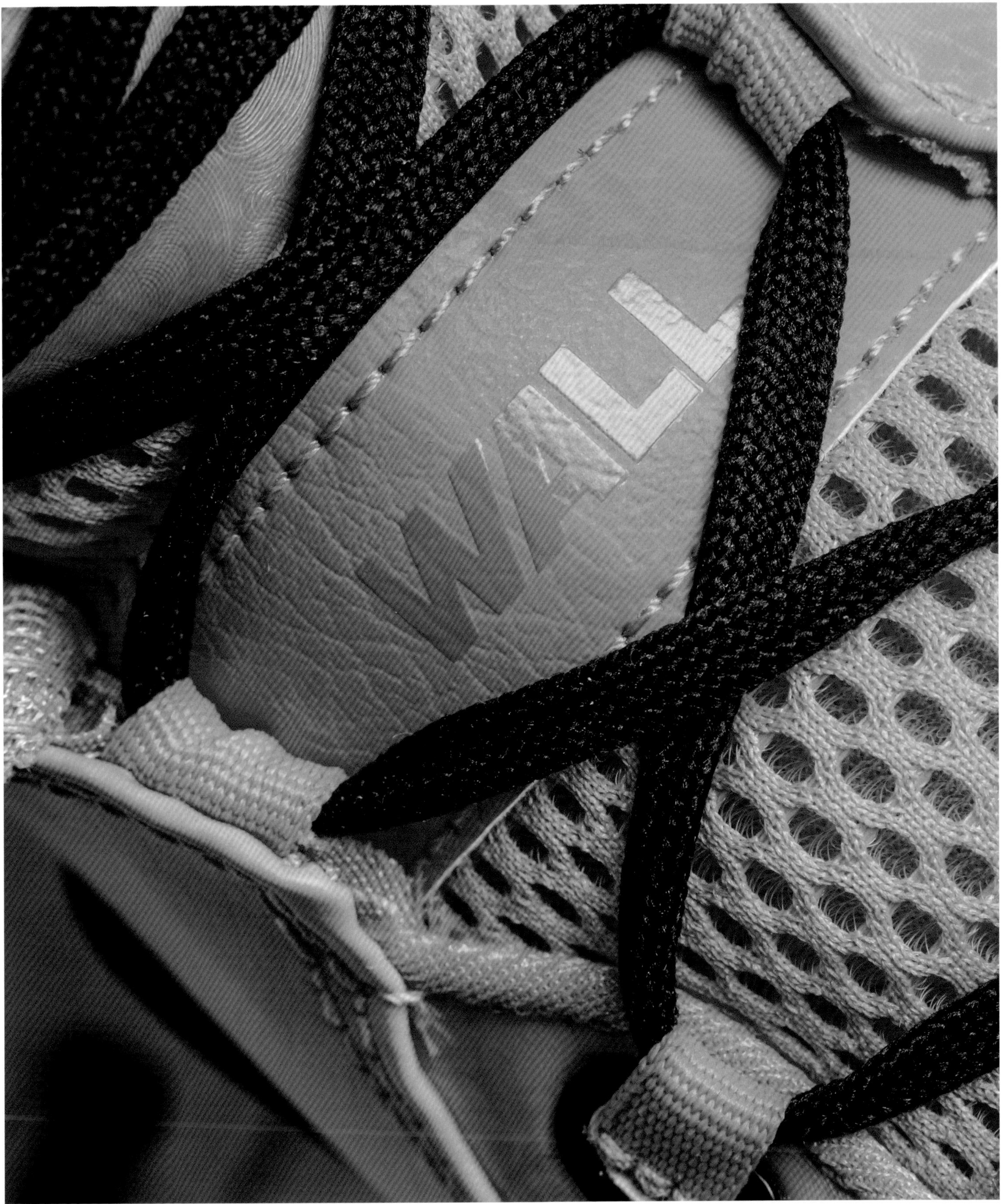

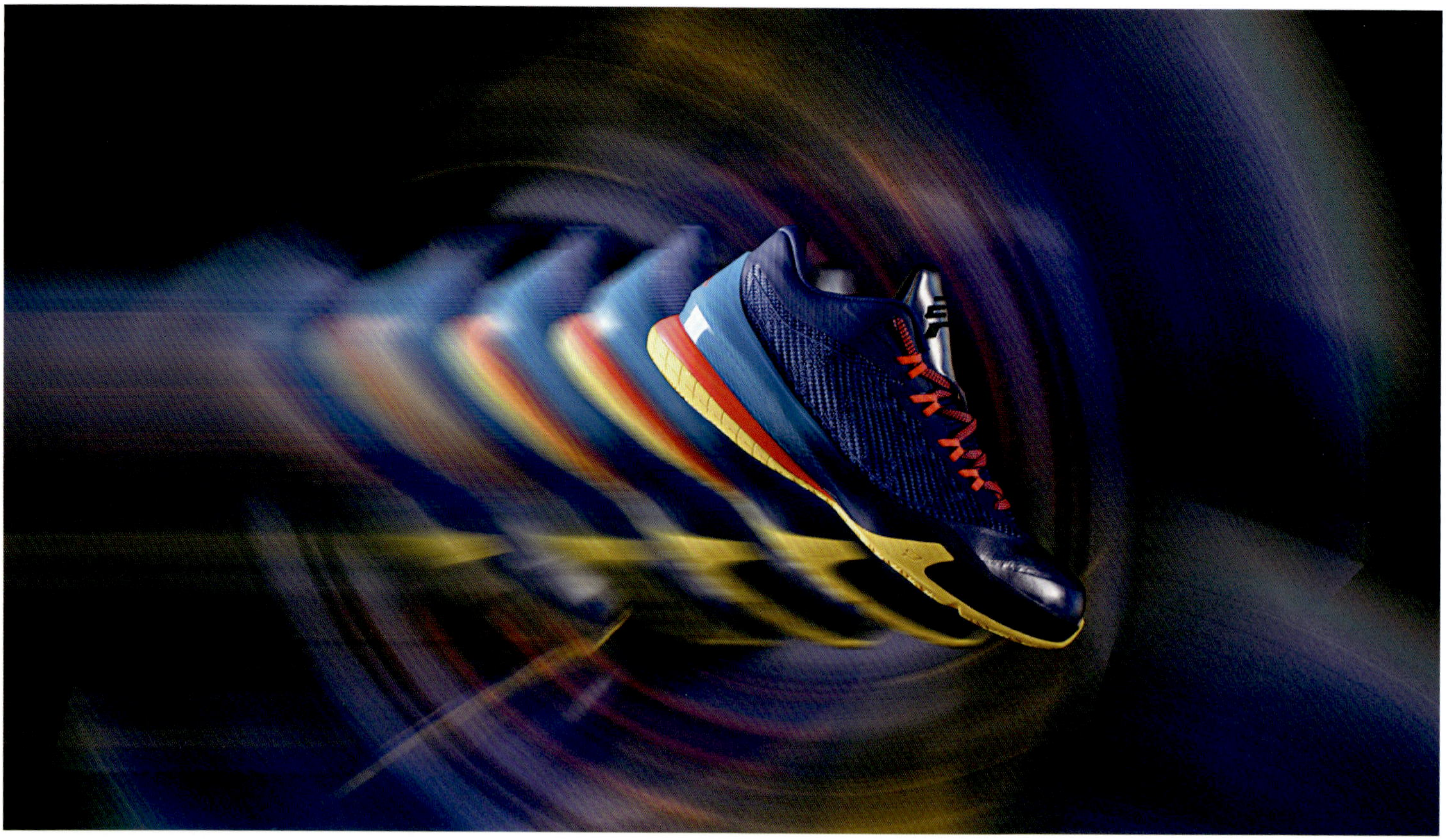

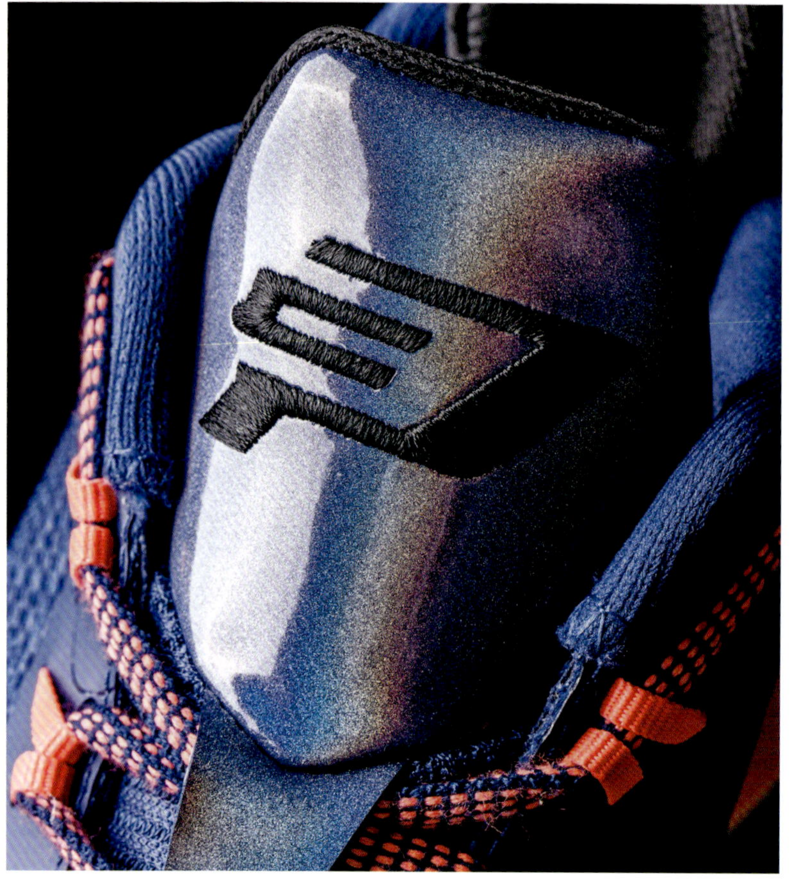

JORDAN CP3VIII

In 2014, the Jordan Brand debuted the eighth iteration of Chris Paul's signature shoe. A unique 5/8 height, coupled with an inner sleeve, delivers a sock-like fit in a model that is made for players with an up-tempo game.

Details

The tongue, with sleek and synthetic overlays, has Chris Paul's trademark on it and his family tree on the inside.

Details

The shoe includes custom Sneaker Freaker branding on the tongue, a common practice for collabratively released shoes.

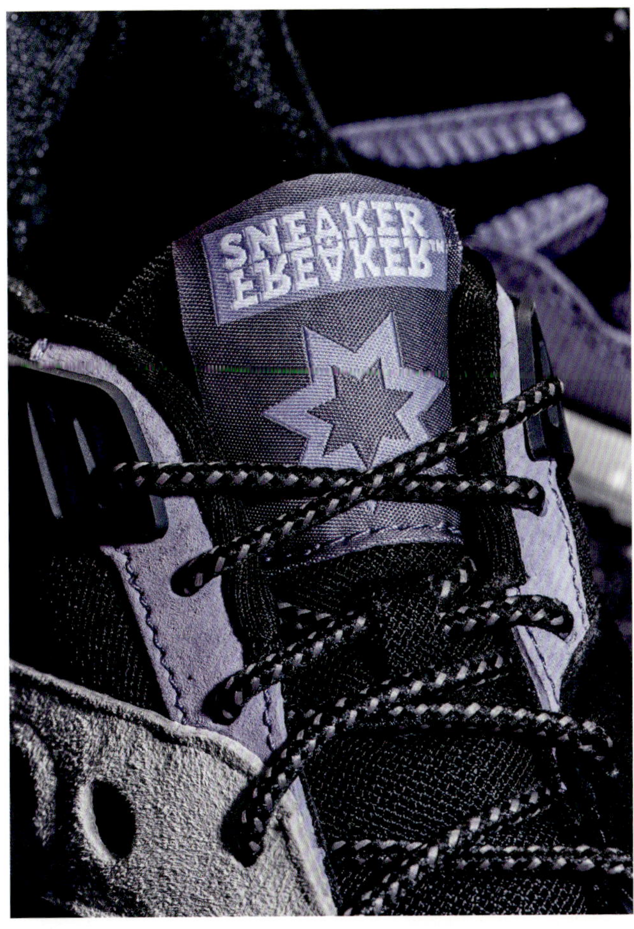

SNEAKERFREAKER × SAUCONY GRID SD [KUSHWACKER]

This project is a collaboration between Saucony and Sneaker Freaker (a sneaker magazine) in 1991.

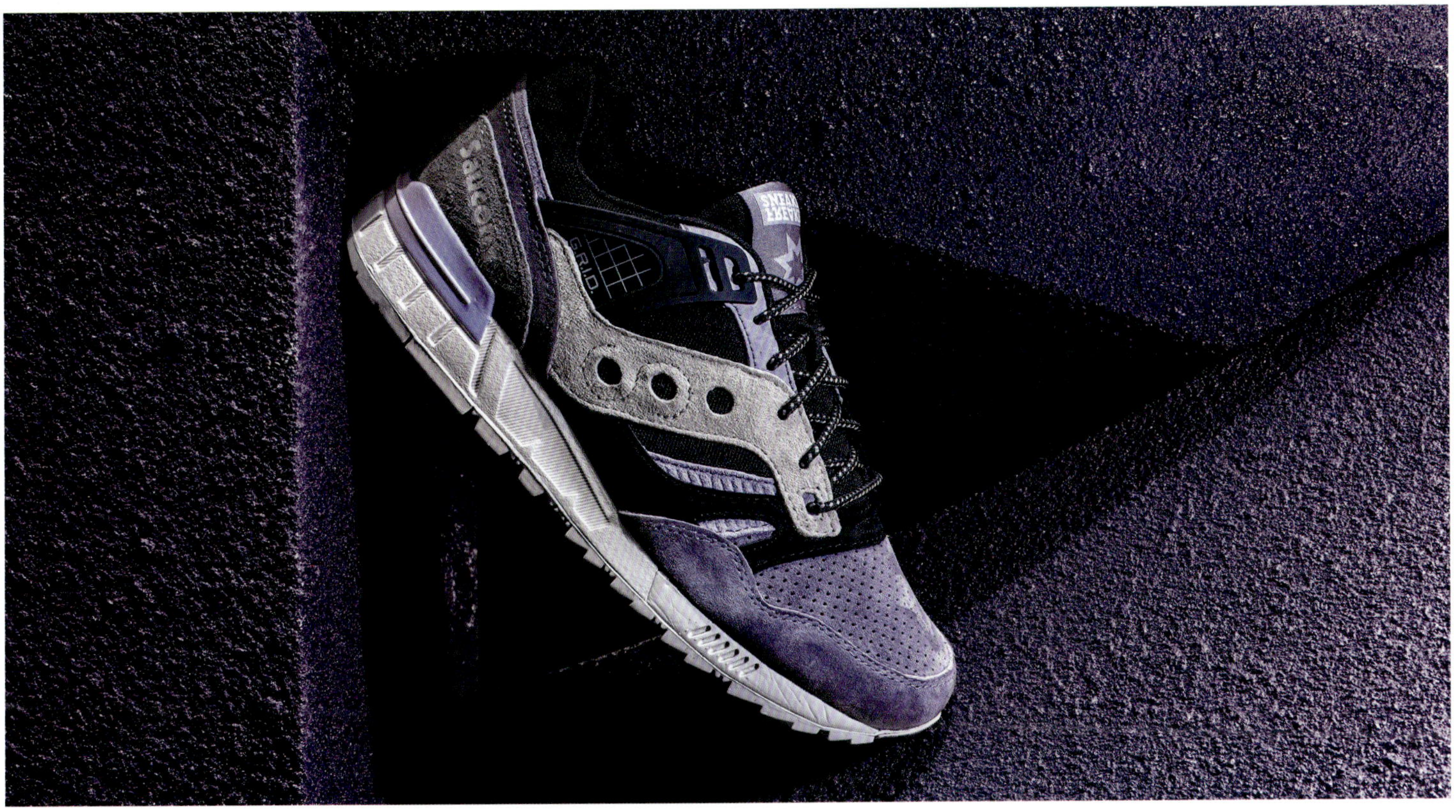

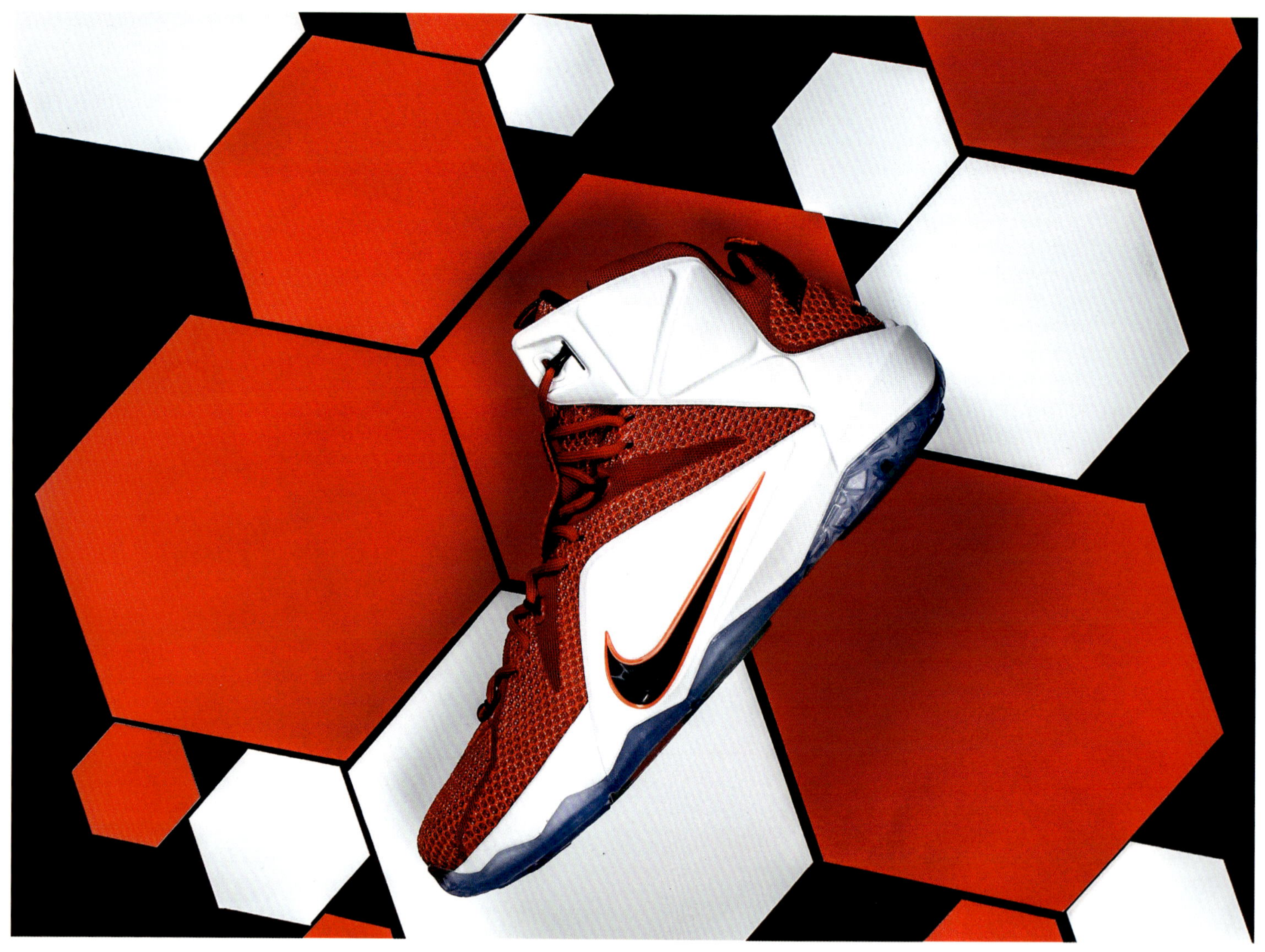

NIKE LEBRON XII [HEART OF A LION]

NIKE LEBRON XII [HEART OF A LION] , a.k.a. the LEBRON 12, is a Jason Petrie work. It is designed to enhance LeBron James' explosiveness while combining three key benefits: superior cushioning, harnessed support and natural flexibility. N.S.R.L. has run in-depth scientific analysis about its performance. It is a proven new generation of sneakers capable of delivering cushioning, support and flexibility.

Details

The tongue bears the singature of LeBron James and his personal trademark. The 12 black dots indicate it is a LEBRON 12.

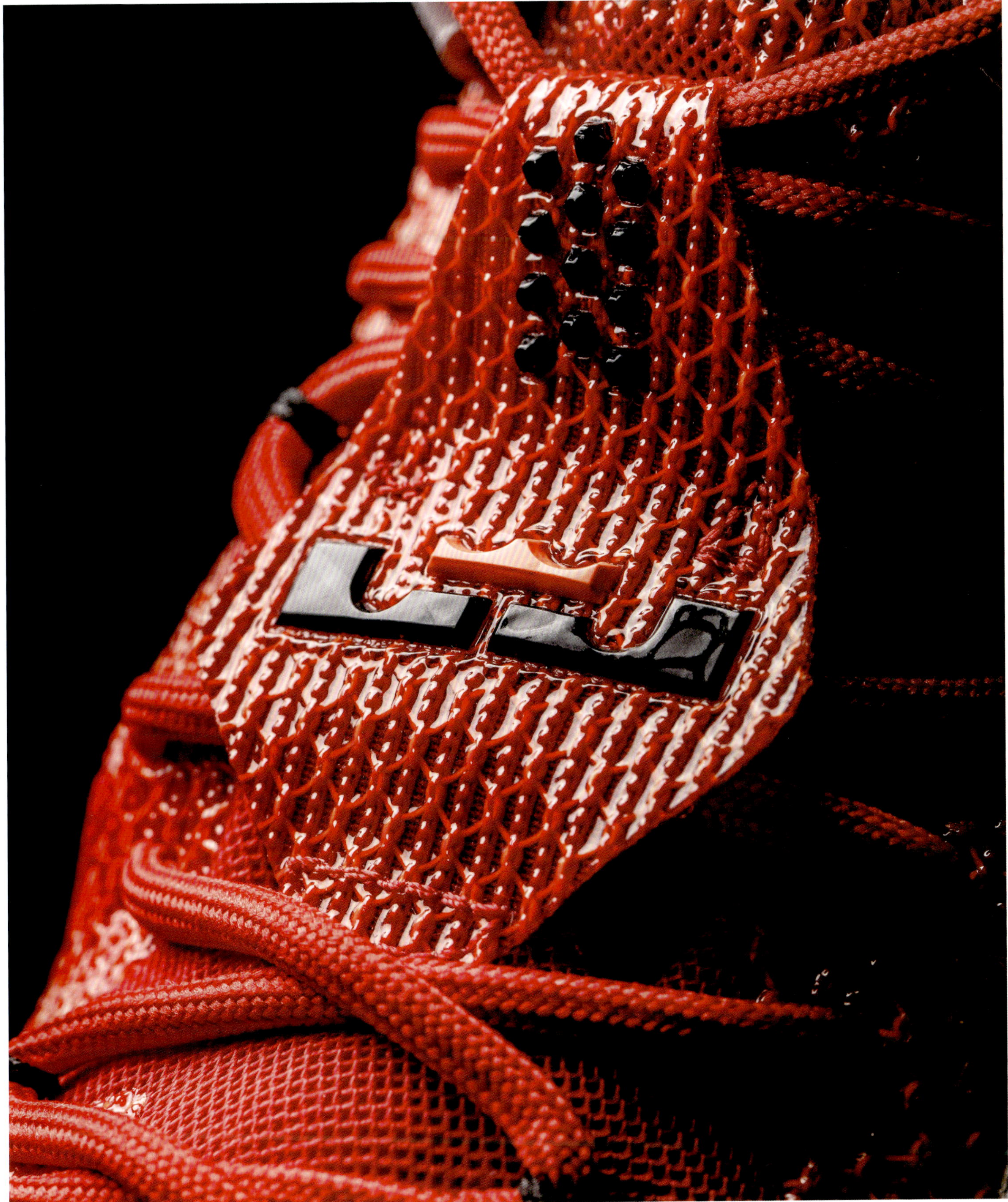

AIR JORDAN 4 RETRO [CEMENT]

The original Michael Jordan 4 was designed by Tinker Hatfield and released in 1989. The pair in the picture was the remastered Air Jordan 4 Retro 2016. The paint splattered speckles against gray on the midsole, pristine nubuck leather and the conspicuous NIKE AIR all made it the closest one to original pair Jordan debuted 28 years ago.

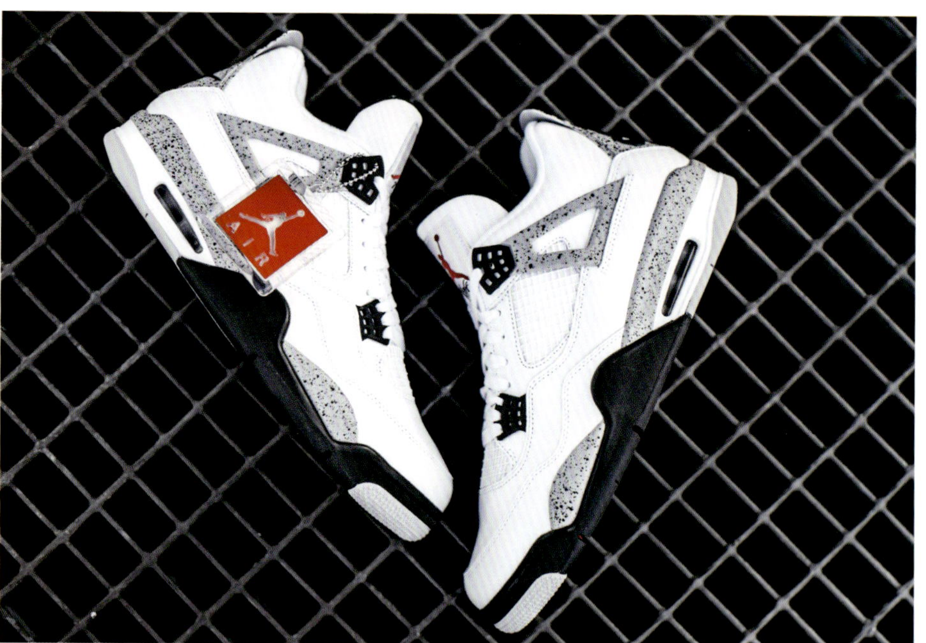

Details

The combination of the Jumpman logo and the "Flight" script is the classic icon of Air Jordan 4.

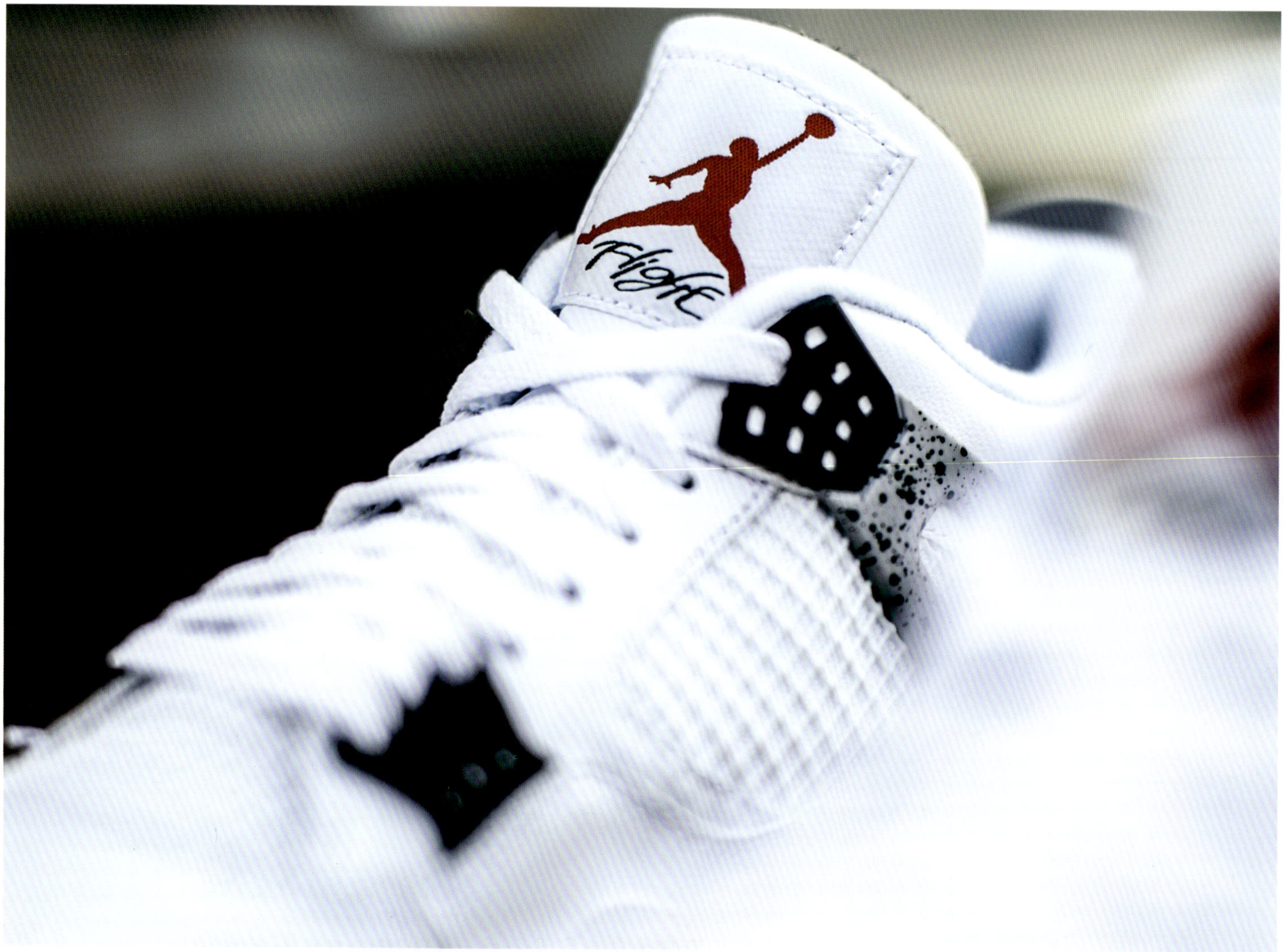

Details

The leather tongue has thc embossed "LeBron James" signature and "XIII." Echoing the Summer Olympics with the metallic gold "LJ" overlay, the Nike LeBron XIII Low has surfaced in a new "USA" colorway.

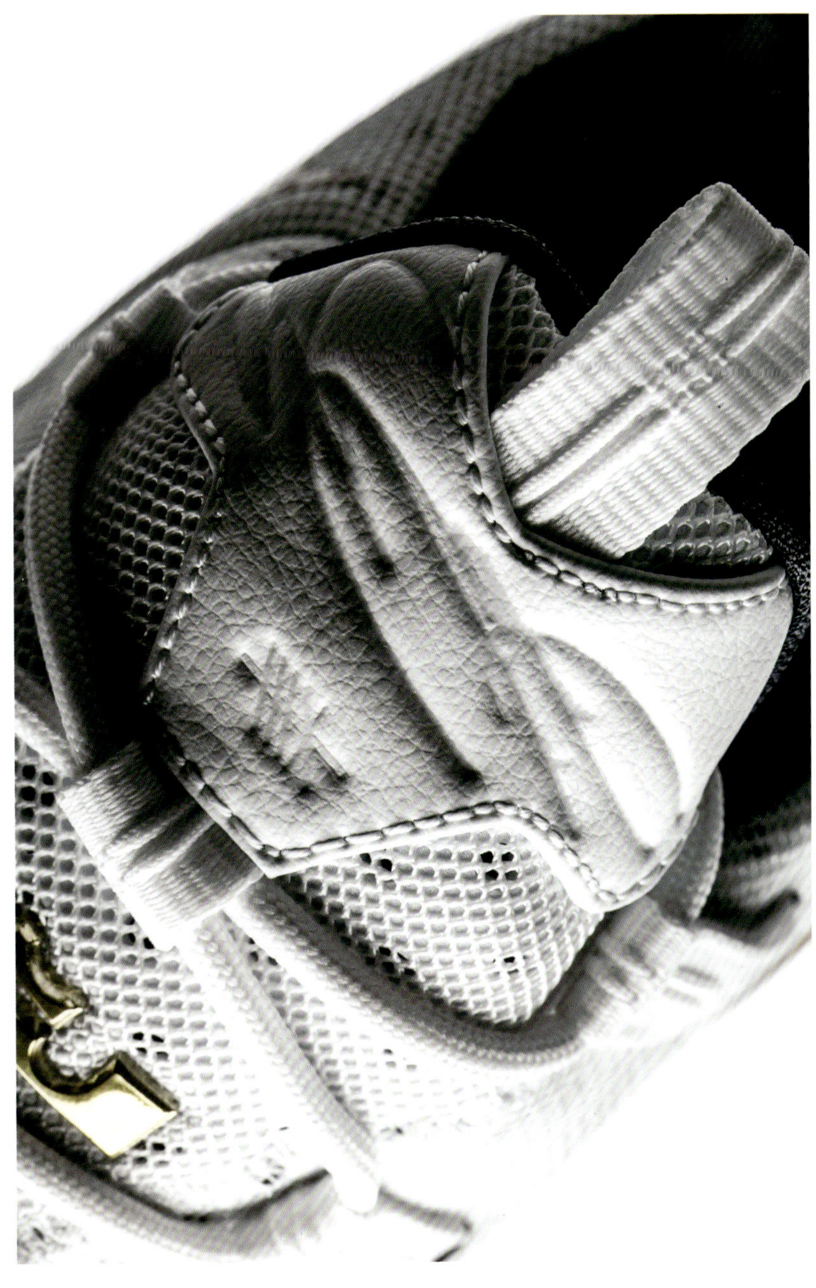

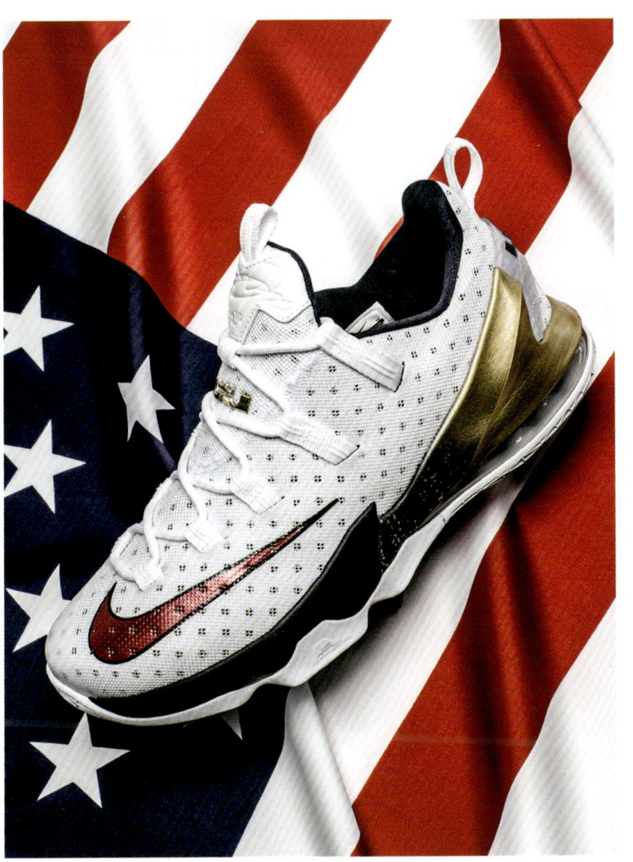

NIKE LEBRON XIII LOW [USA]

Released in 2016 and designed by Jason Petrie, LeBron XIII is a cutting-edge low top. It features Nike Zoom Air cushioning units, Max Air 180 unit for shock-absorbing cushioning and full-length injected Phylon for lightweight cushioning. It has got everything for maximum explosiveness on the court.

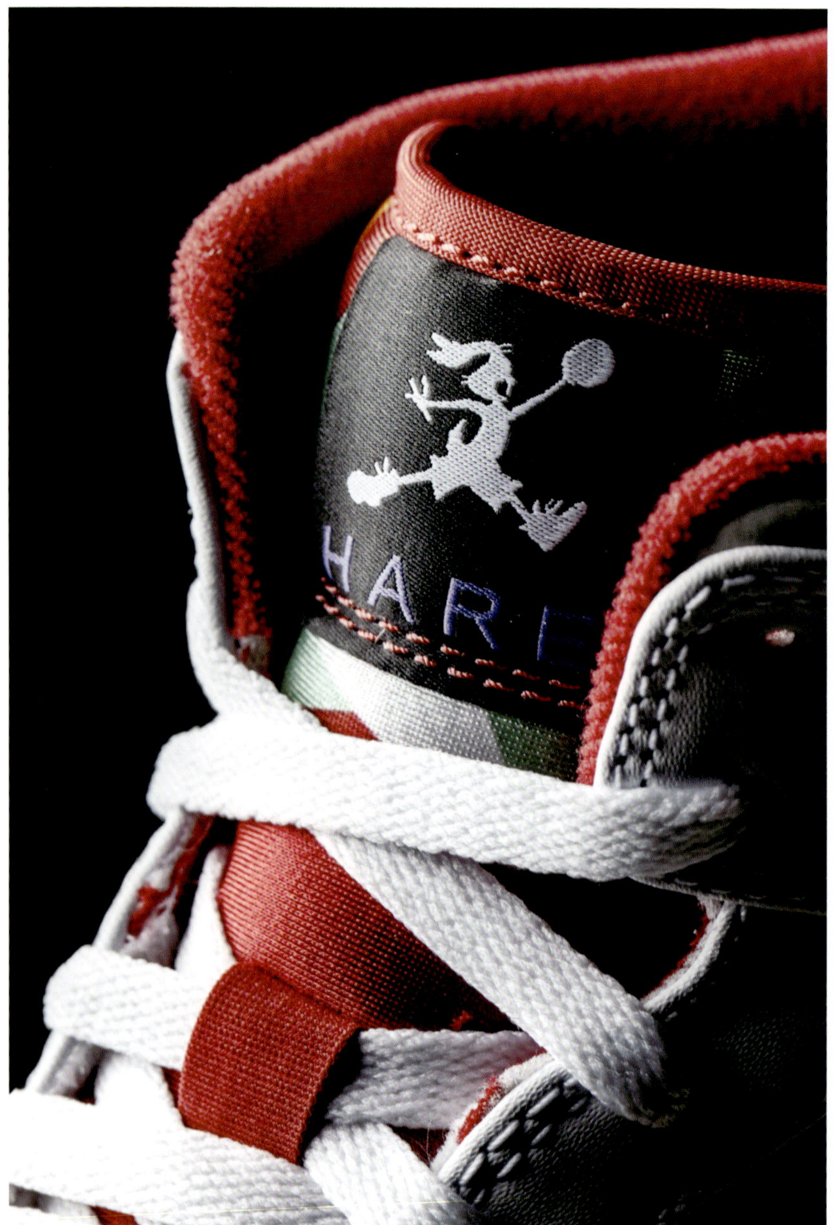

Details

With a multicolor tongue inspired by Bugs' signature carrot, the "Hare Jordan" logo occupies the central tongue instead of the original Jumpman.

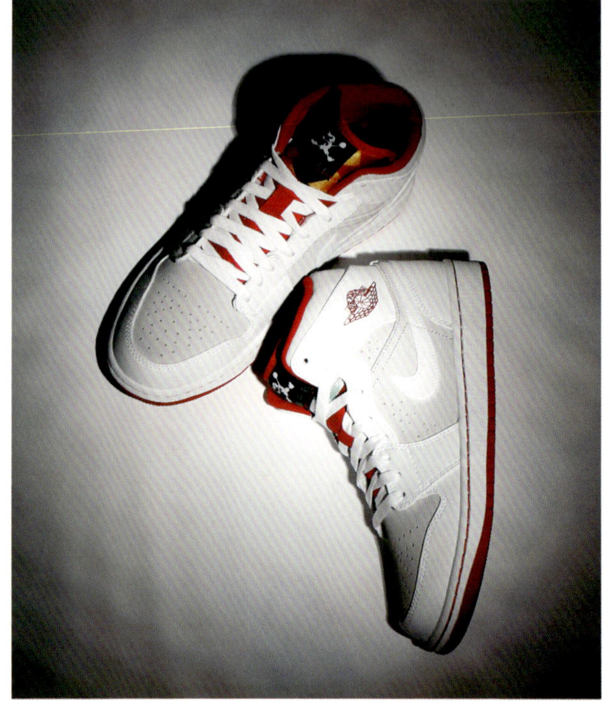

AIR JORDAN 1 MID [HARE]

Released in 2015, it is a replica of the eight-hole Air Jordan 1. It is inspired by the iconic cartoon character Bugs Bunny, a co-star of Michael Jordan in a 1992 commercial.

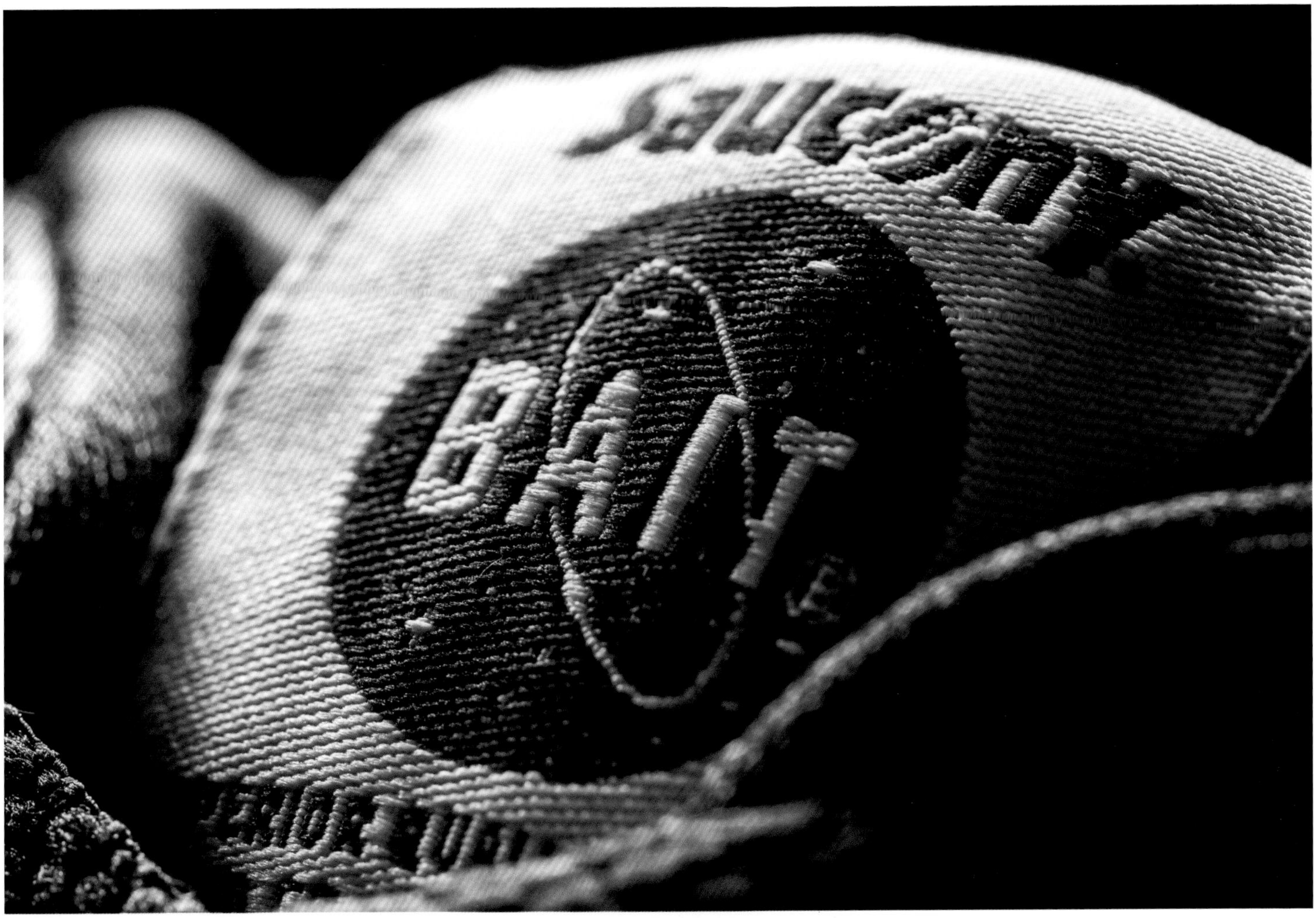

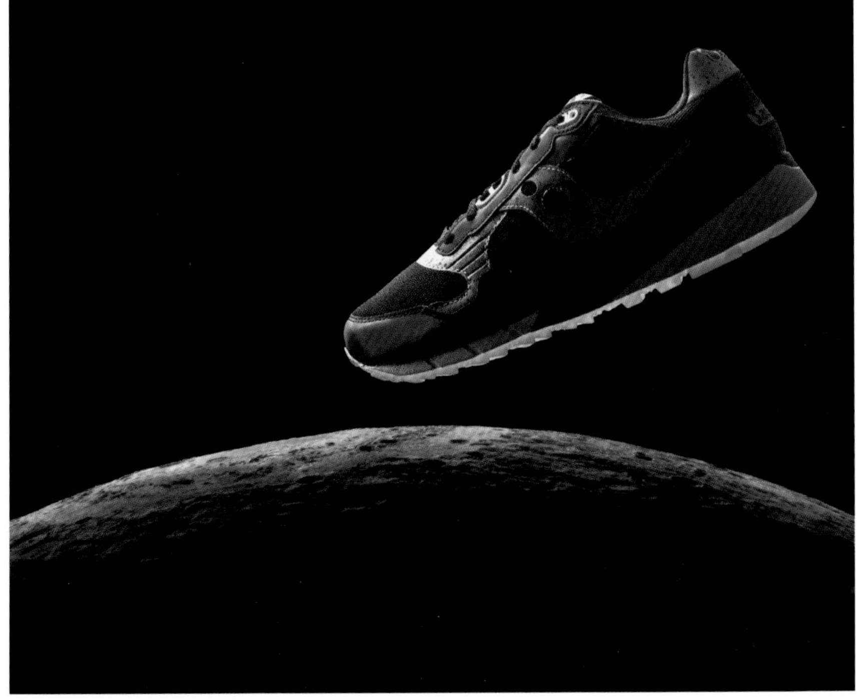

Details

BAIT and Saucony branding appears on a NASA-inspired woven label at the tongue, along with photographs of the moon and earth tucked away on the insoles.

BAIT×SAUCONY SHADOW 5500 CRUEL WORLD6 [GIANT LEAPS]

Saucony, a classic American sneaker manufacturer, together with BAIT, a California-based premium brick-and-click concept retailer in footwear, co-launched Shadow 5500 Cruel World 6 "Giant Leaps." Its colorway was inspired by the "moon-landing."

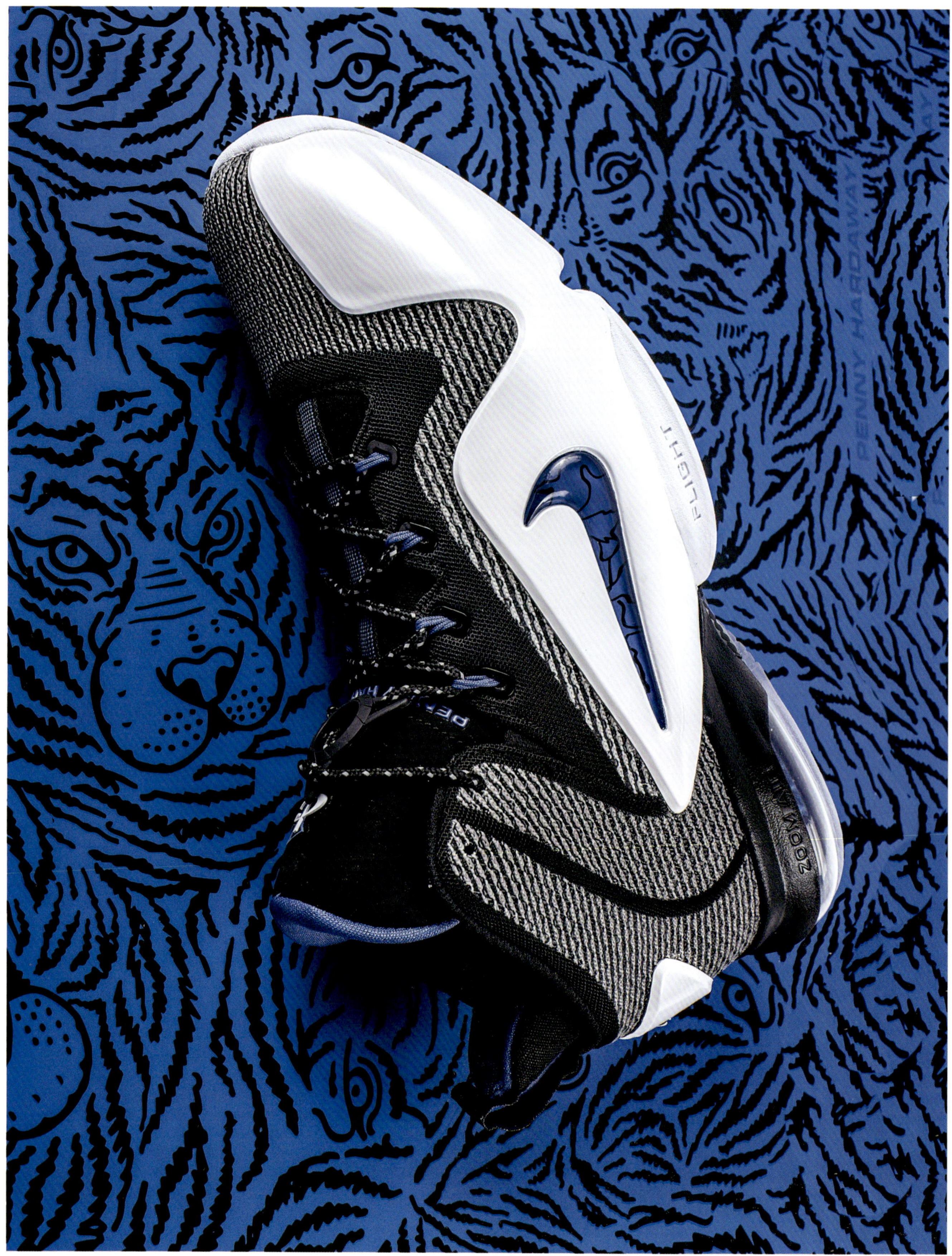
FLIGHT
PENNY HARDAWAY

Details

The plastic triangle shoelace buckle is the unique accessory of this pair. The "1 Cent" symbol on the tongue and "SIX" on the inside of the tongue indicate this is the sixth generation. And it also carries the signature of Penny Hardaway.

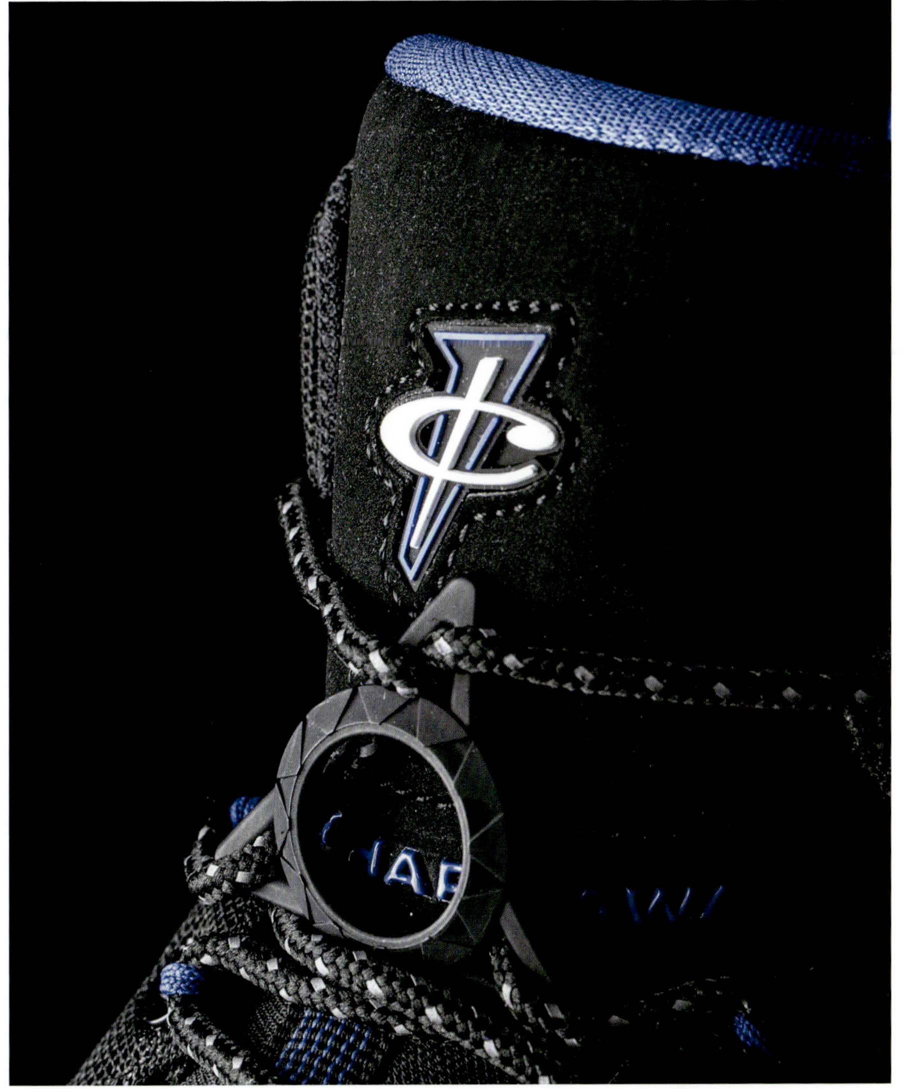

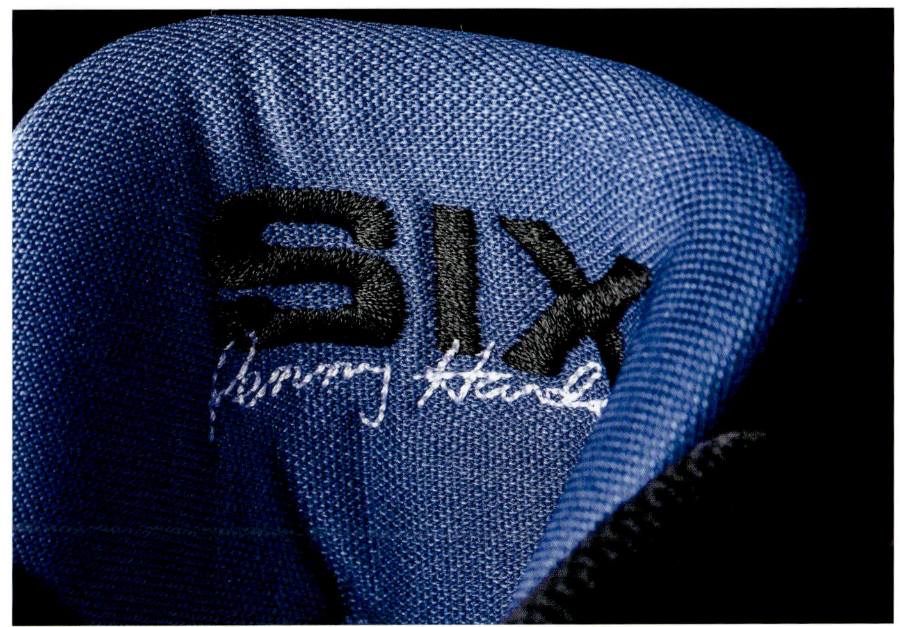

NIKE ZOOM PENNYVI [PENNY PACK]

In 2015, PENNY PACK paid homage to Air Foamposite One and Zoom Penny VI. Designed by Marc Dolce, it is the third pair of Penny Hardaway signature shoes. The color scheme is inspired by young Penny's days hooping at Memphis Tigers.

Details

The dragon-scale-like leather on the tongue creates a three-dimensional lace shoe.

JORDAN CP3 IX [YELLOW DRAGON]

Unveiled in 2015, it is the ninth signature shoe of Chris Paul. The colorway in the picture is inspired by the dragon dance, a celebration for the Chinese new year.

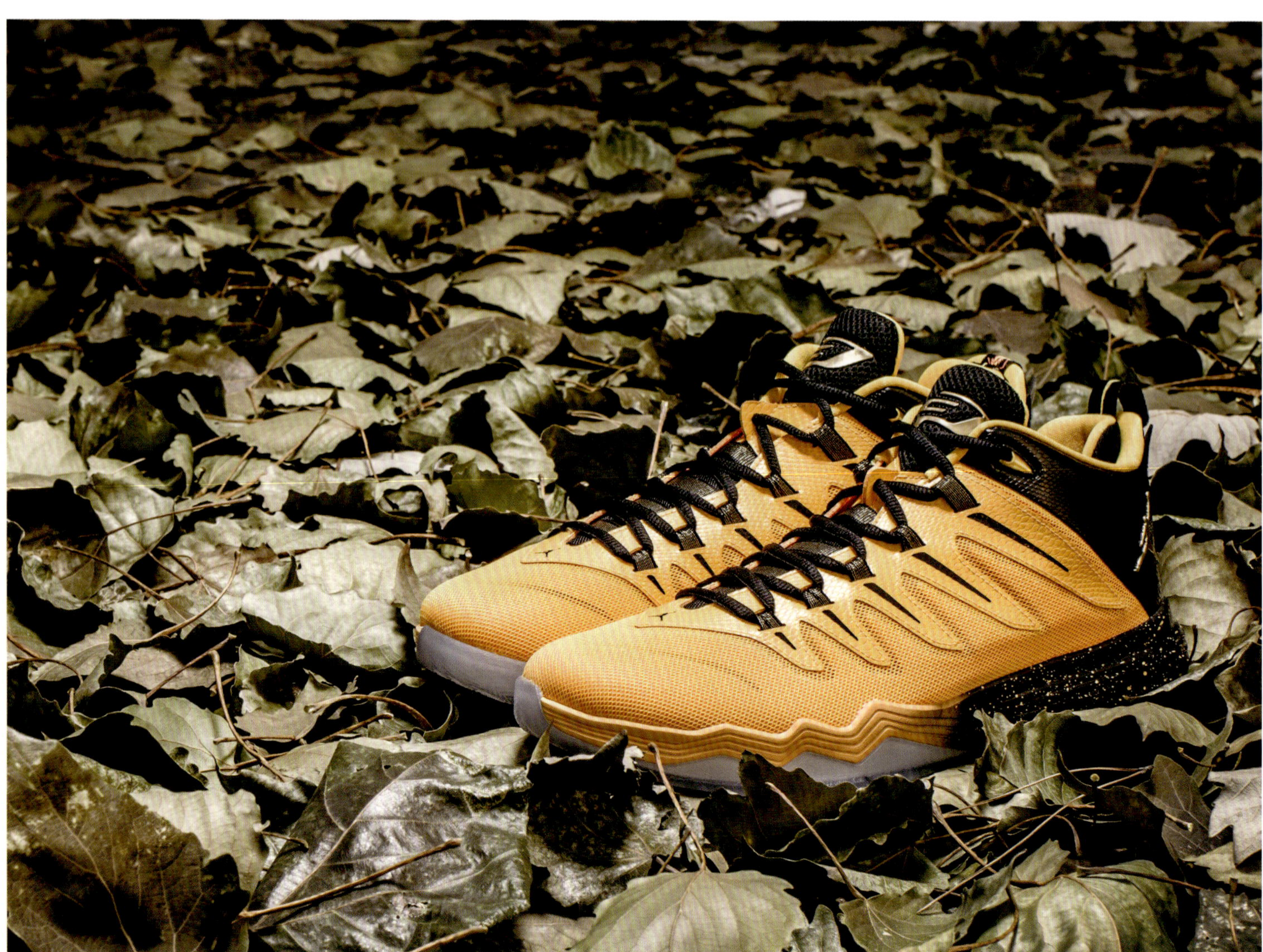

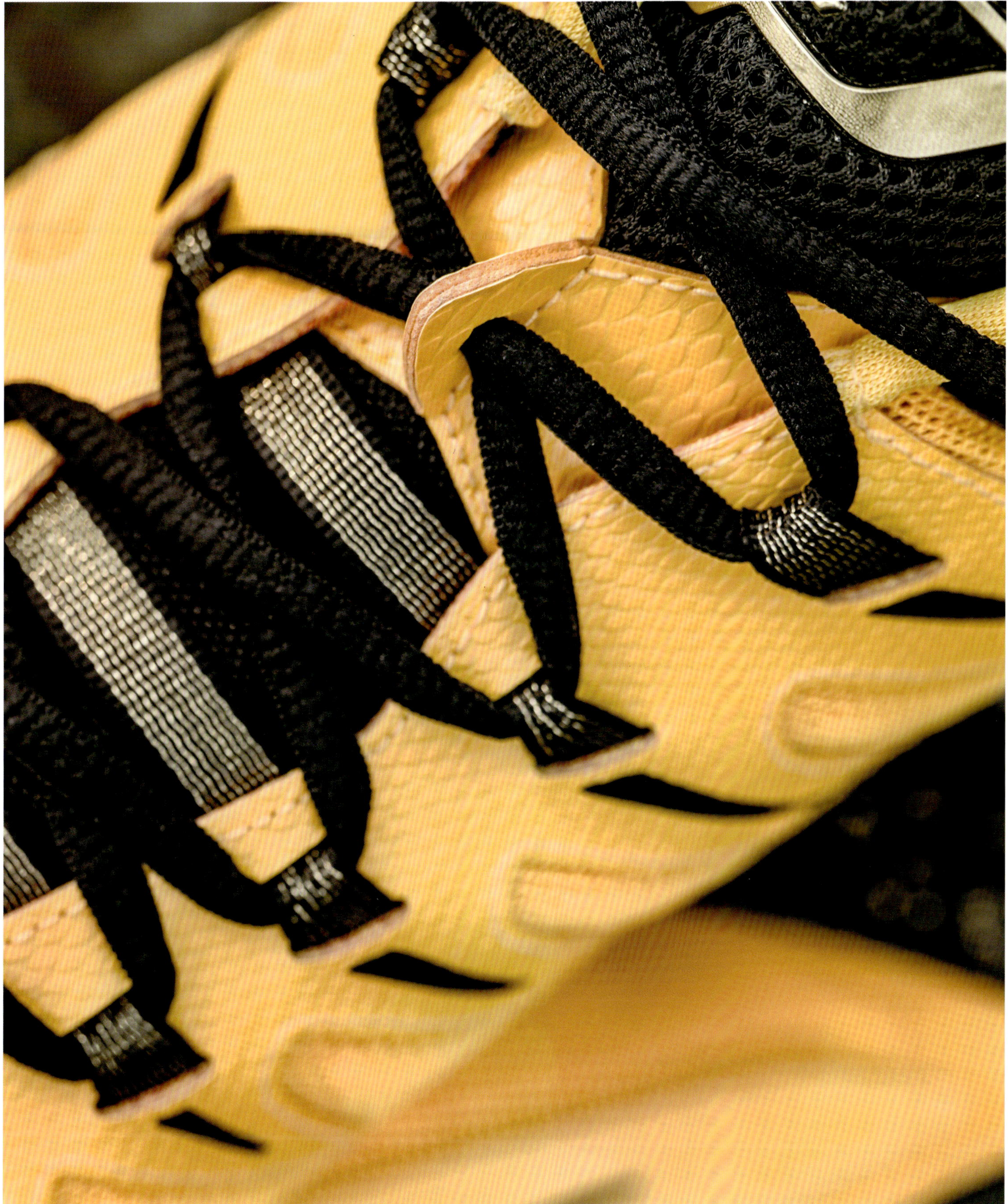

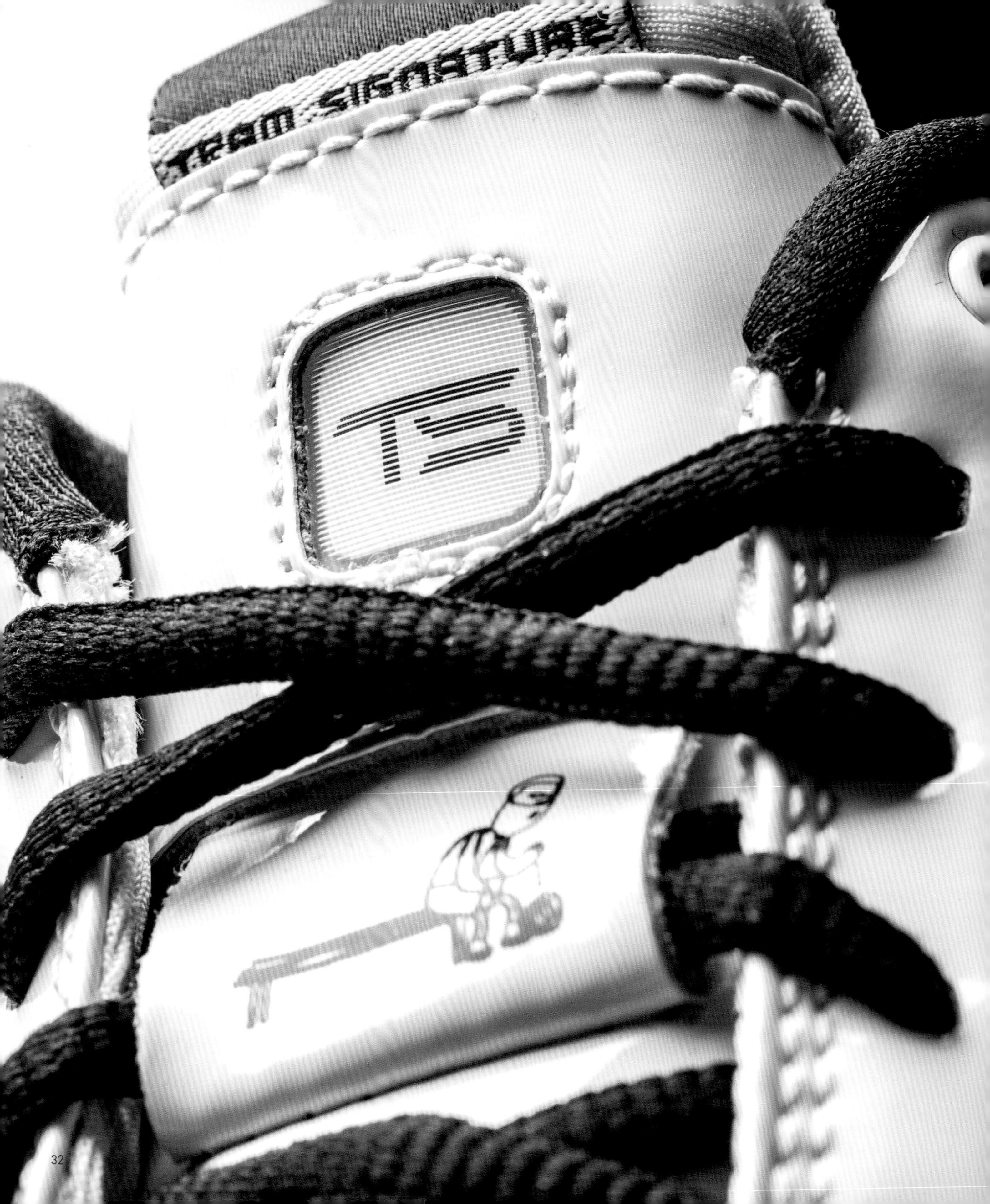
TEAM SIGNATURE
TS

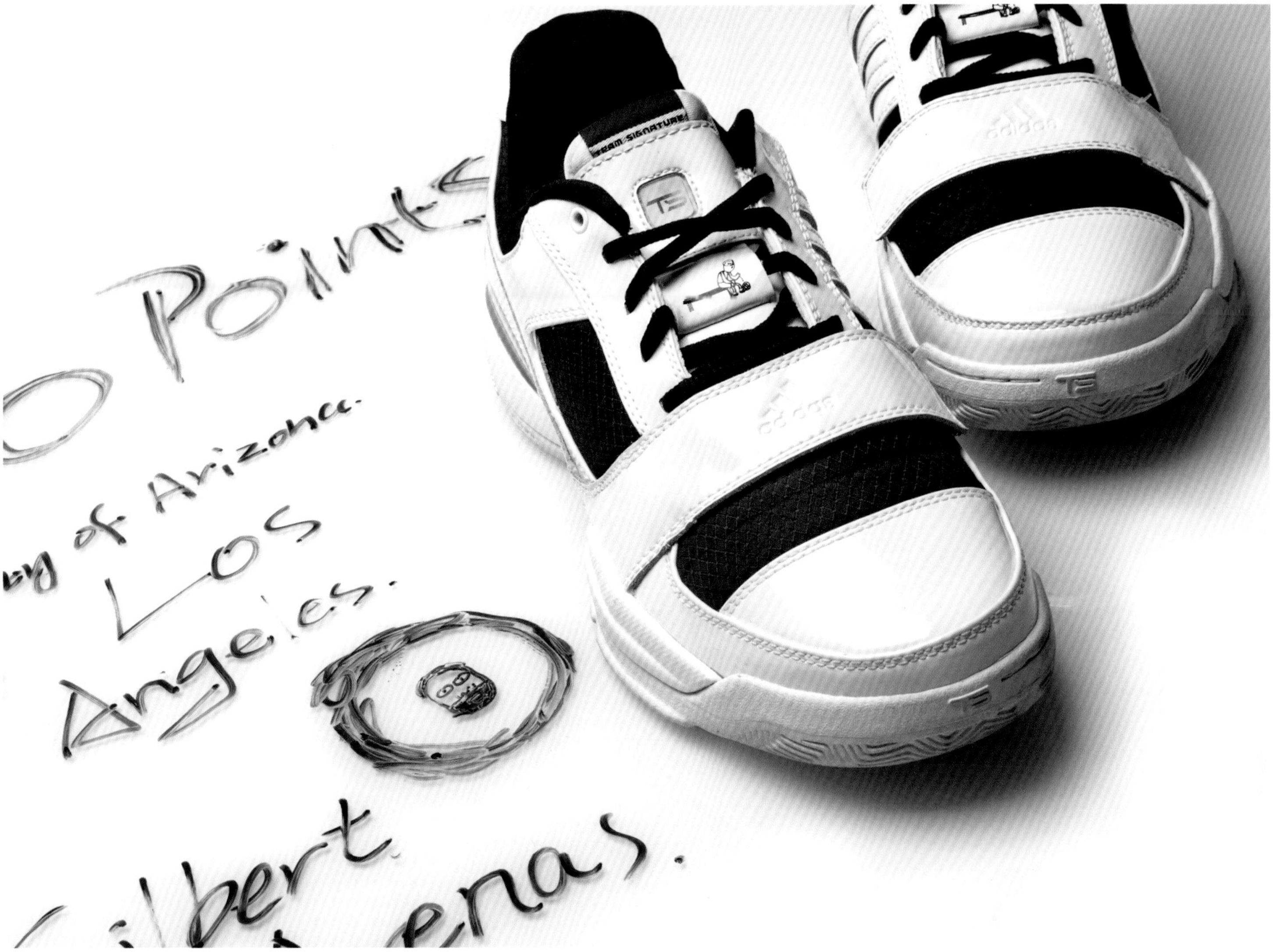

ADIDAS TS LIGHTSWITCH GIL [CUSTOMIZE]

Launched in 2007, this is a customized pair of Gilbert Arenas. The colorway is inspired by a 2007 TV commercial. The white quarter uses some material akin to whiteboard. Gilbert Arenas also gets a marker pen with the shoes.

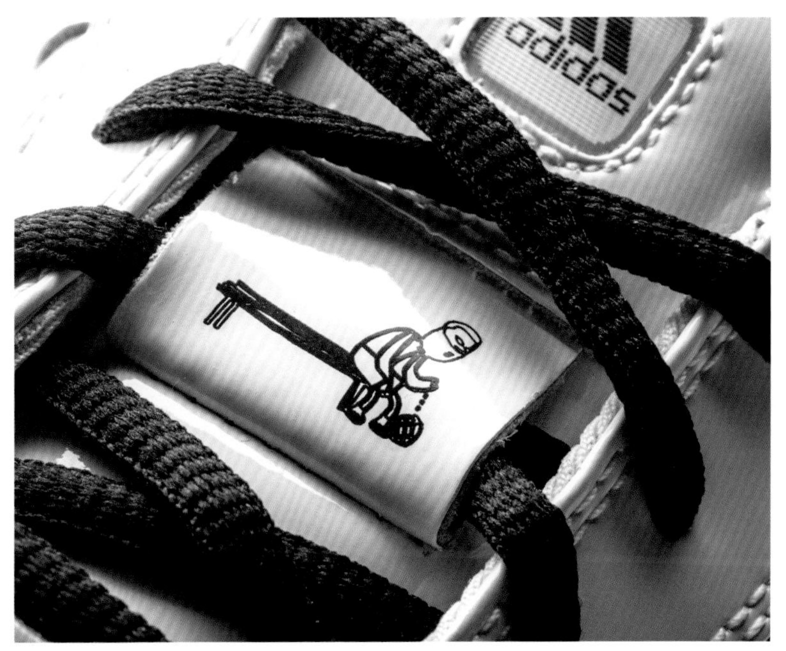

Details

The tongue features a cartoon image of Gilbert Arenas bouncing a ball on a bench. Its hologram materials create a partially visible adidas logo and "TS" trademark.

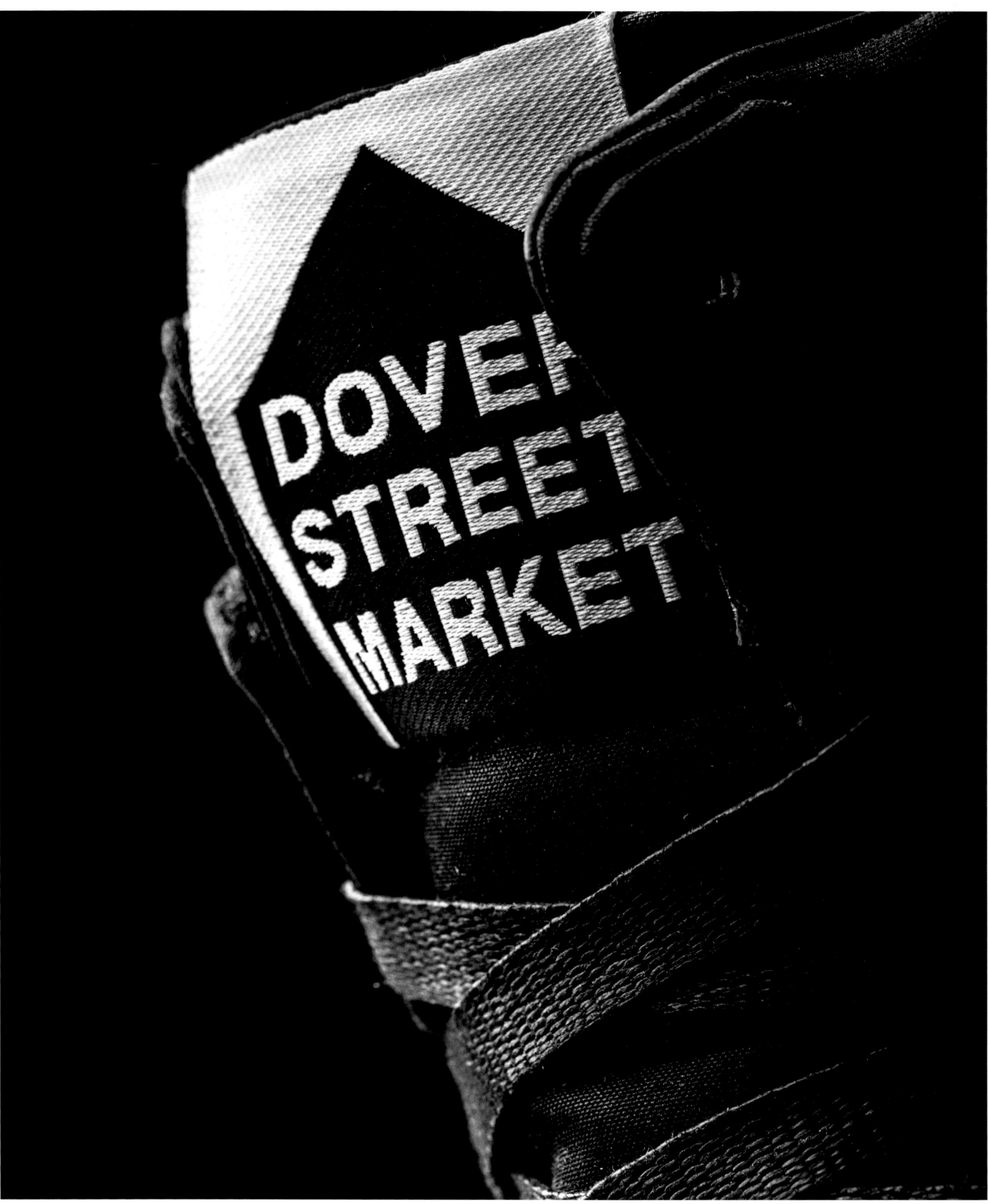
DOVER
STREET
MARKET

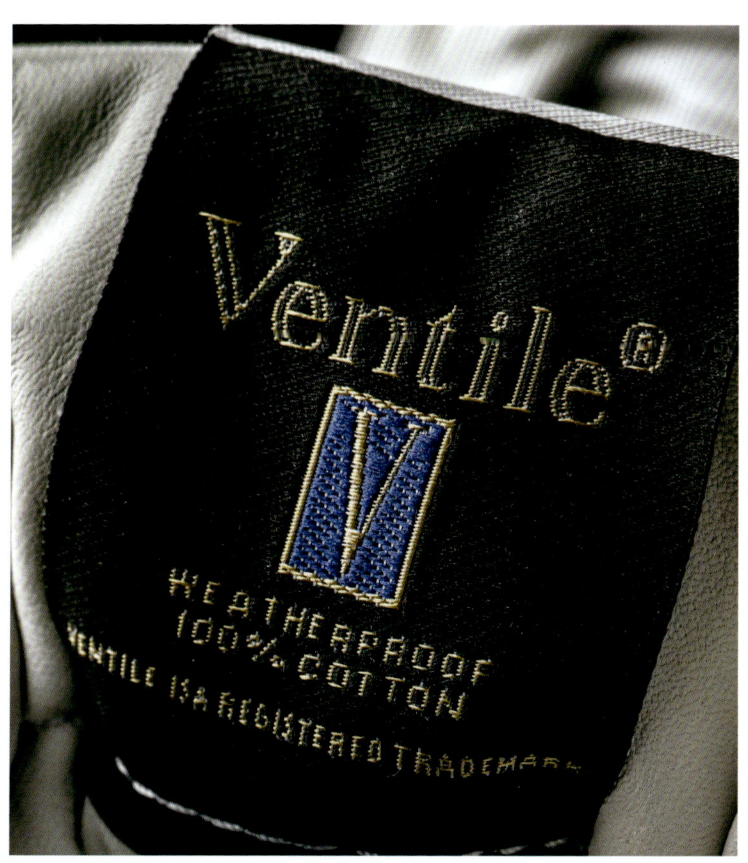

Details

The tongue has a DSM logo and a "Ventile®" mark inside, which indicates the use of a waterproof ventile fabric upper.

NIKELAB DUNK LUX SP/DSM

In 2015, the 30th anniversary of the well-established Nike Dunk Shoe, NikeLab and Dover Street Market — the fashion landmark in London — together launched the two-iteration Dunk Lux.

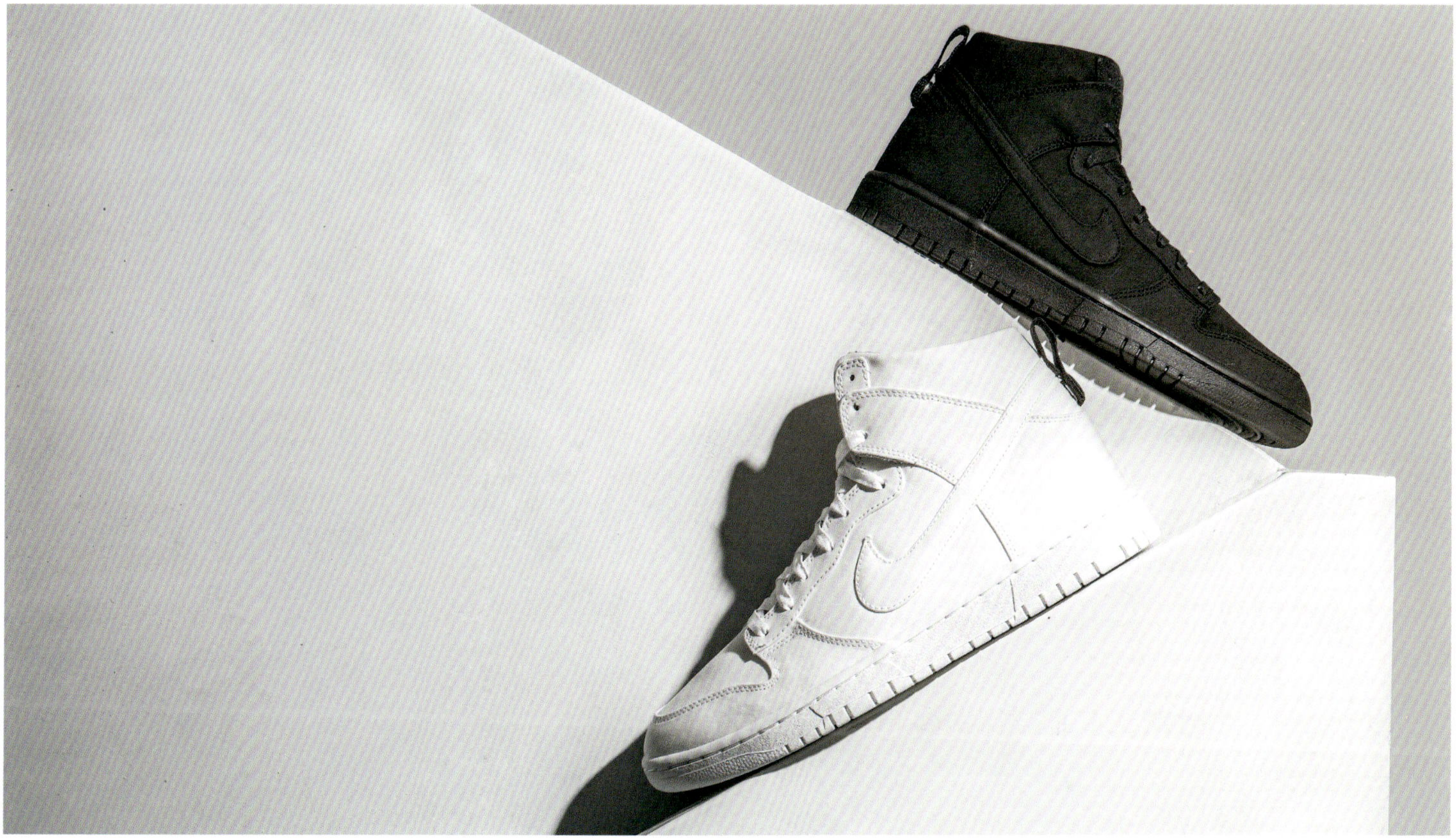

Details

Custom tongue tags and Solebox's embossed branding on the heel denote the special status of this Consortium release.

SOLEBOX × ADIDAS CONSORTIUM ULTRA BOOST UNCAGED

In March 2016, the famed Berlin sneaker shop Solebox had the privilege of creating a custom version of the popular Ultra Boost sneaker for the adidas Consortium World Tour. This pair gives up the silhouette TPU design.

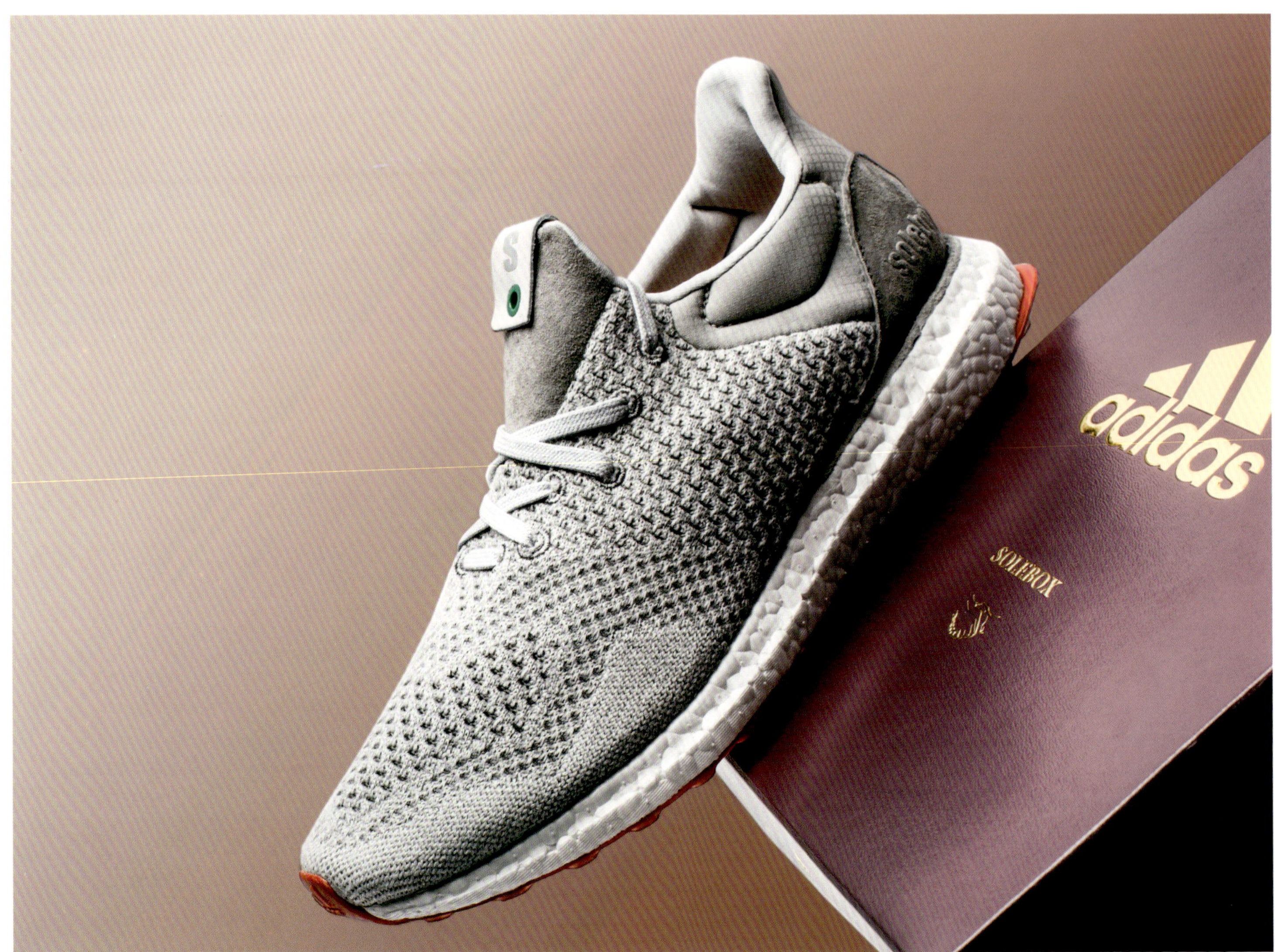

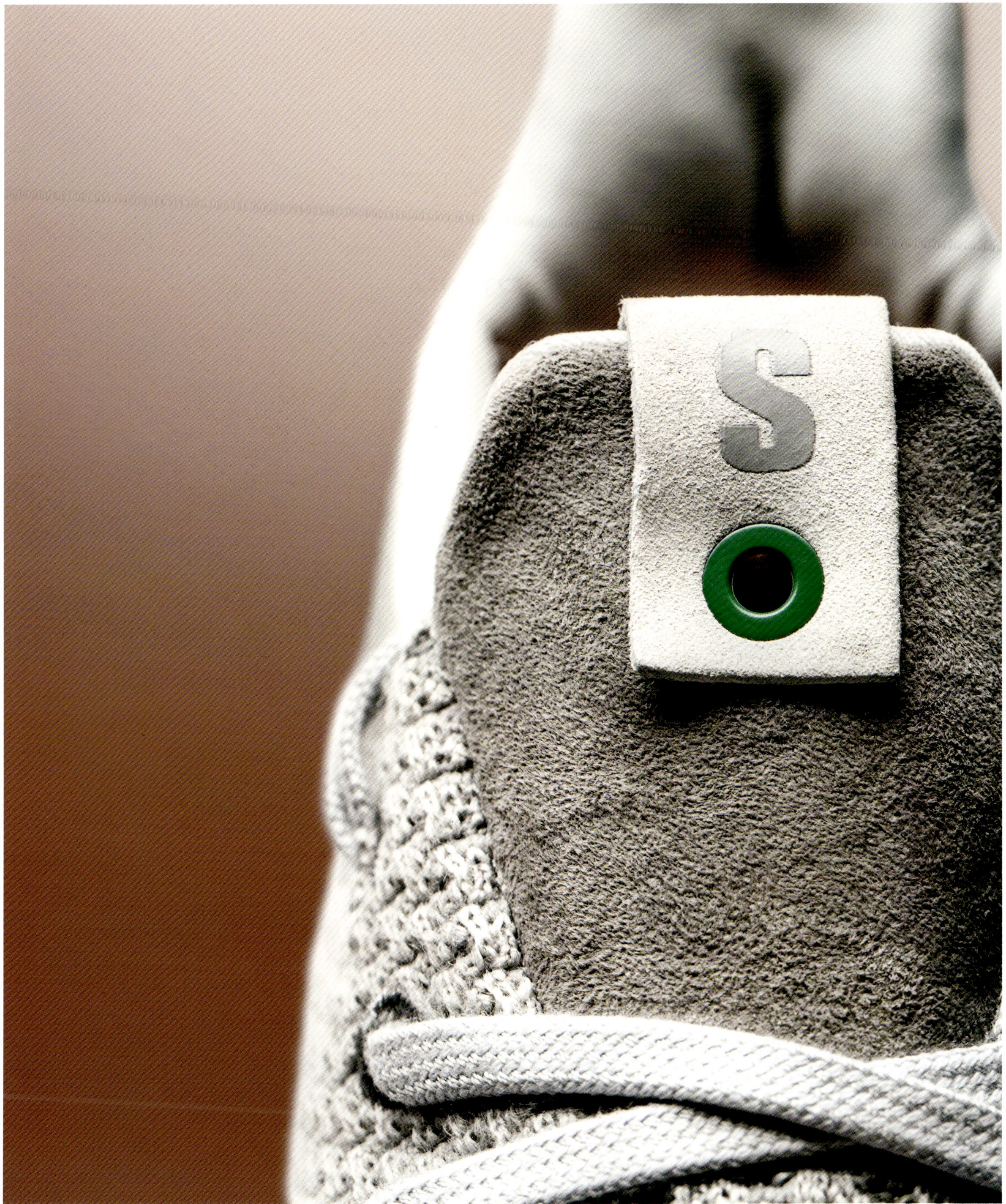
S

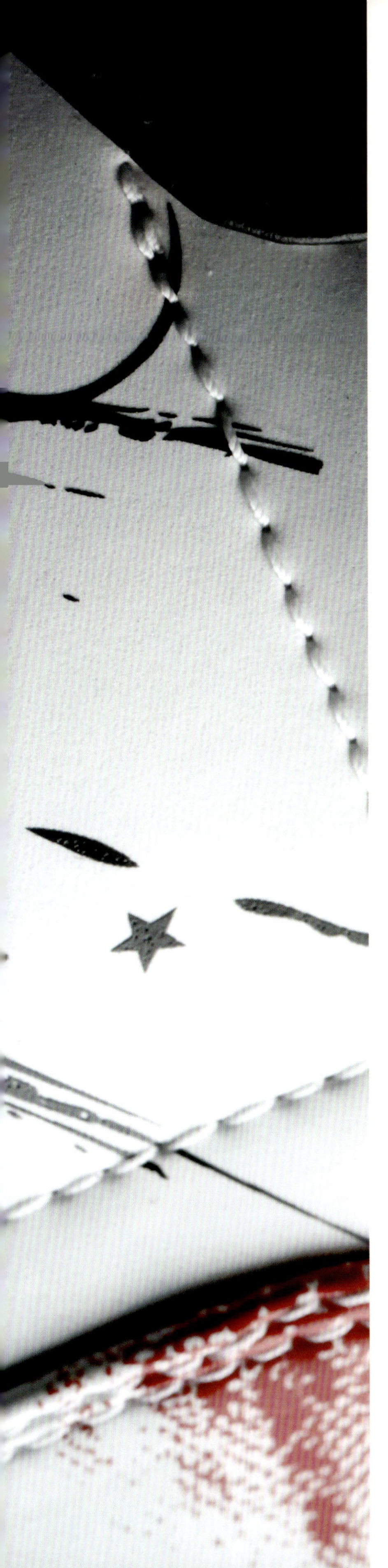

Upper, which mostly tells about the design of a shoe, usually impresses people first and foremost. It has become more vocal and powerful to express designers' thoughts, as new technologies, materials and techniques present more choices.

UPPER

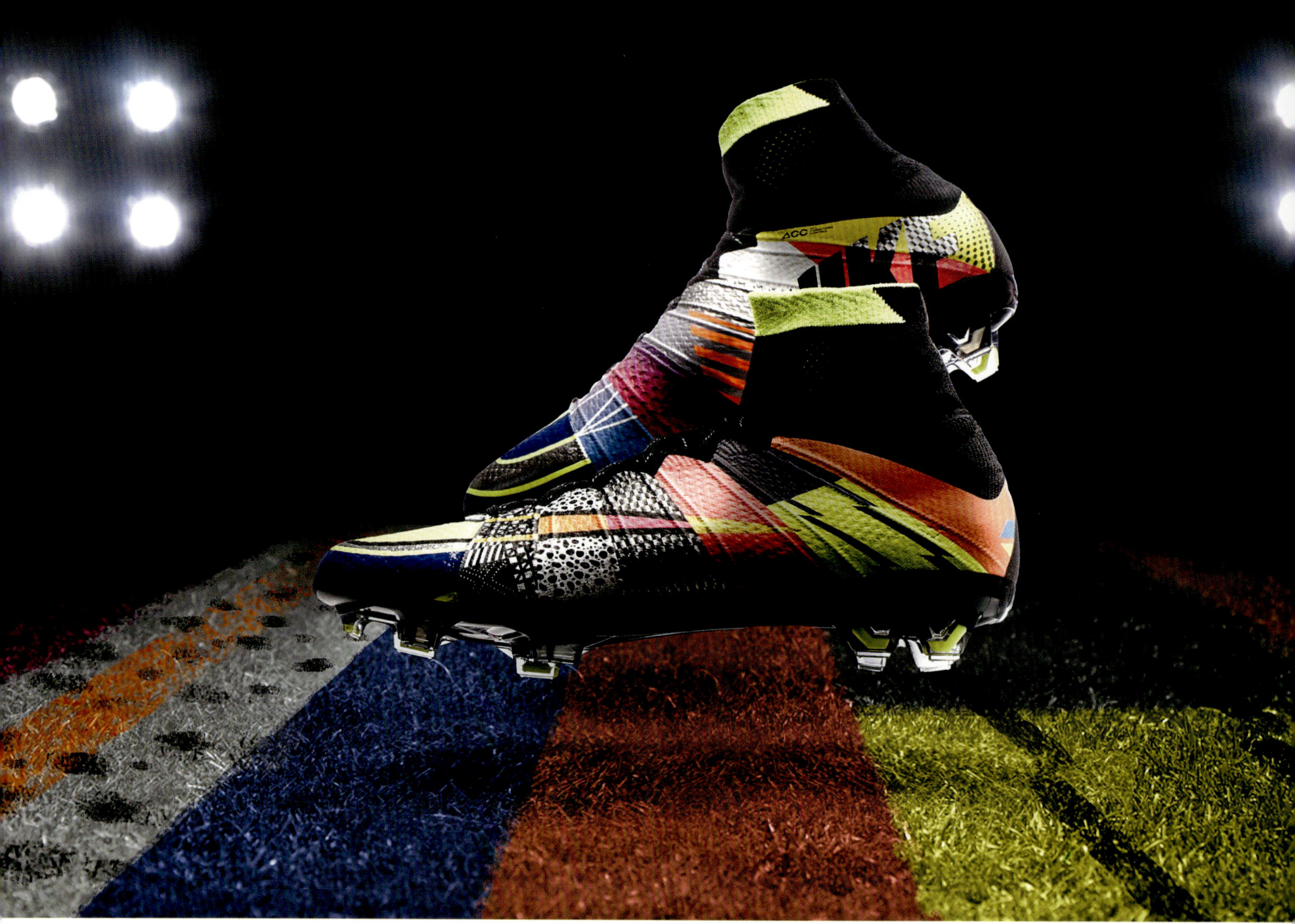

NIKE MERCURIAL SUPERFLY IV SE FG [WHAT THE?]

Released in 2016, NIKE MERCURIAL SUPERFLY IV SE FG pays homage to the previously released 16 Mercurial Shoes. It is a limited version: only 3,000 pairs are available worldwide (the quotas for the Chinese mainland is only 50). It is the first football sneaker that uses the "What The?" theme.

Details

The All Conditions Control (ACC) technology of the upper ensures a consistent performance on both wet and dry courts.

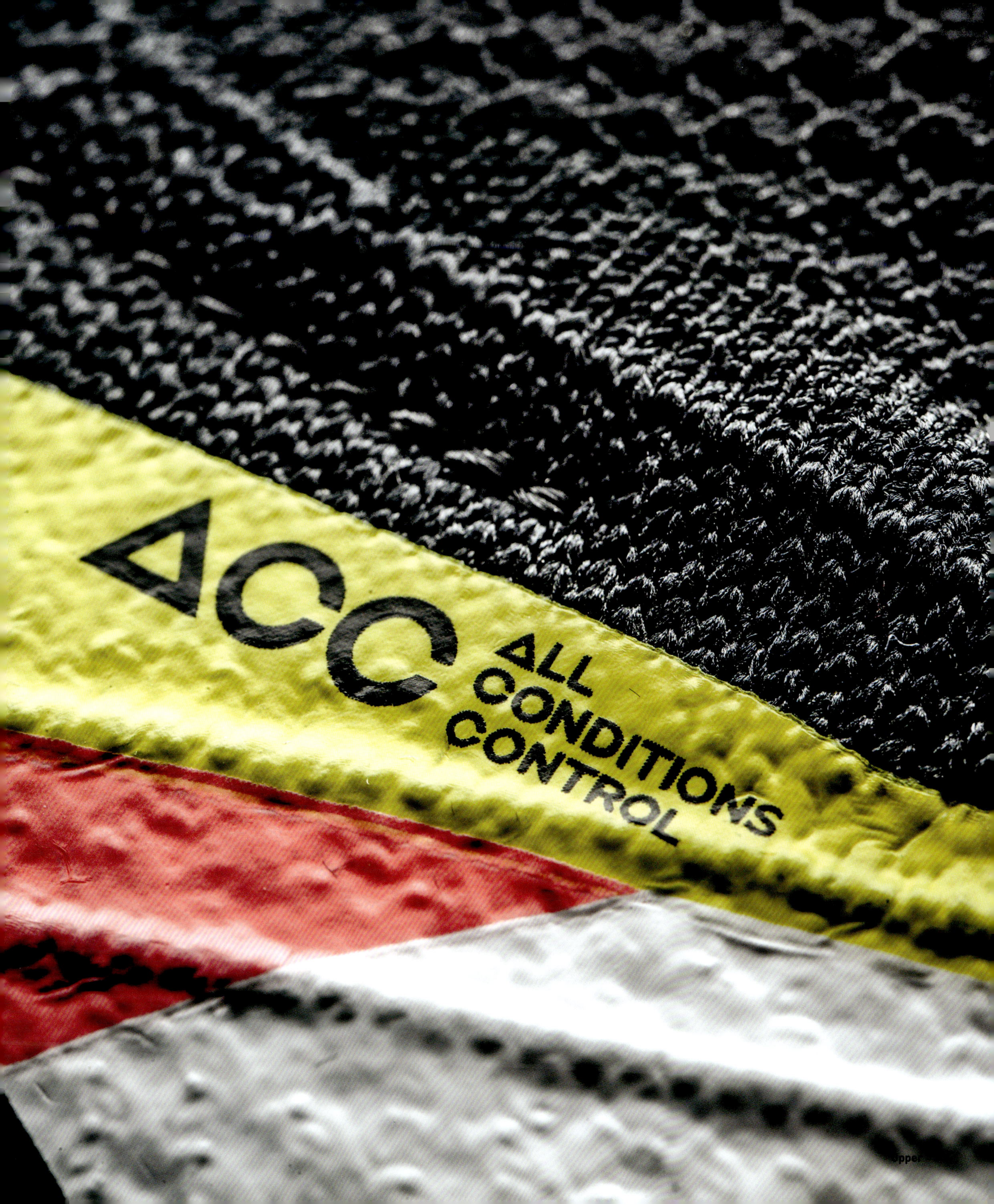
ACC
ALL
CONDITIONS
CONTROL

Details

The upper combines a wealth of materials including mesh and pigskin suede. White, gray and green are the primary tones. The plastic eyelets and the nylon stripes seem to wrap the shoes in their arms.

ADIDAS EQUIPMENT RUNNING CUSHION 93

The 2015 adidas Equipment Running Cushion 93 in this picture remains true to its 1993 predecessor.

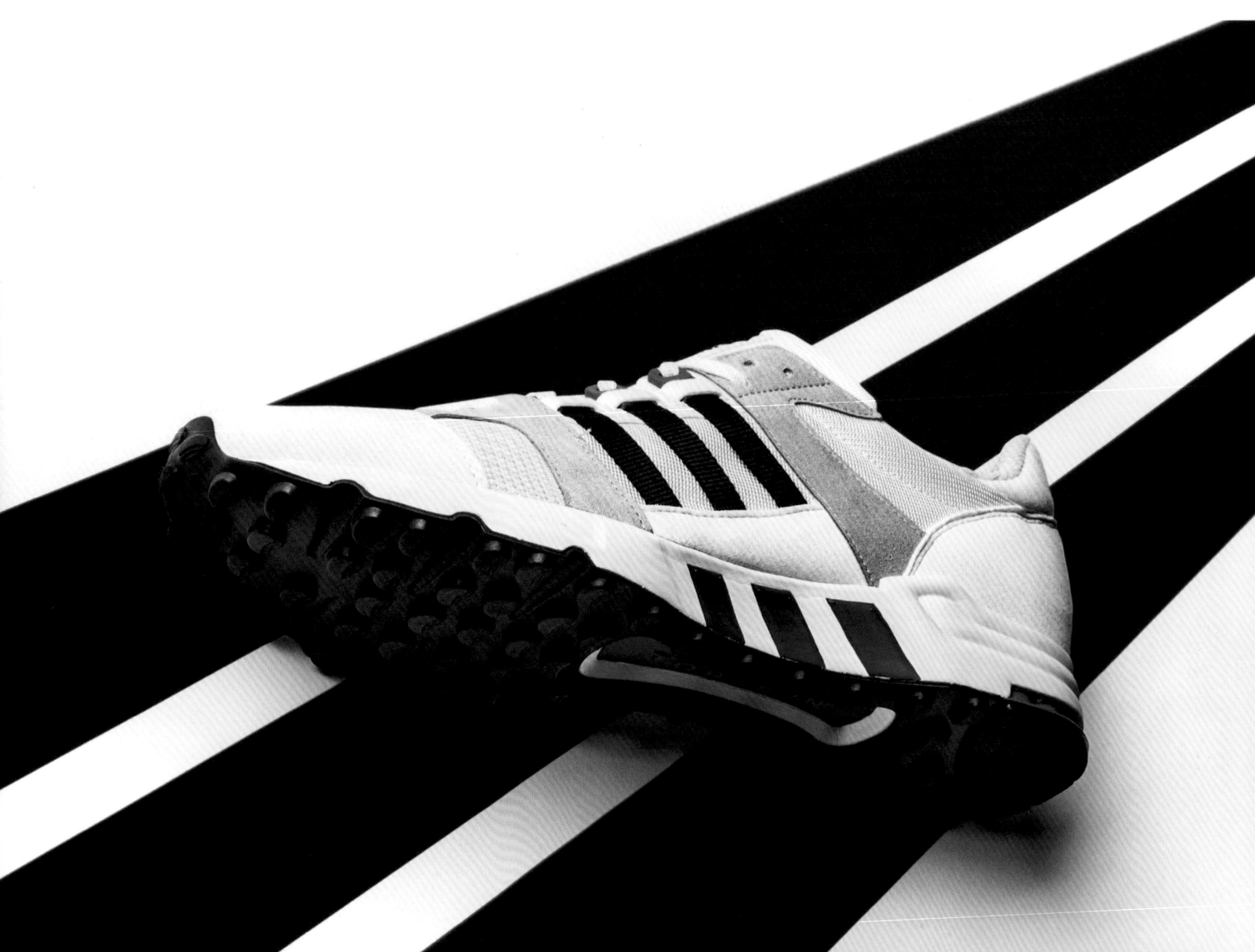

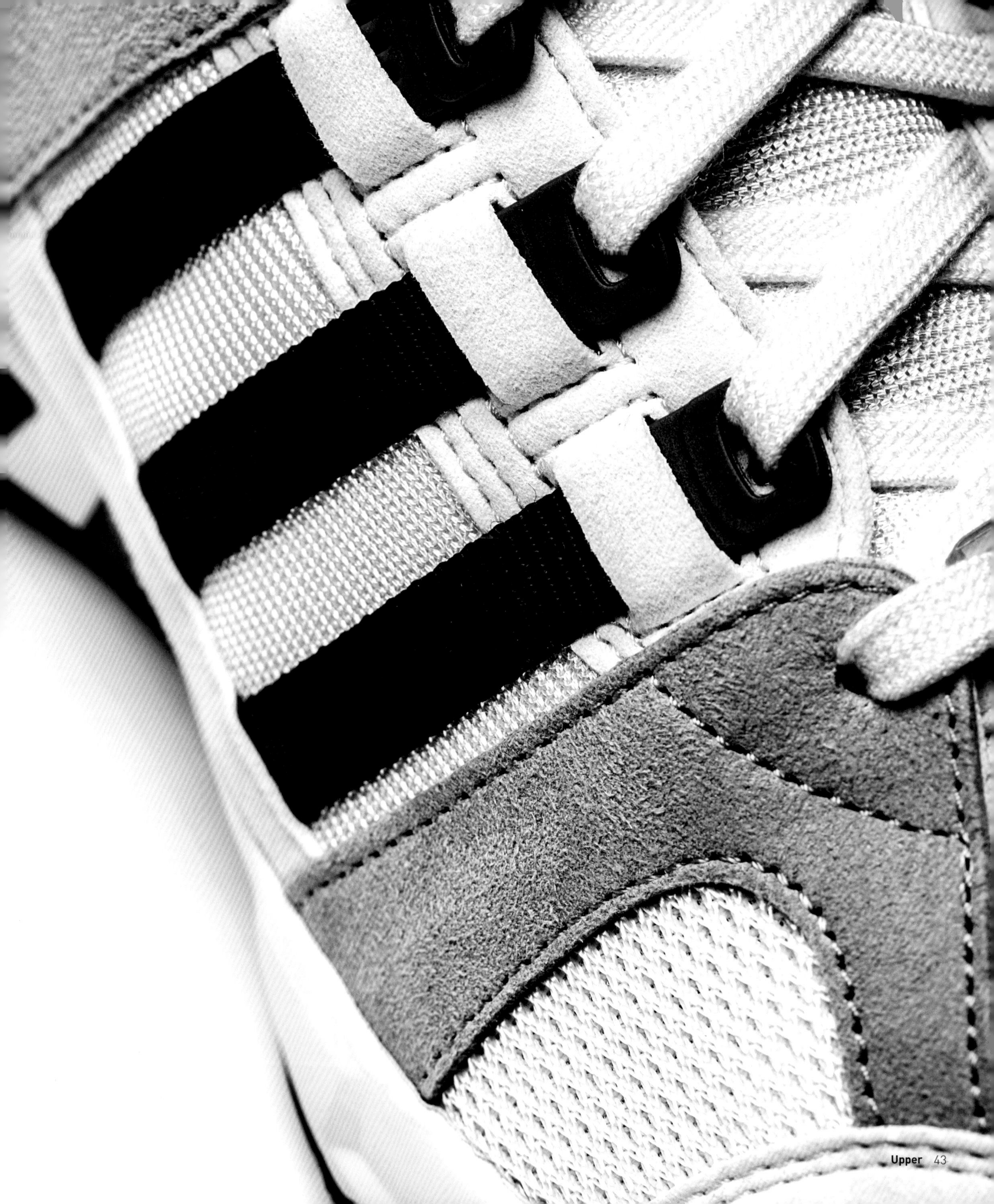

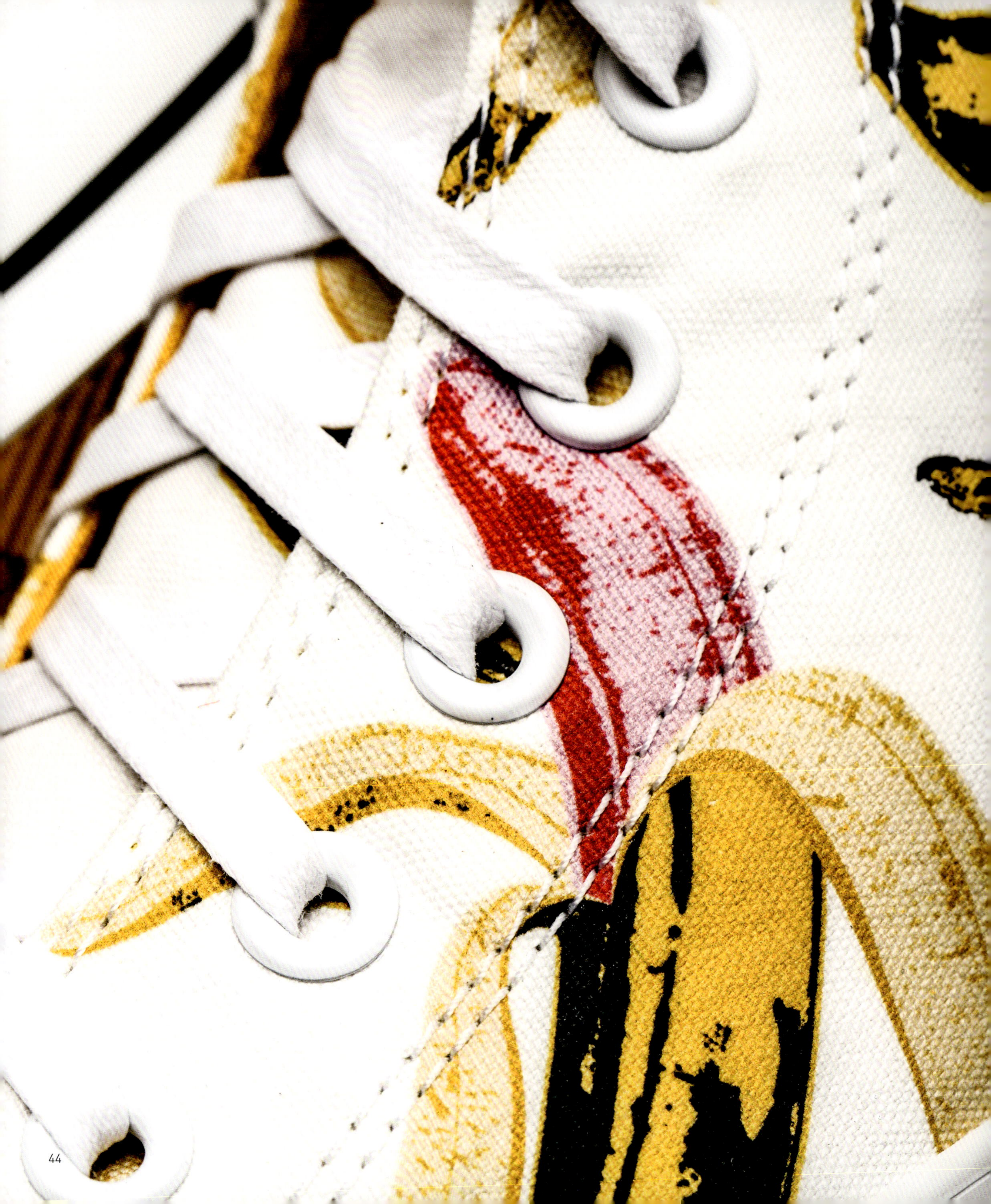

Details

The canvas upper is rendered with a unique take on Warhol's iconic banana artwork.

CLOT × ANDY WARHOL × CONVERSE CHUCK TAYLOR ALL-STAR [YEAR OF THE MONKEY]

In 2016 — the year of the monkey — Converse launched the Chuck Taylor Line with CLOT and the Andy Warhol Foundation for the Visual Arts.

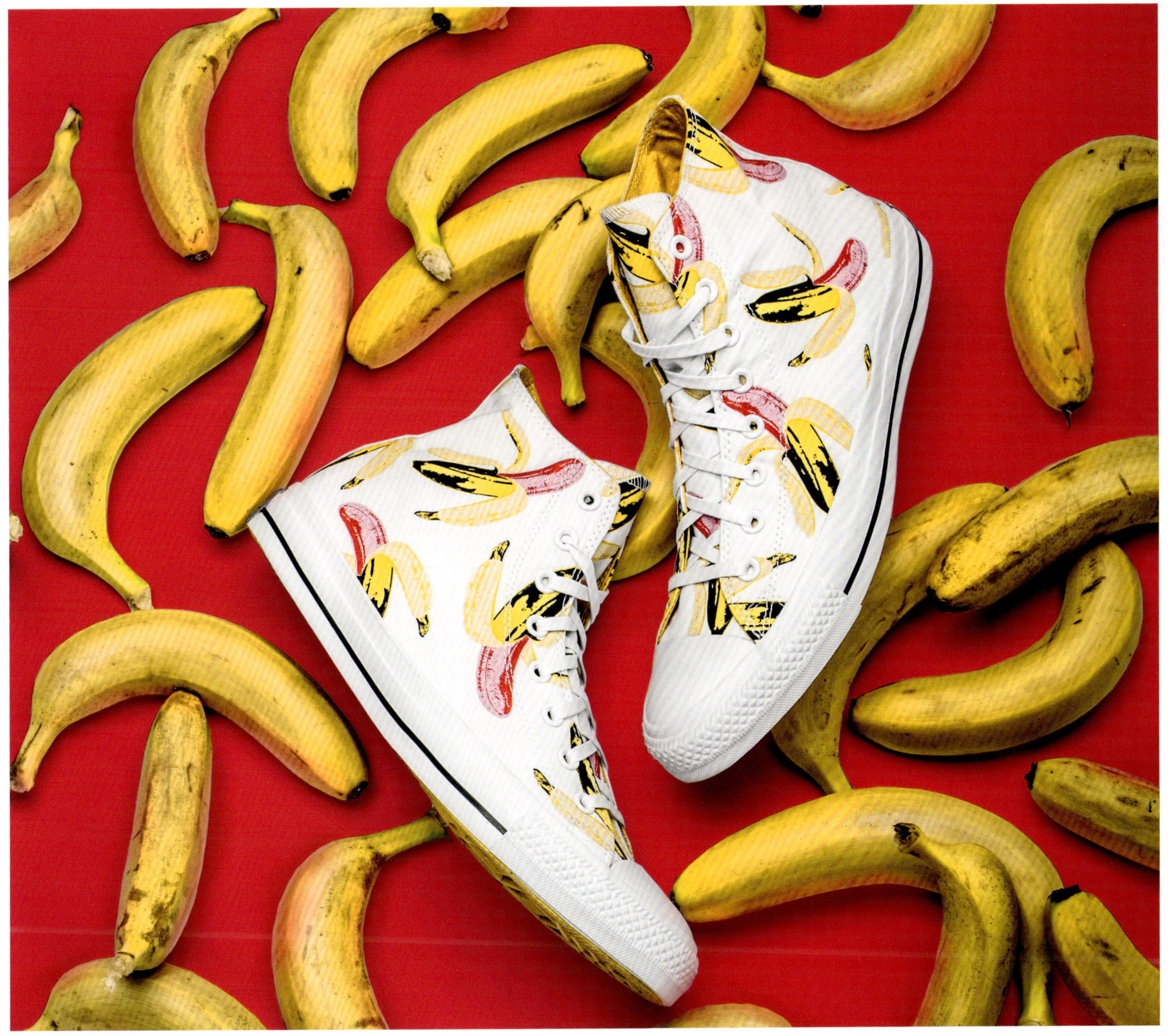

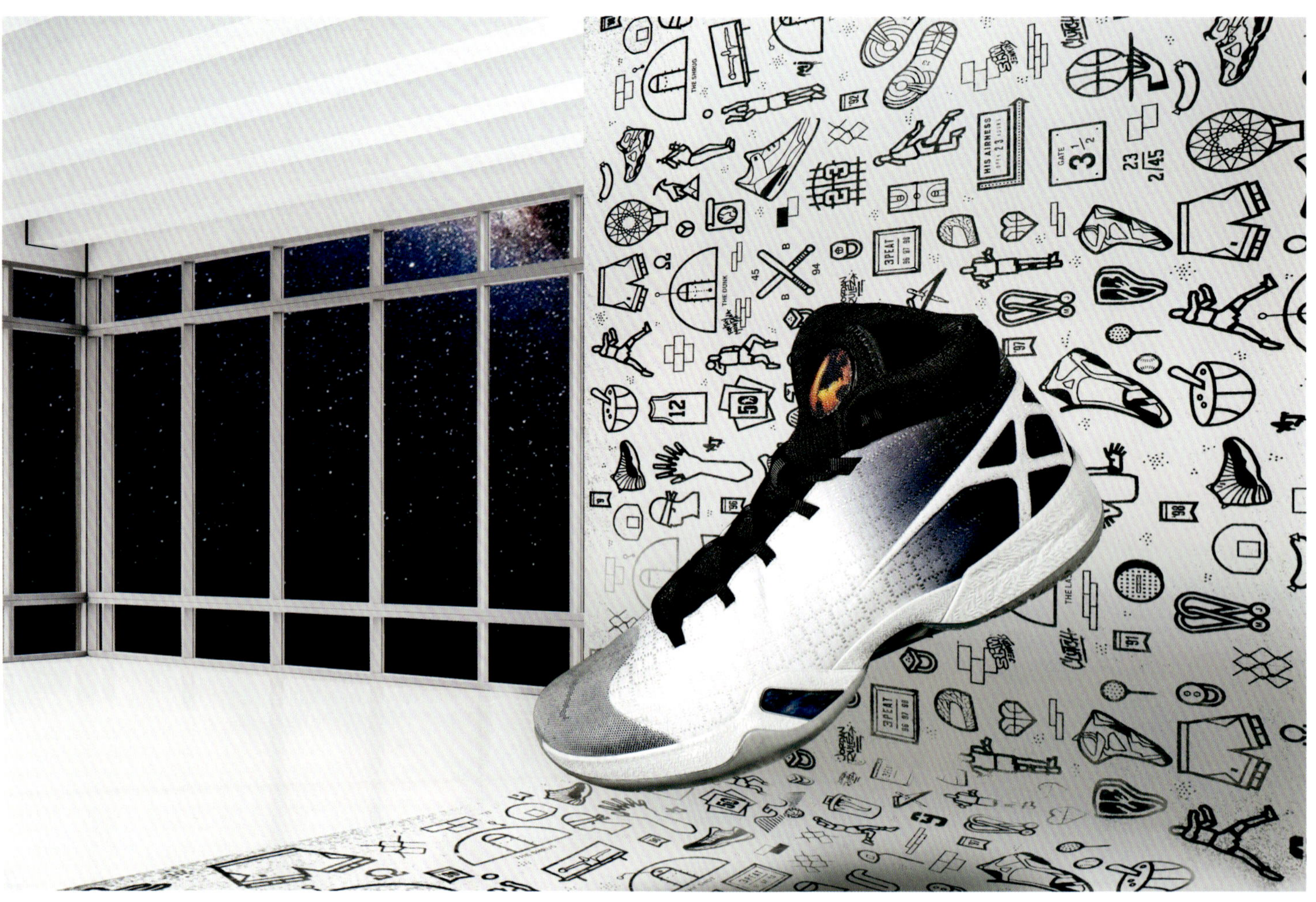

AIR JORDAN XXX

Released in 2016 and designed by Tinker Hatfield, it is the 30th signature shoe for Michael Jordan.

Details

The upper is a mix of woven, knit and 3D printing materials. The "lofted knit" is used for the first time in the Jordan line.

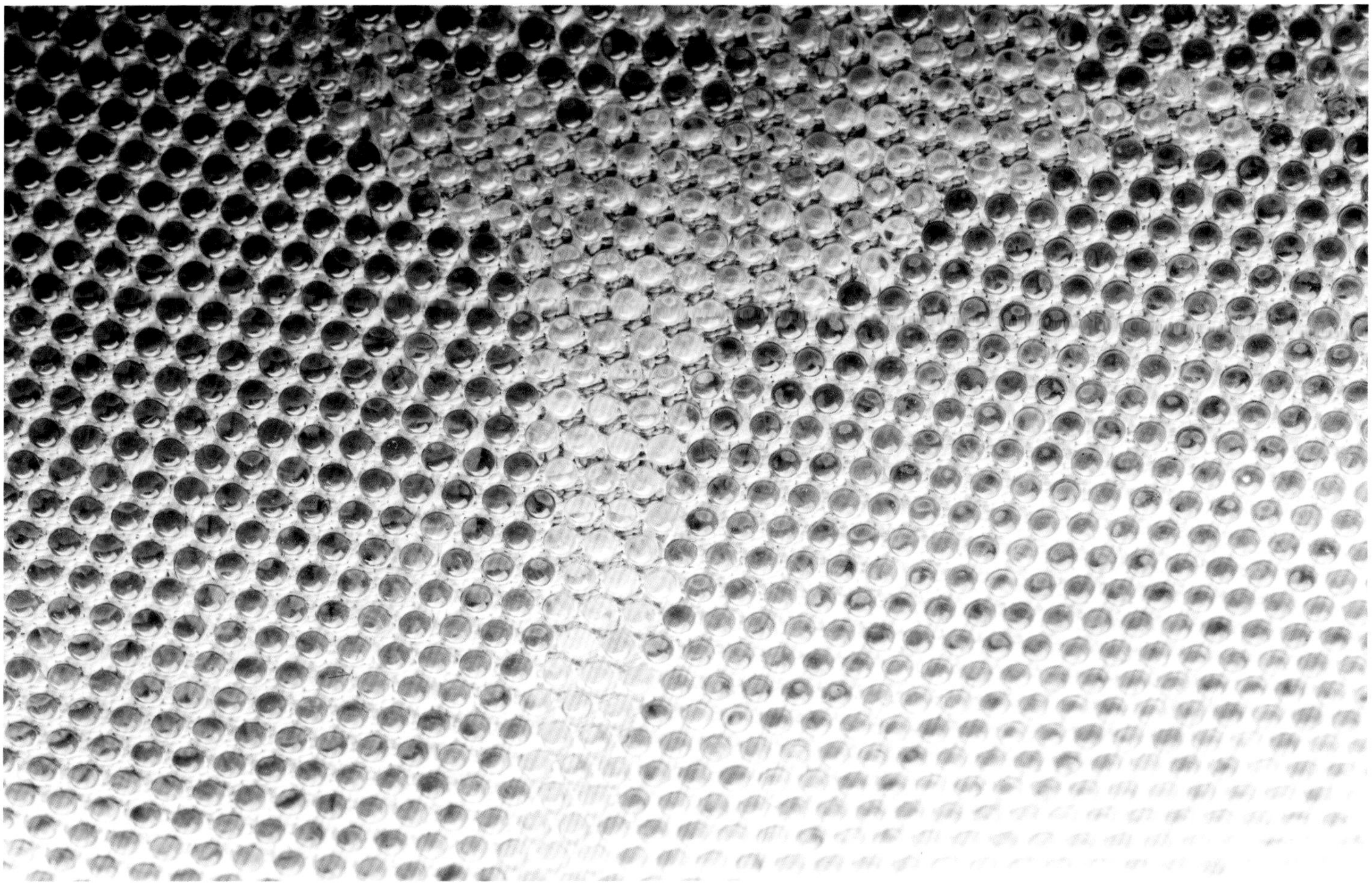

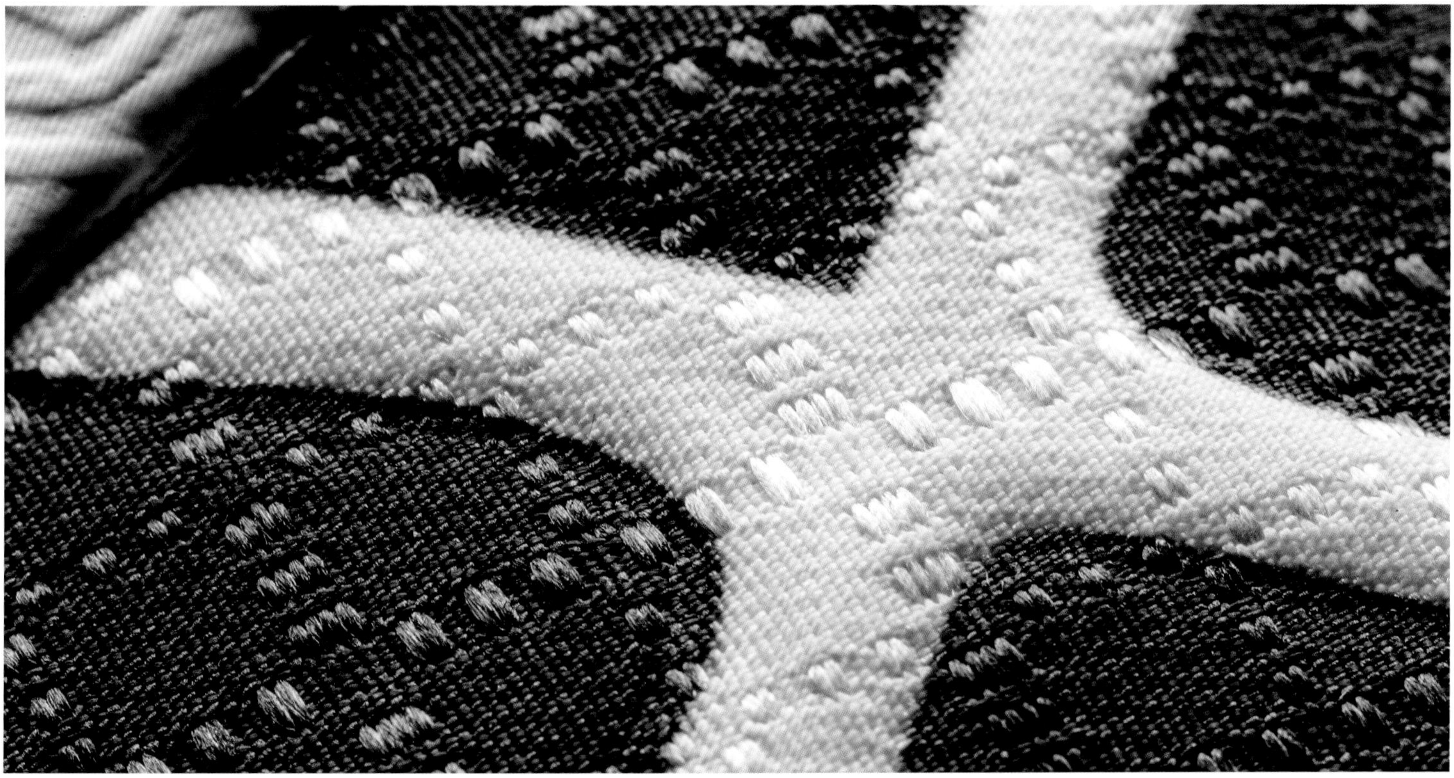

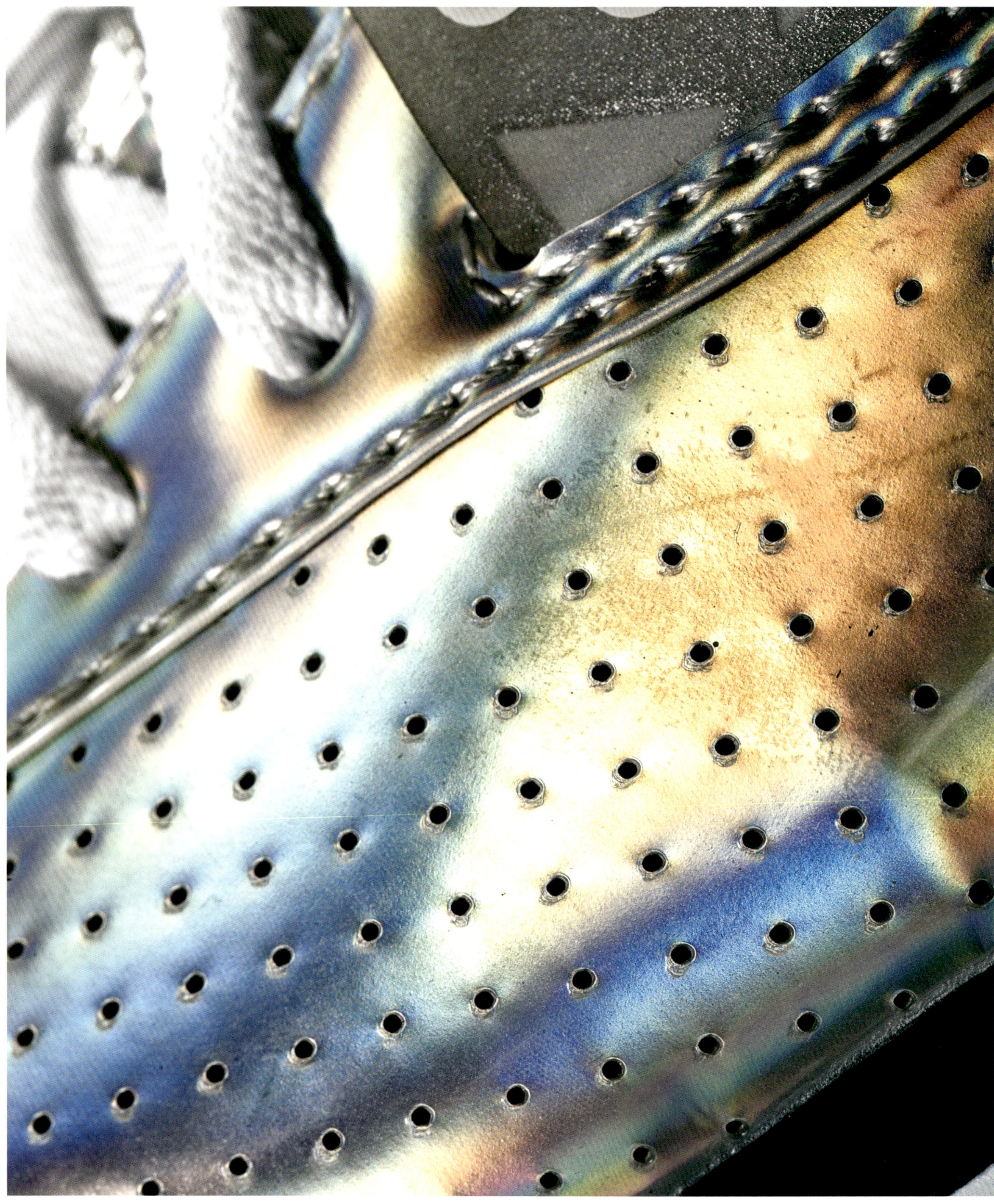

Details

The upper uses coated materials and has many pierced holes, reflecting a variety of colors under the sunshine. What distinguishes this sample from other sneakers in the market are: the middle sole of the sample is black; its reflective effect is weaker.

LI-NING DWYANEWADE 4 ALL-STAR SAMPLE

Dwyane Wade's fourth signature LI-NING sneaker, yet to be released to the public, is designed by Eric Miller.

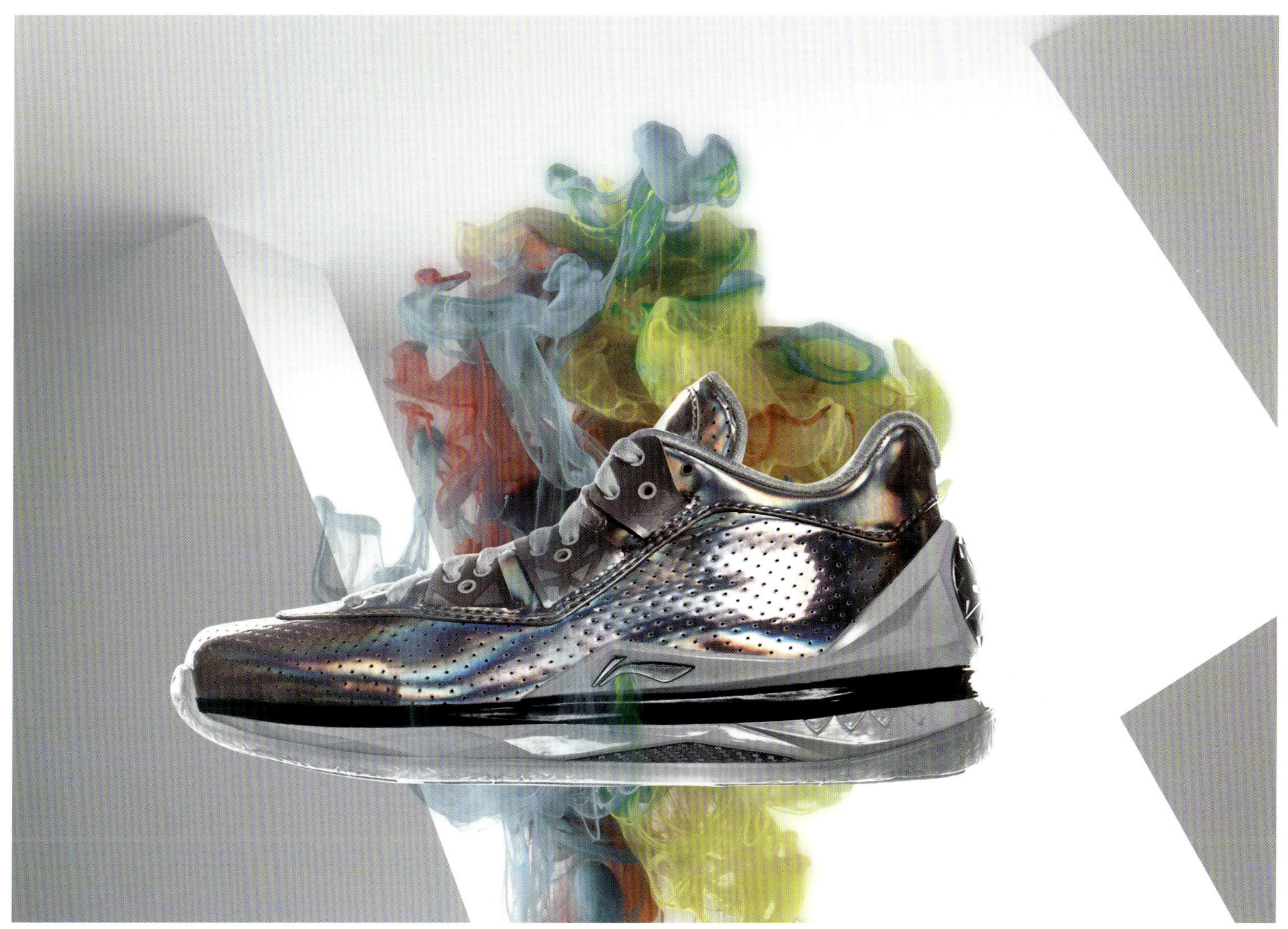

SAUCONY SHADOW 6000 [IRISH COFFEE] PACK

Released in 2016, the color choice of the shoe salutes Joe Sheridan and his 1943 creation and introduction of Irish Coffee.

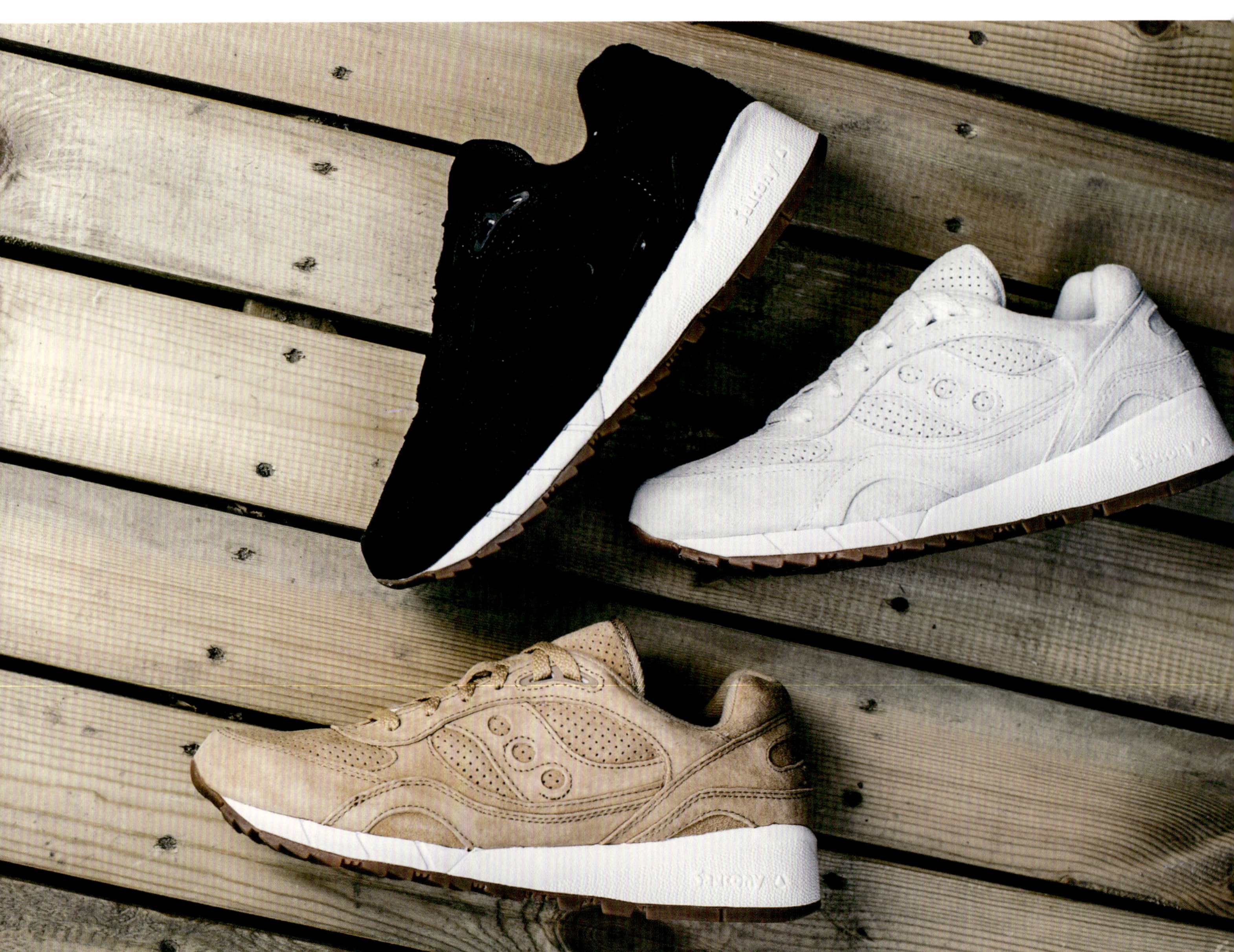

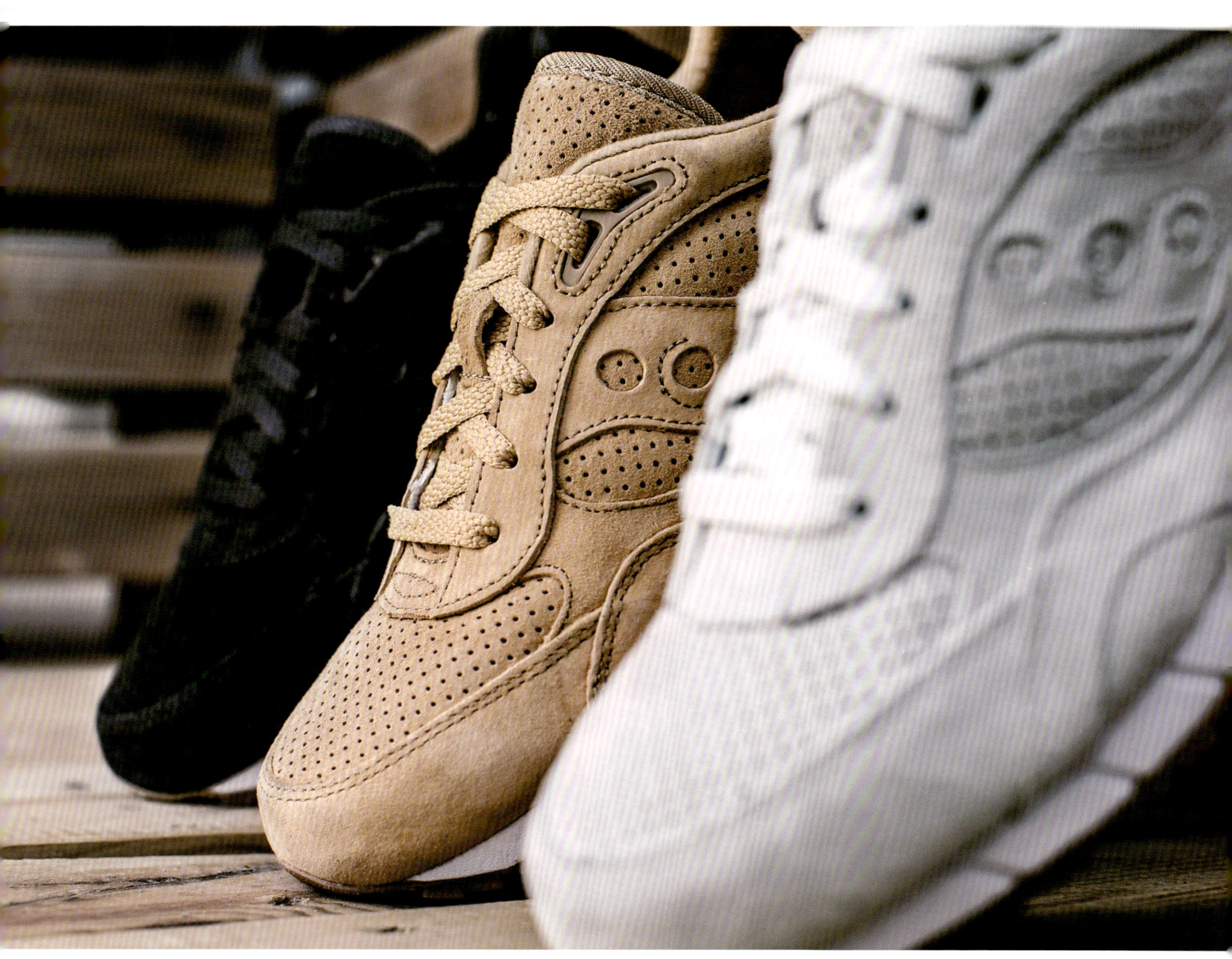

Details

The white-black-brown colorway of its buttery suede uppers is inspired by the key elements required to brew Irish Coffee — coffee, whiskey and cream.

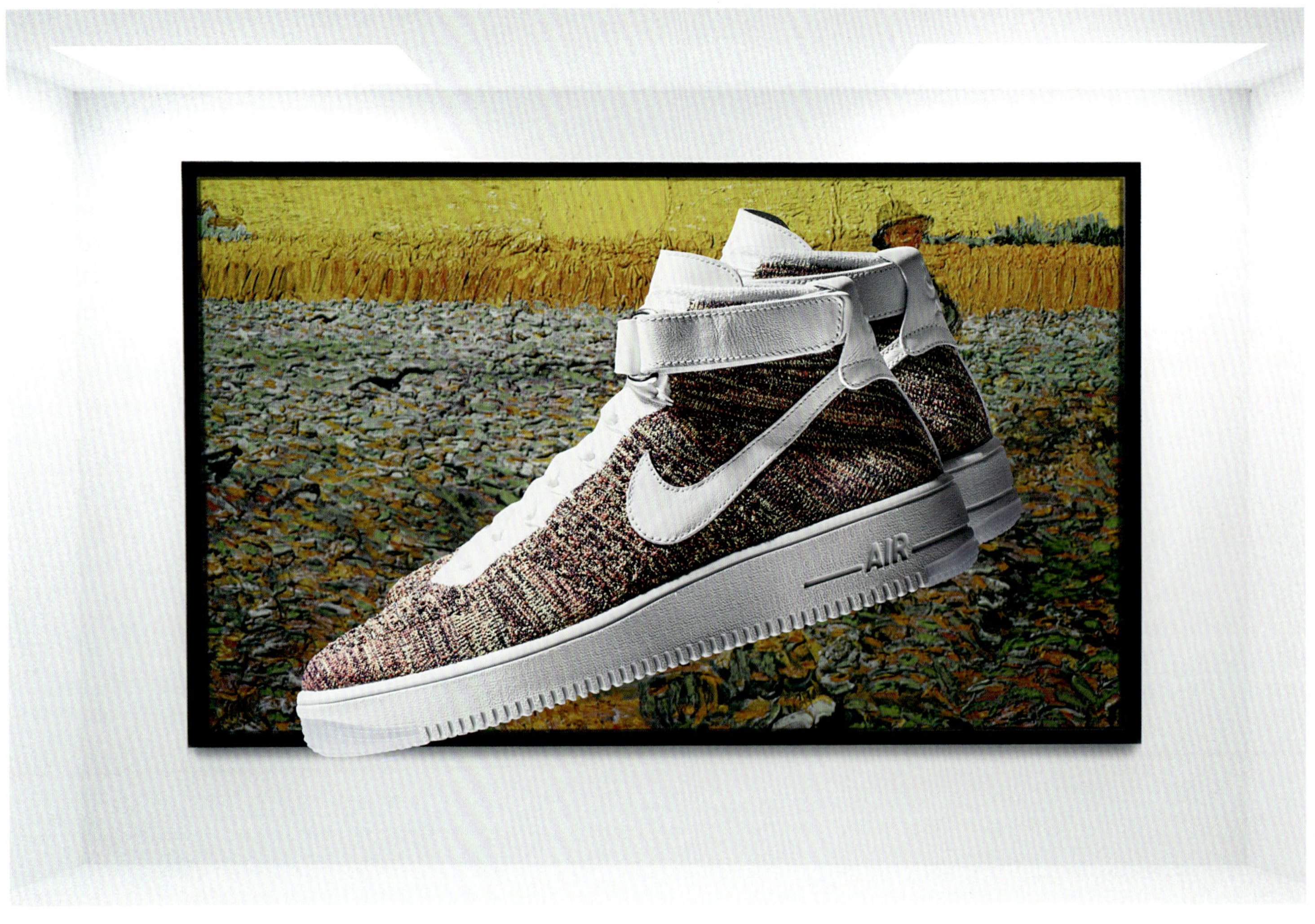

NIKE AIR FORCE 1 ULTRA FLYKNIT MID [MULTICOLOR]

Released in 2016 — which marked the 34th anniversary of the Air Force 1 — the Nike Air Force 1 Ultra Flyknit Men's Shoe weighs 50 percent less than the 82 hoops original thanks to its all-new, ultra-breathable Nike Flyknit upper.

Details

Concerted efforts from the design team ensure that it remains true to the original Air Force 1 aesthetics while using crafted Flyknit panels. They retain the toe, saddle, stitches, punch holes and the upper of the original one and opt for thicker and stronger woven yarns for its toe and eyelets.

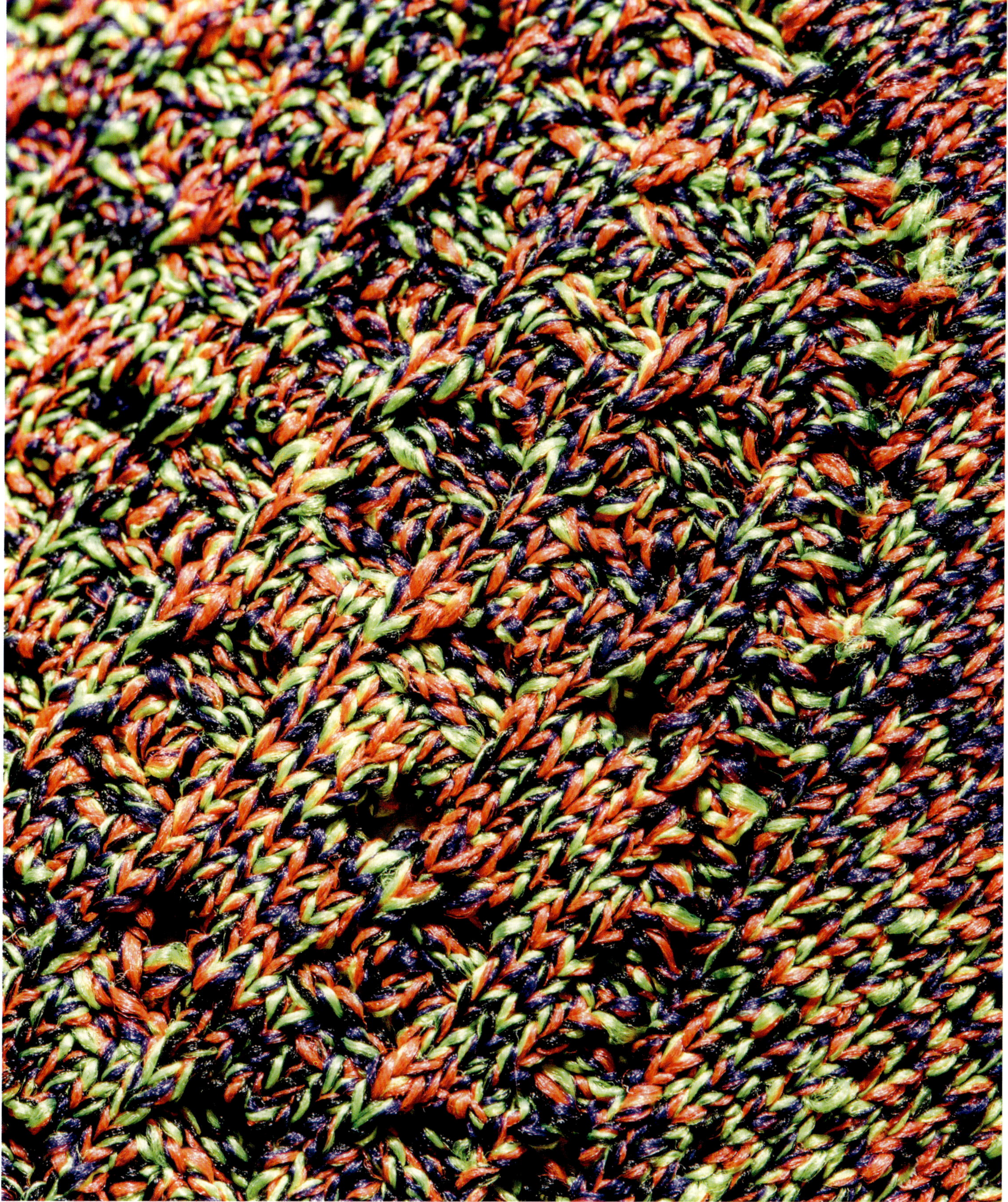

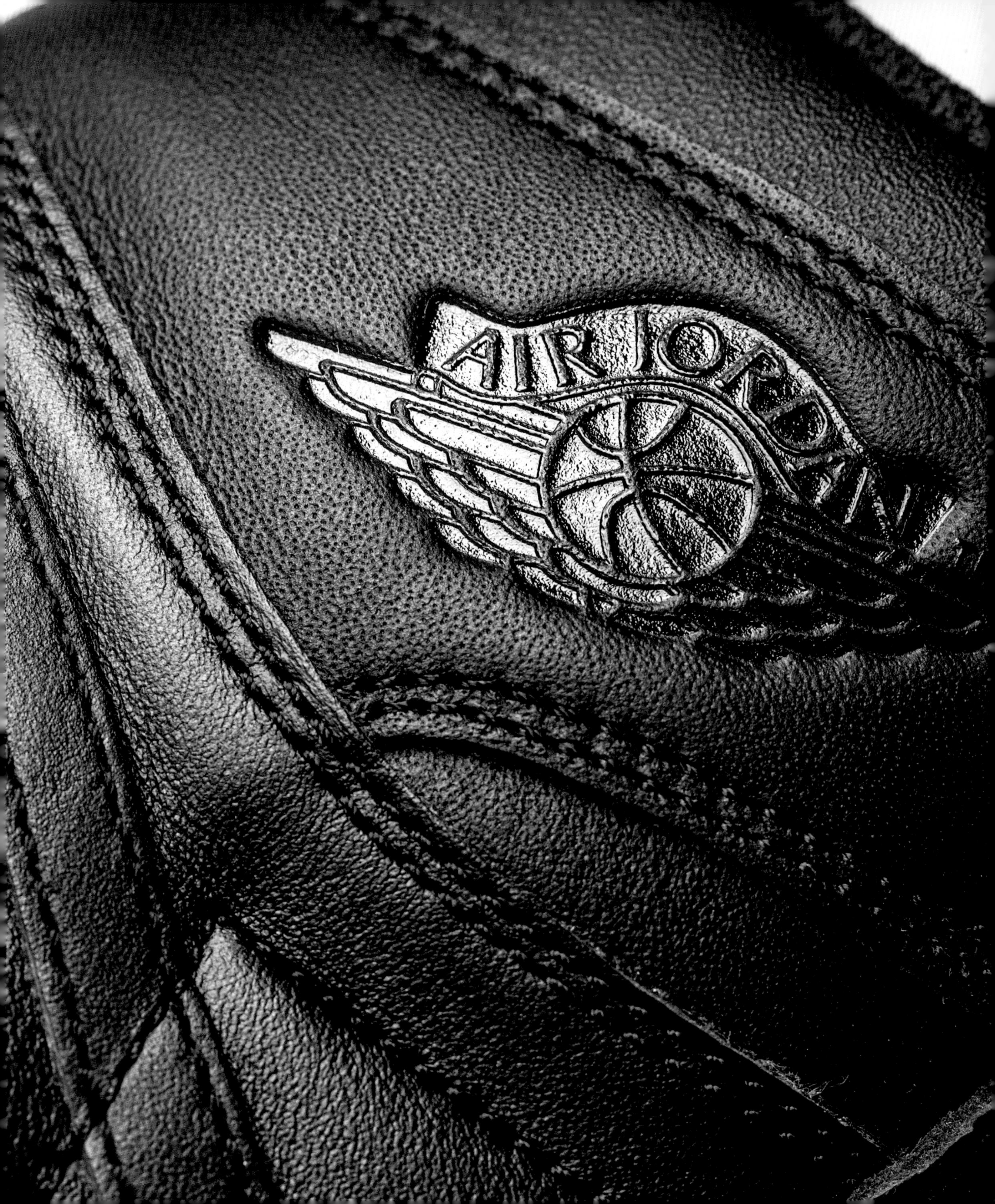
AIR JORDAN

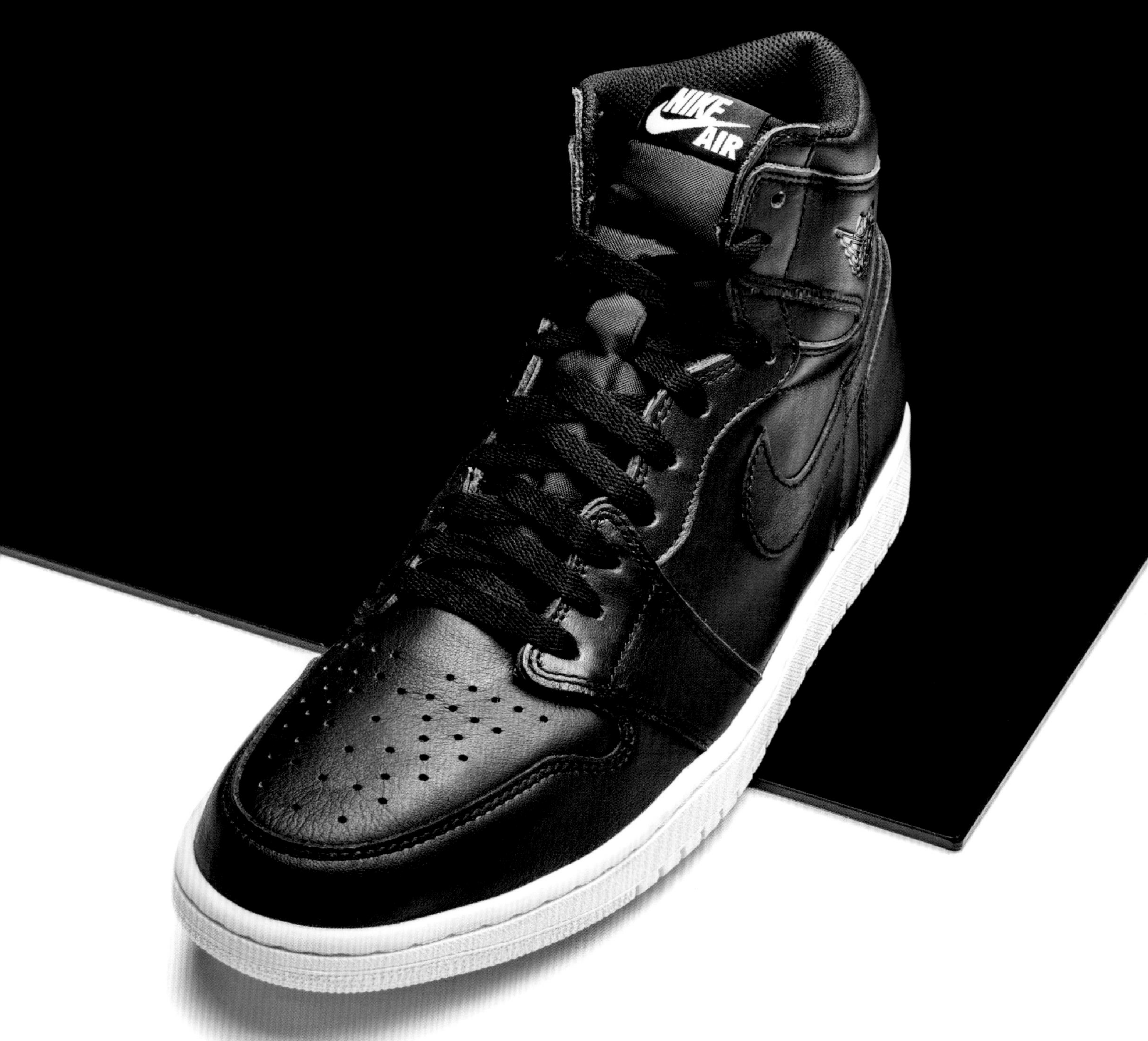

AIR JORDAN 1 RETRO HIGH OG [BLACK/WHITE]

This is the 2015 replica of the first Michael Jordan signature sneaker. Designed by Tinker Hatfield, it incorporates some iconic Nike elements. Air Jordan 1 has joined the club of "the most representative and classic sneakers."

Details

Inspired by classic sneakers like Air Jordan 1 Retro High OG, it uses full-grain leather, delivering premium quality and great durability.

Details

The lightweight, elastic and solid Nike Flyknit, which uses polyester yarns, increases the breathability through the eyelets of the woven threads. For this improved iteration of Flyknit, it has used thermoplastic polyurethane (TPU) for the first time. TPU outperforms previous stiff mesh materials of Kobe X in durability, weight, flexibility and supportiveness.

NIKE KOBE XI ELITE LOW [ACHILLES HEEL]

Debuting in 2015, it is the 11th signature Nike shoe of Kobe Bryant. Meanwhile, this sneaker, designed by Eric Avar, is also the last signature sneaker of Kobe because he was hanging up his shoes soon.

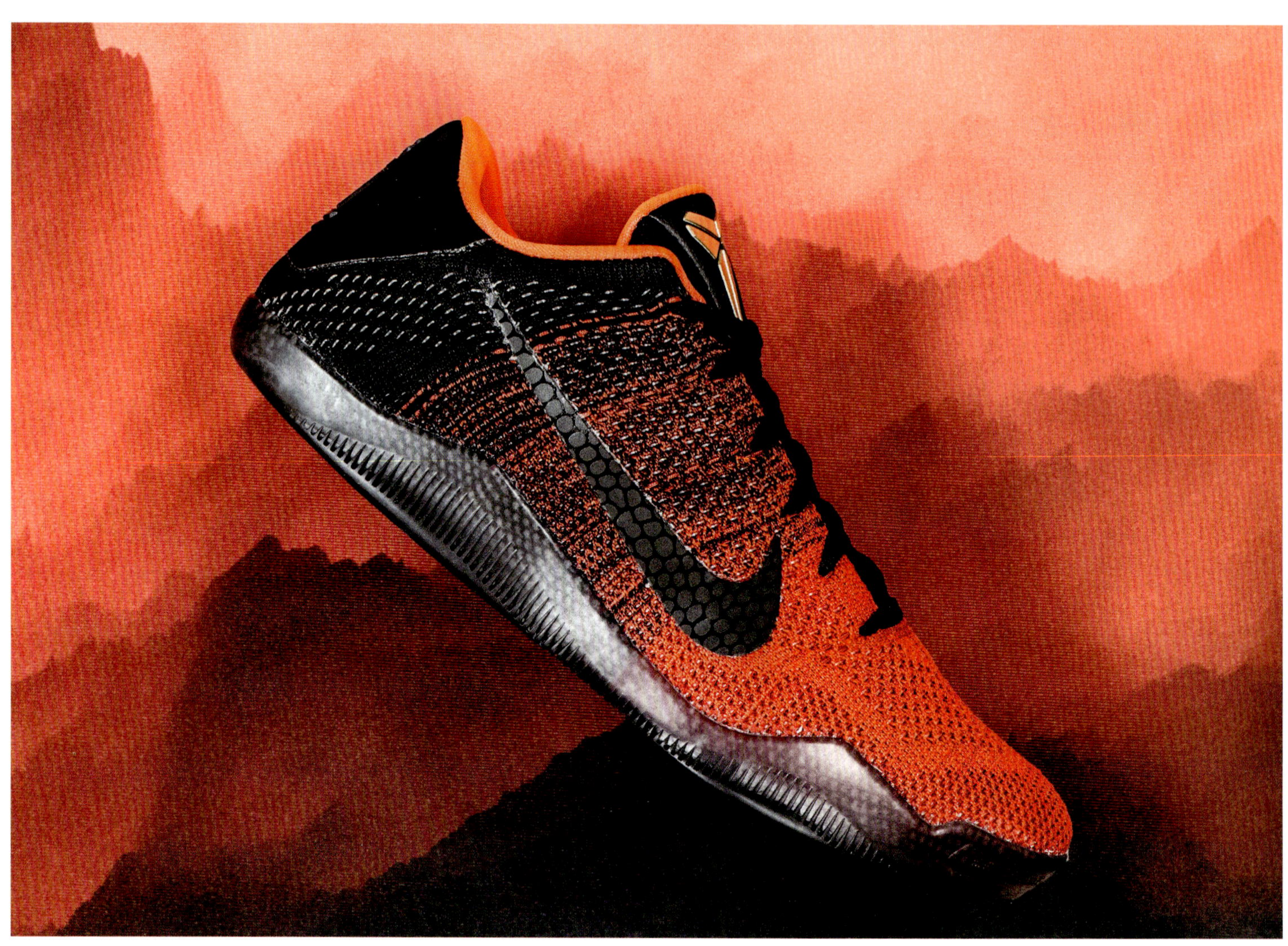

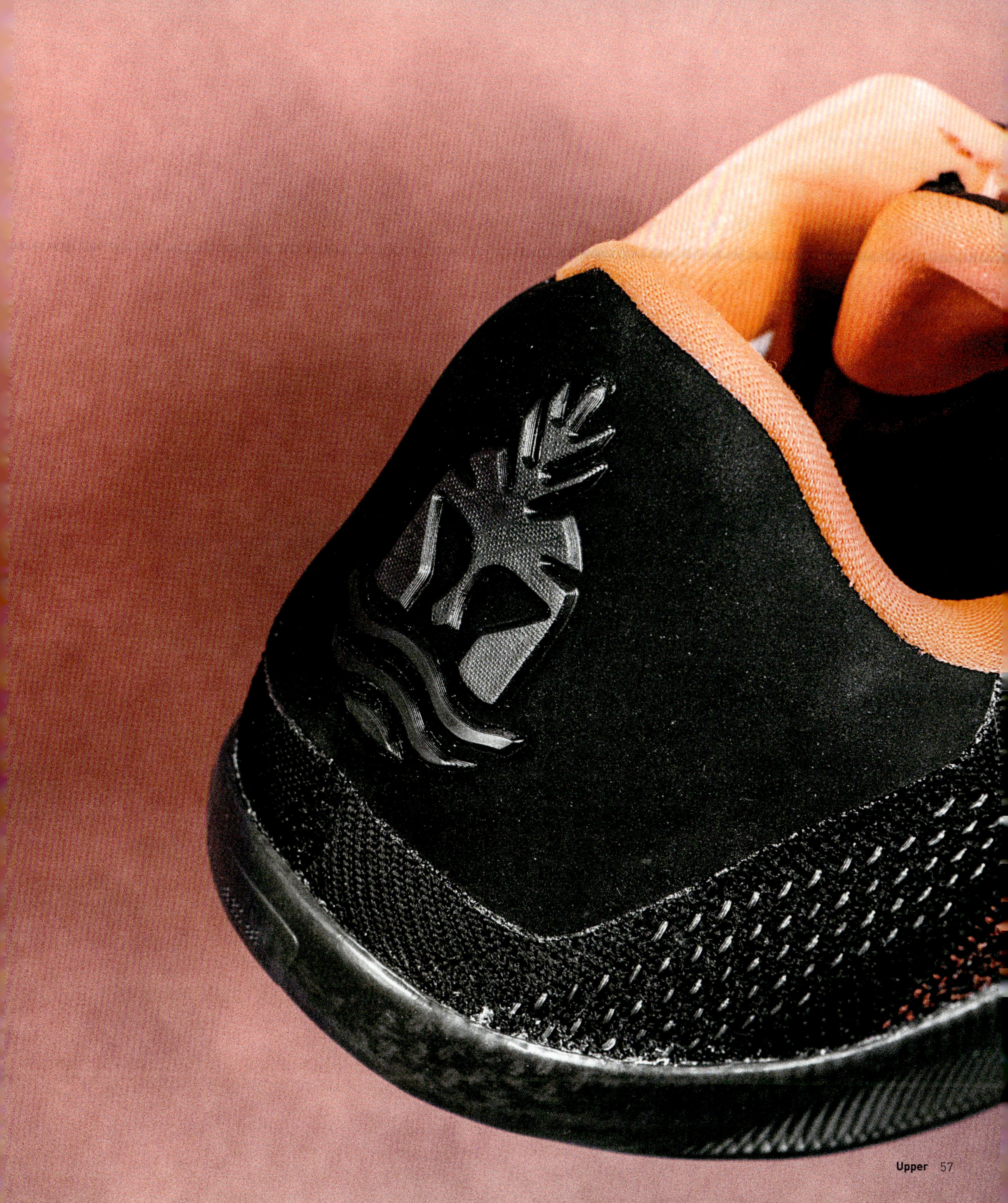

PORTS 1961 BEE SNEAKERS

"Slip-on" Line, launched in autumn 2015, is a retro of the 1961 Ports shoe. Ports is a Canadian luxury brand and Mr. Luke Tanabe, its founding father, is a global traveler, aspiring to "wander and wonder in the Sahara Desert at dawn and wine and dine in the Big Apple at dusk."

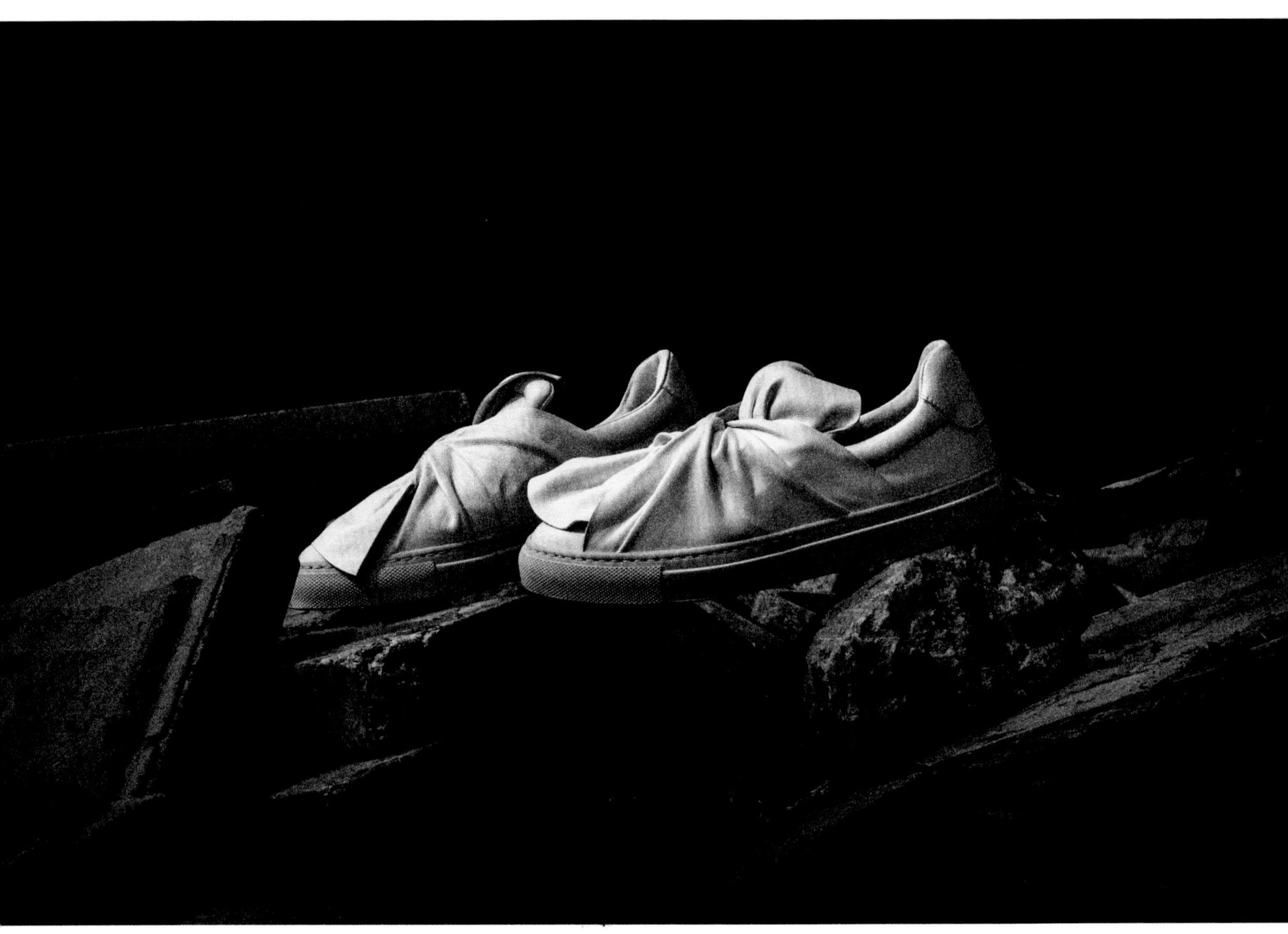

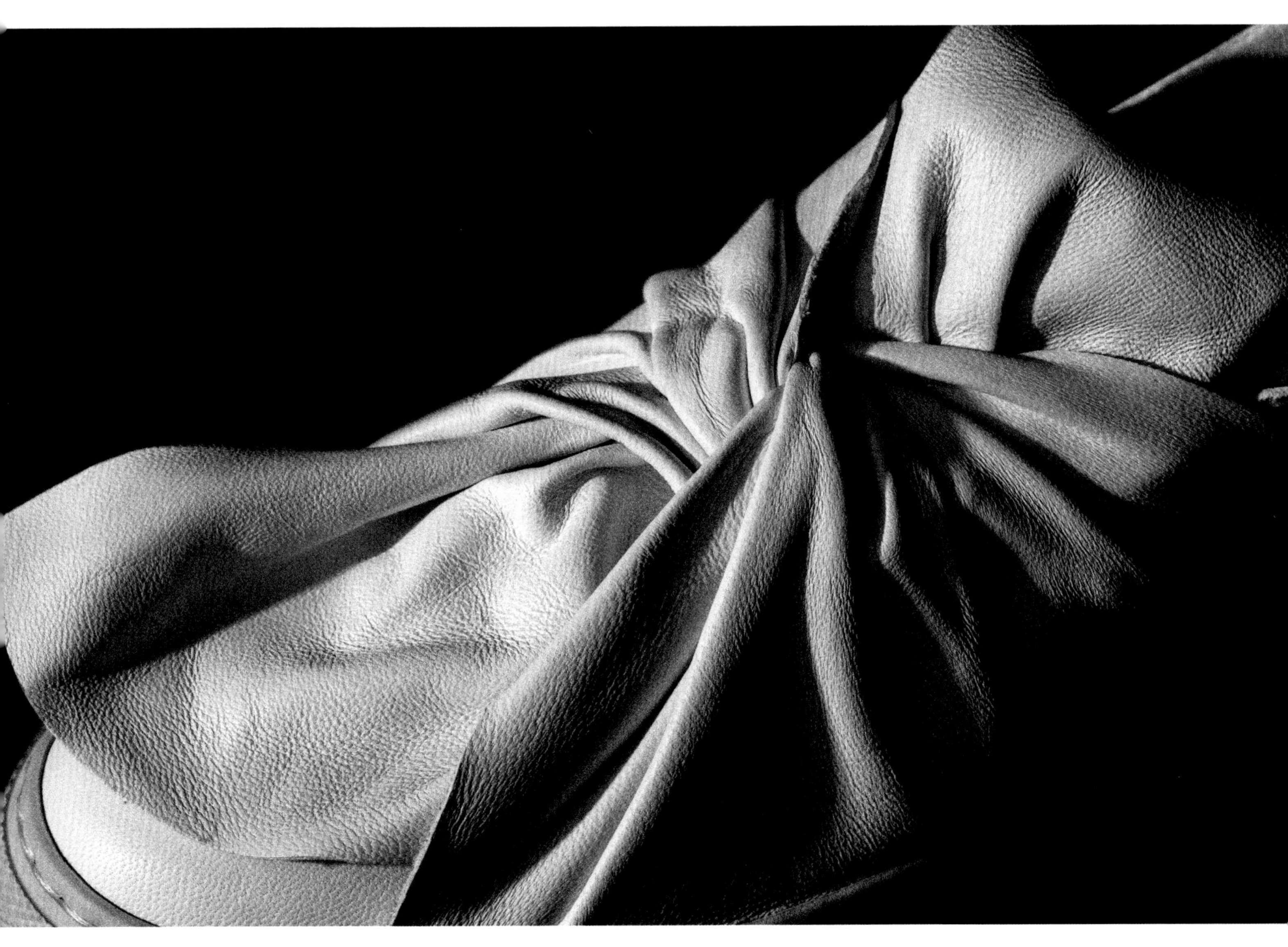

Details

The Bee Sneaker features a sleek lambskin upper with a wrapped ribbon design. This raw-cut style surely says, " Less is more."

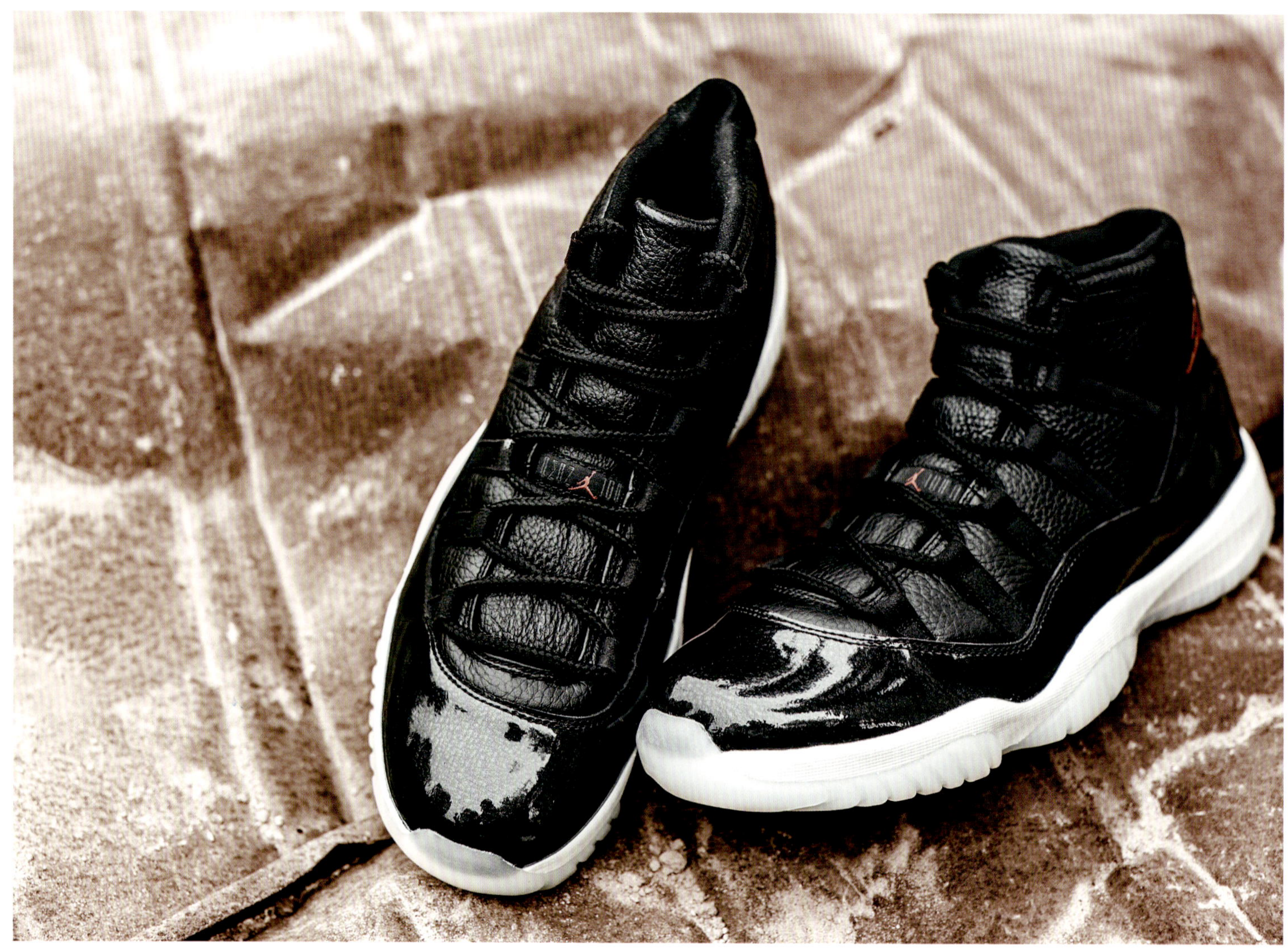

AIR JORDAN 11 RETRO [72-10]

Released in 2015, the take is a Tinker Hatfield-designed shoe modeled after the Air Jordan 11. The colorway is set to celebrate the exceptional 1995-1996 championship season, when MJ and his squad made history with a 72-10 regular season record.

Details

Forgoing the use of nylon, the upper is a mix of nubuck, patent leather and premium tumbled leather. The combination of the three different materials has brought out the best of the multi-textured attributes.

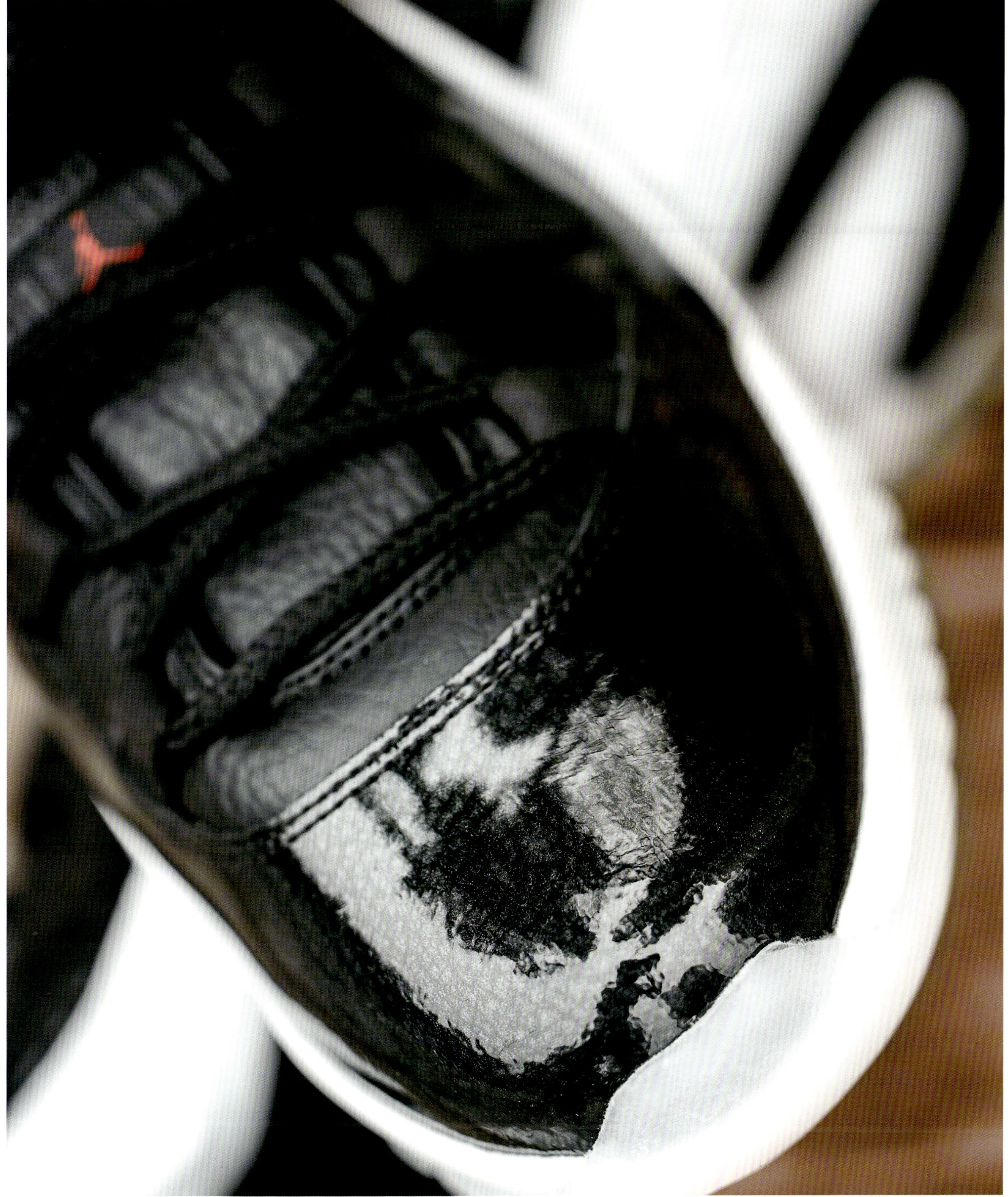

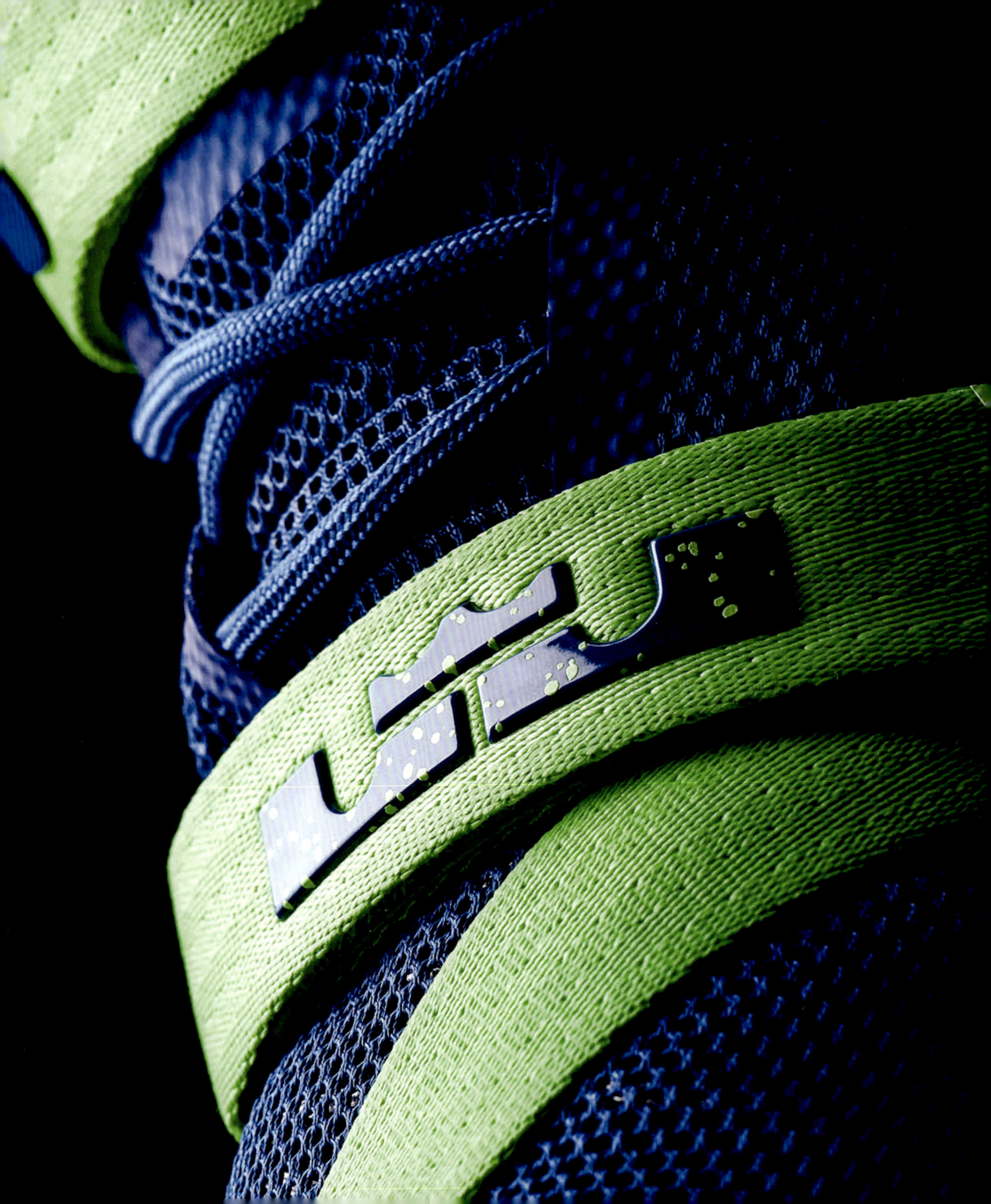

Details

The shoe features a mesh upper with heat-pressed materials, and laces stretching from the mid of the instep to the tongue of the shoe. Two hook-and-loop straps are designed to wrap the ankle and midfoot.

NIKE LEBRON SOLDIER IX

Released in 2015 and designed by Jason Petrie, it is the ninth iteration in the "Soldier" collection, a line of LeBron James' signature shoes.

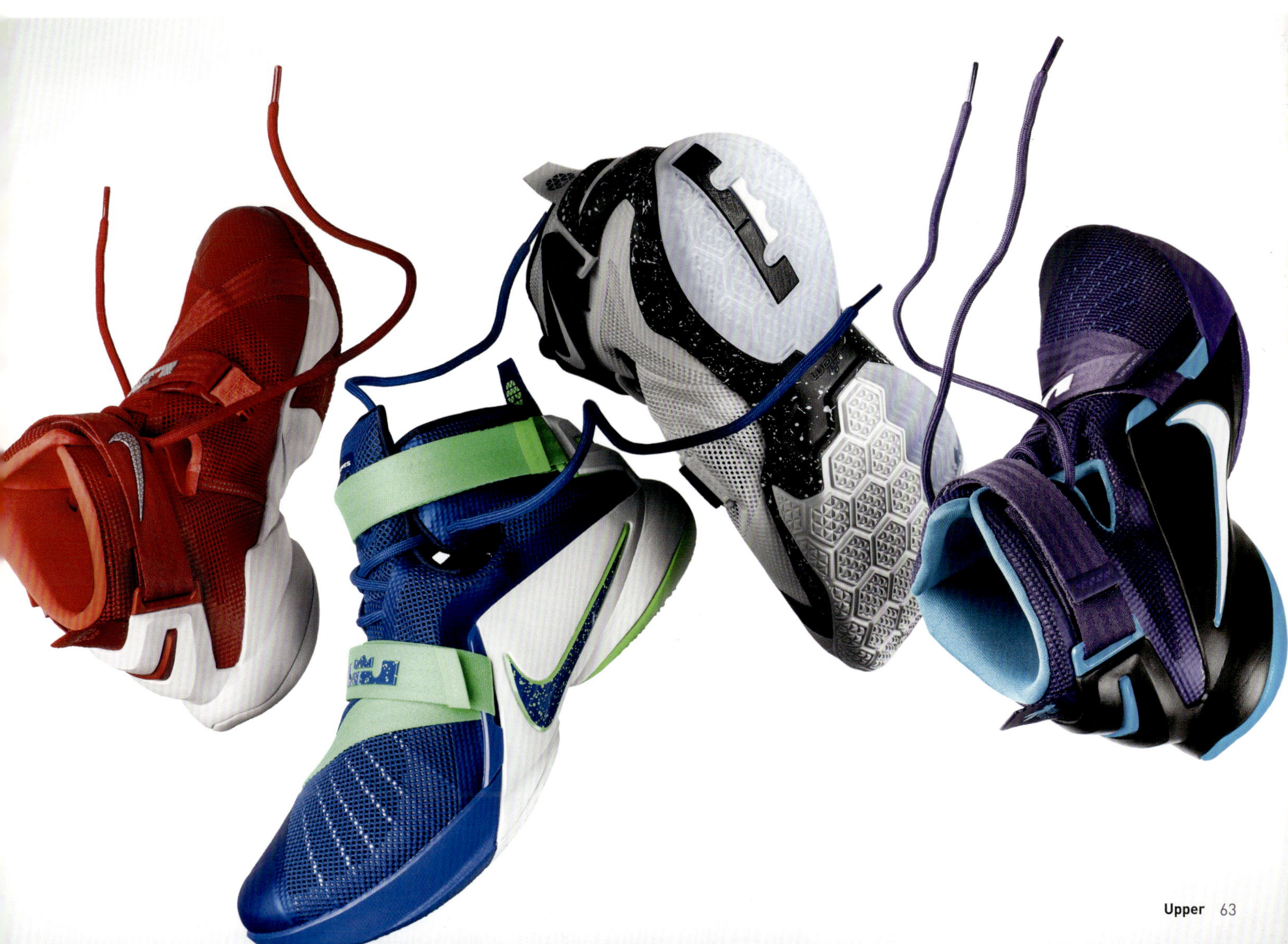

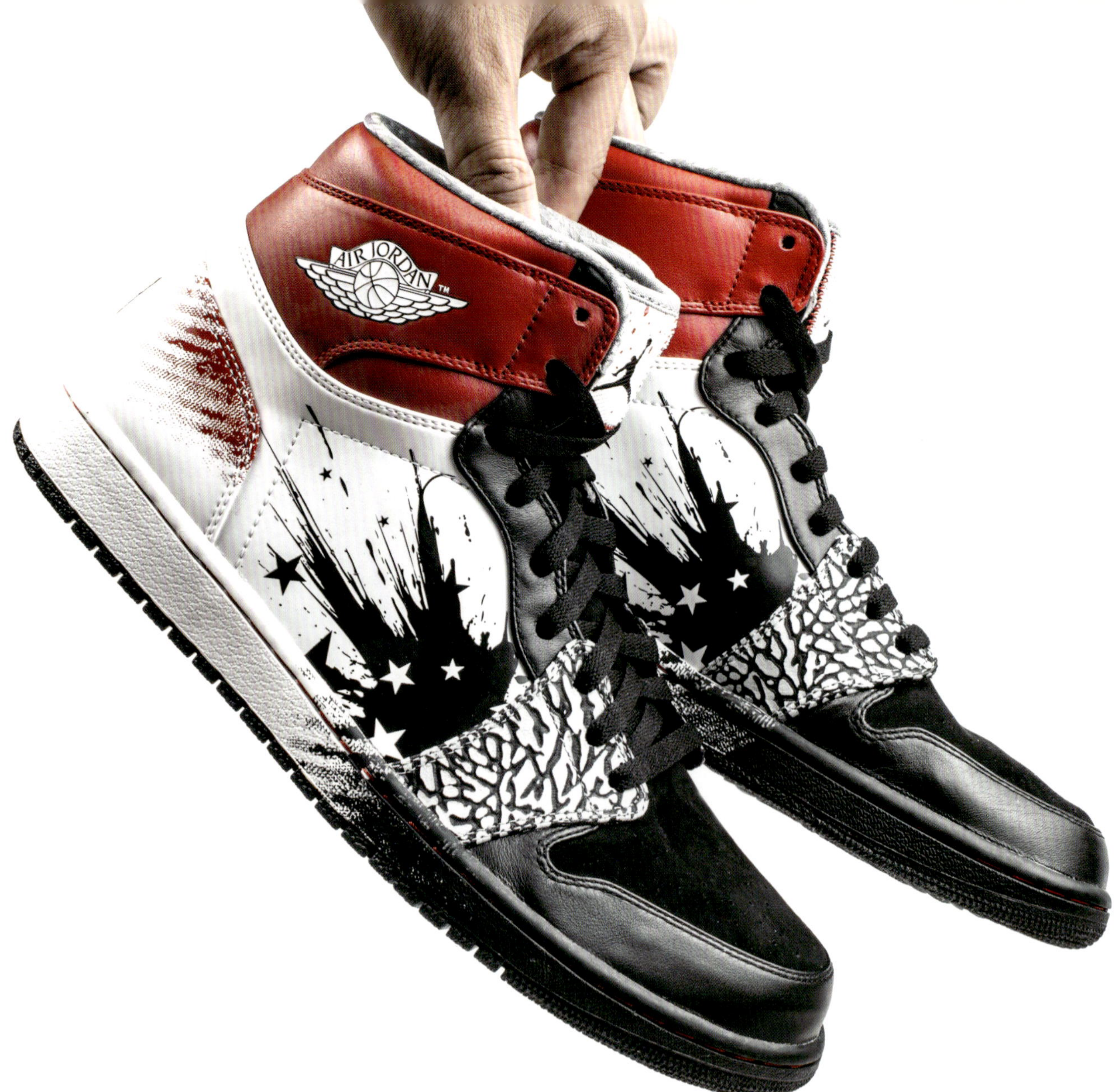

AIR JORDAN 1 HIGH DW

In 2012 Jordan Brand, in conjunction with British artist Dave White, unveiled a limited edition of Air Jordan 1 — a wild redesign of the classic silhouette.

Details

The upper is made of suede. The Swoosh on the lateral side is replaced by the iconic paint splash and stars of Dave White. The elephant print paneling of the Air Jordan 3 is also inherited.

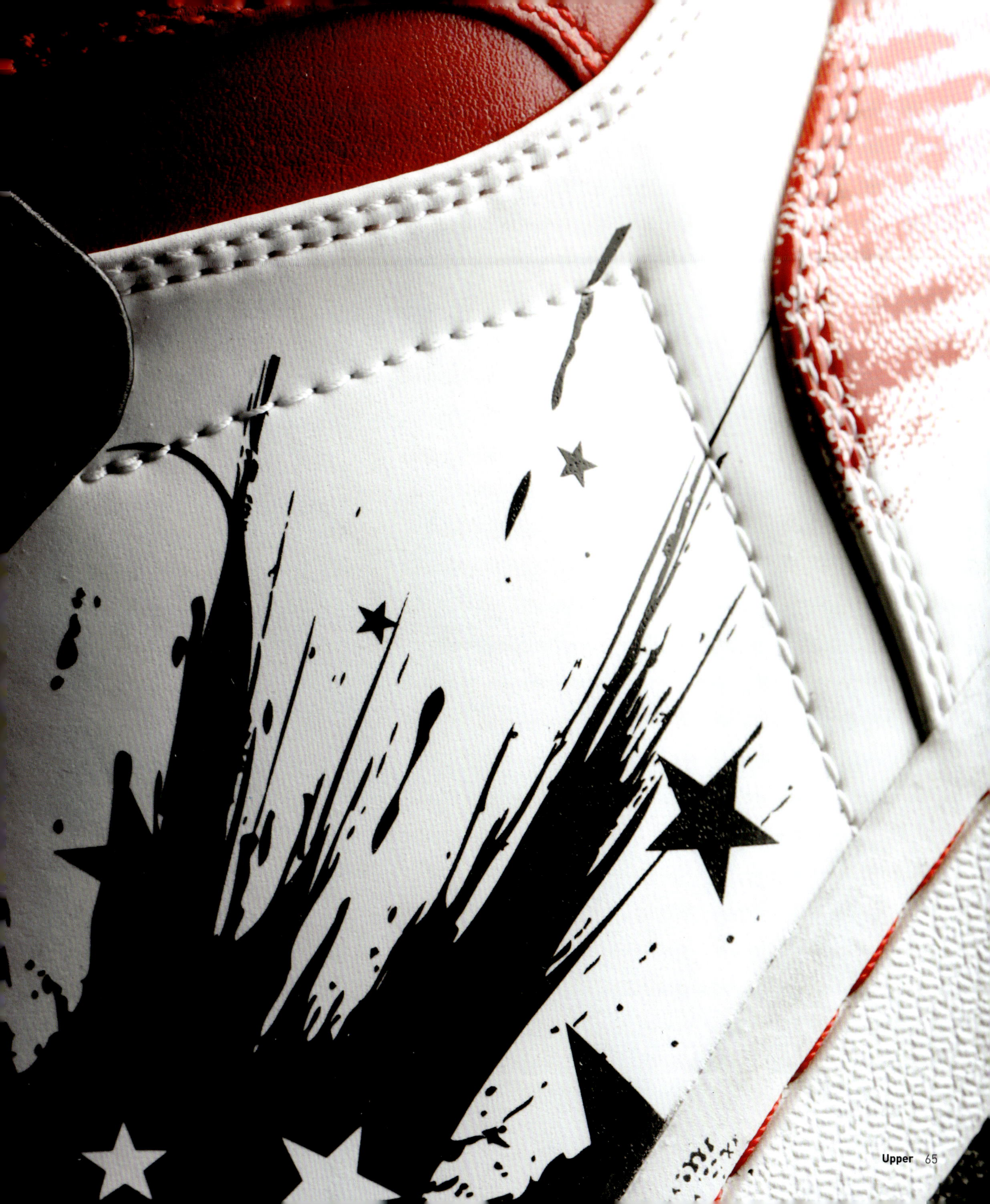

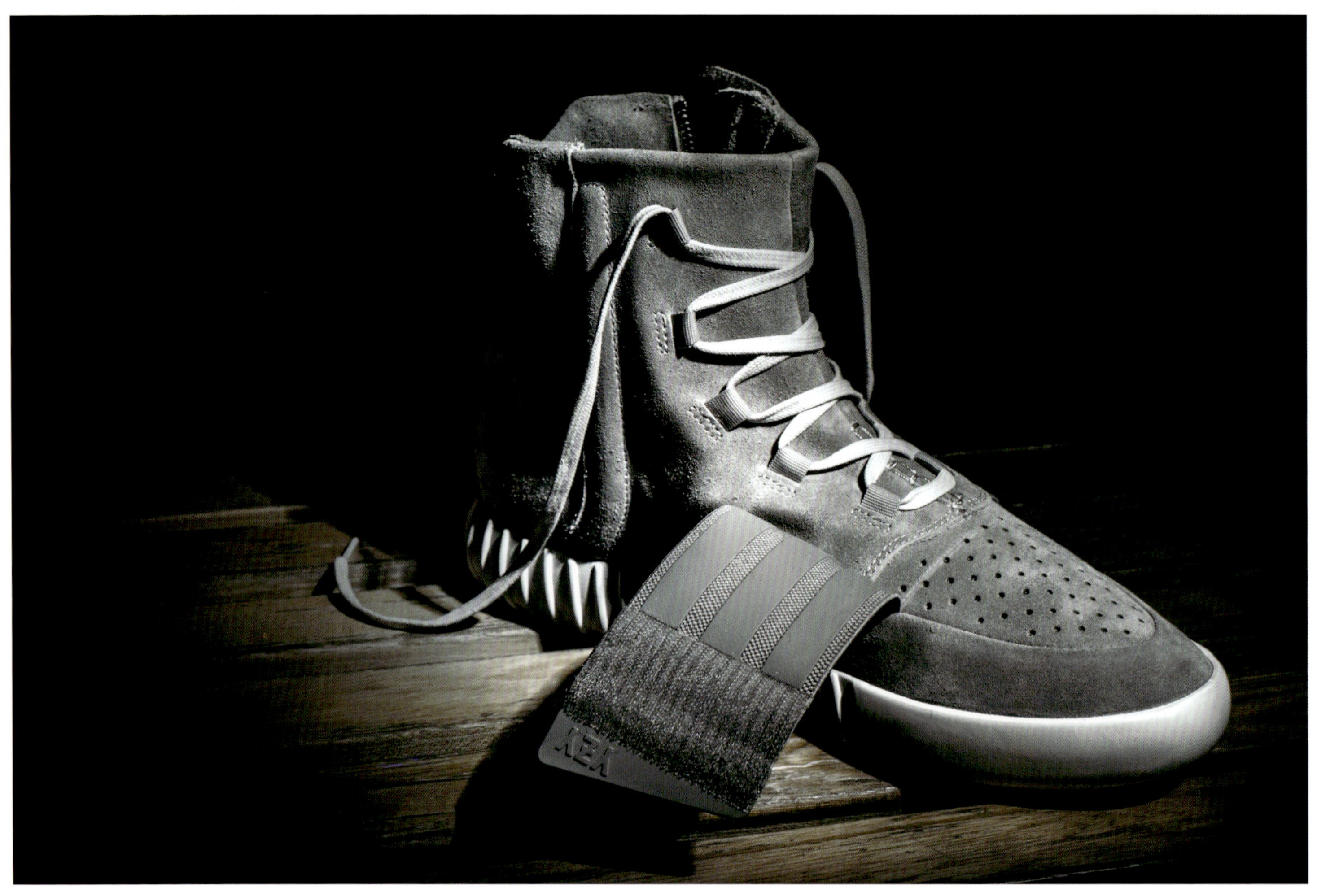

ADIDAS YEEZY BOOST 750

Released in 2015, Yeezy Boost 750 marks the first collaboration between Kanye West and adidas. 750 is more chic than the traditional sneaker, echoing West's distinctive taste in fashion.

Details

Yeezy Boost 750 highlights a high-end style, suede upper and punched pattern. Forgoing the traditional tongue design, the upper is a one-piece. A zipper is built into the ankle part, and on the mid of the upper we see a wide canvas hook-and-loop strap with three elastic stripes attached inside.

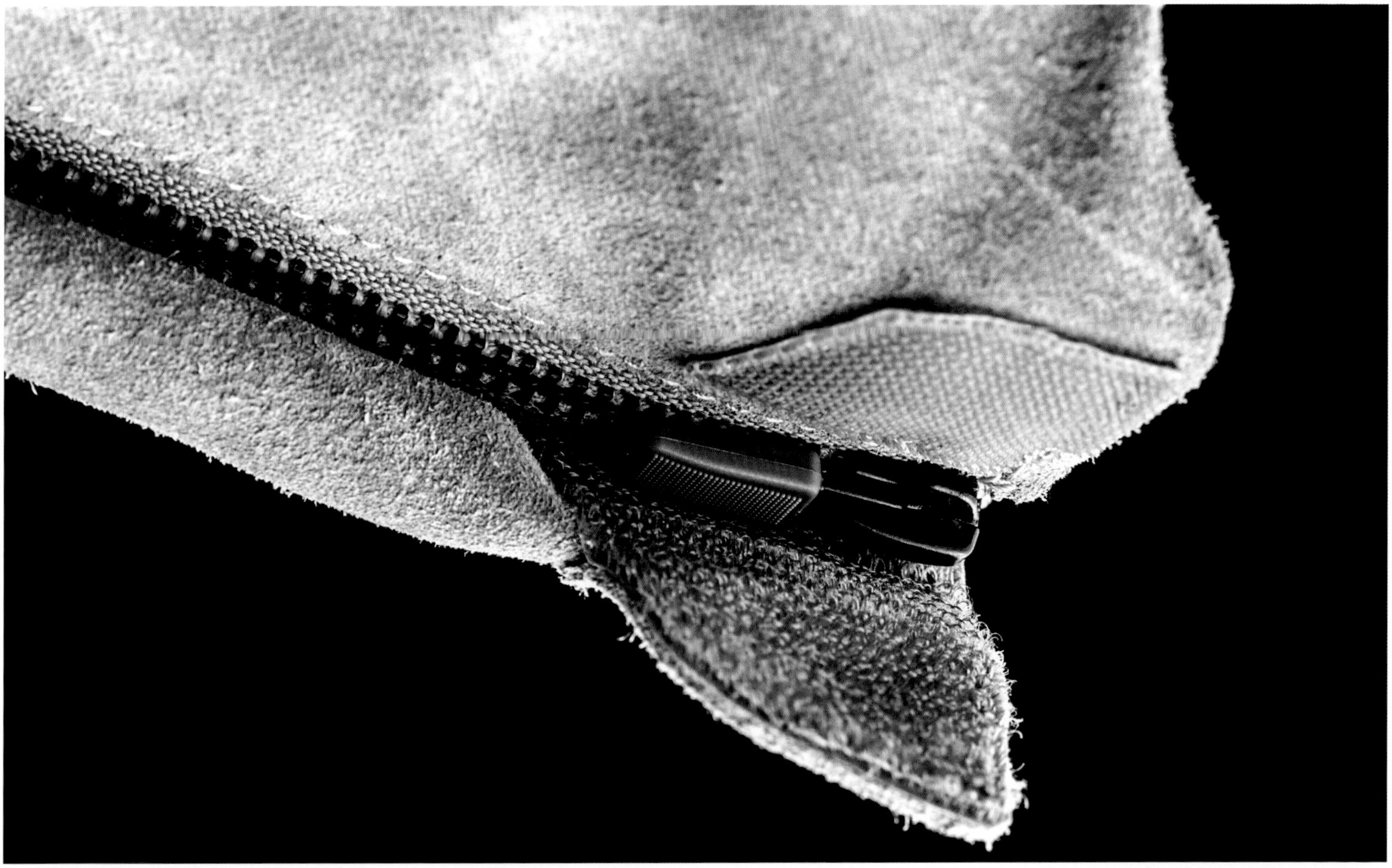

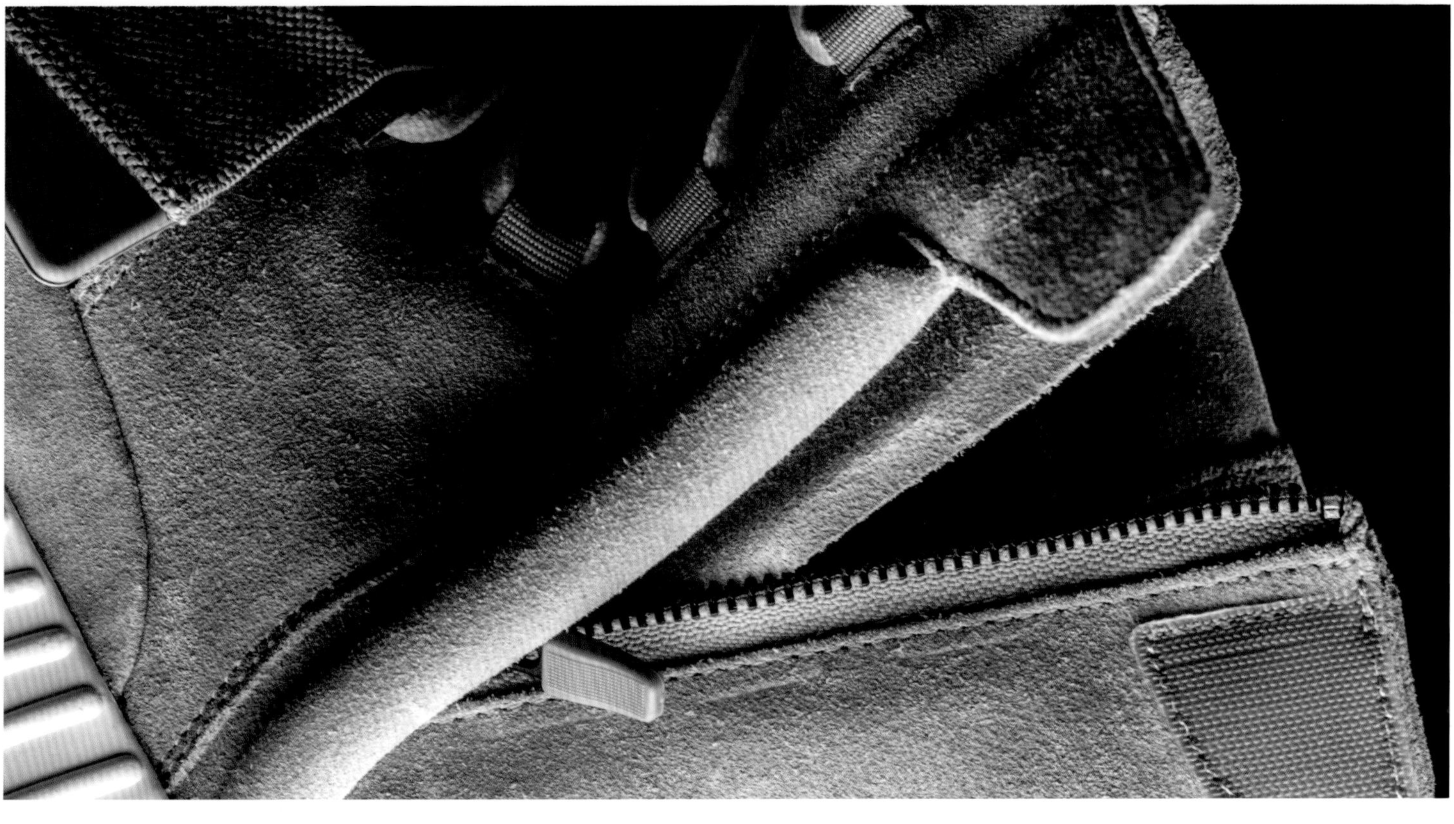

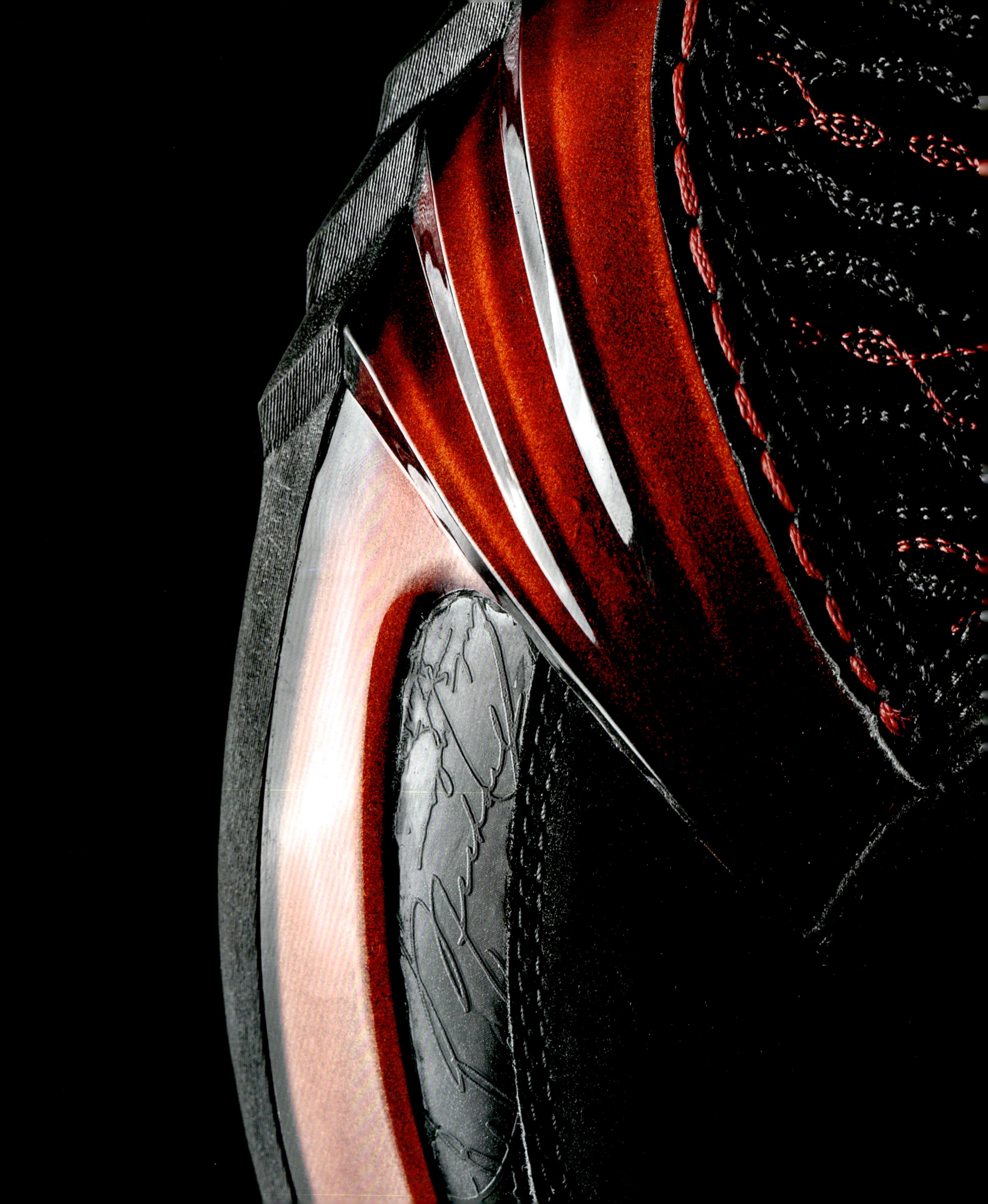

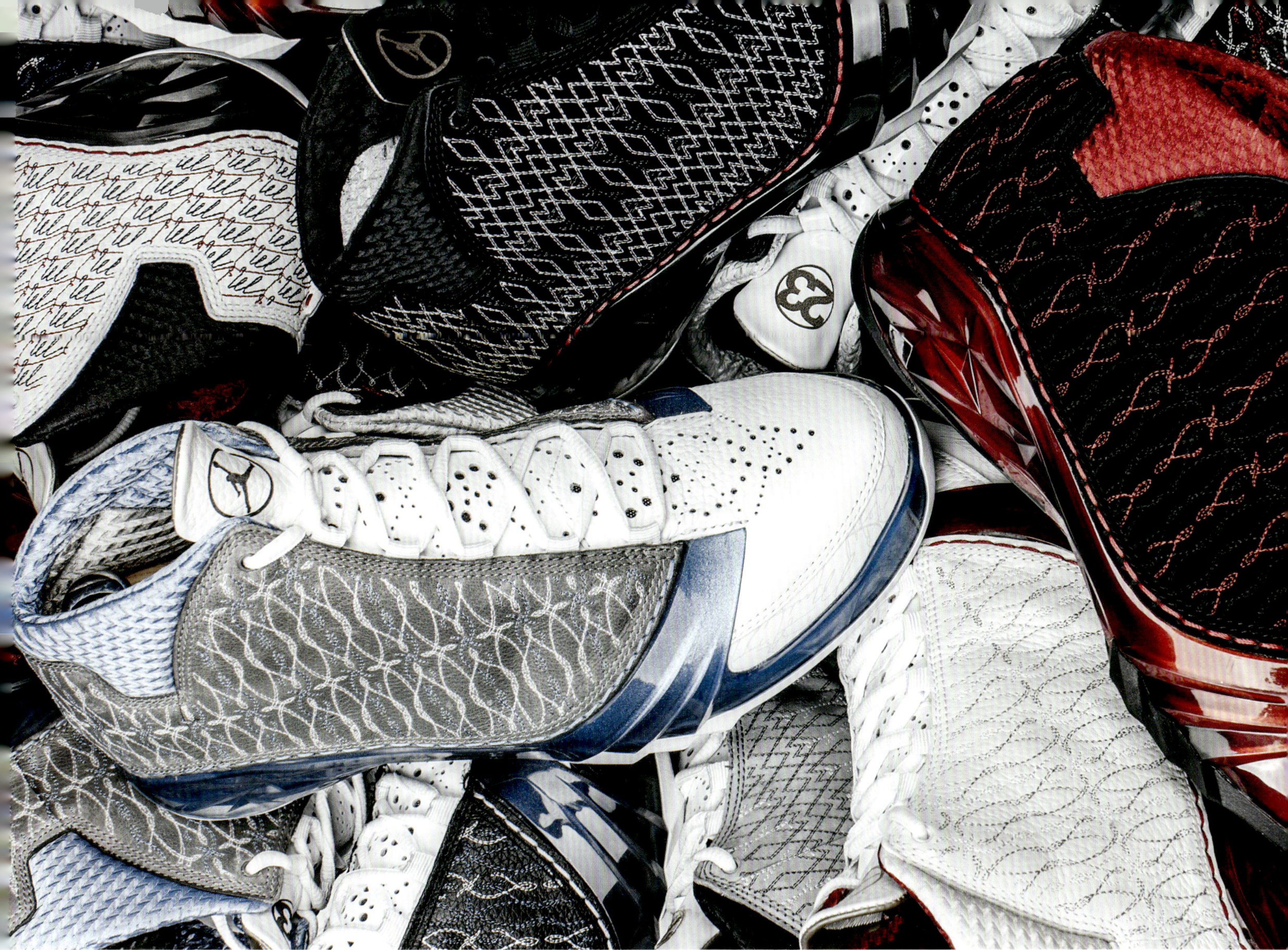

AIR JORDAN XX3

In 2008, Jordan Brand amazed the world with the long-awaited, 23rd iteration in Jordan's signature line. It is another Tinker Hatfield-designed shoe. Because the number "23" is special to Michael Jordan, the shoe thus has a unique position in Jordan Brand's history.

Details

Air Jordan XX3 is the first basketball sneaker in Nike's history to embrace Nike Considered's green design ethos, where details in the development and design of the shoe seek to reduce waste and use environmentally preferred materials wherever possible — all without compromising its athletic performance. The upper and sock liner are a mix of leather and nylon. An embroidery pattern is applied in the lateral side, which differs between colorways. The TPU body in the midsole extends to the sneaker head, and an intricate punched design is dedicated to the head and the tongue.

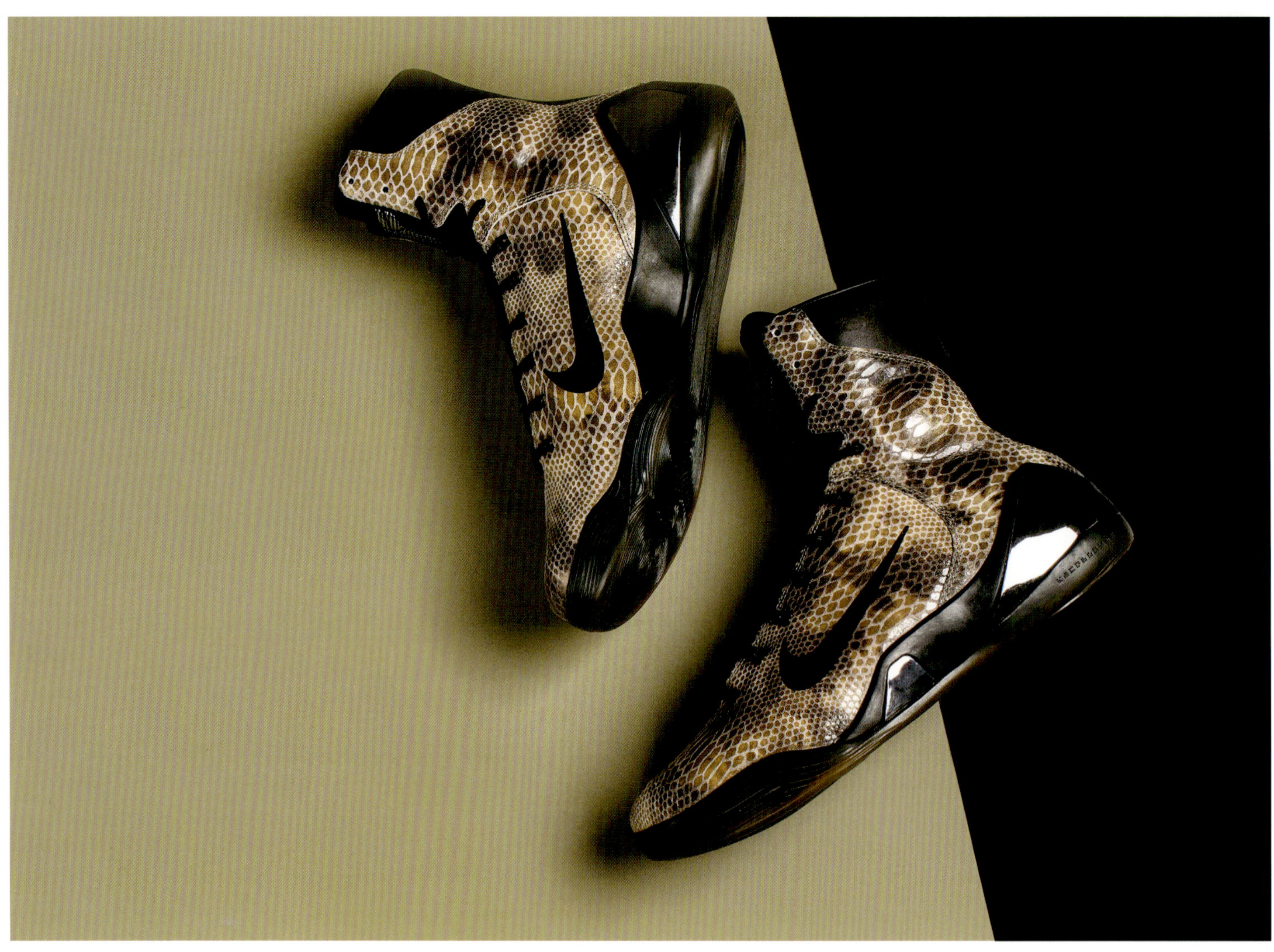

NIKE KOBE IX HIGH EXT QS

Launched in 2014 and modeled after the Nike Kobe 9 Elite, it is a new high-top edition of the Black Mamba's off-court Kobe IX EXT. While continuing to deliver superior performance, the EXT version is enriched with a more fashionable touch.

Details

The special release has a predominantly beige upper coupled with a "snakeskin" texture. The black Swoosh is printed on the quarter panels, and an embossed design is applied around the ankle.

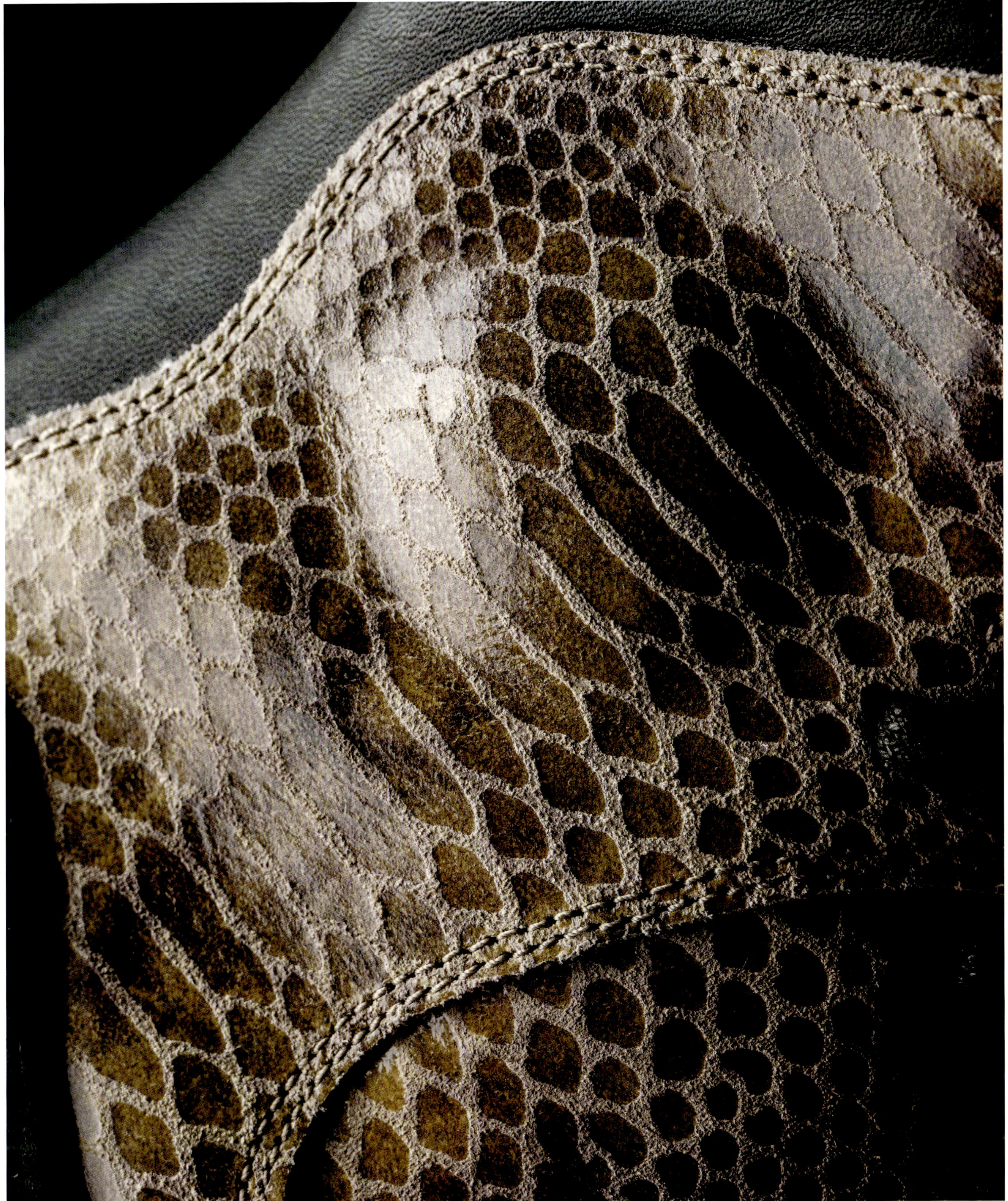

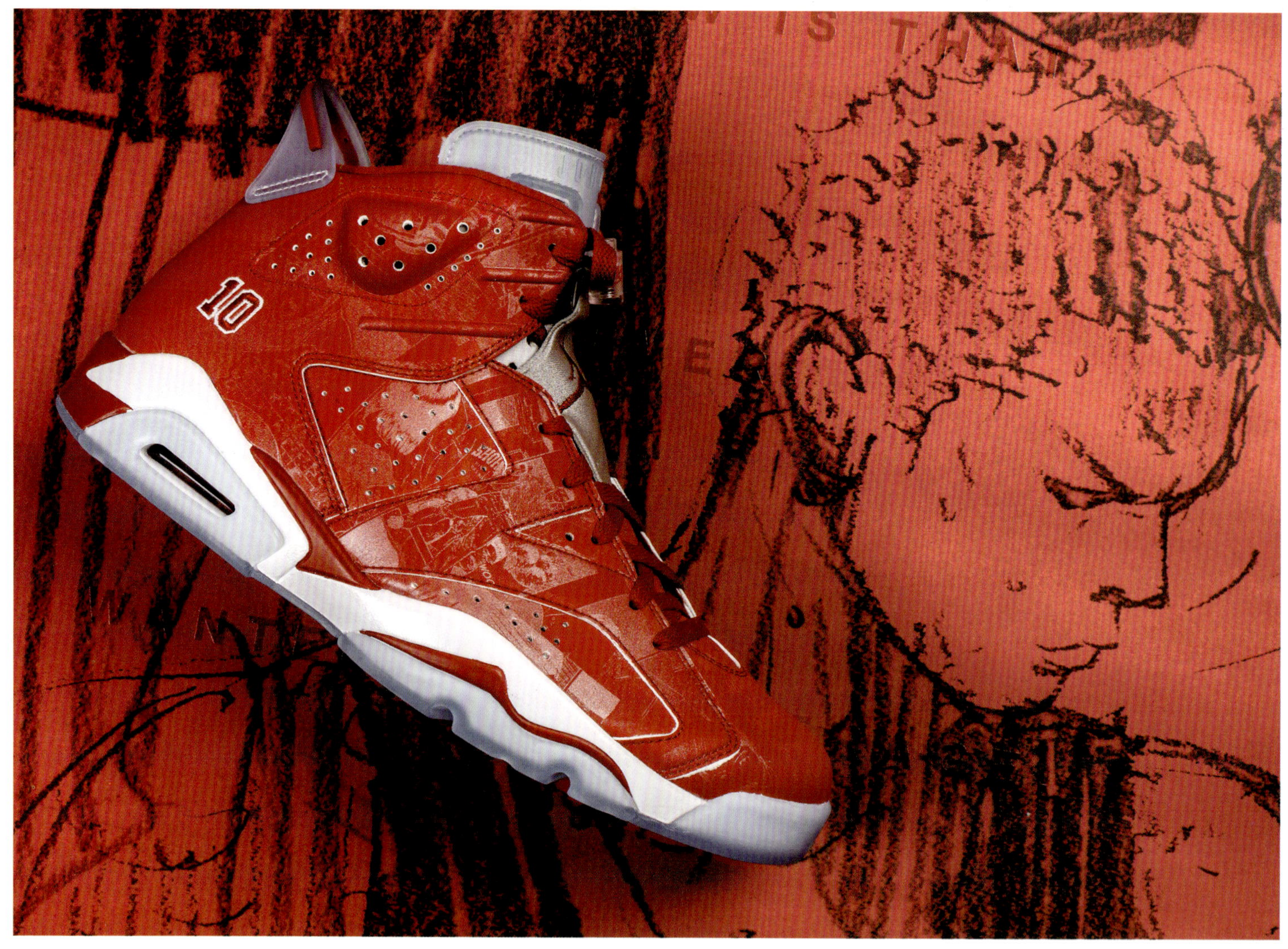

AIR JORDAN 6 RETRO × SLAM DUNK

In 2014, Jordan×Slam Dunk, a collaborative work between Jordan Brand and Japanese caricaturist Inoue Takehiko, debuted in Hong Kong. Air Jordan 6 is the sixth iteration in Jordan's signature line, with which he used to swoosh to his first NBA victory. It is also the shoe that Hanamichi Sakuragi, the main character in *Slam Dunk*, wears in the manga.

Details

The Air Jordan 6 Retro × Slam Dunk features a full varsity red leather base that includes flash with laser detailing and some of Hanamichi Sakuragi's classic images. Instead of Michael's number "23," Sakuragi's jersey number "10" is embroidered on the counter, with a white translucent rubber tongue and sock liner sitting atop.

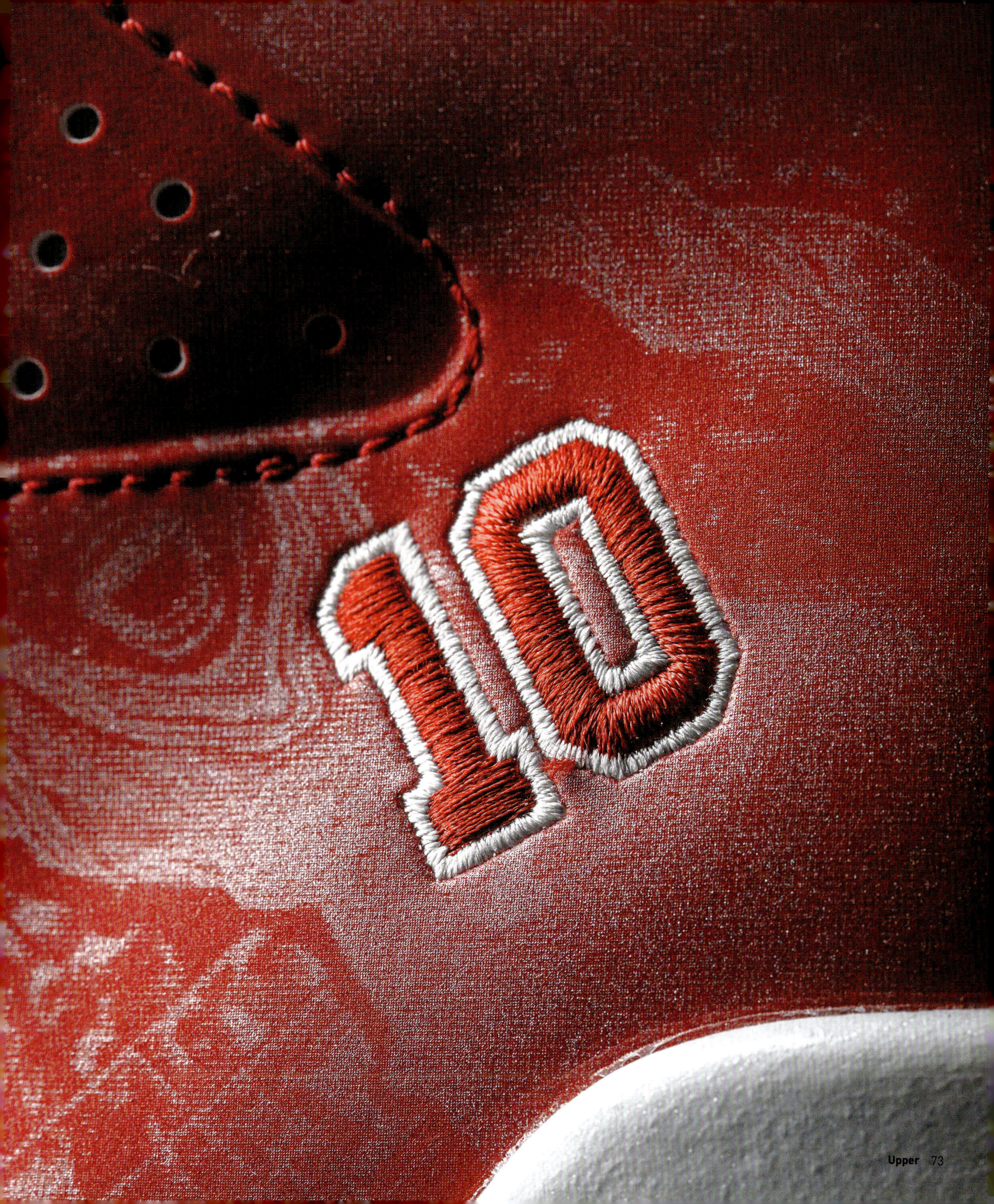
10

Details

With a simple shape and exaggerated bright silver color, the shoe became a sensation the moment it hit the market. Distinguished from traditional leather material, the shining chrome tech gives the upper a bold and futuristic look. It is also the shoe that Webber wore during his All-Star games.

DADA SUPREME C-DUBBZ

Launched in 2002 and co-designed by Chris Webber and Lantz Simpson, C-Dubbz is Webber's signature sneaker in DADA Supreme.

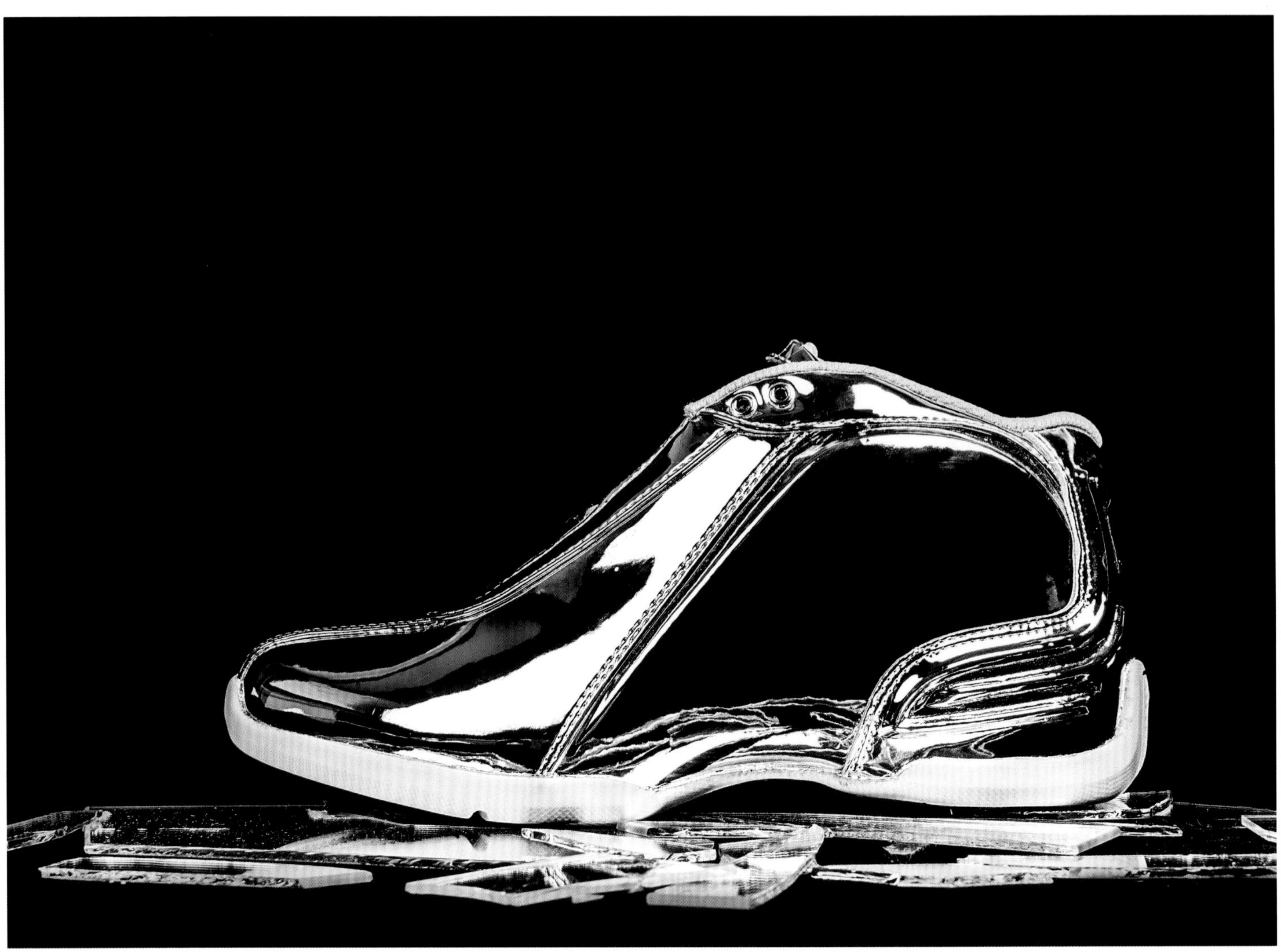

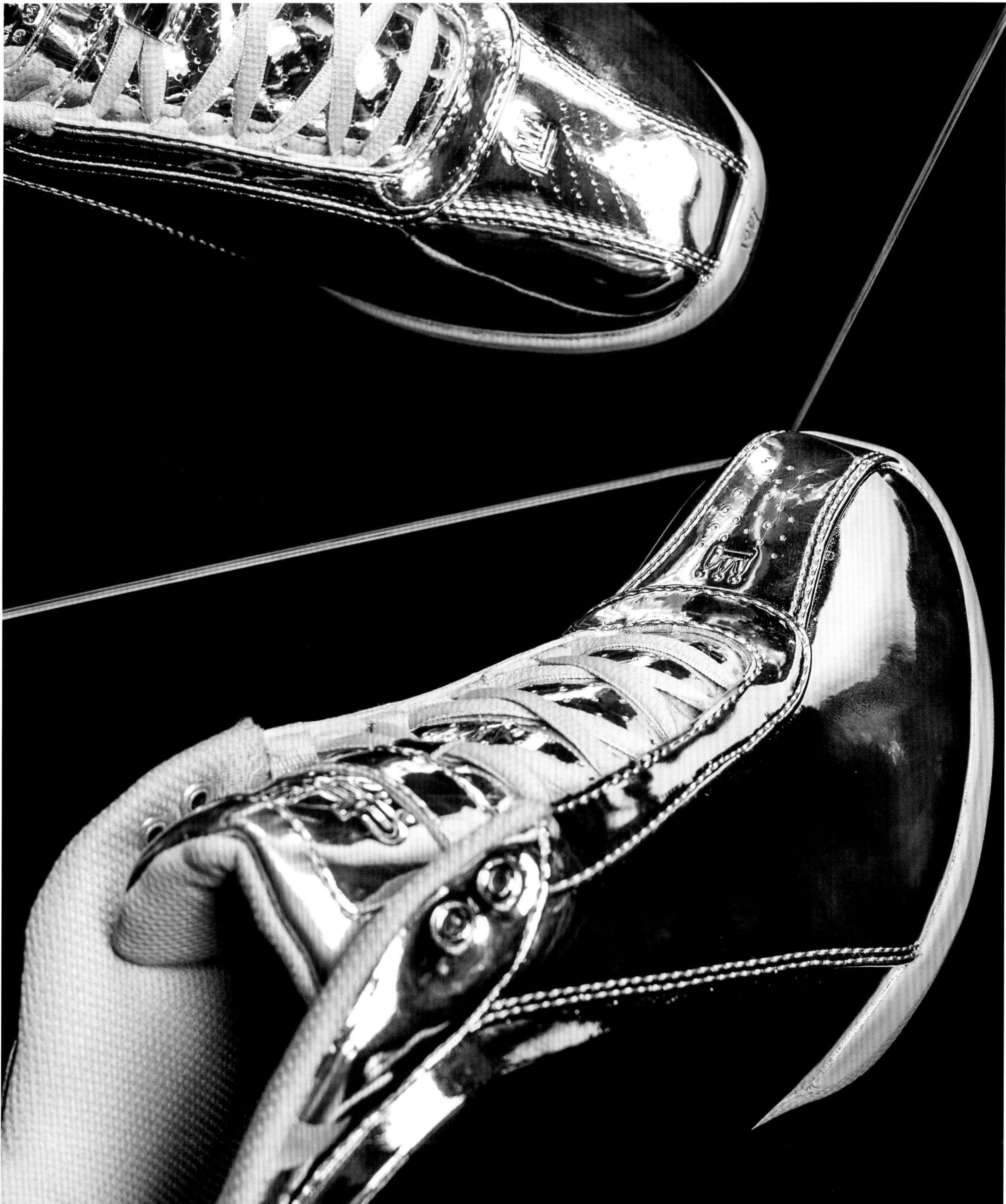

UNDRCRWN × ADIDAS GIL ZERO LOW PE

As part of the collaborative project between adidas and UNDRCRWN in 2007, Gil Zero Low is the signature sneaker of Gilbert Arenas.

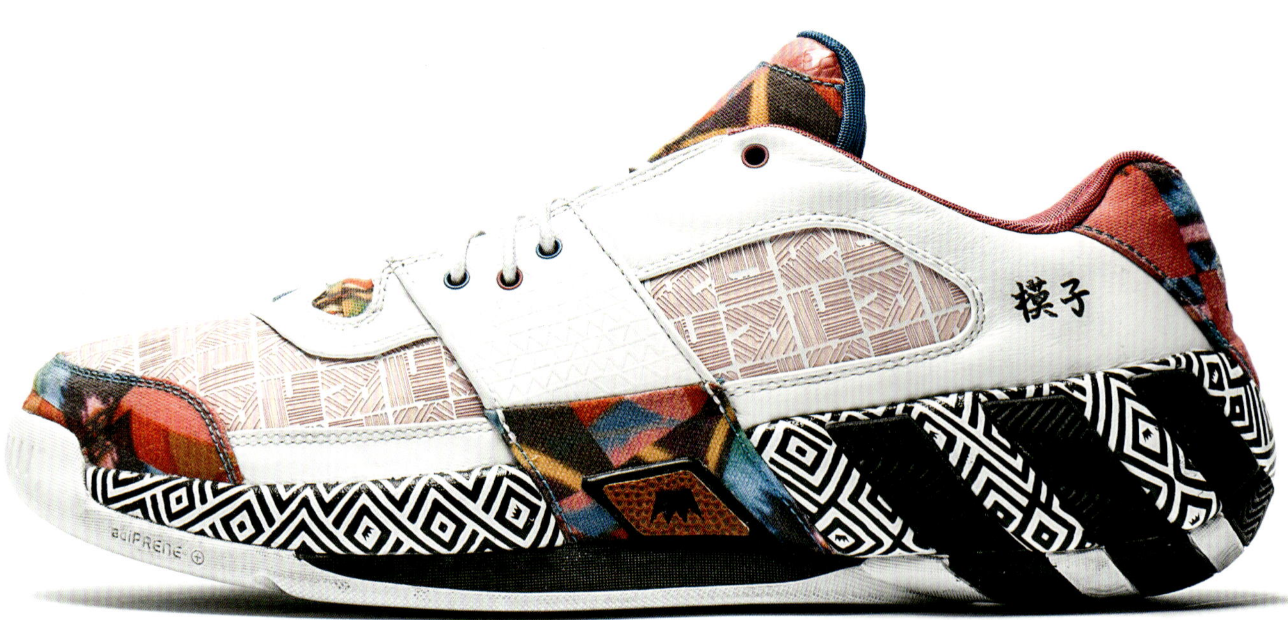

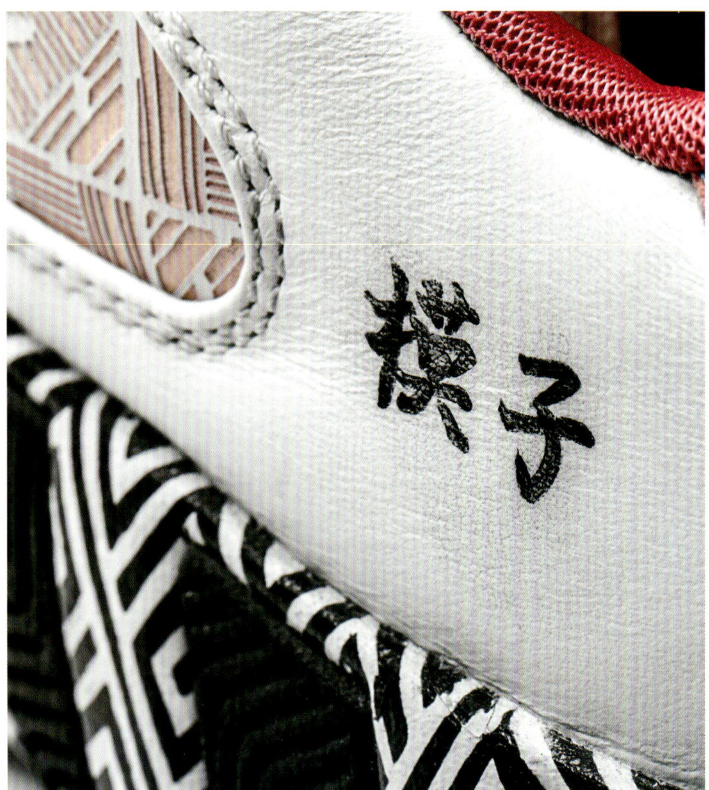

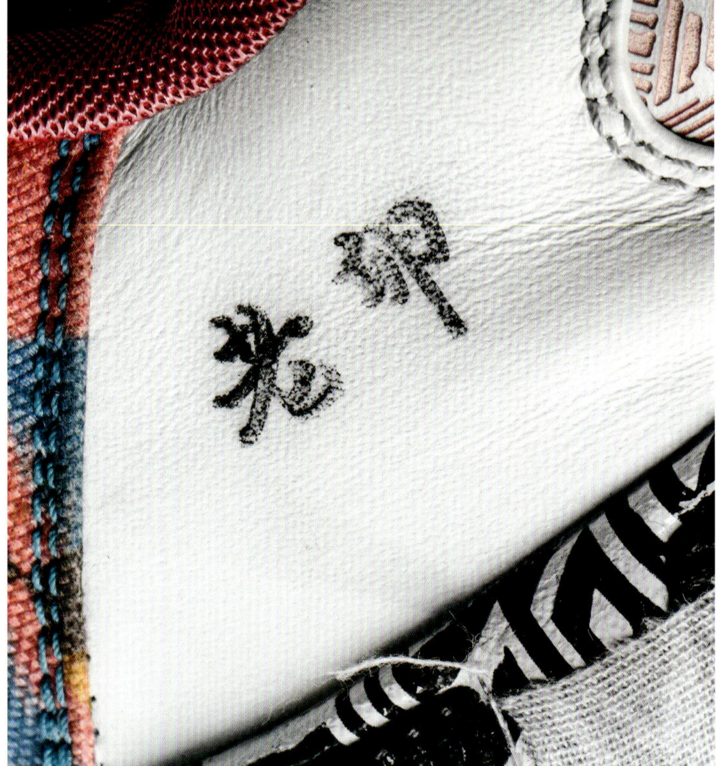

Details

Designed in a 1990s' fashion style, the shoe is a remix of white leather and colorful tapestry. The laser-cut "UNDRCRWN" logo appears on both the sneaker head and lateral sides. The shoe showcased in the picture is the one Arenas wore in the CBA.

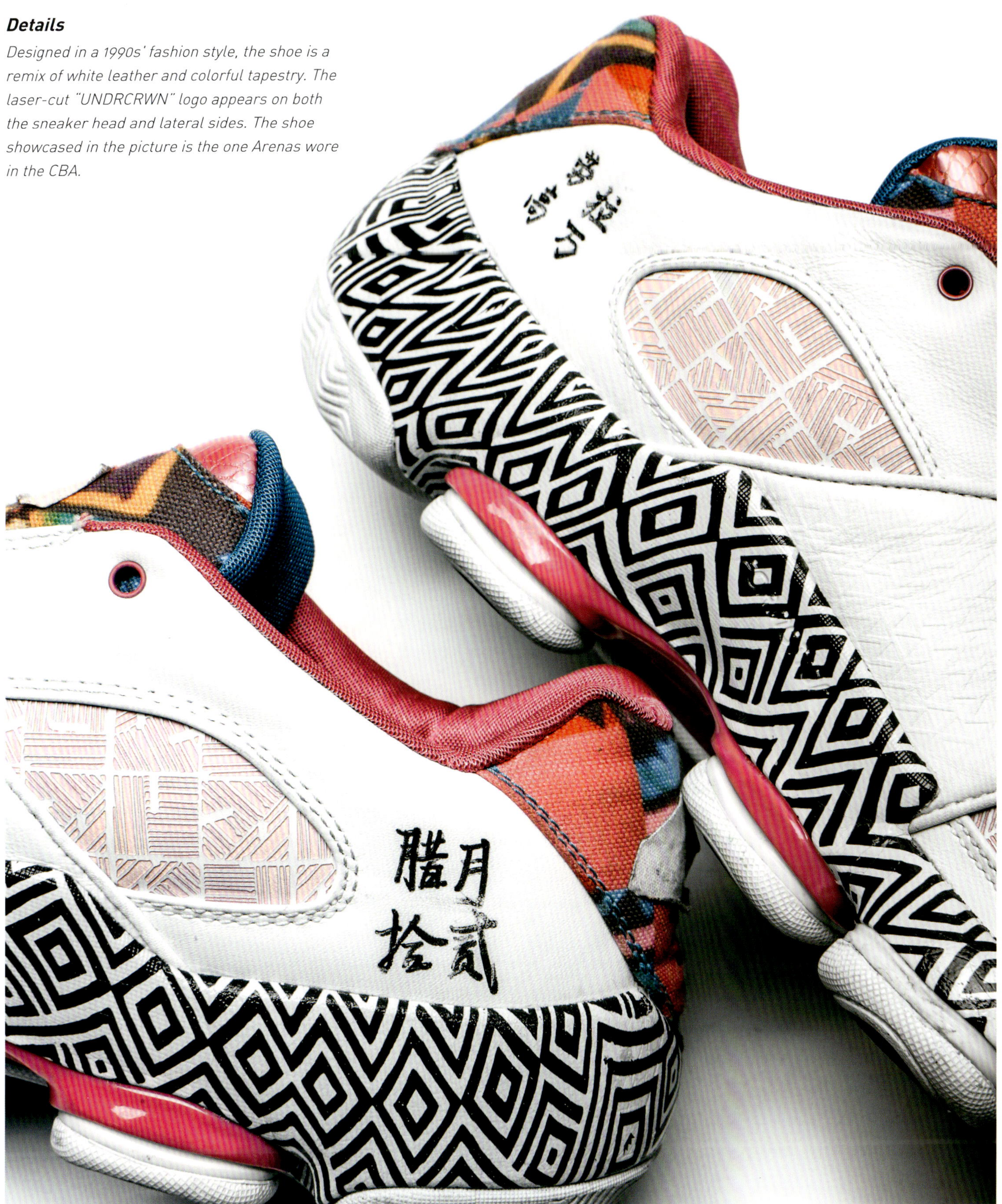

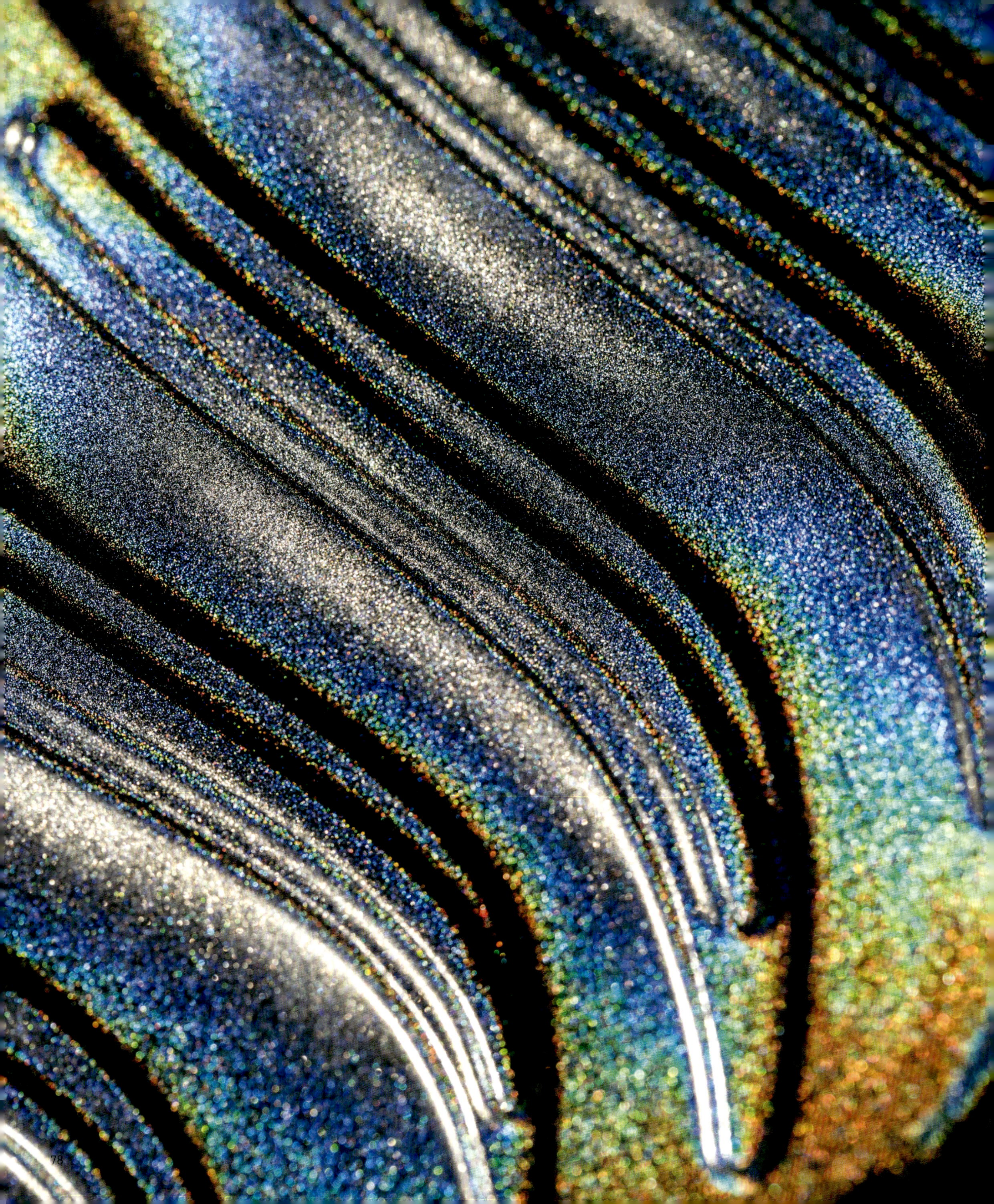

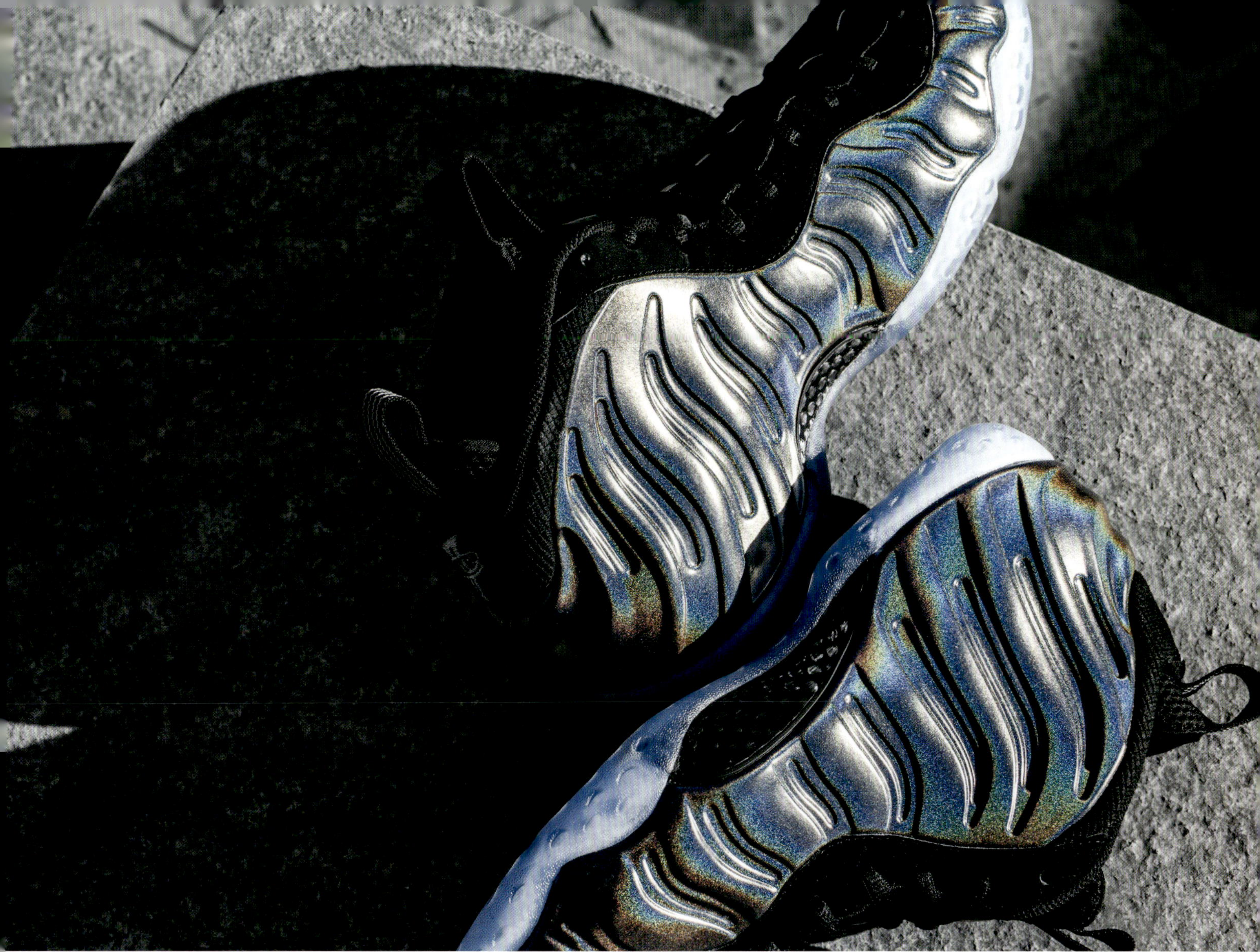

NIKE AIR FOAMPOSITE ONE [HOLOGRAM]

The model was built by Eric Avar in 1997 for Anfernee "Penny" Hardaway. Boasting a pioneering design, the shoe utilizes Foamposite material in a groundbreaking manner. "Hologram" is a new colorway for its retro version in 2015, inspired by holography.

Details

The shoe features a full holographic color-changing Foamposite upper. Aside from the iridescent upper, you can also see black detailing on the tongue and inner liner.

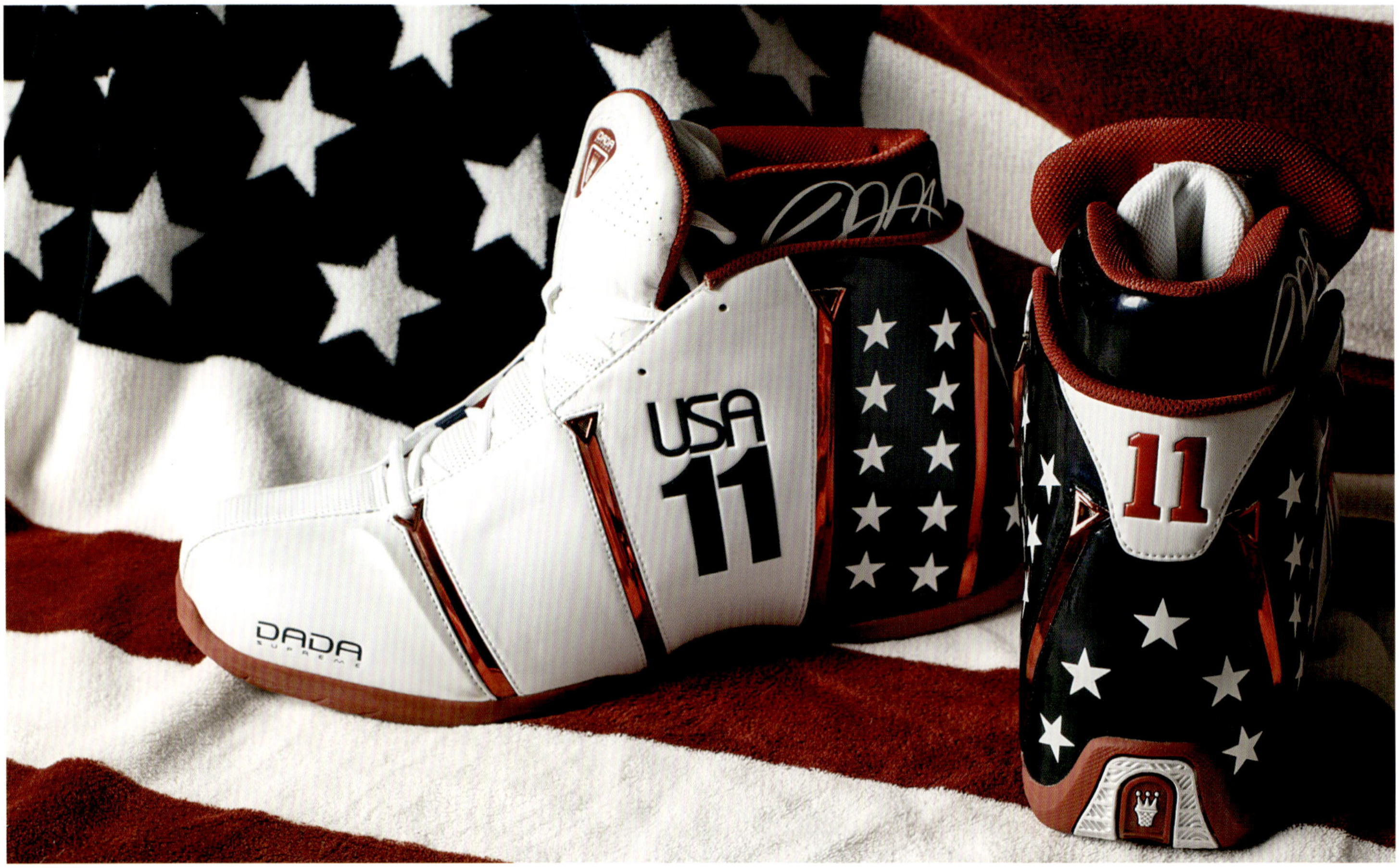

DADA SUPREME 4TH QUARTER [USA] KARL MALONE PE

Released in 2002, it is a signature sneaker of Chris Webber, who is a signed player of DADA Supreme. Webber himself together with Lantz Simpson co-designed the shoe.

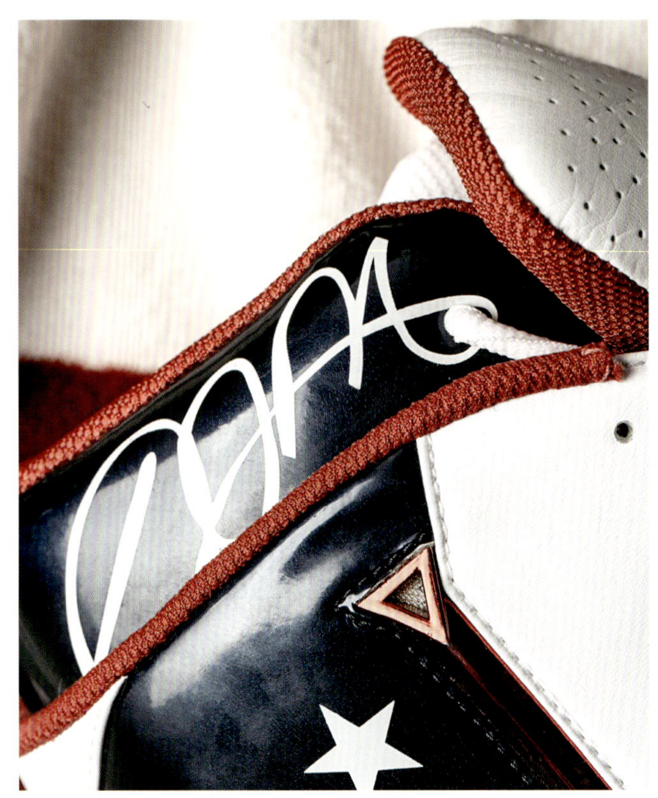

Details

The model boasts a colorway of red, blue and white, which is also the color scheme of the American national team. The star pattern and electroplated TPU stripes on the upper are inspired by the national flag. "USA" and "11," Karl Malone's number on the national team, are printed on the exterior of the shoe. A "DADA Supreme" logo is placed at the sneaker head.

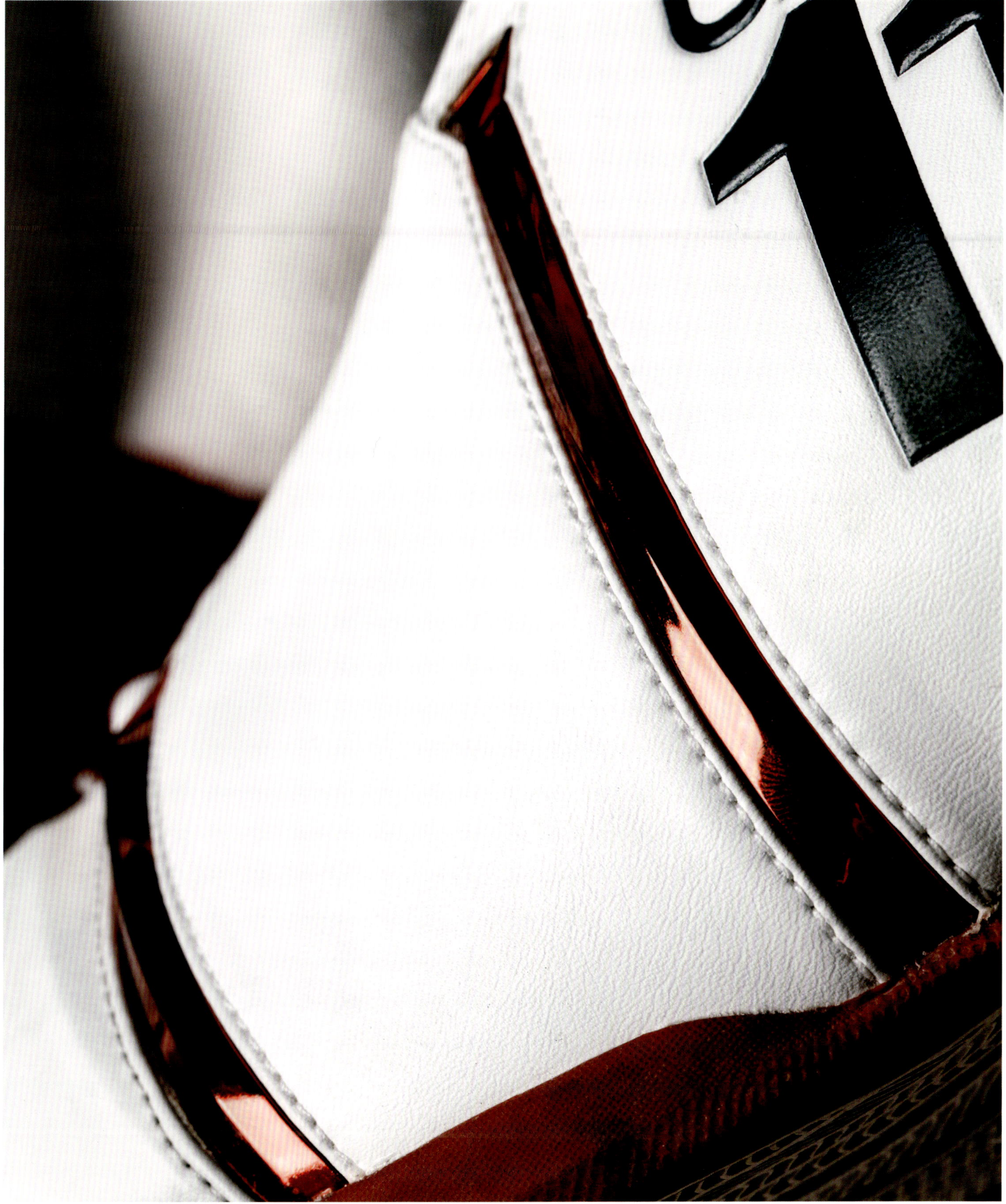

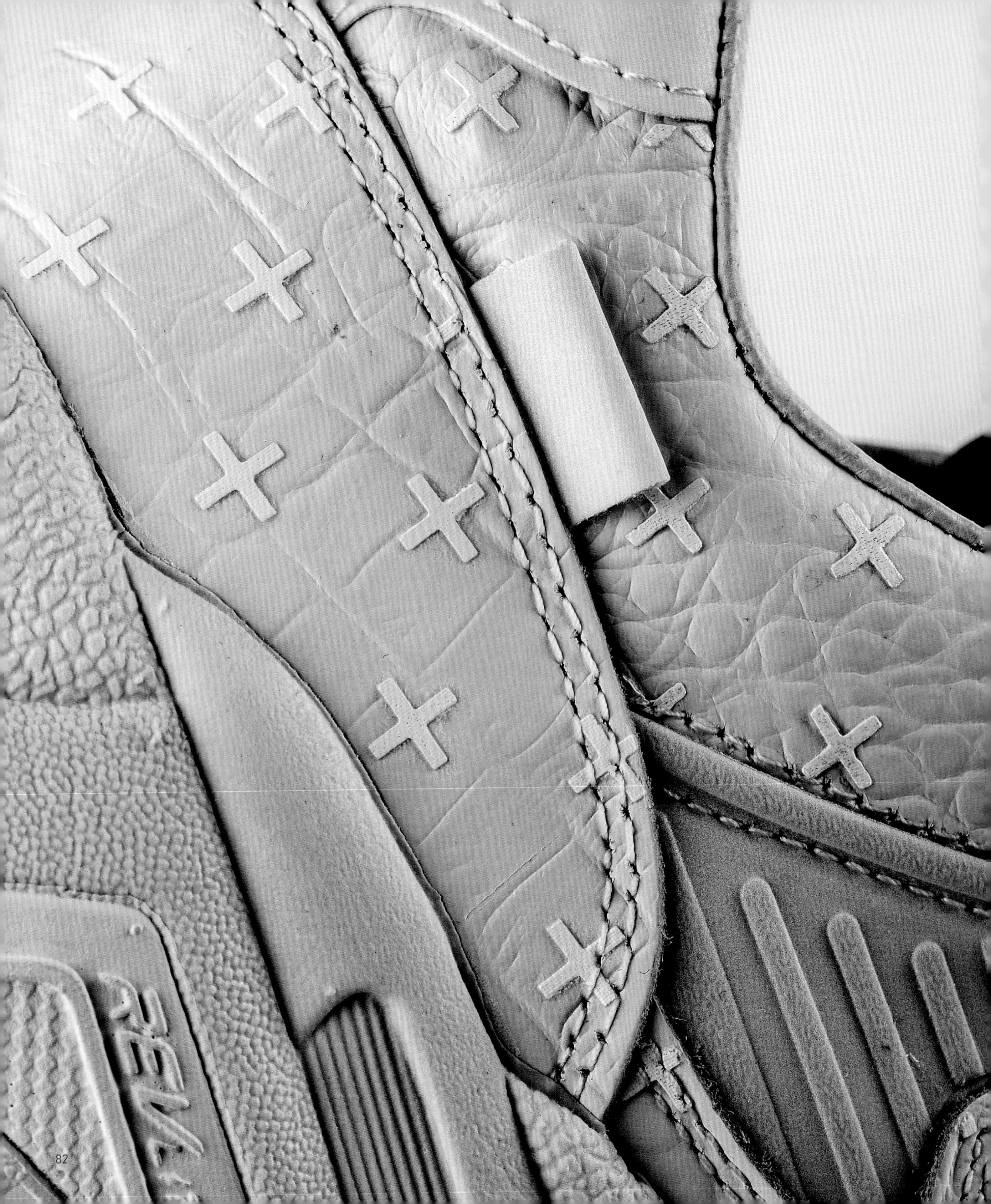

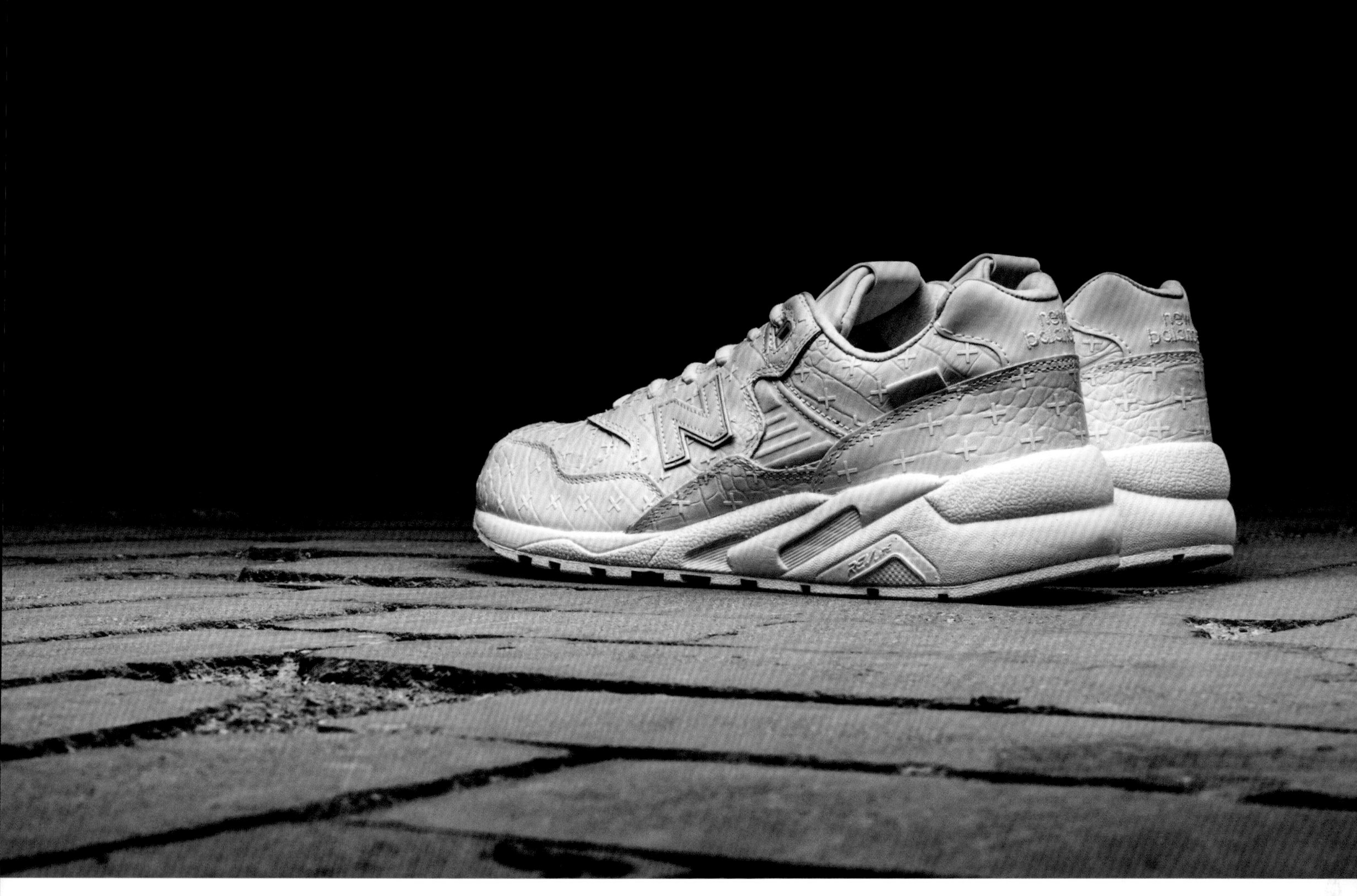

NEW BALANCE MRT580XX

Released in 2015, New Balance MRT580XX is the special edition of the classic MRT580. Its all-white silhouette and dashing has become a new vogue.

Details

Falling right in line with two of the sneaker world's biggest trends right now, monotone colorways and reptile textures, the simple yet sophisticated MRT580XX receives an all-white croc-embossed treatment with an added unique touch of reflective "X" shapes across the upper.

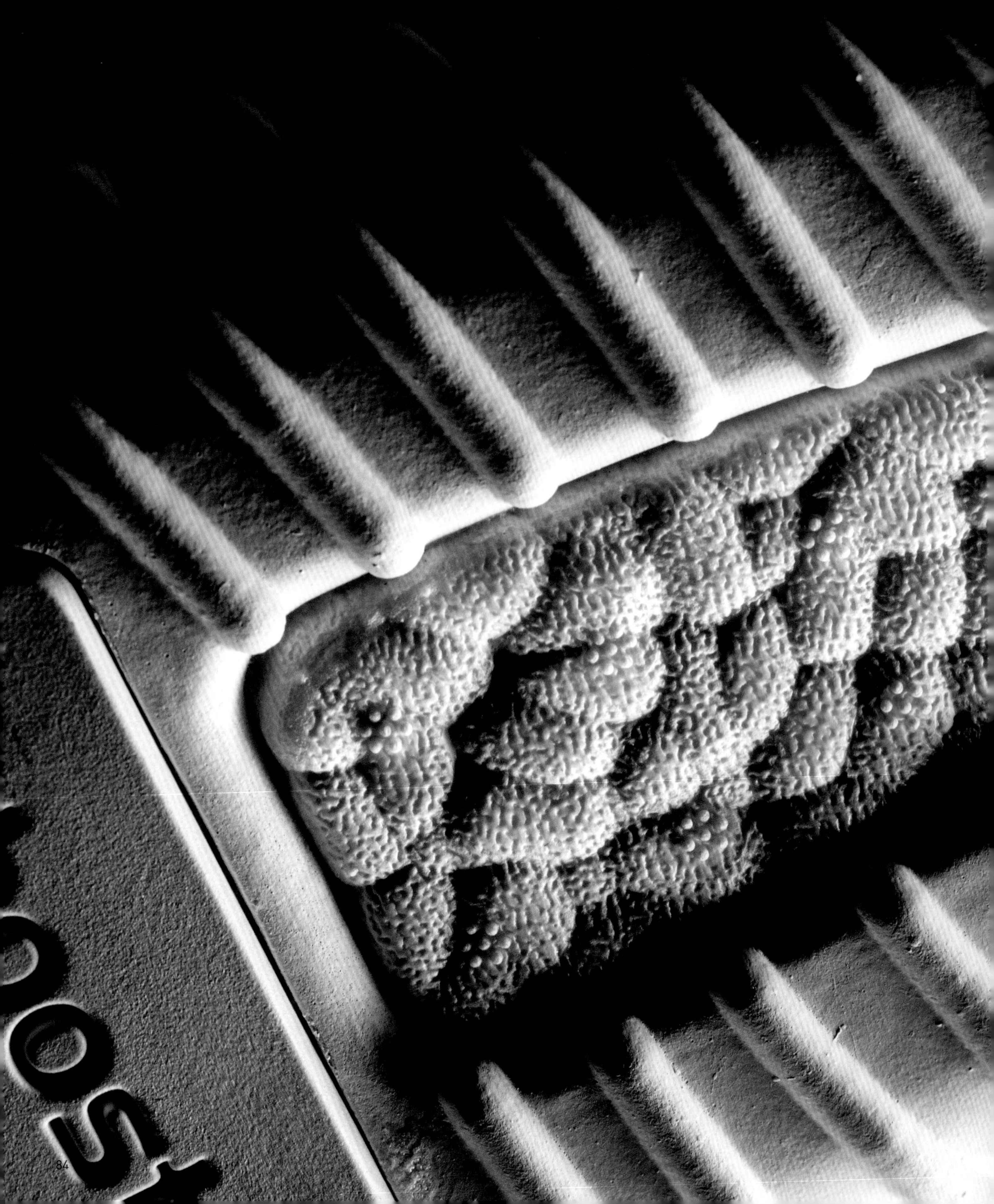

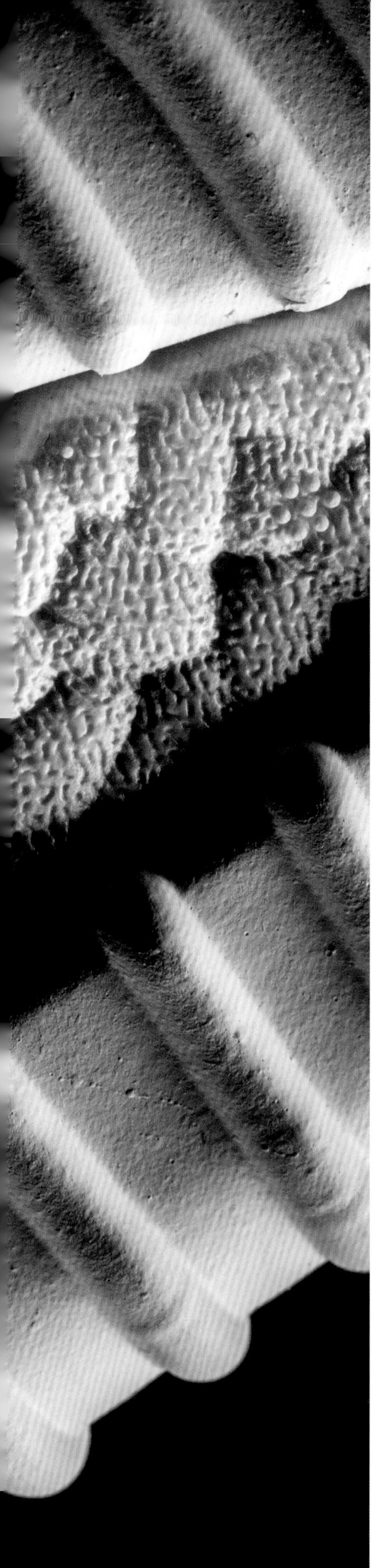

A shoe's fit and feel is determined by its sole, the soul of every pair. To deliver unmatched wearer experience, a sole is usually packed with the proudest technologies of each brand.

OUTSOLE

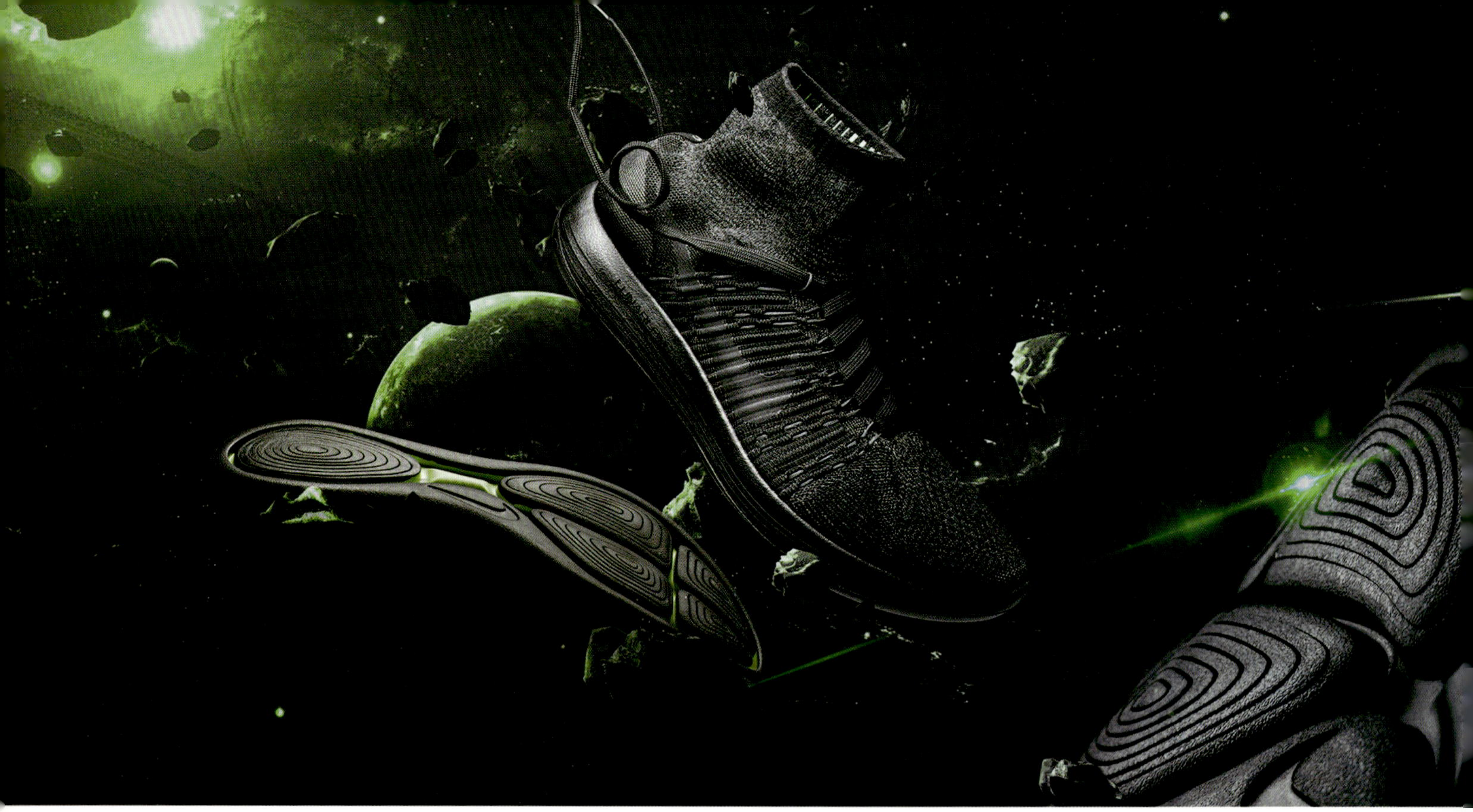

NIKELAB LUNAREPIC FLYKNIT

Lunarepic Flyknit is Nike's latest flagship running shoe in 2016. The high-cut profile is rarely seen in traditional running footwear, and the Flyknit tech is utilized in the upper. Tae Yong Lee, Design Director of Nike running shoes, came up with the new design.

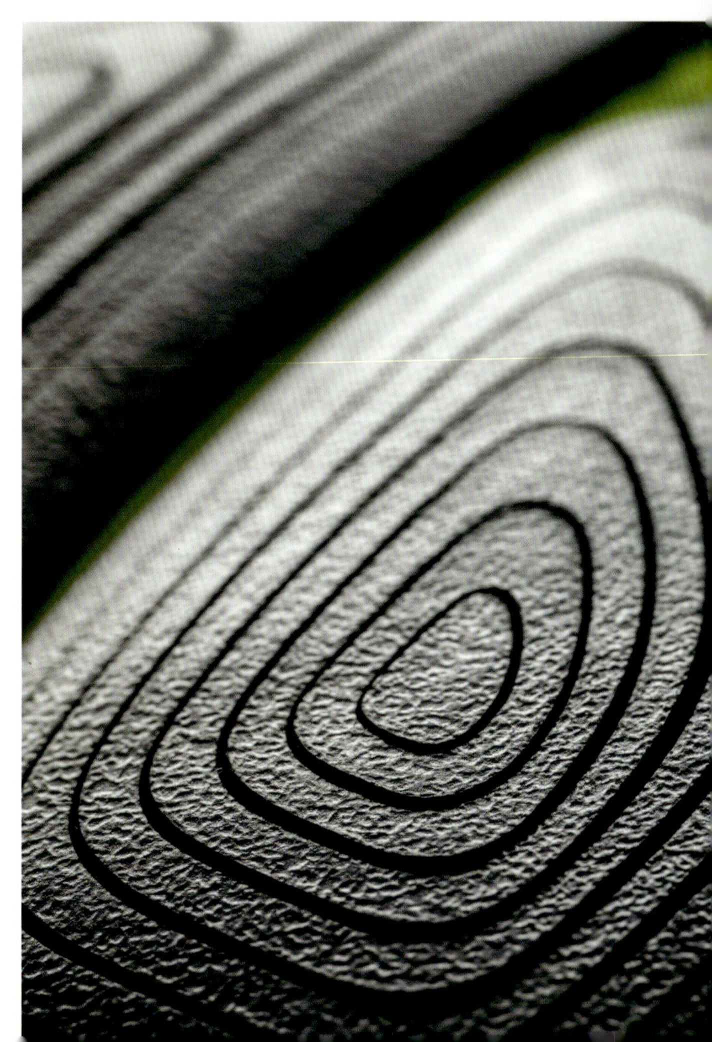

Details

A brand new technology, bi-jection, is introduced to the midsole. Drawing strength from the heating technique, the soft Lunarlon is encapsulated in a container of the harder Phylon foam, without using a drop of glue; the manufacturing has minimized environmental pollution. Moreover, the laser-cut grooves on both the midsole and outsole function as a buffer.

ADIDAS YEEZY BOOST 350

In 2015, Kanye West and adidas came back with the highly anticipated new adidas Yeezy Boost 350. Unlike the 750, the 350 is designed for everyday wear. The Primknit upper also delivers added comfort.

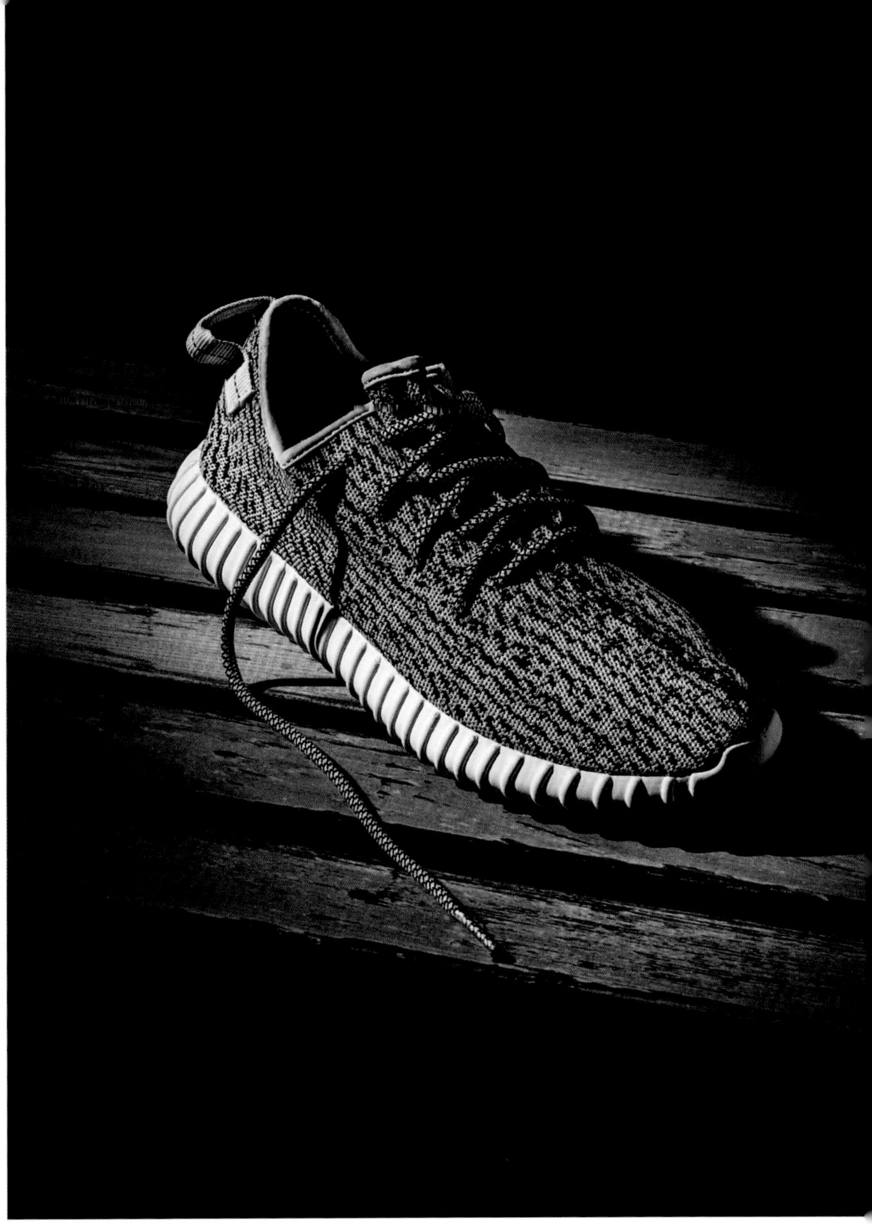

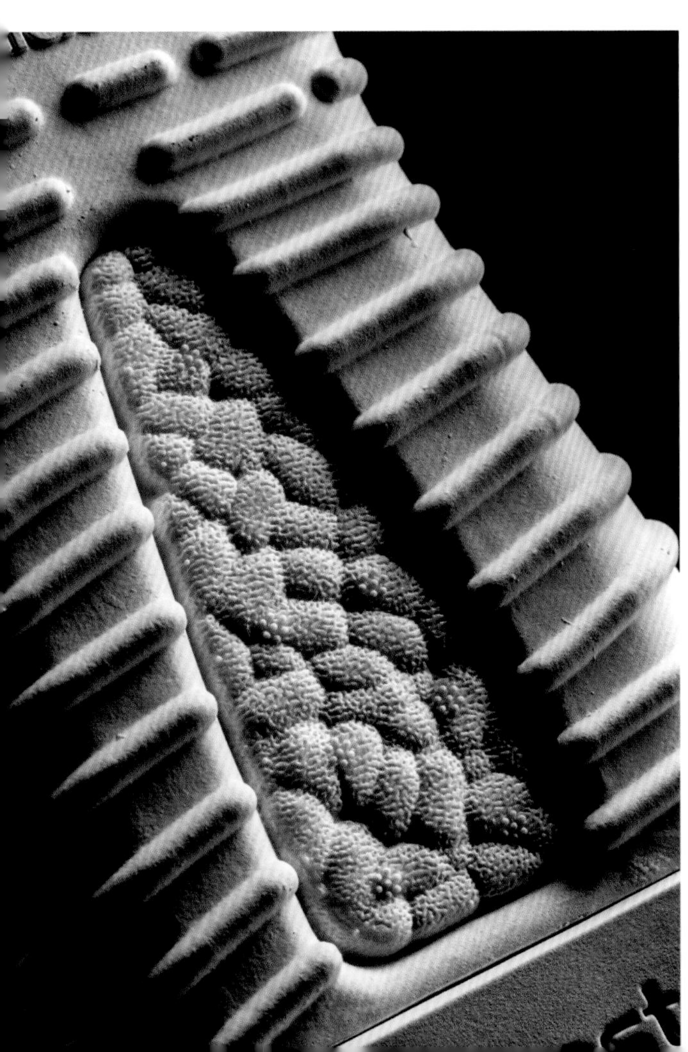

Details

The sole features a rubber frame in a full-length ribbed pattern. The Boost cushioning system is embedded in the base, and a hollow-out design is introduced to the heel.

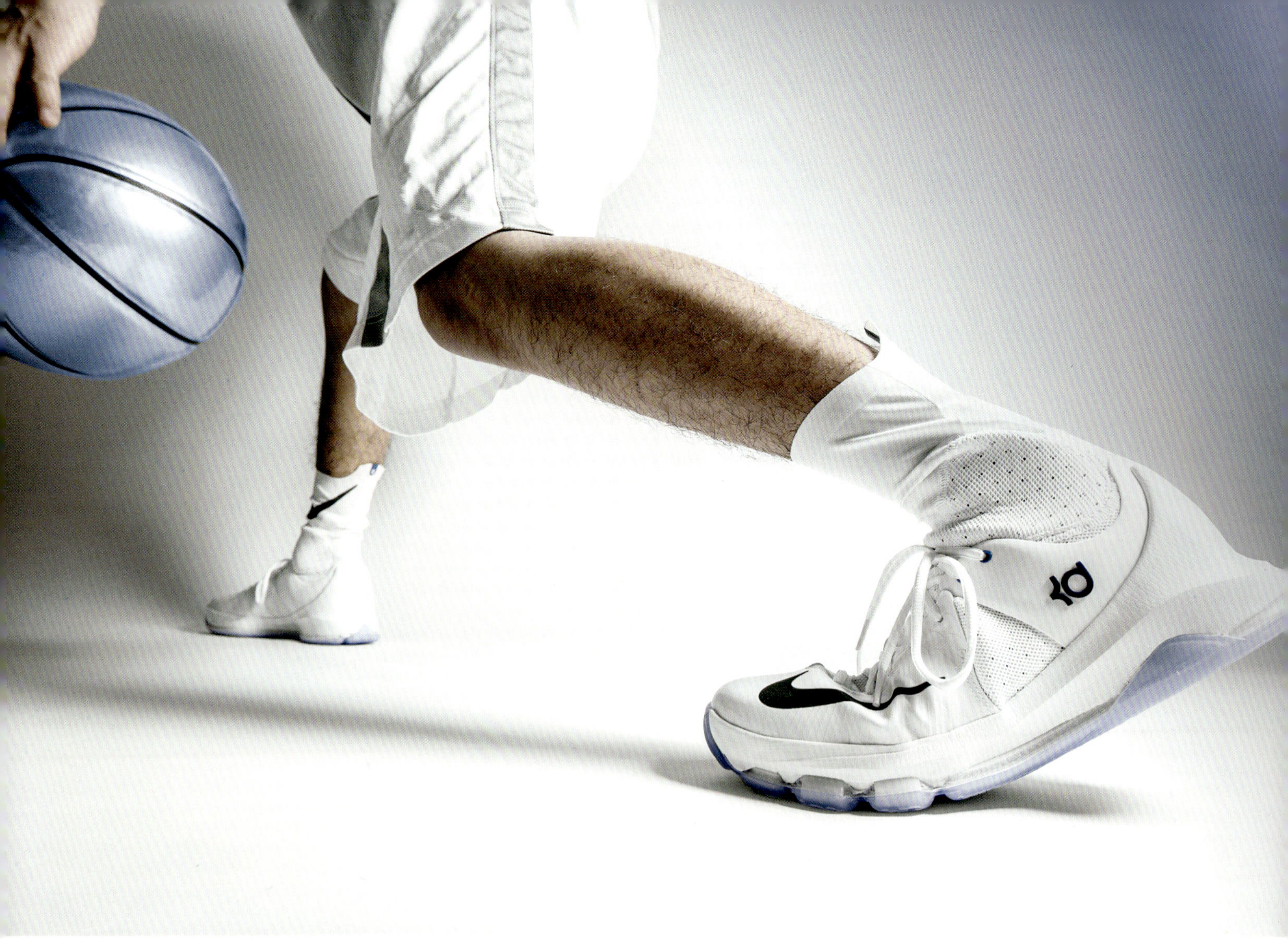

NIKE KD8 ELITE

Released in 2016 and co-designed by Kevin Durant and Leo Chang, KD8 Elite is a technically advanced and eye-catching new version of KD's eighth signature shoe.

Details

The built-in, calf-length compression sock is inspired by KD's "Sabretooth Tiger" tattoo. The midsole is equipped with full-length visible Nike Zoom Air cushioning, and the outsole boasts a design of flex grooves in the heel and the forefoot.

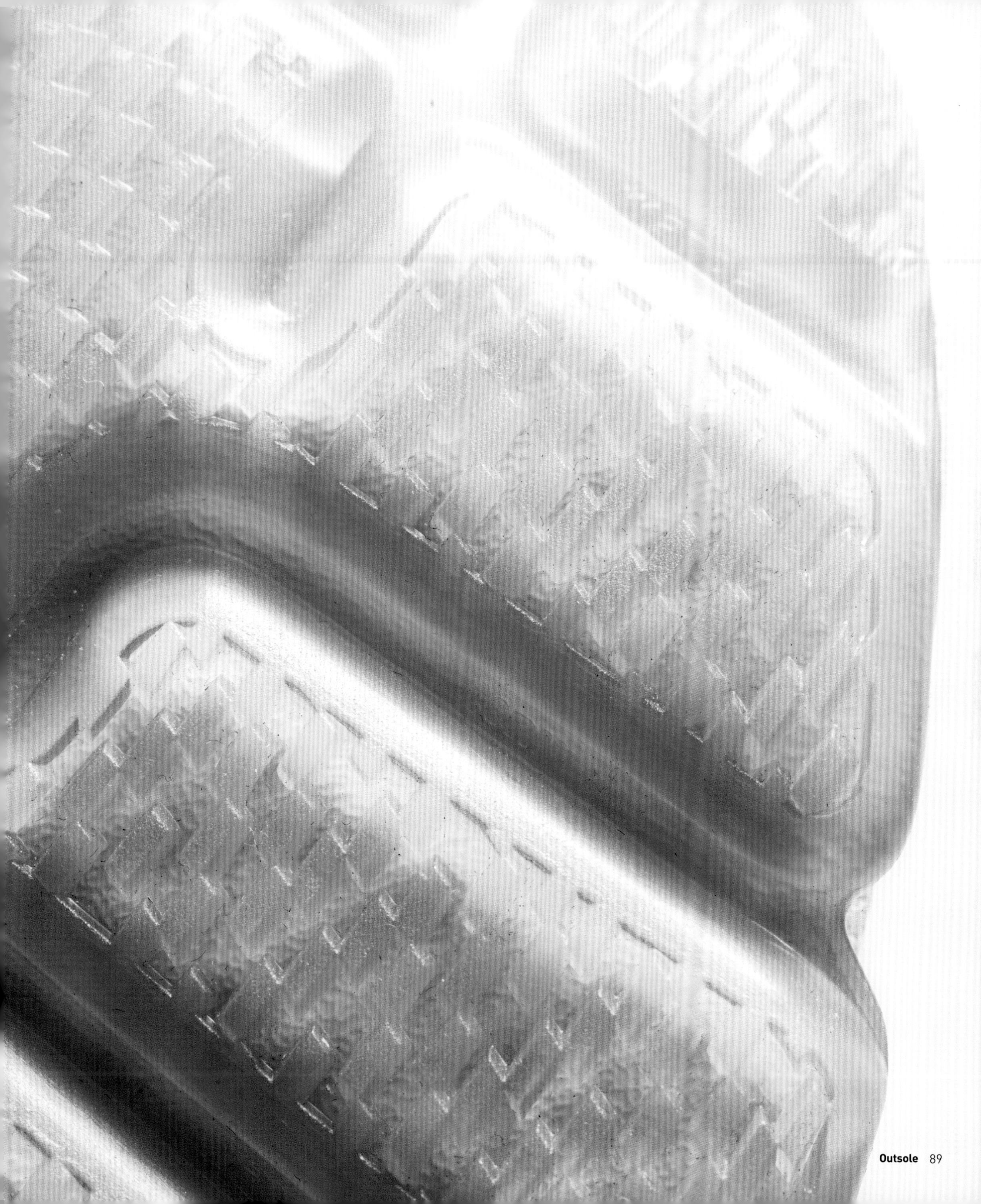

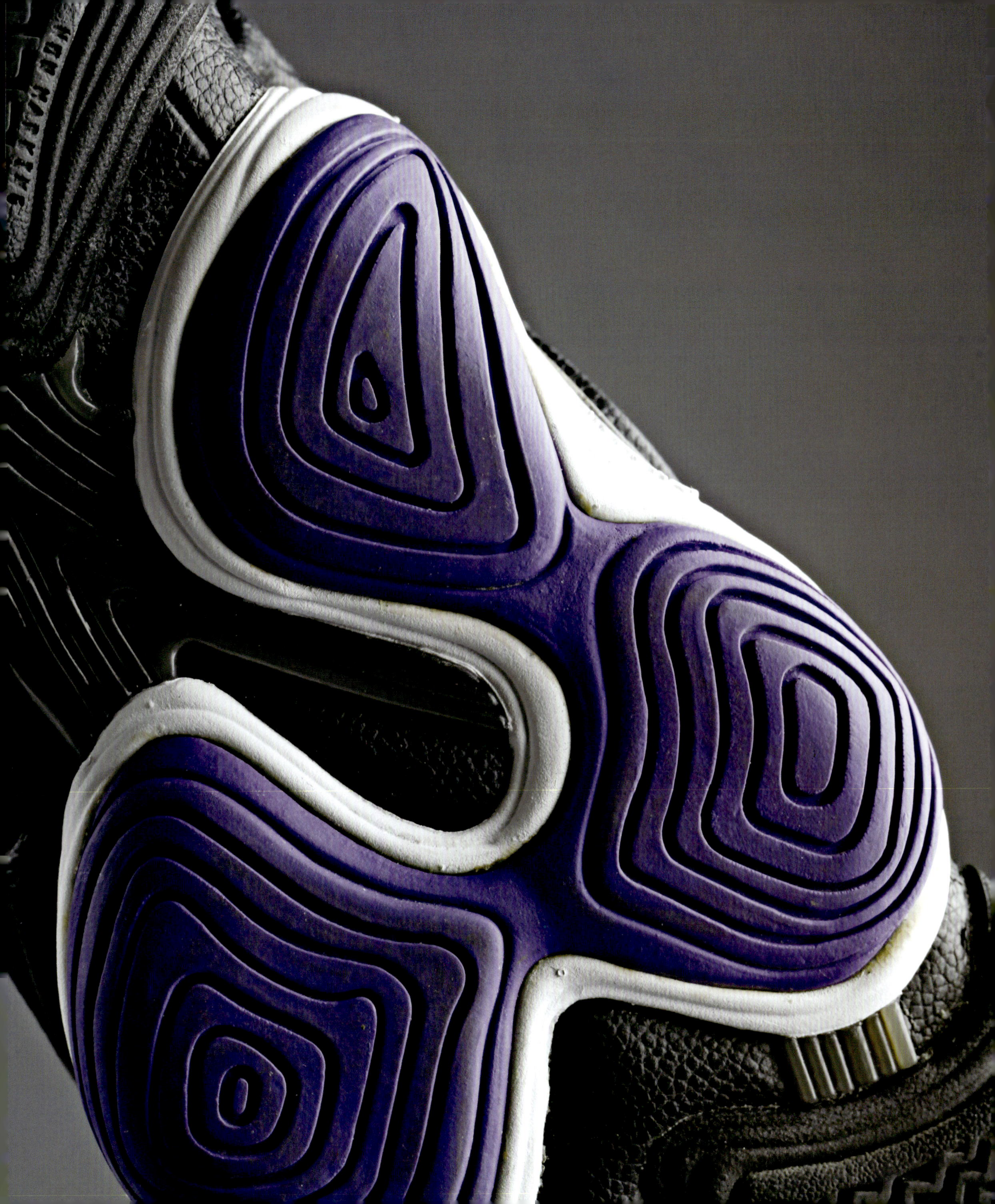

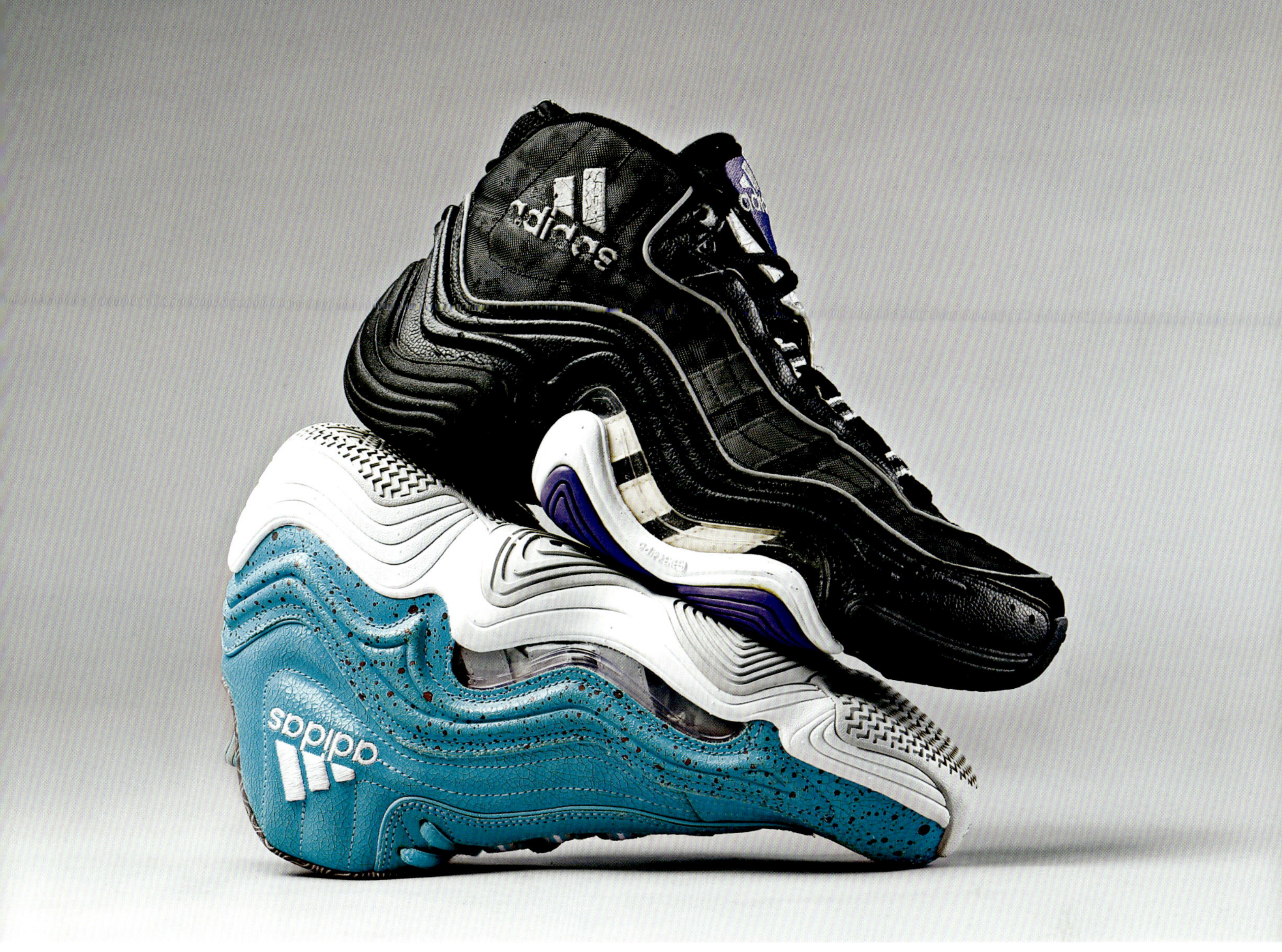

ADIDAS EQT KB8 II [CRAZY 2]

Launched in 1998, KB8 II is Kobe Bryant's second adidas signature shoe. The upper is improved by its large use of "Breathable Metallic Mesh." This revolutionary fibre has enhanced its breathability. The snug fit and excellent performance make the pack a great hit on the market. We have every reason to say it is one of Kobe's best adidas sneakers.

Details

The sole features the FYW (Feel Your Wear) tech, ADIPRNE+ cushion and adiLux pad, with Torsion System in the midsole for increased stability.

Details

Rumor has it that the array of green and orange was created to honor Bugs' carrot addiction. A geometric design is applied to the entire outsole, with round dents scattered on the surface. The midsole is embedded with Air Sole cushioning units.

AIR JORDAN 7 RETRO [HARE]

The Air Jordan 7 "Hare," released in 1992, is the seventh signature sneaker of Michael Jordan. The shoes are inspired by Bugs Bunny, a classic cartoon character in an official Jordan X Looney Tunes ad campaign in 1992.

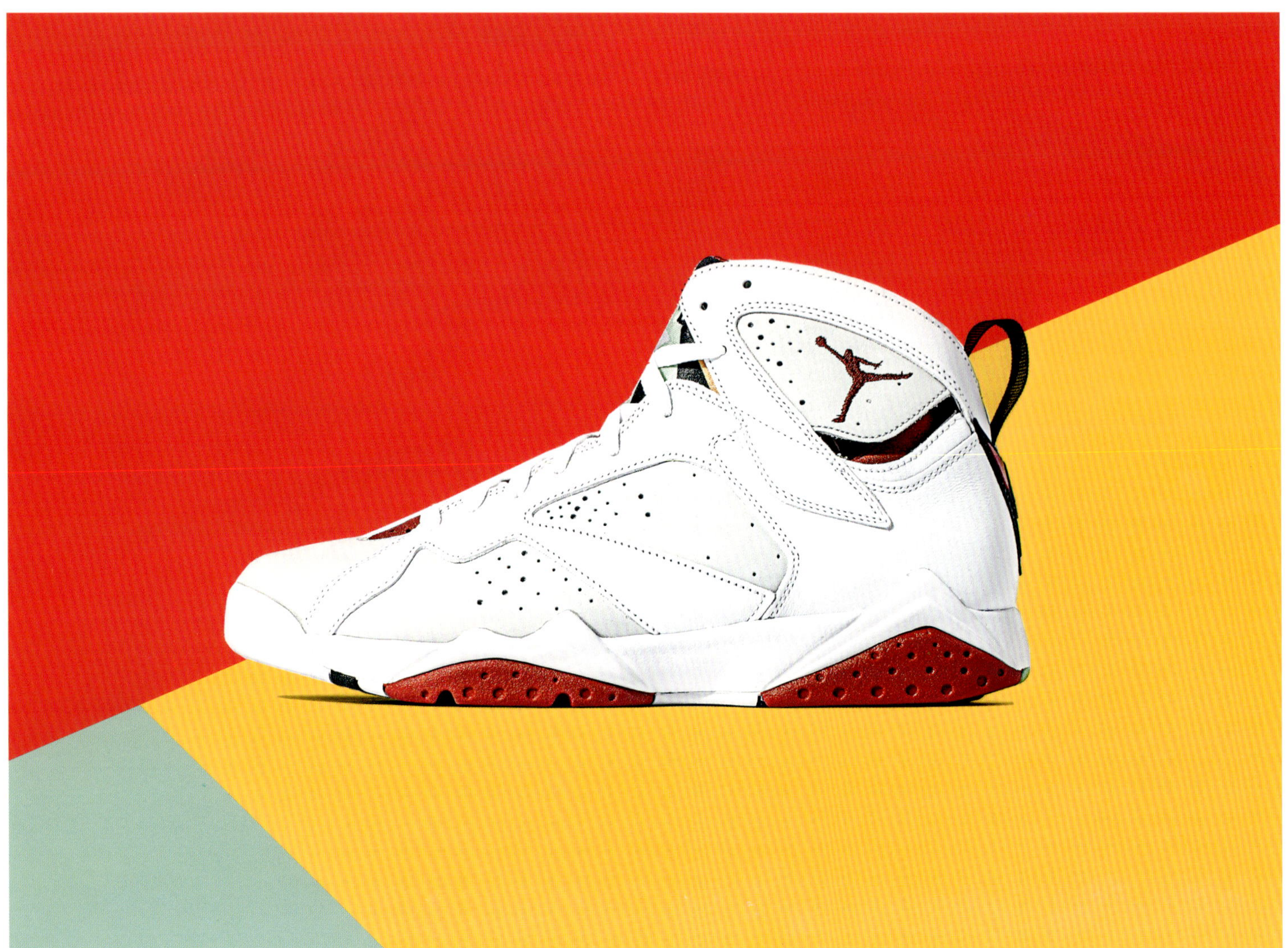

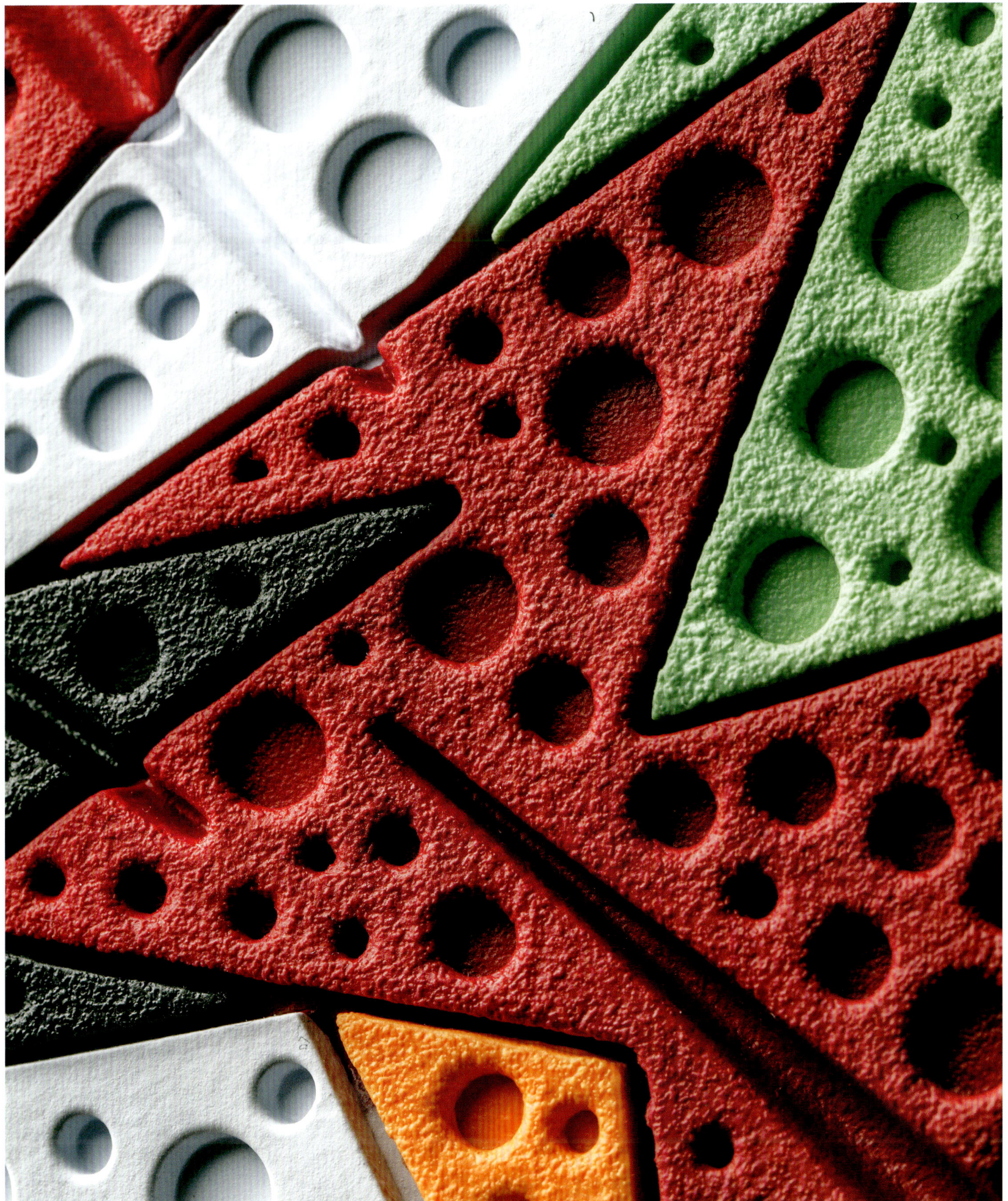

Details

The entire outsole is divided into eight units for more accurate cushioning. Thanks to the Hex Nike Zoom Air technology, designers are now able to use pressure mapping and sport-specific testing data to place the Zoom cushioning where it best serves the athlete — the forefoot. Unlike previous Zoom Air, this new application is engineered to be highly agile and responsive when off the ground.

NIKE ZOOM HYPERCROSS

Released in 2014 by Nike, the shoe is designed for intense training exercises. An innovative Flywire system with a Hyperfuse construction delivers superior lockdown and stability. The low-cut profile boosts greater mobility.

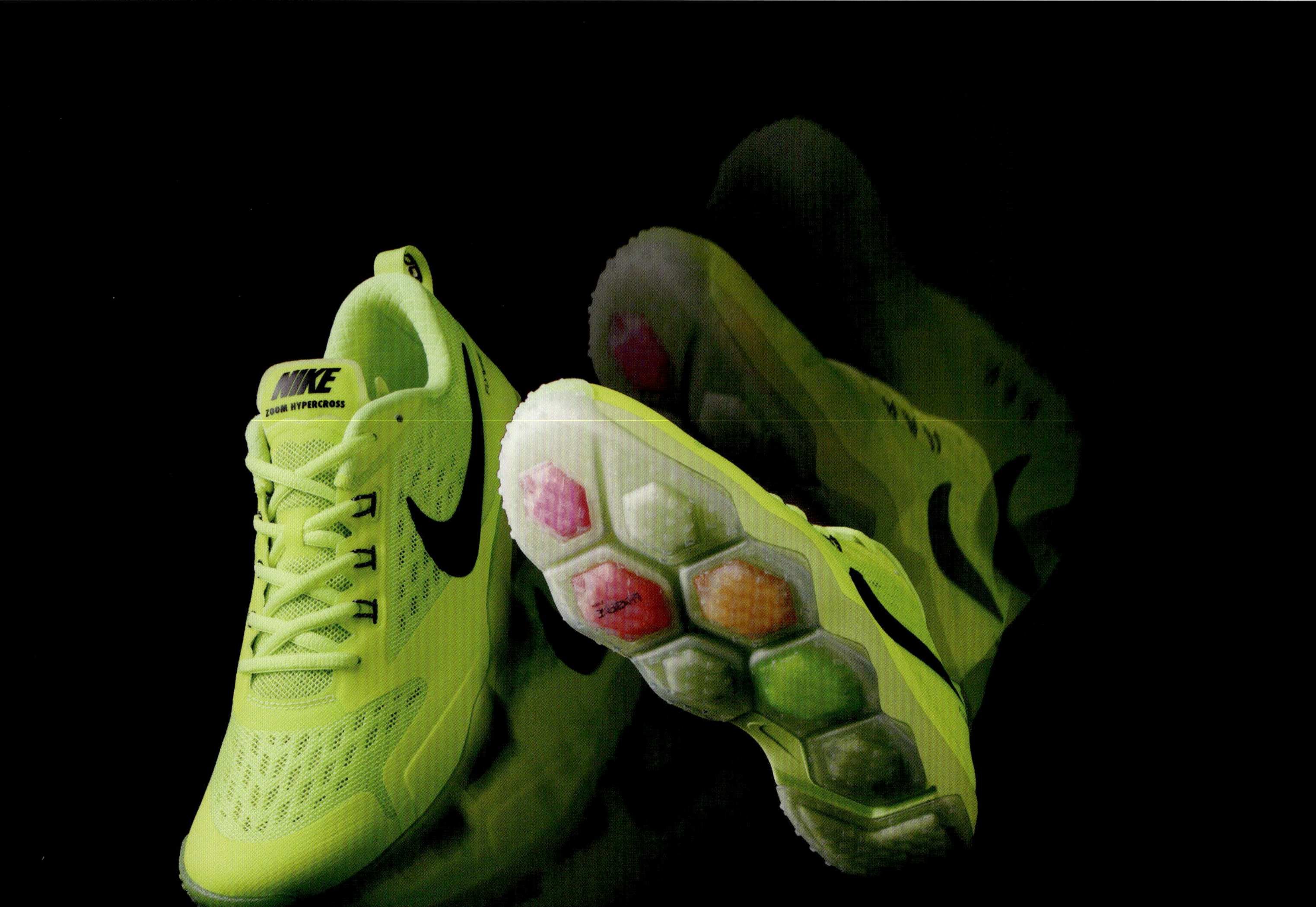

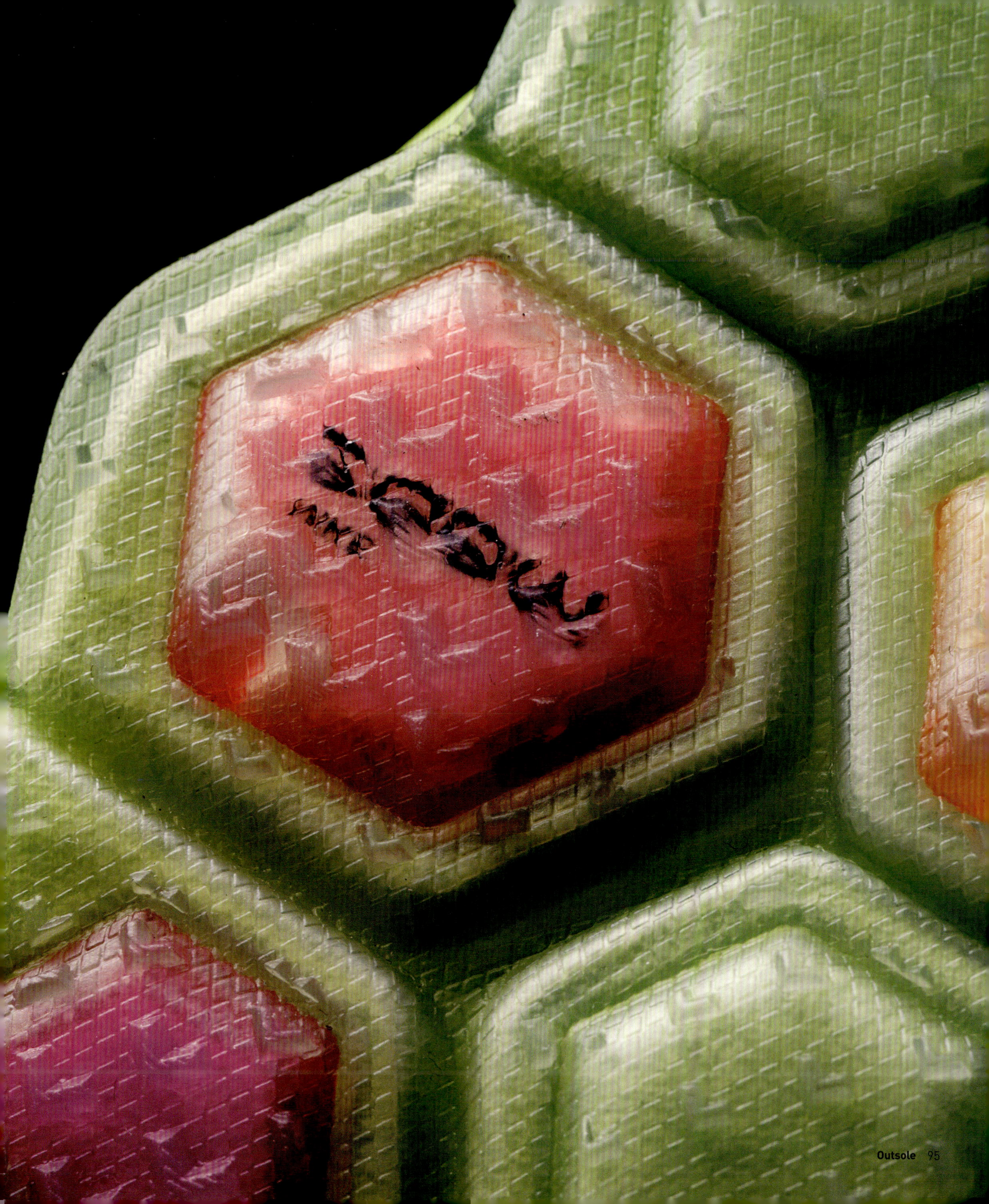

NIKE FREE SPECIAL FIELD BOOT

The inspiration derives from Nike's co-founder Bill Bowerman, who served in the Army during World War II. Inspired by his extraordinary experience, Nike has invented the old wheels and rocked the world again with this Special Field Boot.

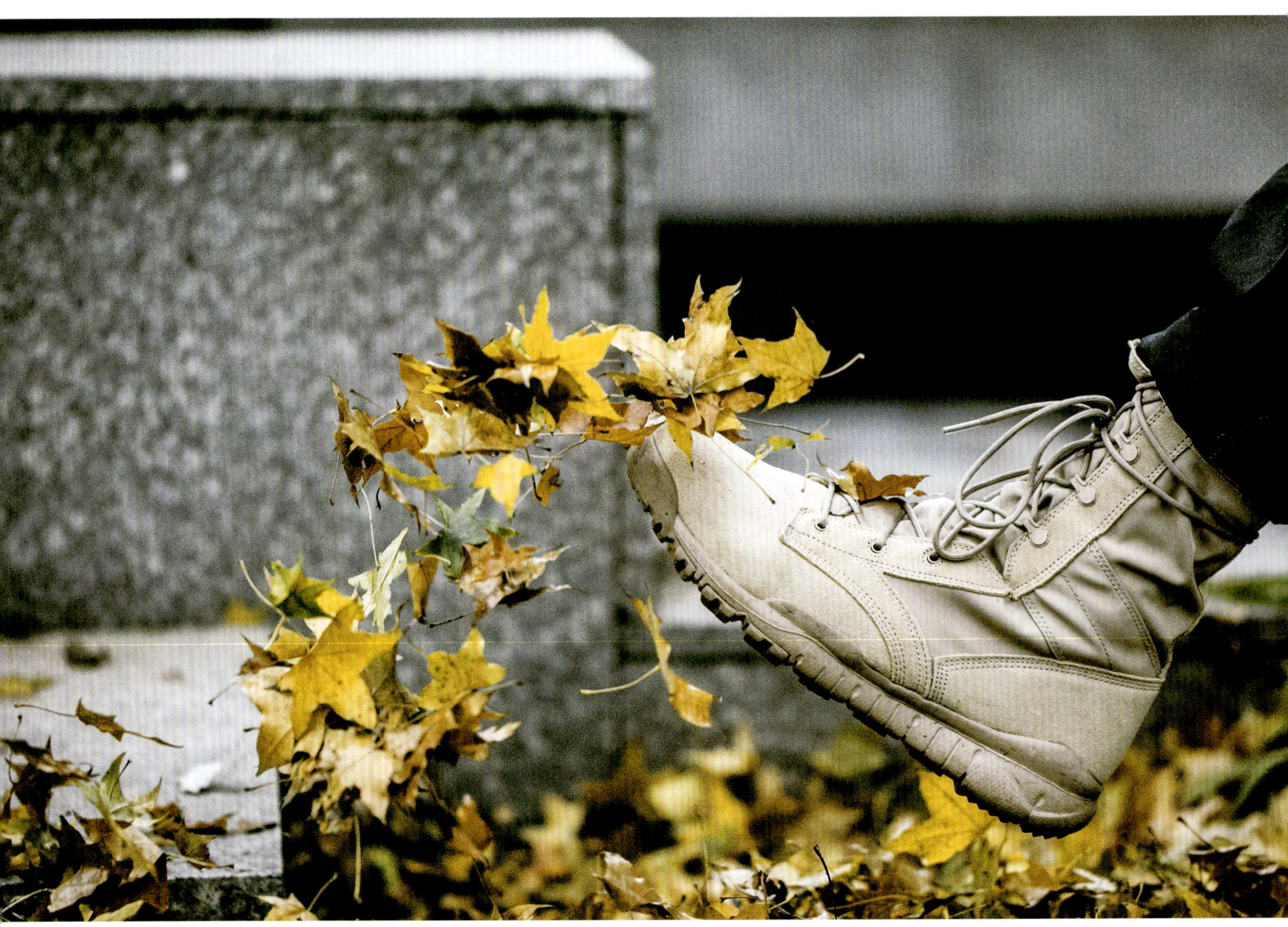

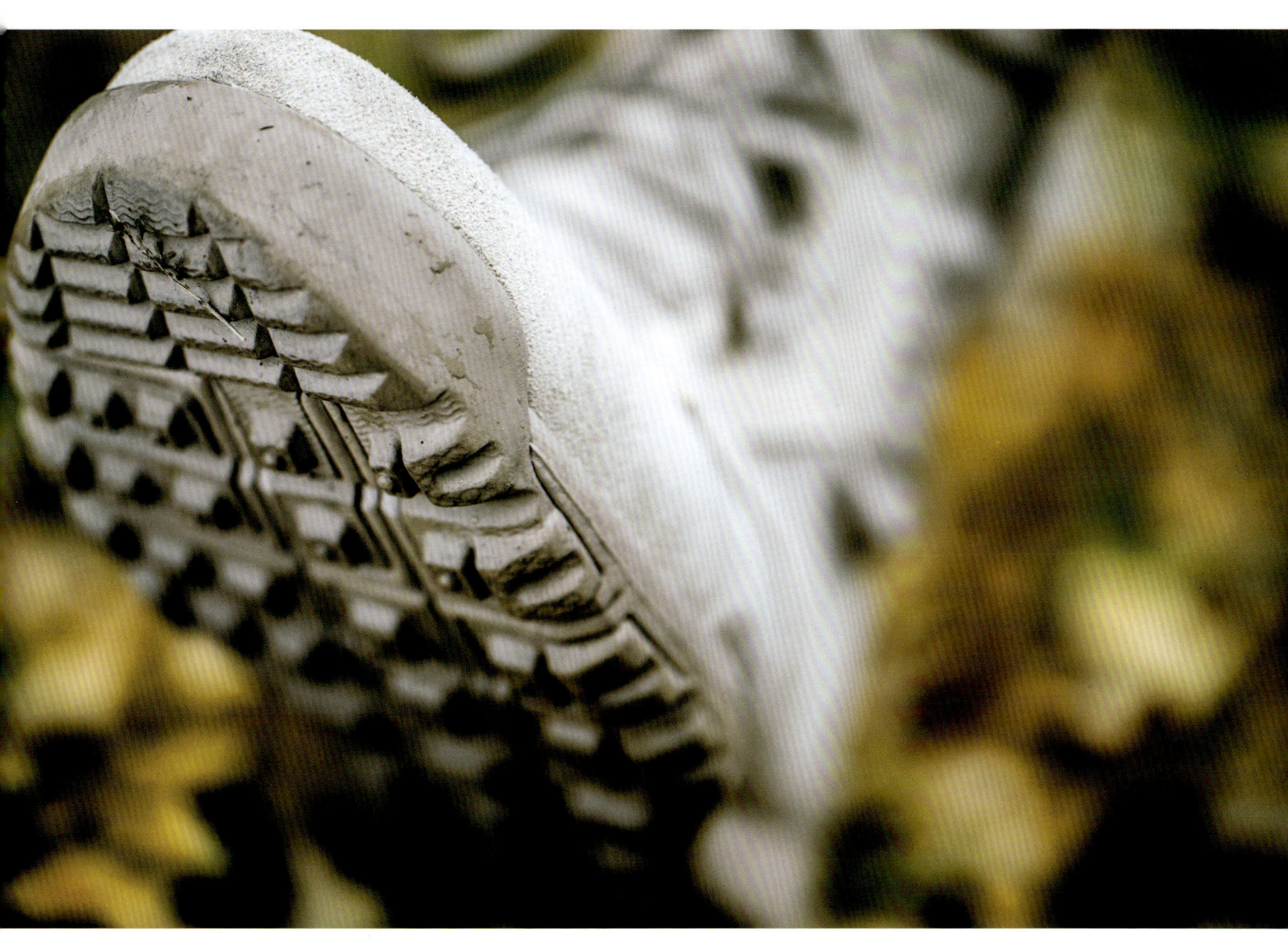

Details

In this hybrid of traditional boot and Nike Free running shoe, the sole is both lightweight and flexible. The design is particularly important for a seasoned soldier, who has to weather and endure so much on the battlefield. Its effective water-and-dirt-proof is another selling point of the boot.

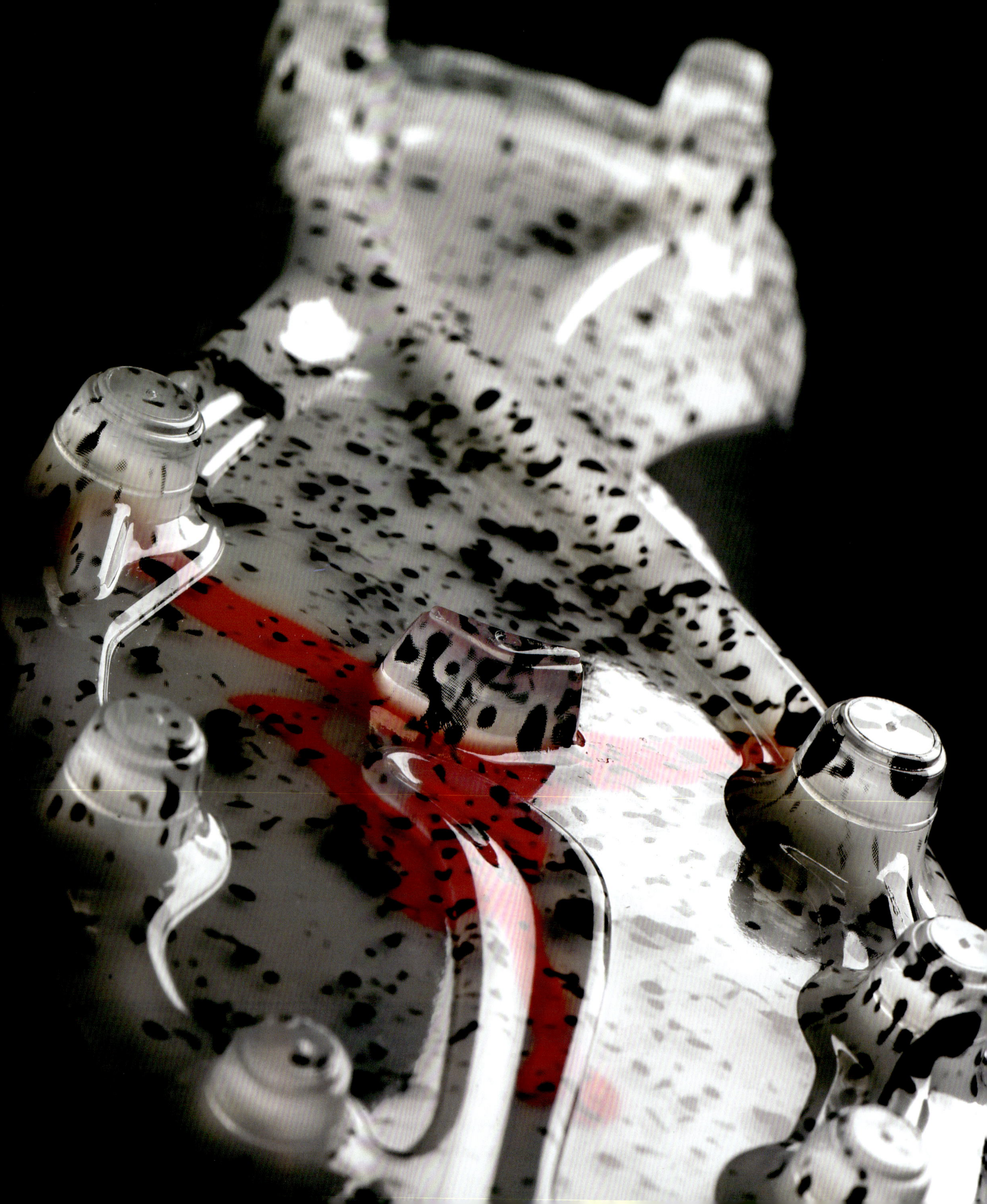

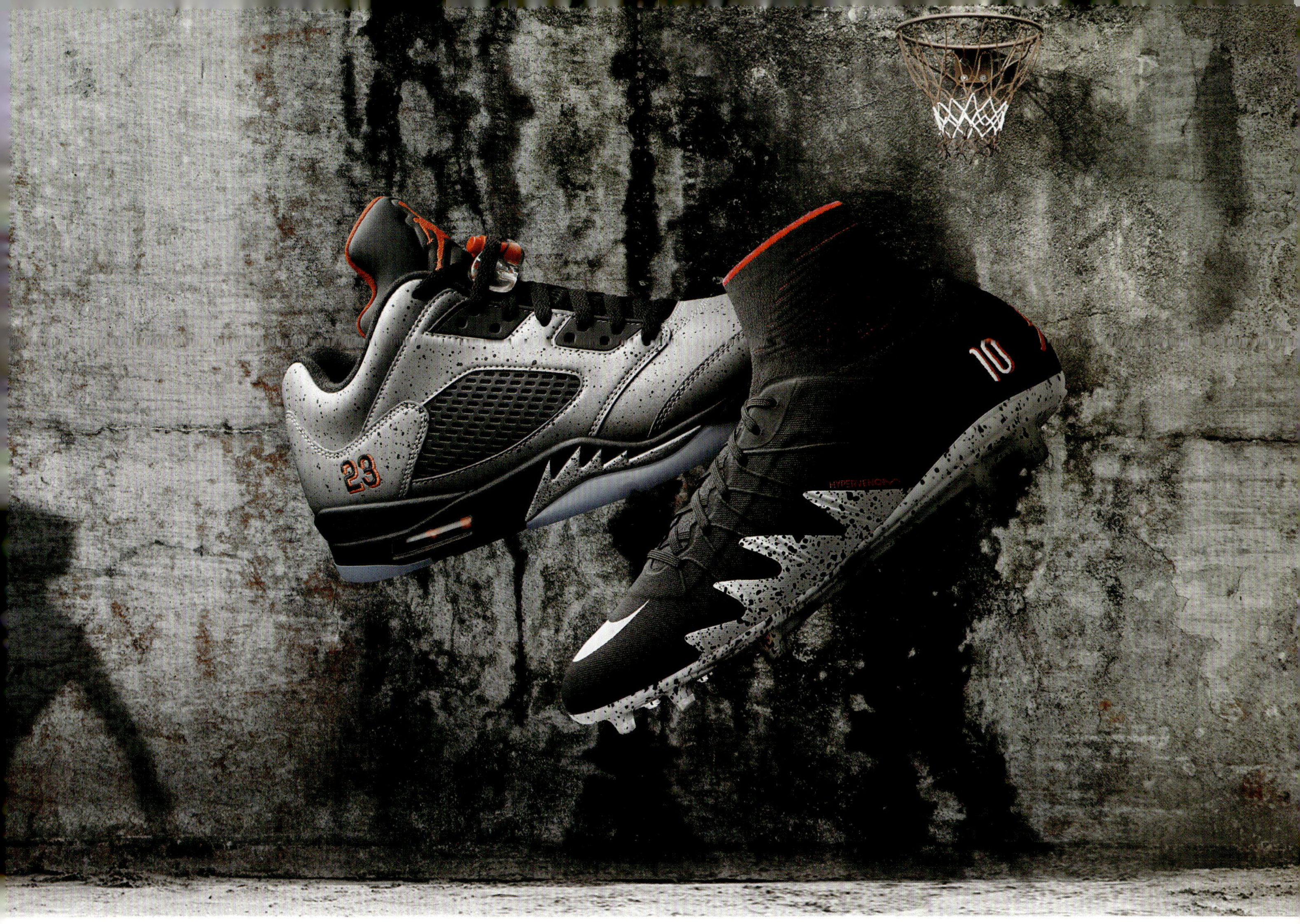

NJR × JORDAN HYPERVENOM

In 2016, Jordan Brand in conjunction with Nike released a reinvented Hypervenom collection for the Brazil football superstar, Neymar Jr. The new pack takes inspiration from the Jordan V, which is Neymar Jr.'s favorite sneaker.

Details

Neymar Jr.'s Brazil number "10" appears on the lateral side of the left black boot and the number "23" on the right boot, which pays tribute to Jordan. The sole features a paint-speckled design with a big Jumpman logo. And a pattern of fighter jet shark teeth, one iconic element of the Jordan V, is also retained in the model.

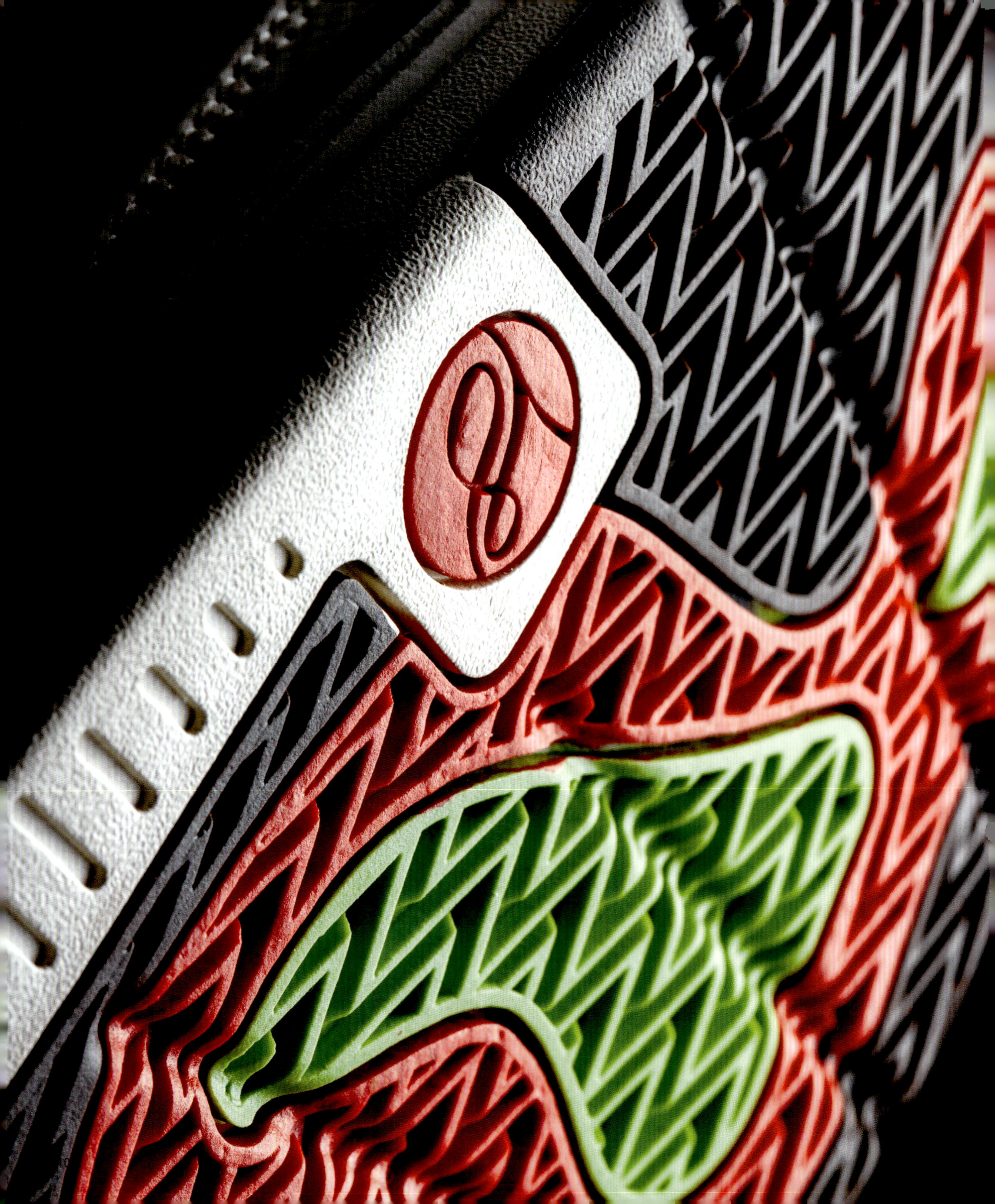

Details

The red and green areas on the outsole utilize the Gradient Dual technology. The midsole is comprised of materials in various density for a more responsive cushion. For added flexibility, the forefoot highlights a groove design. The initials of Tony Parker appear on the surface.

PEAK TONY PARKER II [CHRISTMAS]

Launched in 2014, it is Peak's second signature sneaker for Tony Parker. The inspiration behind the silhouette comes from the famous French Christmas cake Buche de Noel, or the Yule log cake.

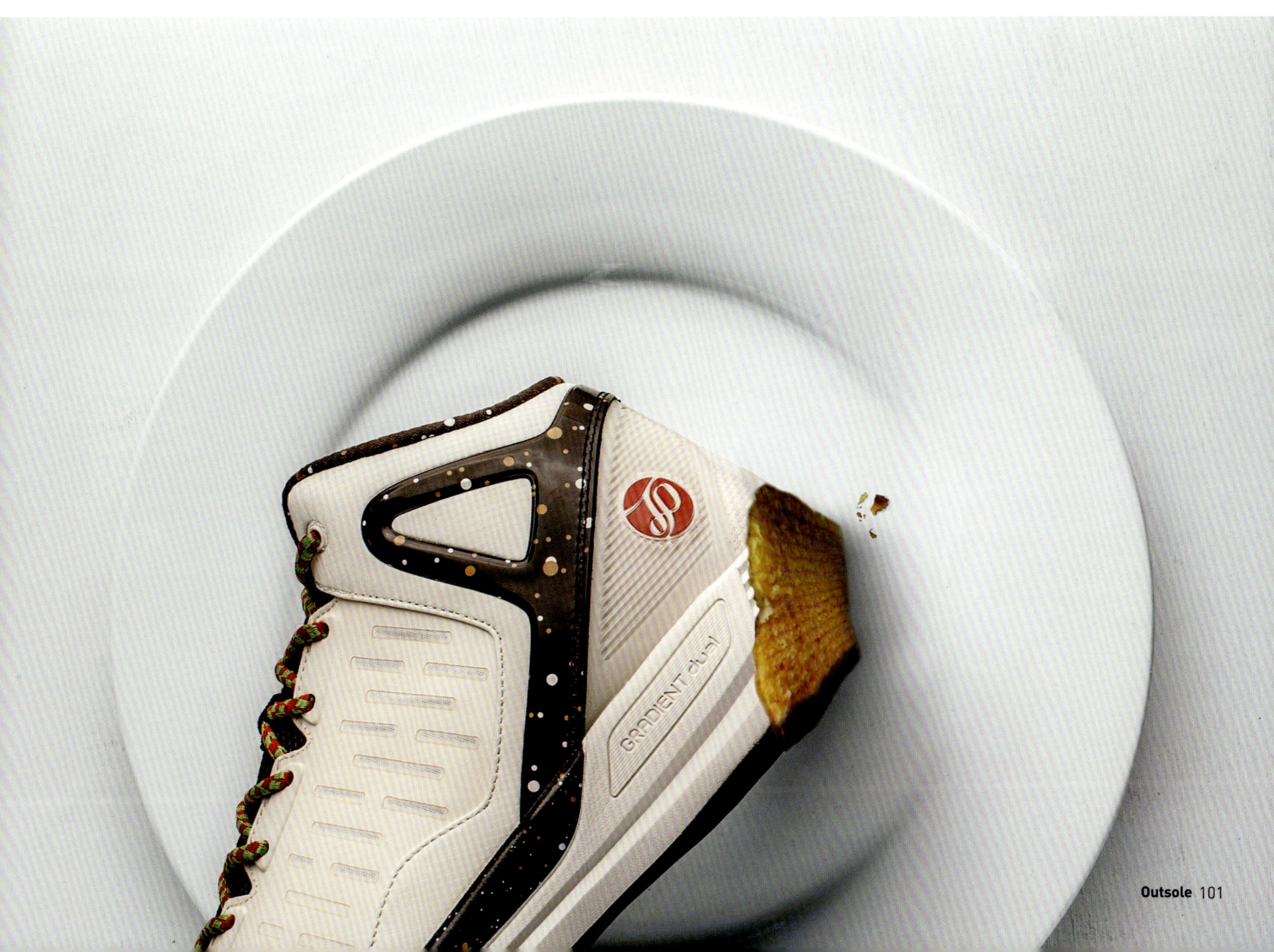

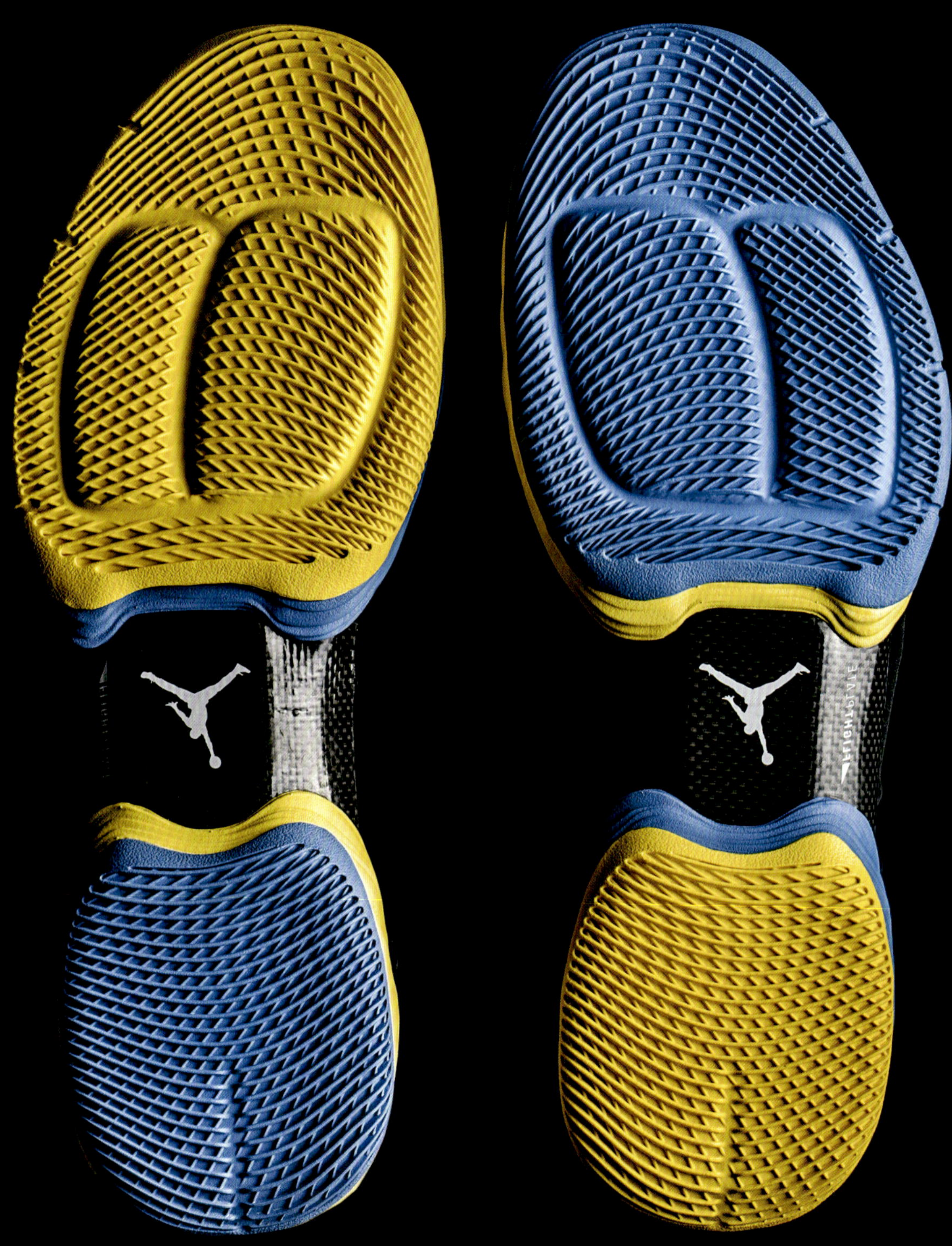

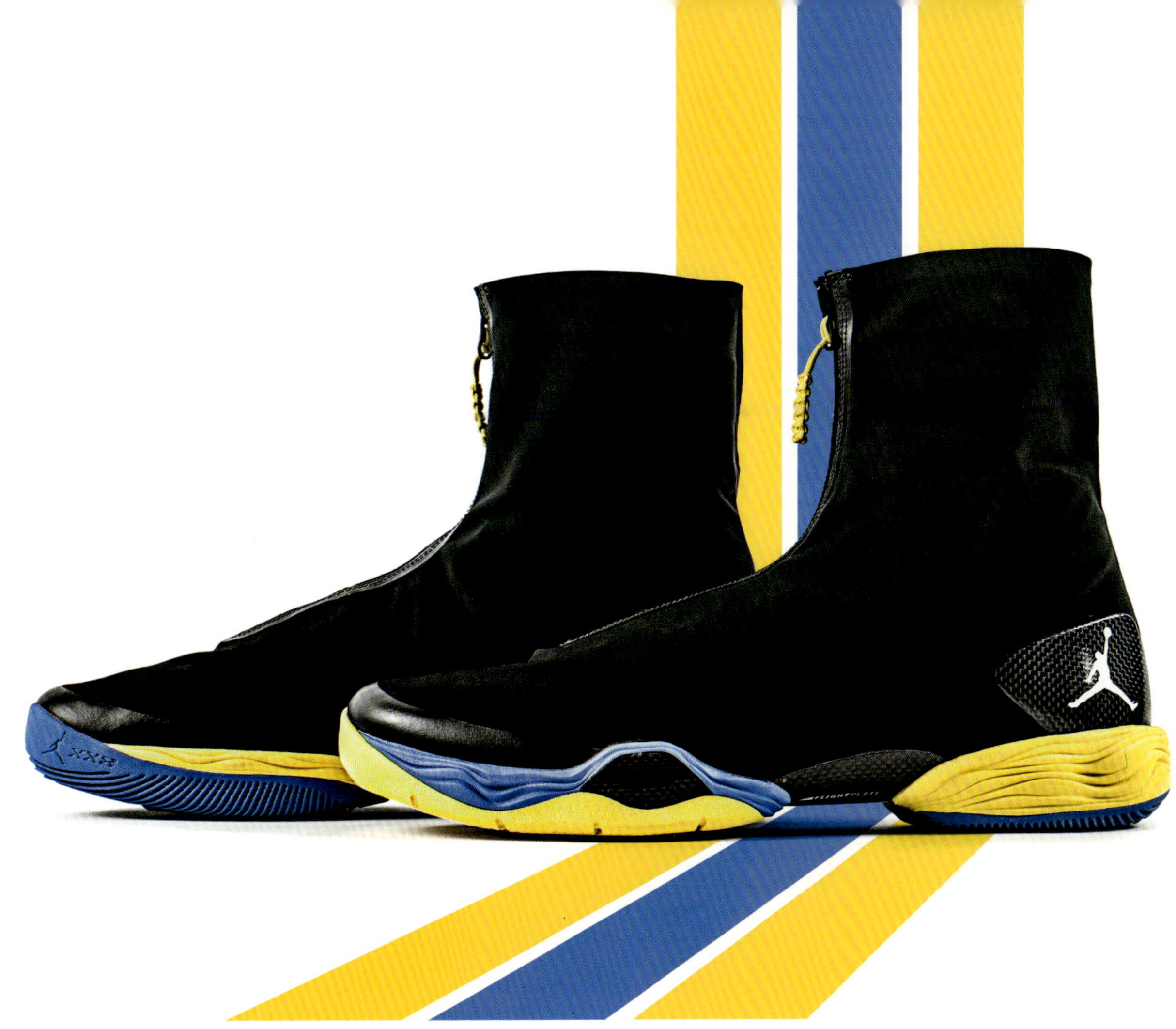

AIR JORDAN XX8 [PLAYOFFS] RW PE

Released in 2013 and designed by Tinker Hatfield, Playoffs is Jordan Brand's 28th sneaker in Michael Jordan's signature line. Unlike other Jordan Brand shoes, Playoffs has a high-cut profile, which is unprecedented. The colorway in the picture is an exclusive for Russell Westbrook in his post-season games.

Details

The Air Jordan XX8 introduced the Flight Plate, a supportive Pebax plate which brings out the best of Zoom Air's capabilities. The outsole boasts a contrasted blue-and-yellow pattern, with a web-shaped texture for reinforced grip. The carbon fiber material around the midfoot and the heel both give you a more harnessed support.

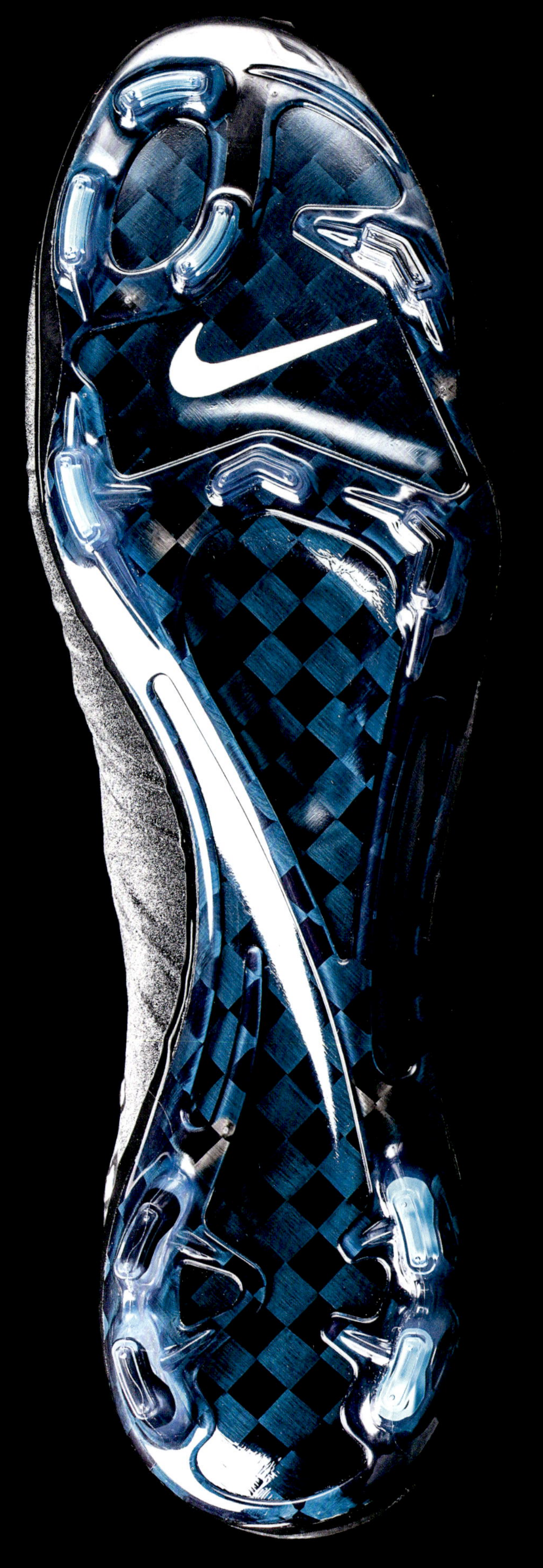

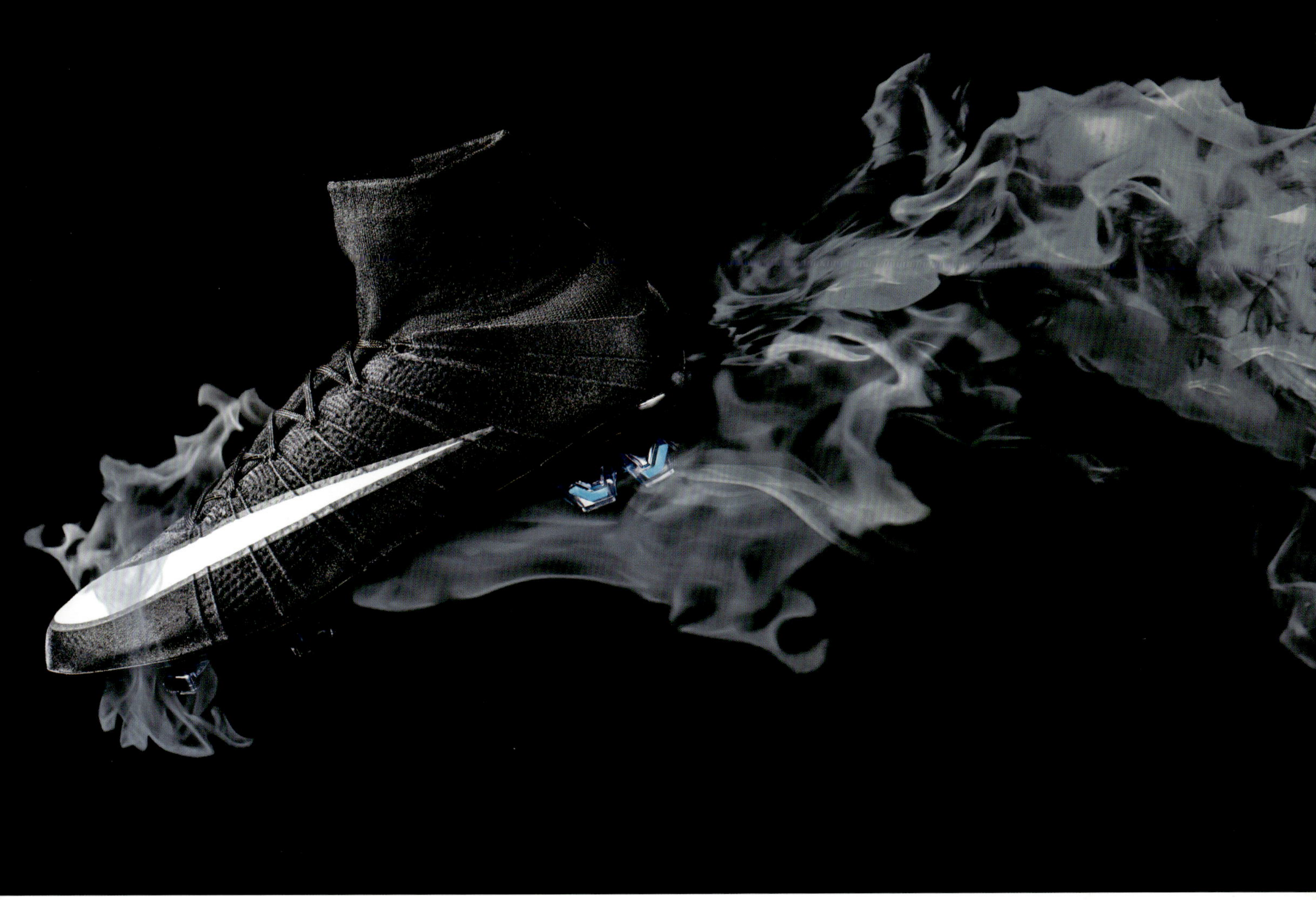

NIKE MERCURIAL SUPERFLY CR7

Tailor-made for Portuguese superstar football player Cristiano Ronaldo, Nike Mercurial Superfly CR7 debuted in 2014. Pursuing a lightning speed and feather-like weight, Mercurial Superfly is designed for players with exceptional explosiveness and speed.

Details

The sole is made entirely of carbon fiber, which makes it both lightweight and flexible. Matched with a Flyknit upper, the shoe is truly light as air.

Details

The midsole is designed to be a fin-shaped structure for better support, and the air bags in the heel bring more stabilized cushioning. The upward extension of the outsole is another added dimension.

NIKE AIR MAX P2 ULTIMATE PE

Launched in 2007, it is Paul Pierce's signature sneaker and is not available on the market. A mix of patent leather and nubuck, together with a design of Velcro, constitutes the most eye-catching element of the shoe.

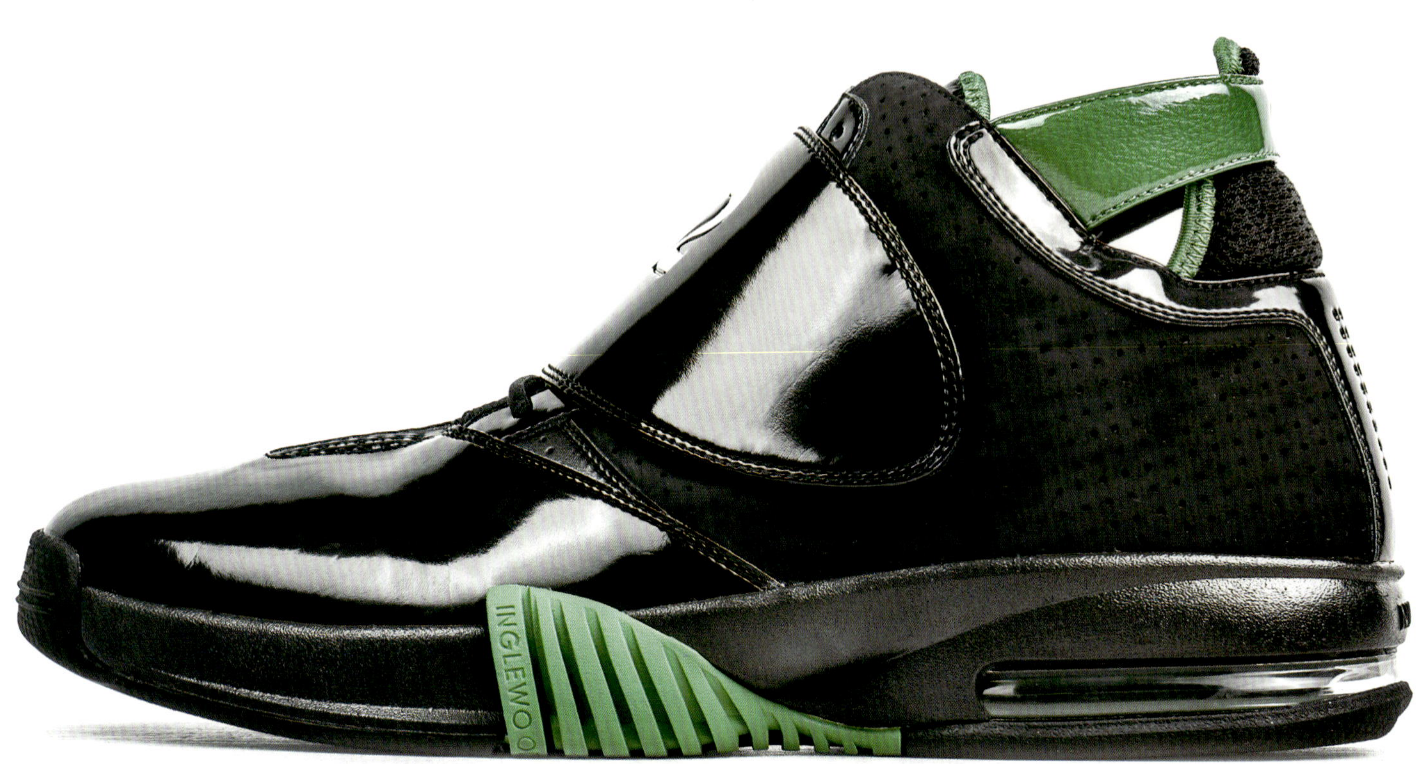

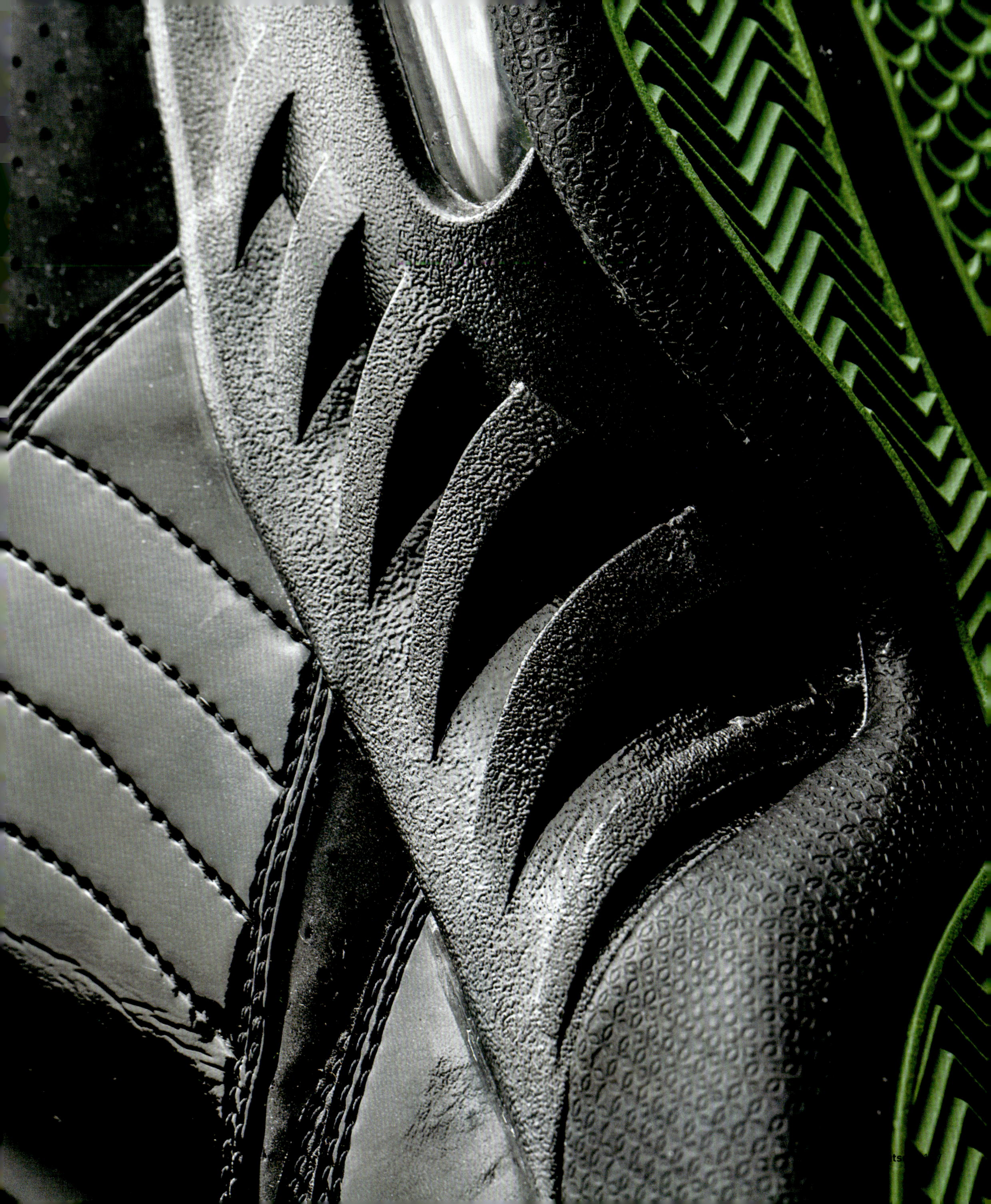

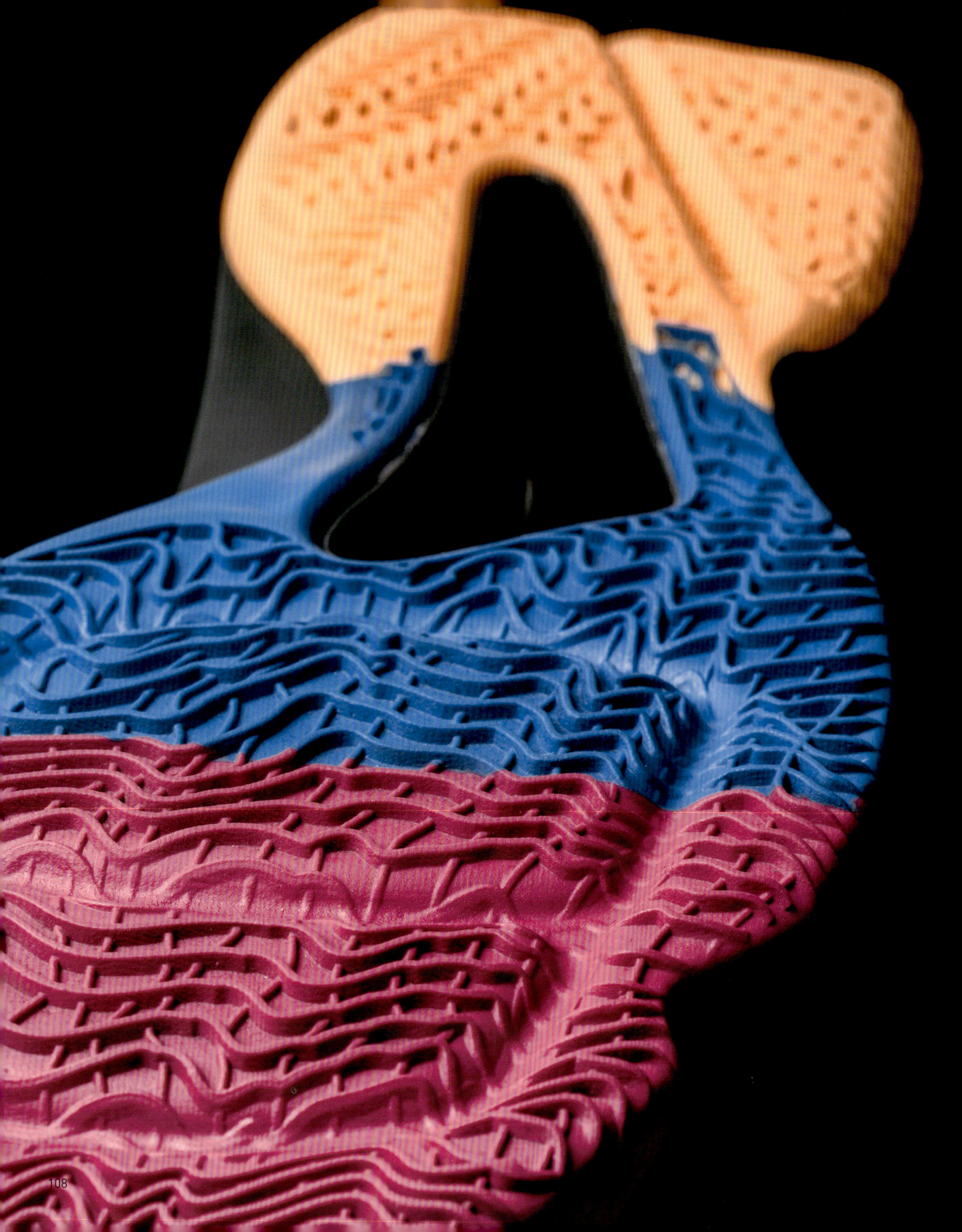

Details

Melo M12 has been updated with new and improved performance features, like the two Zoom Air units that offer responsive cushioning and FlightSpeed technology for an explosive first step.

JORDAN MELO M12 [THE DUNGEON]

Released in 2016, the Dungeon, with its design inspired by a big lizard, is the 12th iteration in Carmelo Anthony's signature line. The colorway, as is showed in the picture, pays tribute to a Baltimore Rec Center, where Carmelo honed his basketball skills as a youngster.

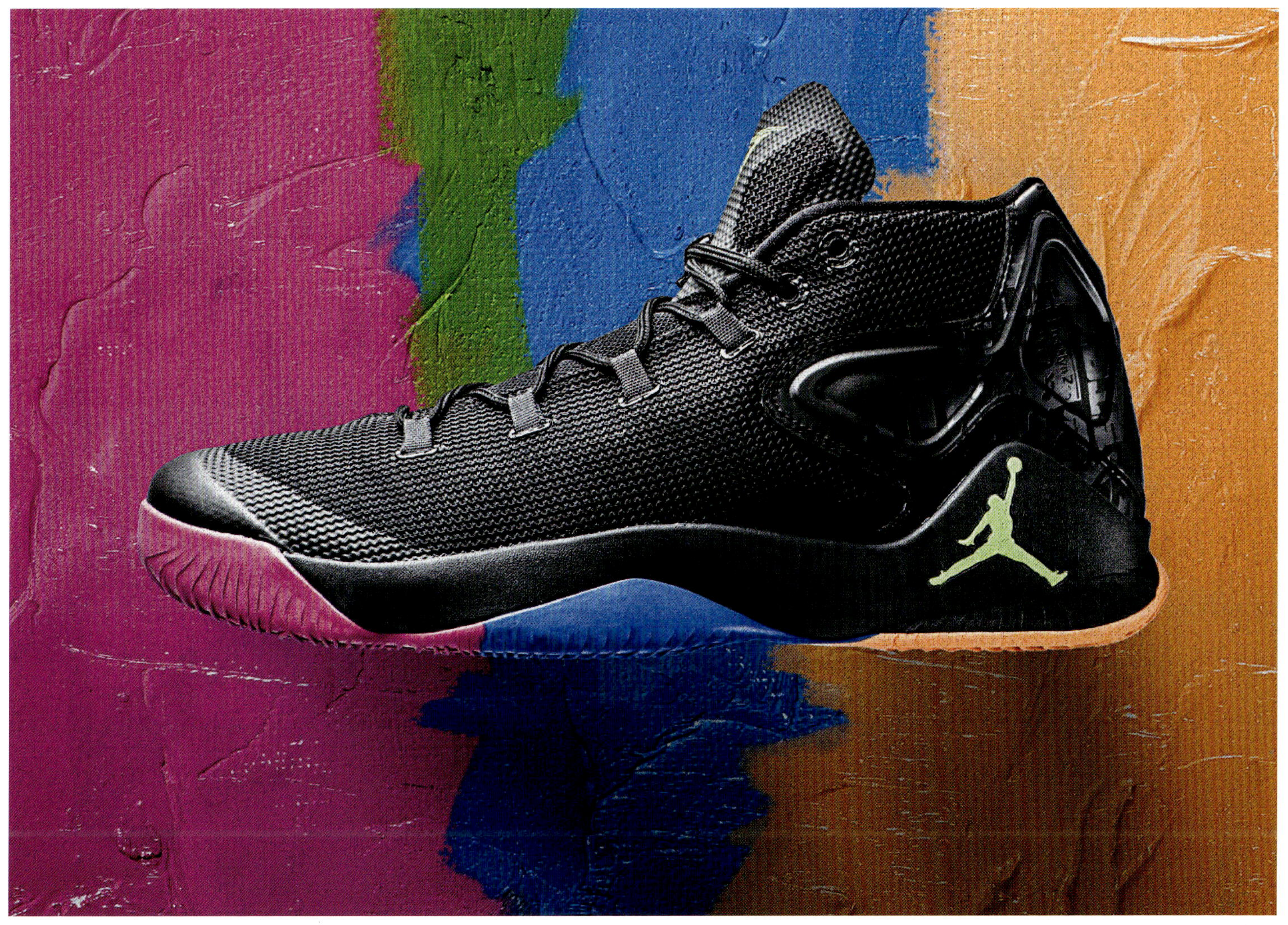

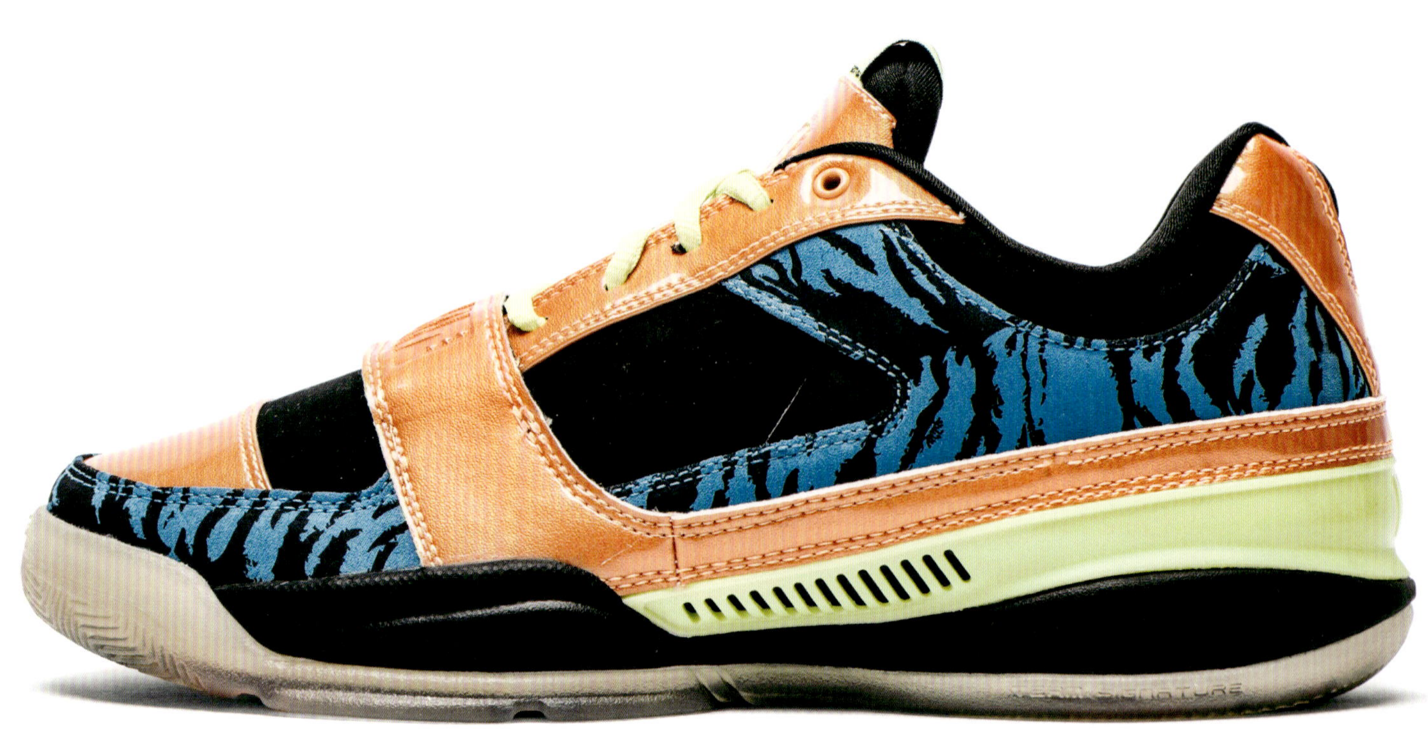

ADIDAS TS LIGHTSWITCH GIL × [SLAM]

The model was co-launched by adidas and SLAM in 2008. The tiger-striped upper is inspired by Gilbert Arenas' tiger tattoo.

Details

Through a crystal-clear outsole, you can see a SLAM cover image of Gilbert Arenas.

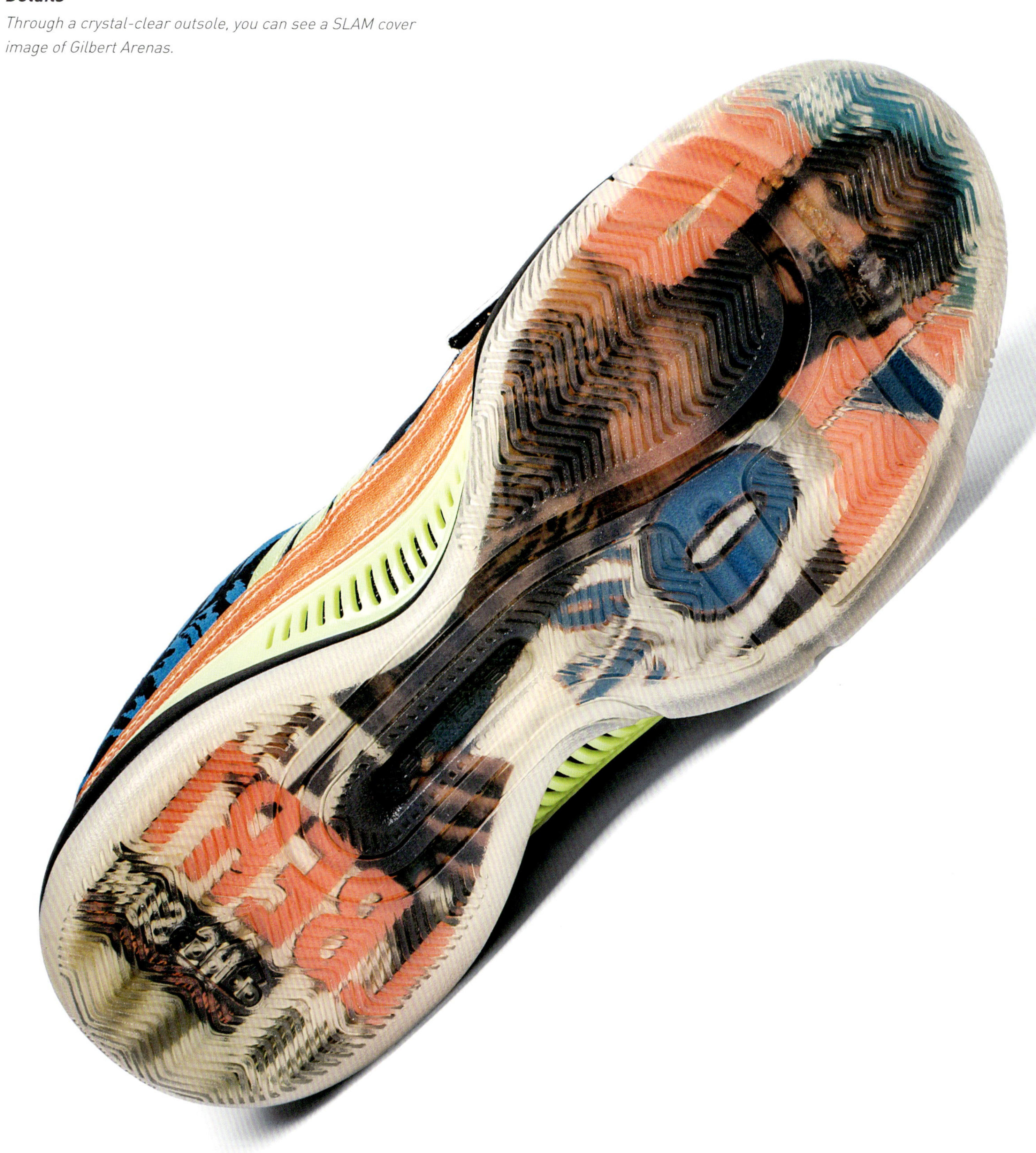

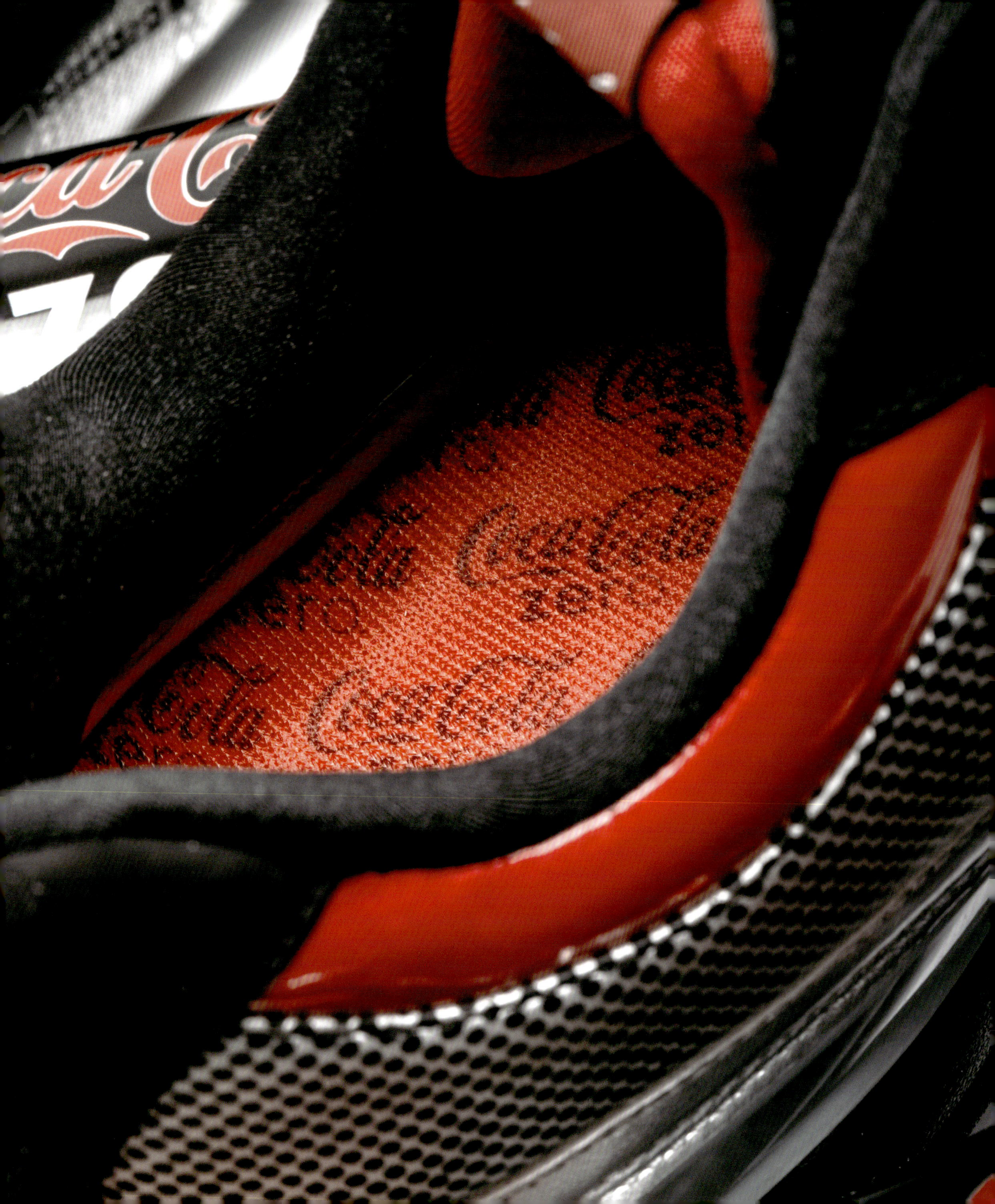

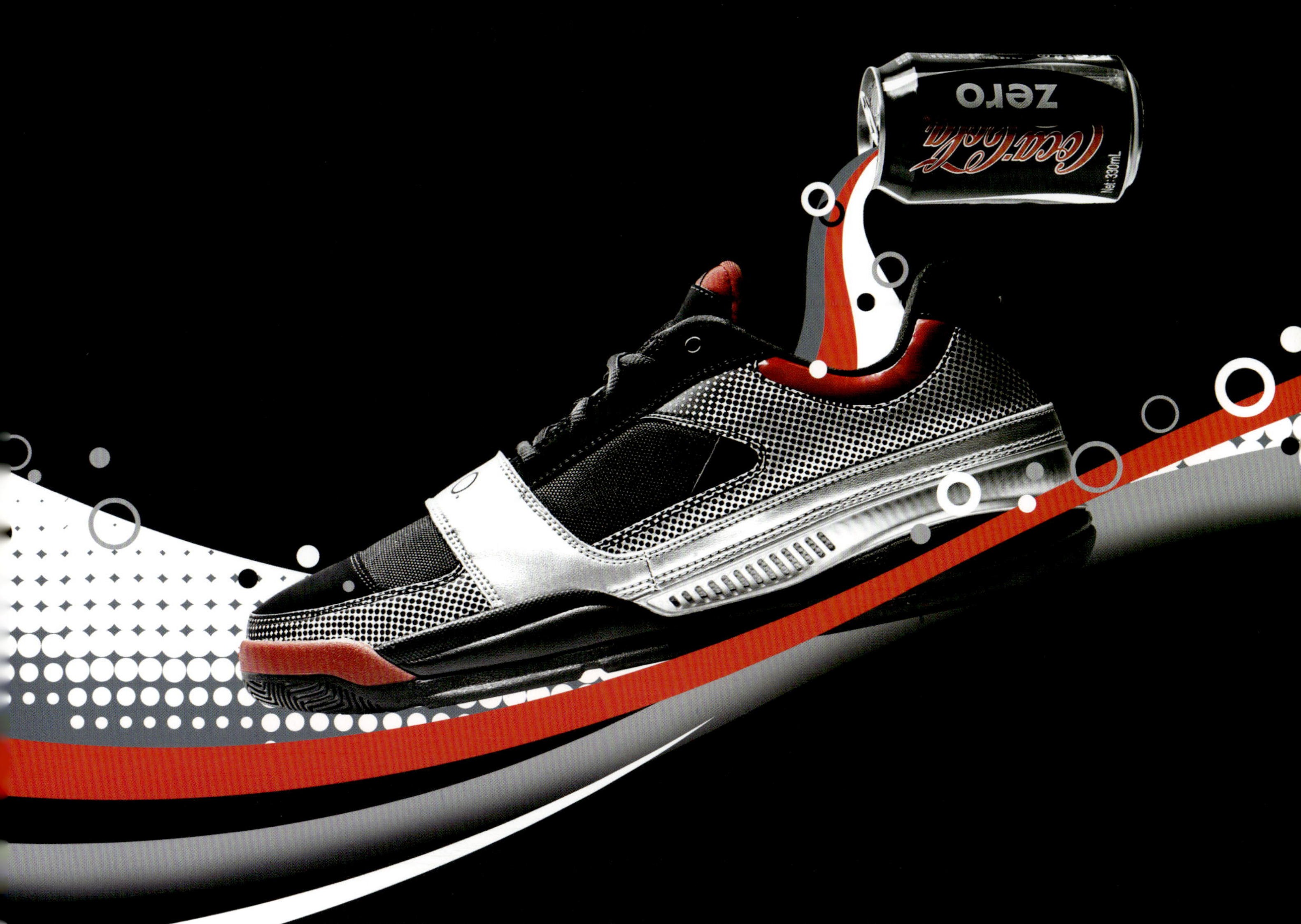

ADIDAS TS LIGHTSWITCH GIL × COCA COLA ZERO SAMPLE

Not sold to public, the sample is a collaborative project of adidas and Coca Cola for Arenas' exclusive collection, TS Lightswitch Gil. The black, red and silver colorway resembles the primary colorway of Coca Cola Zero.

Details

The black logos of Coca Cola Zero constitute a major pattern for the red insole, and the black outsole is equipped with a silver TPU plate in the midfoot.

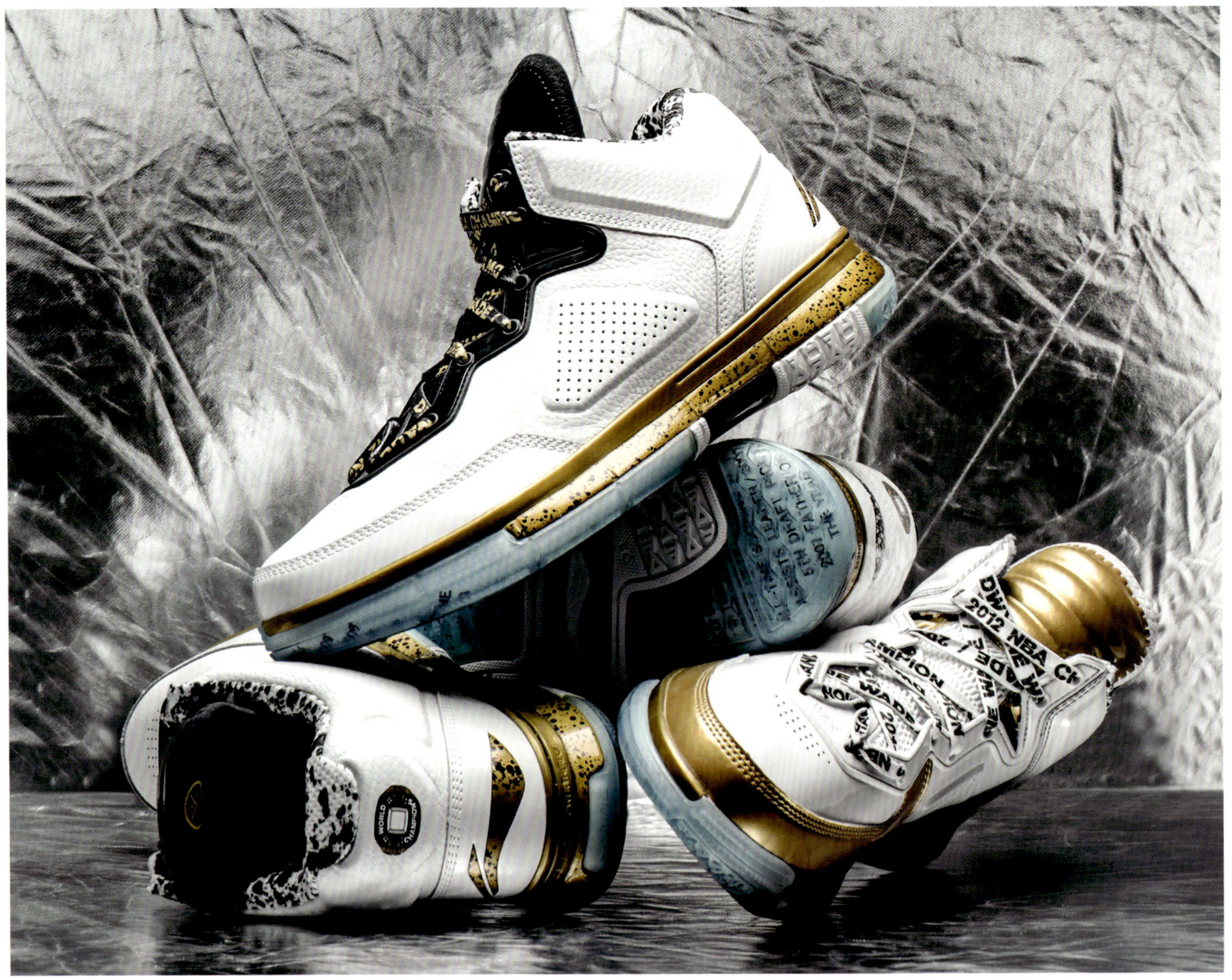

LI-NING WAY OF WADE [DYNASTY]

The Dynasty debuted in 2012, with only 40 pairs available in North America. As Dwyane Wade's first signature Li-Ning sneaker, the new basketball shoe designed by Eric Miller consists of two models, one in a home colorway and the other in an away scheme.

Details

The shoe features an icy blue outsole with various accolades from Wade's career (as of 2012) inscribed on the bottom. His name in red lies beneath the round "WADE" trademark, with the Li-Ning logo printed on the carbon fiber midfoot. The heel's "ZZDG" are the initials of his sons Zaire and Zion, nephew Dada and wife Gabrielle; "91" on the sole indicates the age of his grandma; and "11105" on the mid stands for his 11-year-old son Zaire, 10-year-old nephew Dada and 5-year-old son Zion.

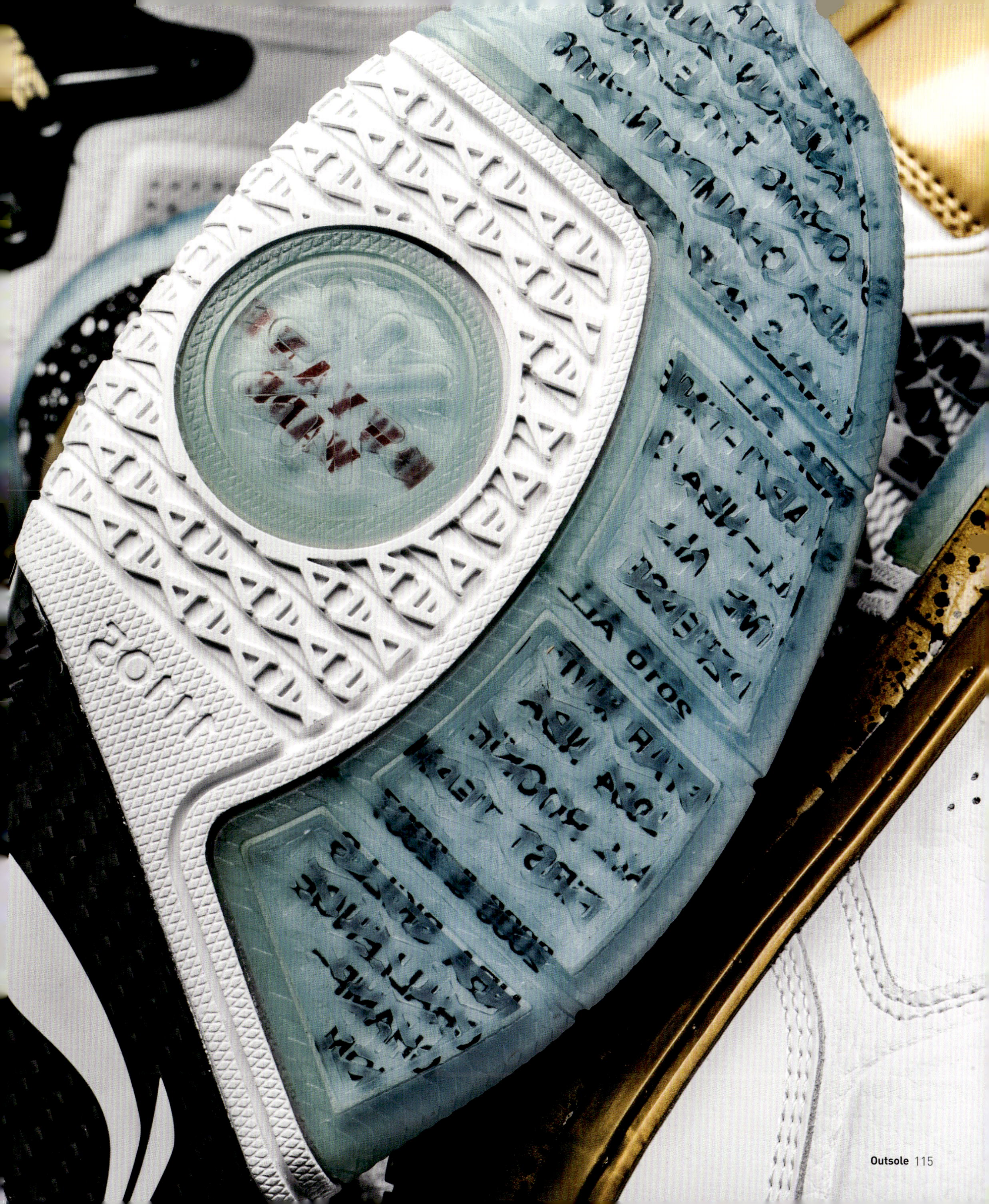

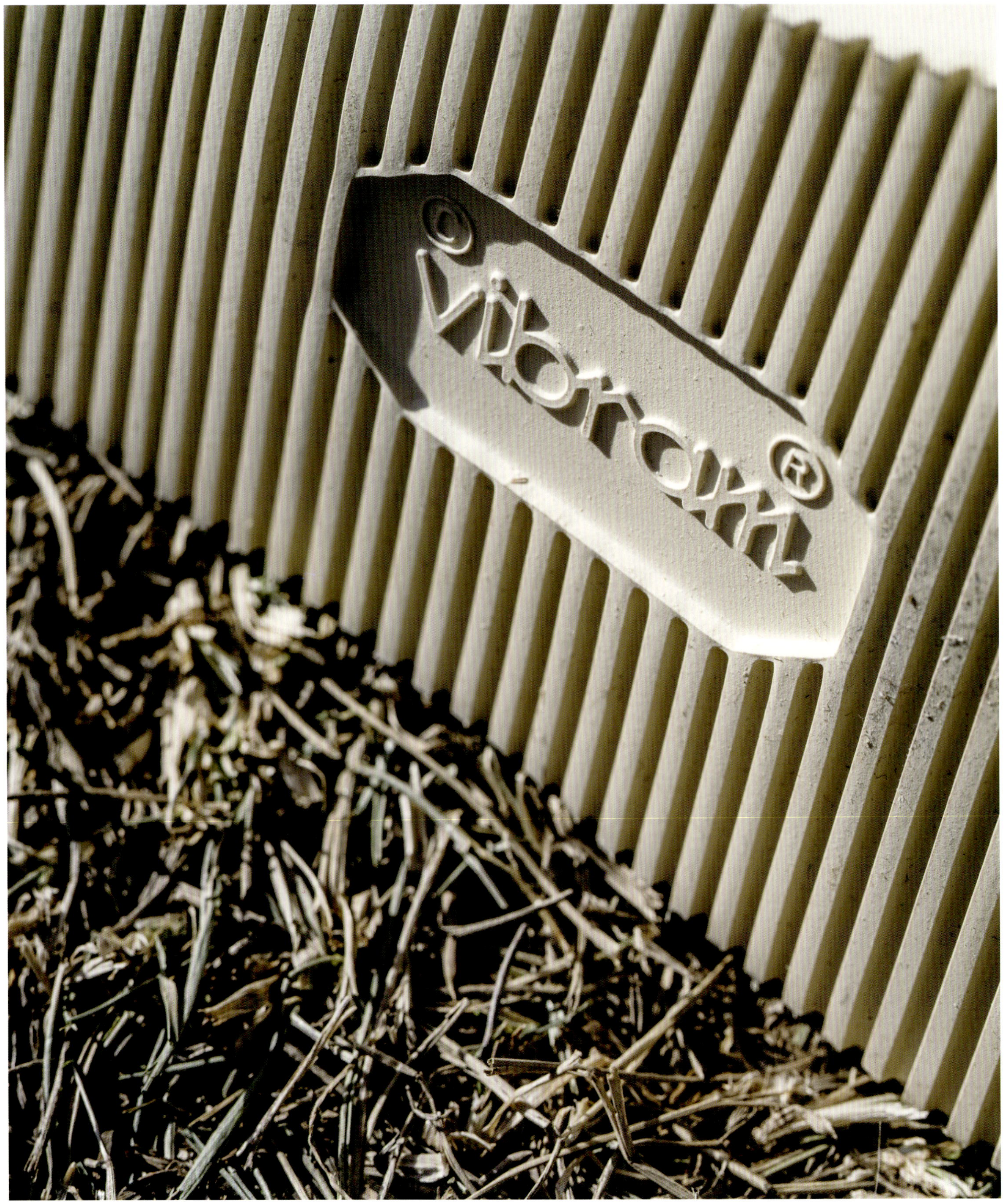

Details

The Chelsea Boot flaunts a Vibram rubber sole with a striped pattern that ensures great grip and durability.

PUBLISH × TIMBERLAND [REINVENTING CALIFORNIA] CHELSEA BOOT

In 2015, Publish Brand — known for delivering premium, timeless "streetwear" — teamed up with Timberland to create this limited-release collection of Chelsea boots. While retaining the key elements of previous Chelseas, the new collaboration is based on the concept of "Reinventing California."

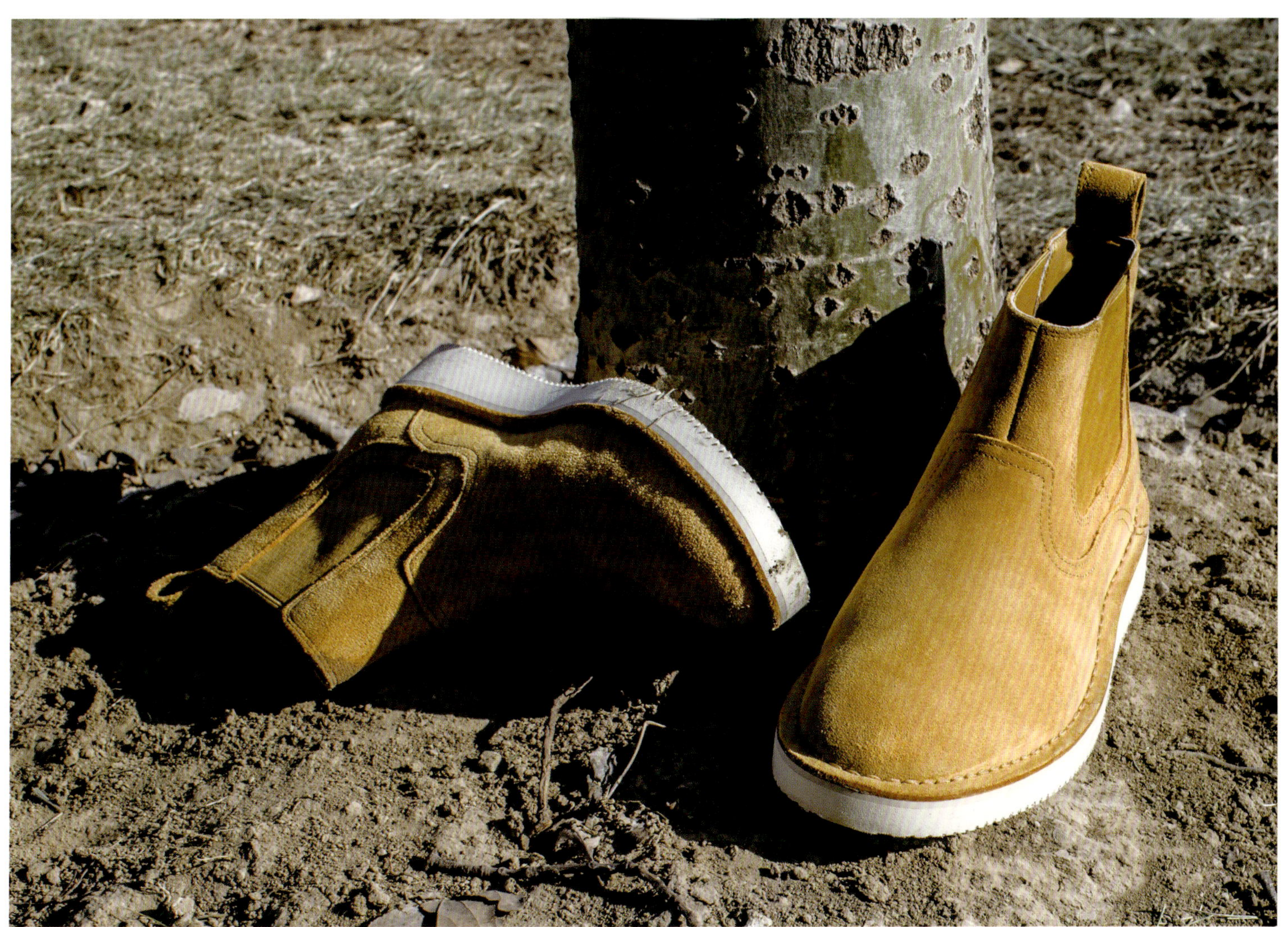

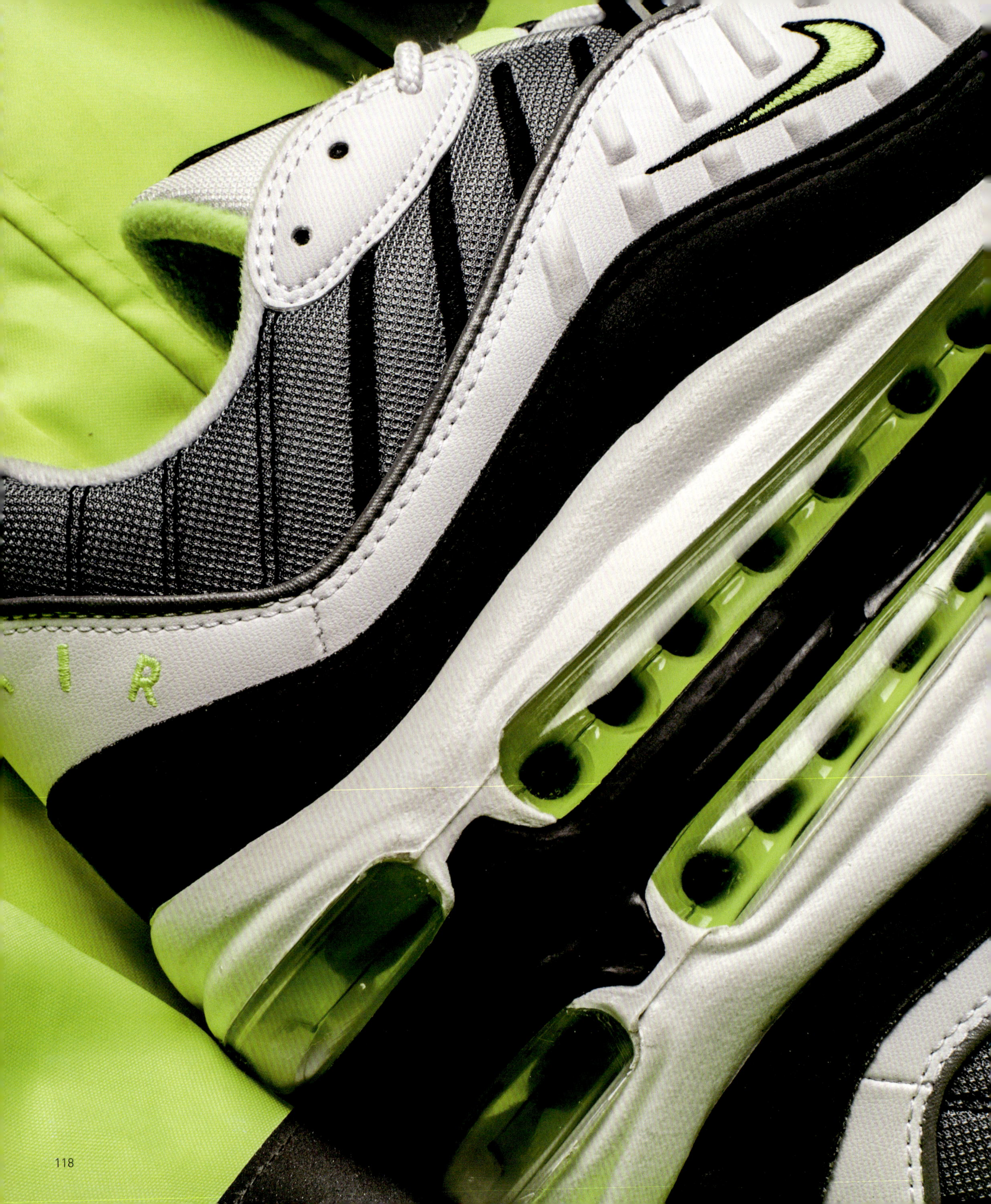

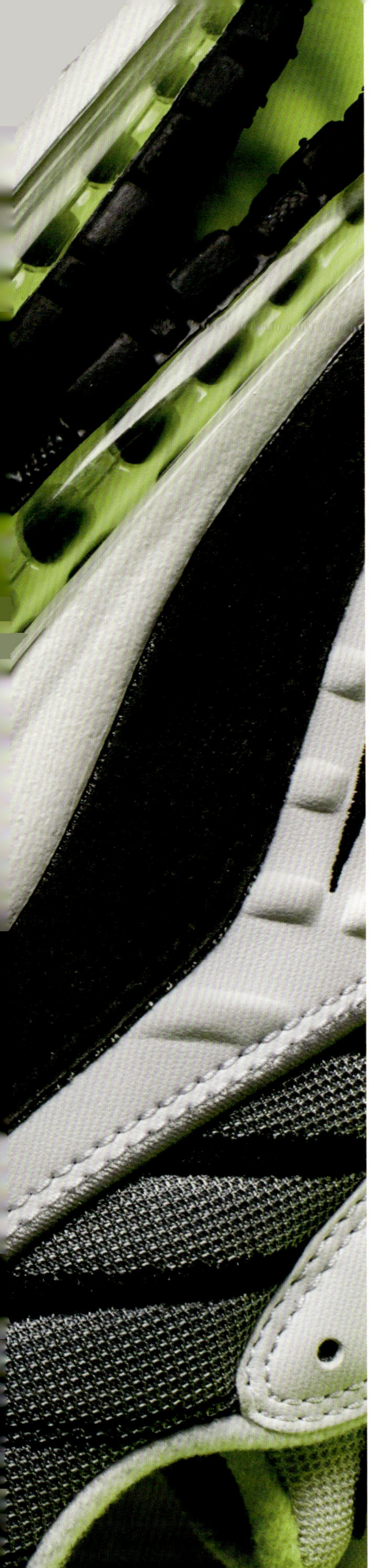

A pro sneaker beats a common sneaker in its sports-enhancing technologies. Through endless trials and tribulations, brands have innovated a variety of technologies, only to deliver greater comfort and stronger protection.

TECHNOLOGY

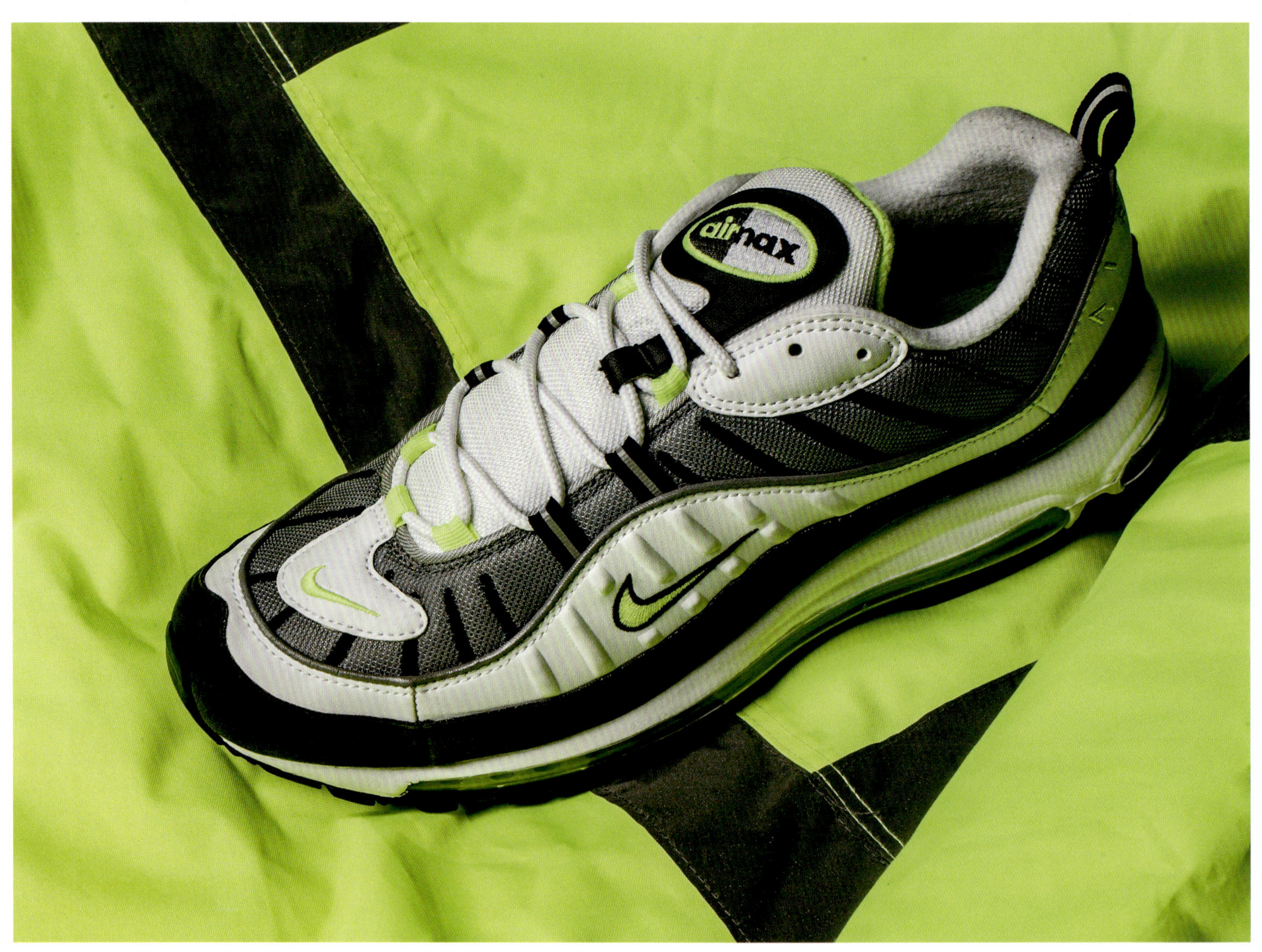

NIKE AIR MAX 98

In 1987, Tinker Hatfield created Nike Air Max with a visible air bag.

Details

Launched in 1998, Air Max 98 features a full-length Air Max cushioning. As time goes by, this technology has matured with more visual impact.

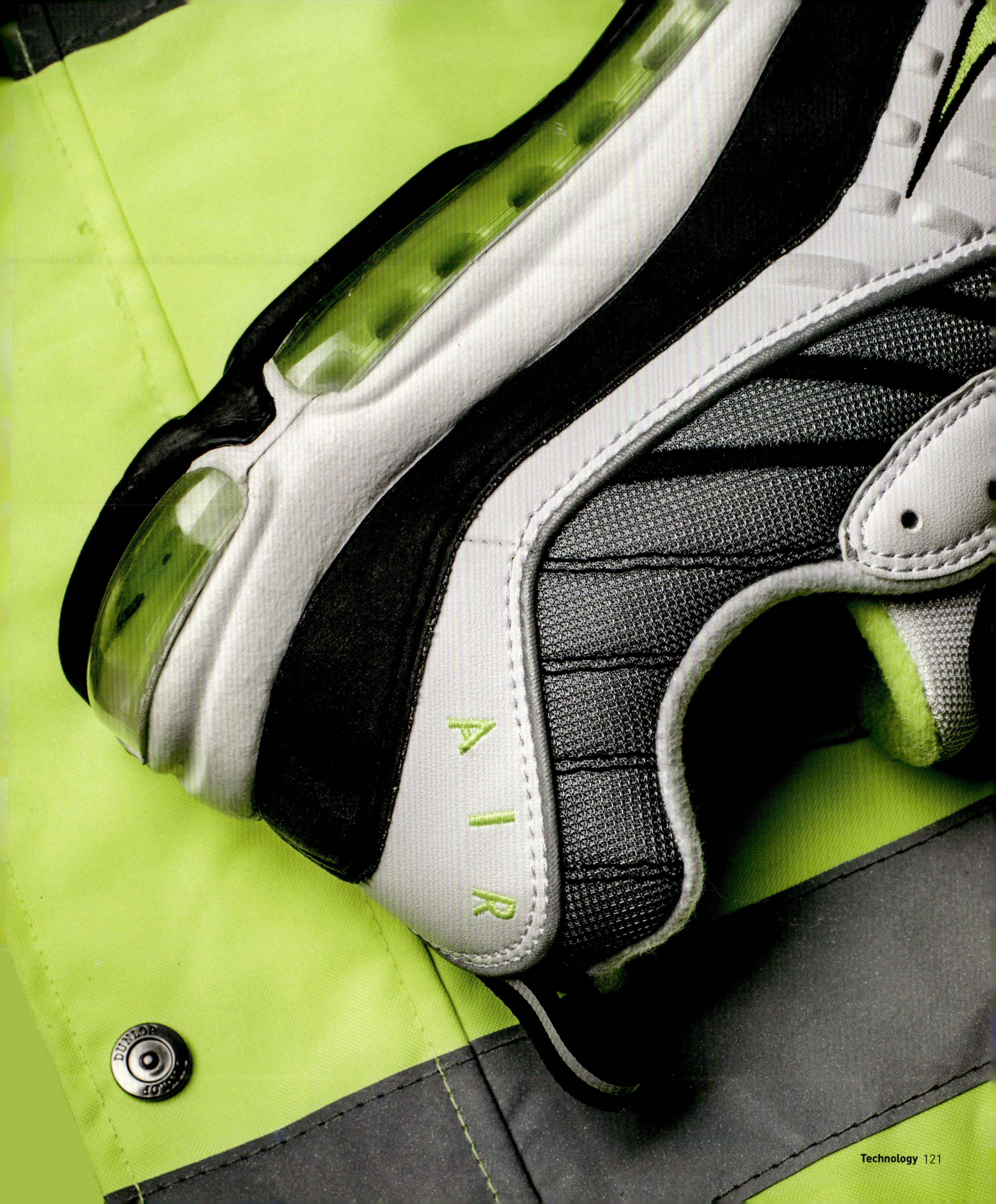
AIR
DUNLOP

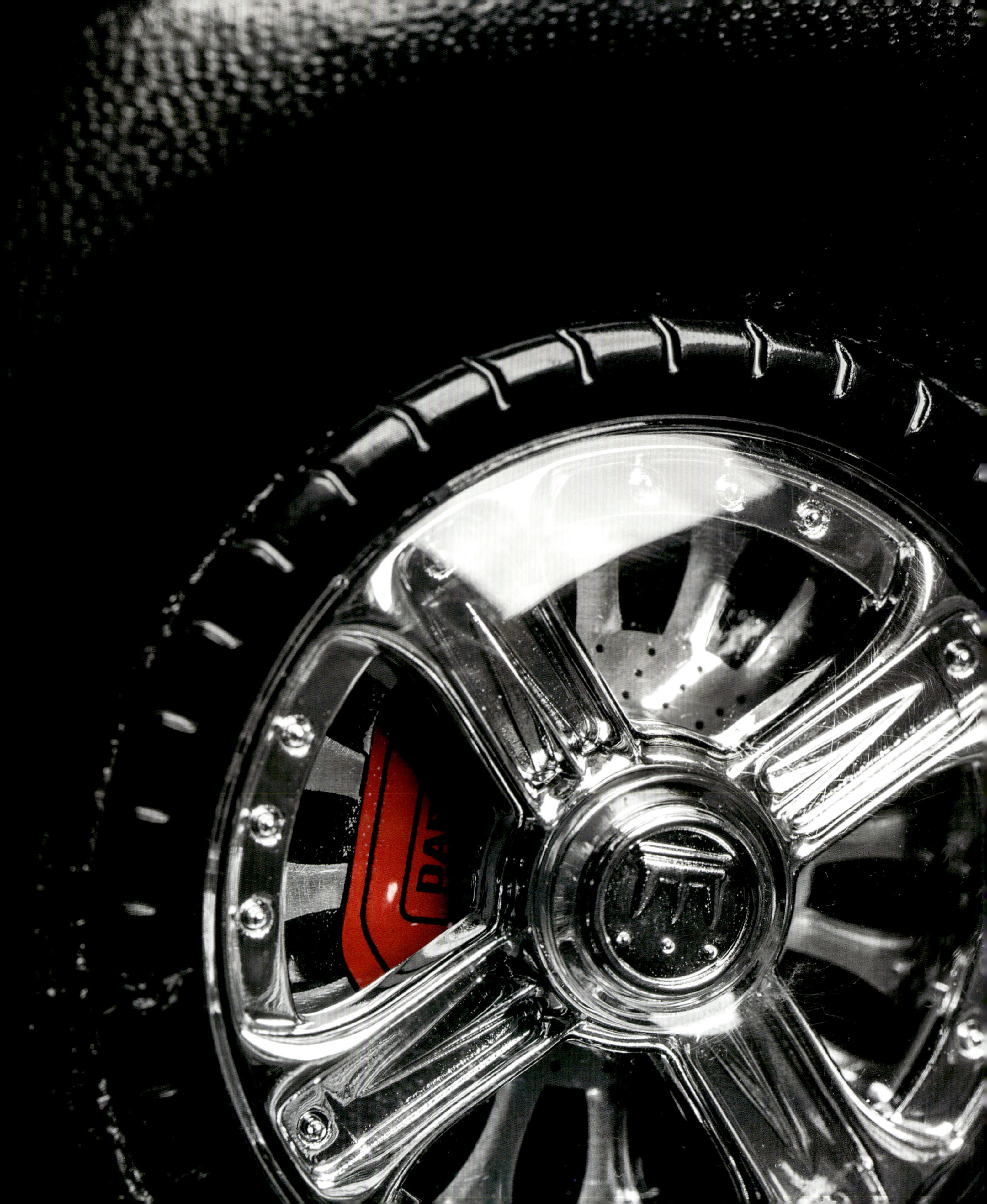

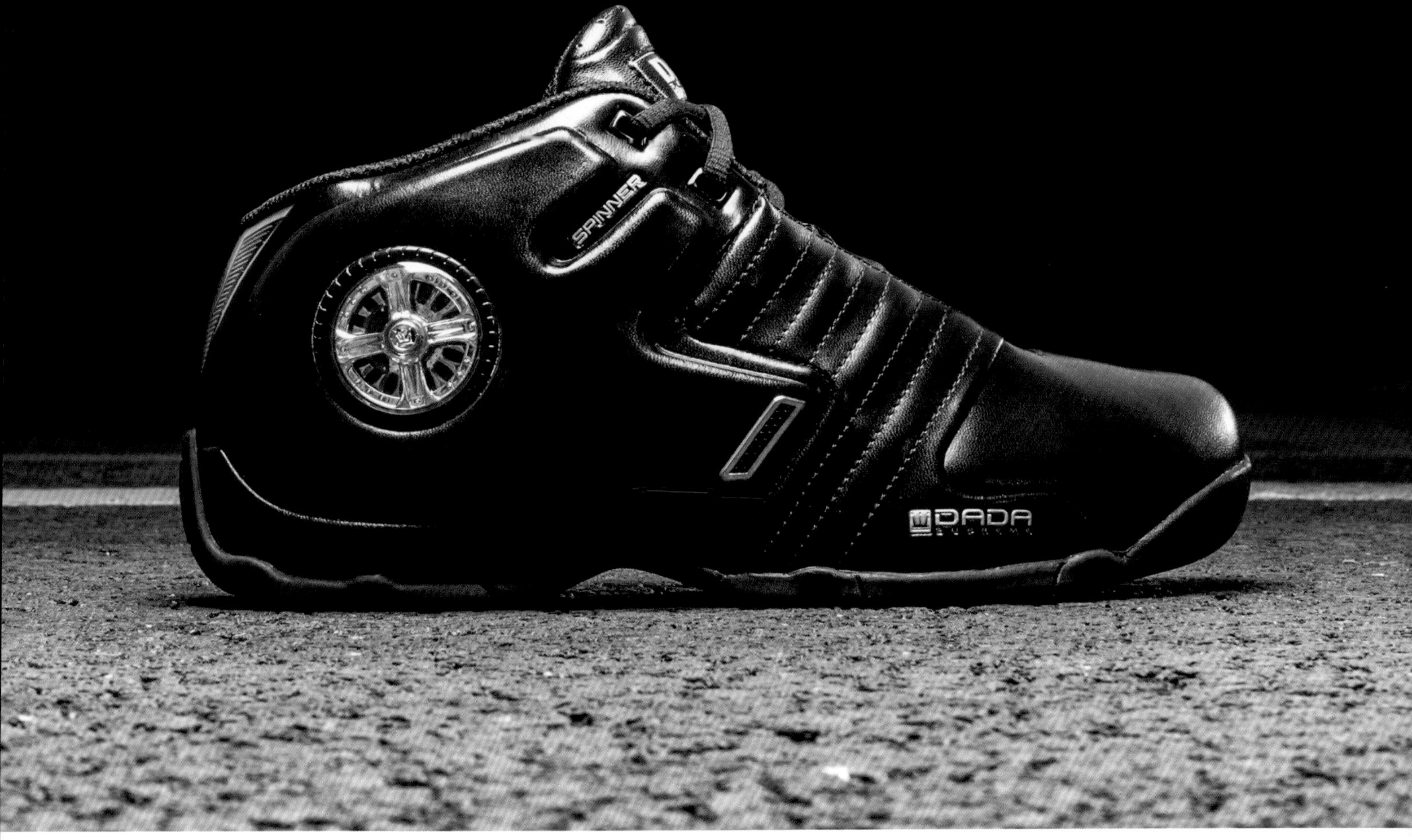

DADA SUPREME SPINNER I

Released in 2005, the inspiration for the model comes from Latrell Sprewell, the company's passionate spokesman for sports cars.

Details

The sneaker is built with DADA's LS Air Exchange technology system, which incorporates both air cushioning and shock springs in the sole. As the air cushion dampens shock, it creates airflow to spin a set of wheels on the exterior of the shoe. That is why it is called "Supreme Spinner."

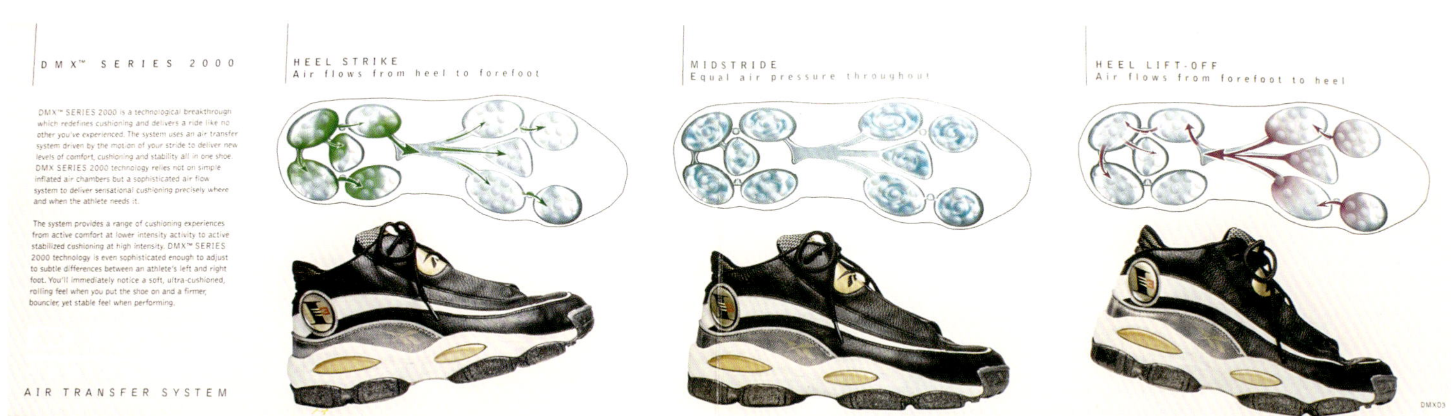

REEBOK ANSWER DMX 10

Released in 1997, DMX 10 is the first signature sneaker of the renowned basketball player Allen Iverson in his Answer pack.

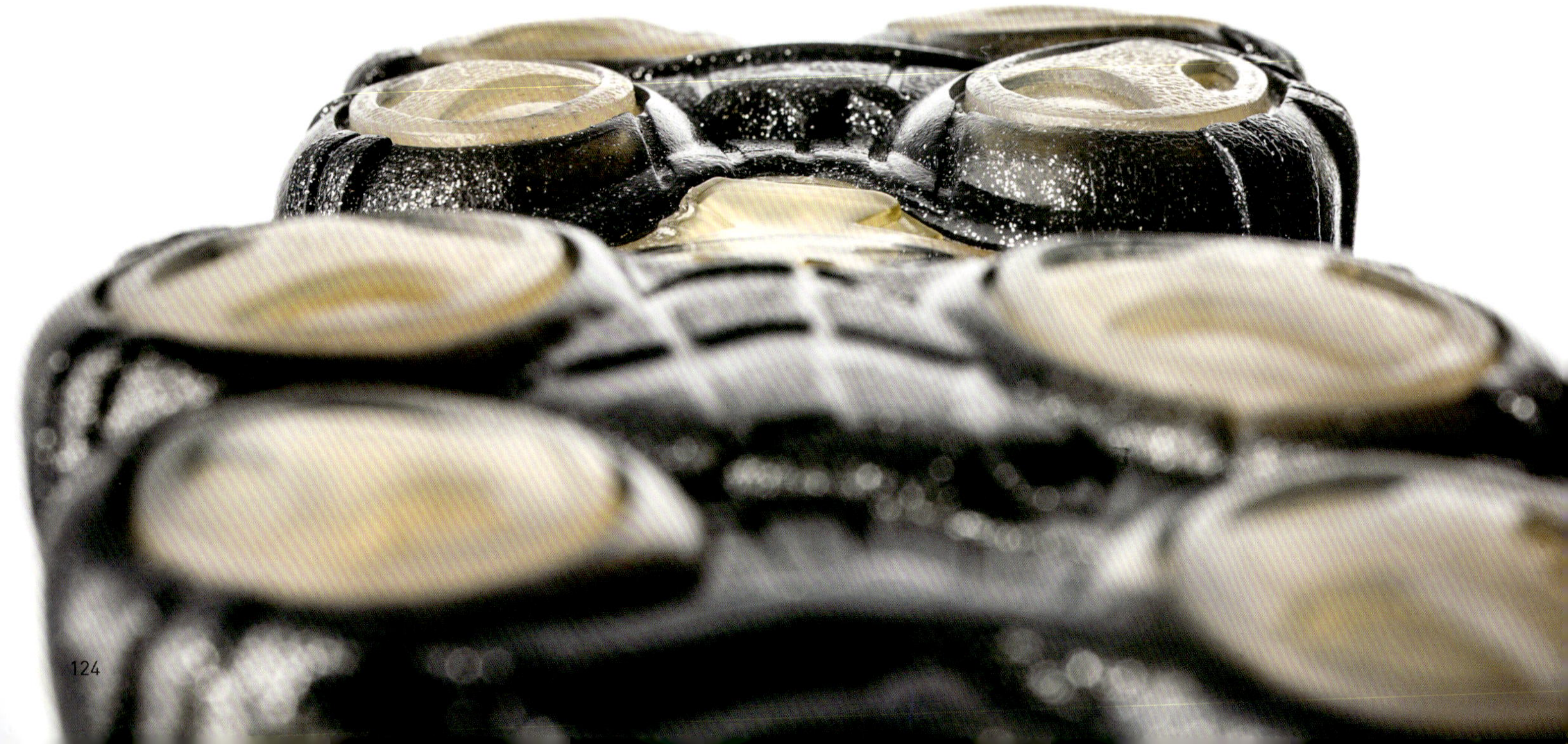

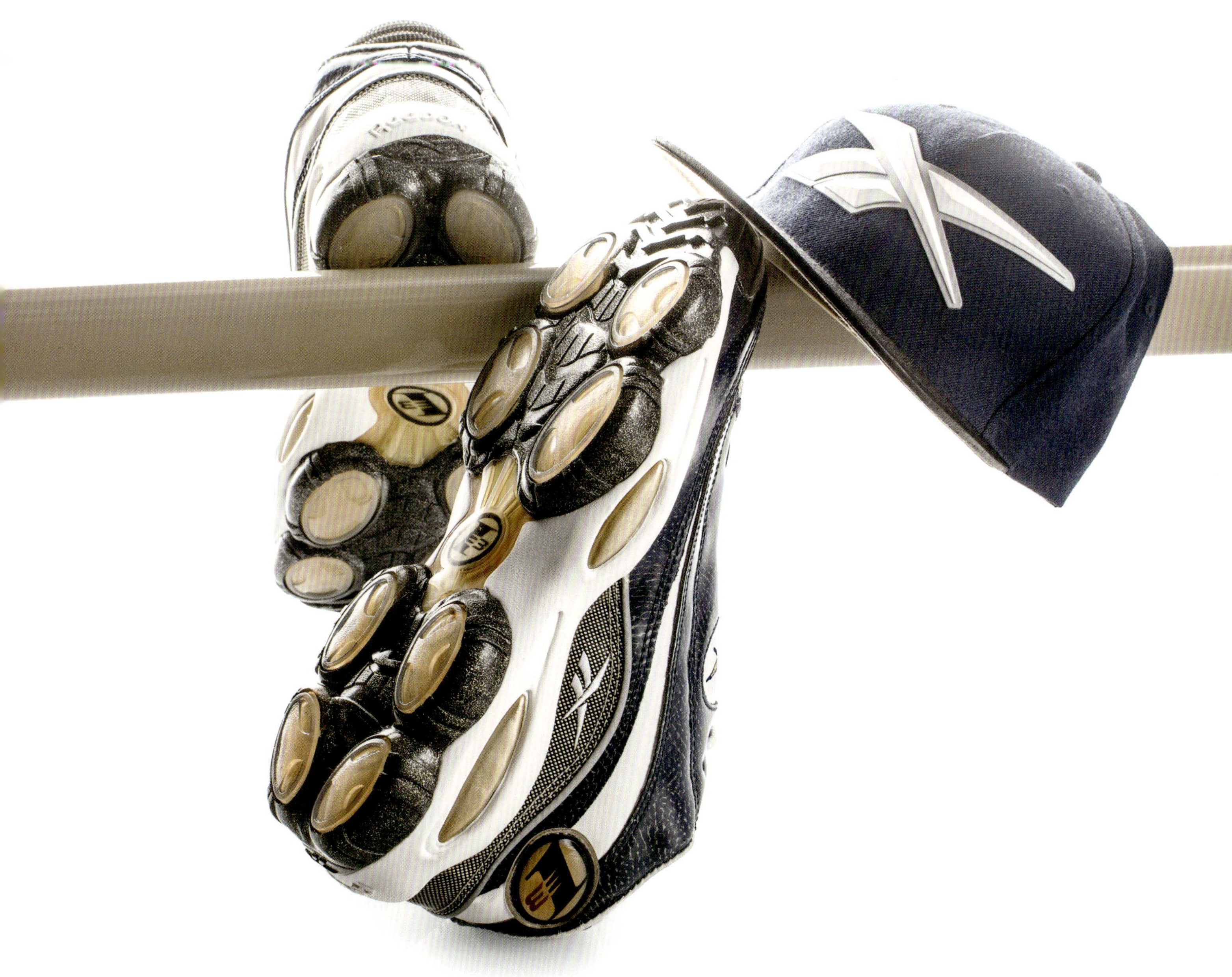

Details

The DMXTM SERIES 2000 technology is utilized in the outsole design. The sole consists of 10 connecting air bags. Each bag reacts to external pressure in a unique manner, thus rendering a supportive cushion.

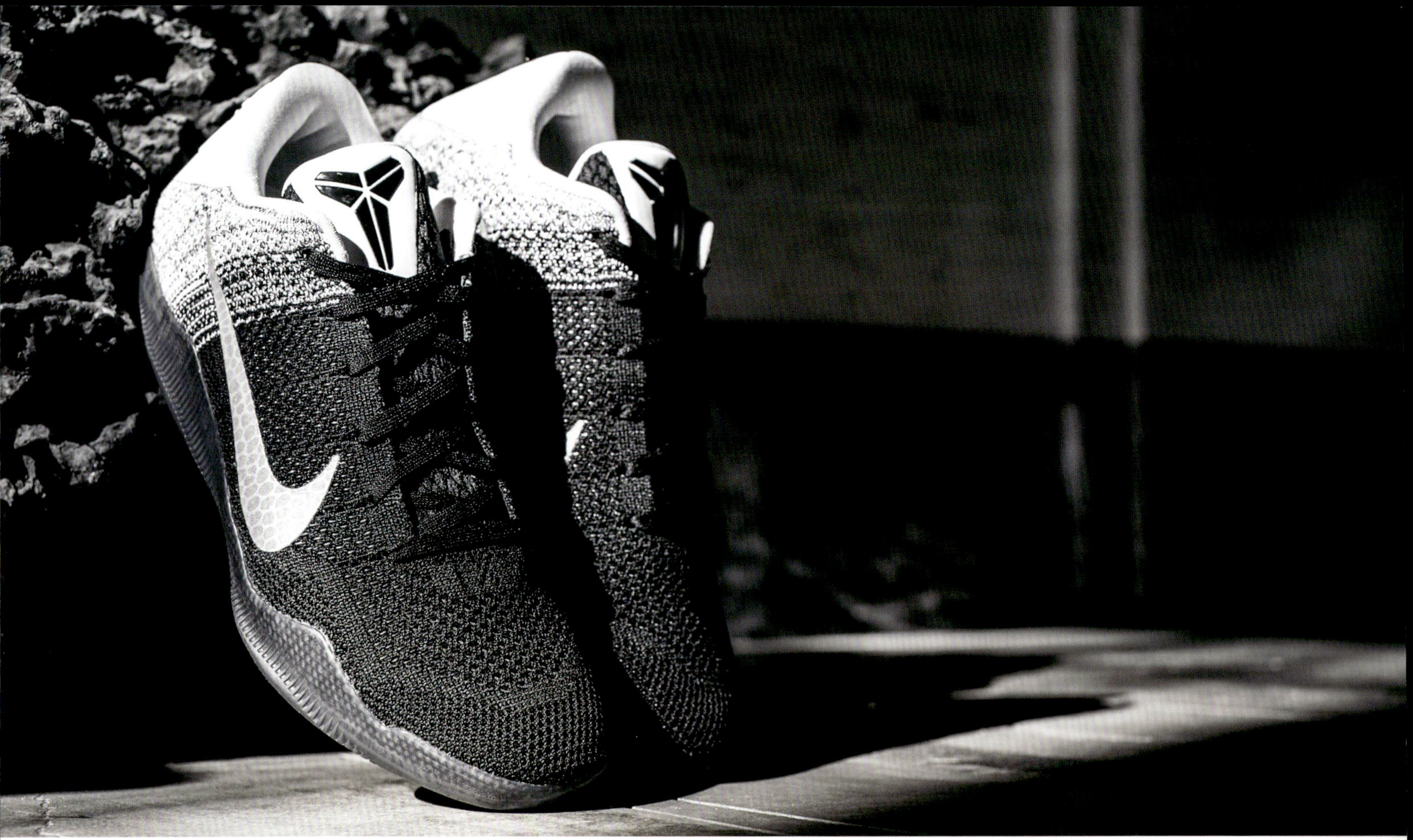

NIKE KOBE XI ELITE LOW [LAST EMPEROR]

The Last Emperor debuted in 2016 and was designed by Eric Avar. It is Nike's 11th installation into Kobe Bryant's signature line. The colorway is a salute to Kobe's legendary career.

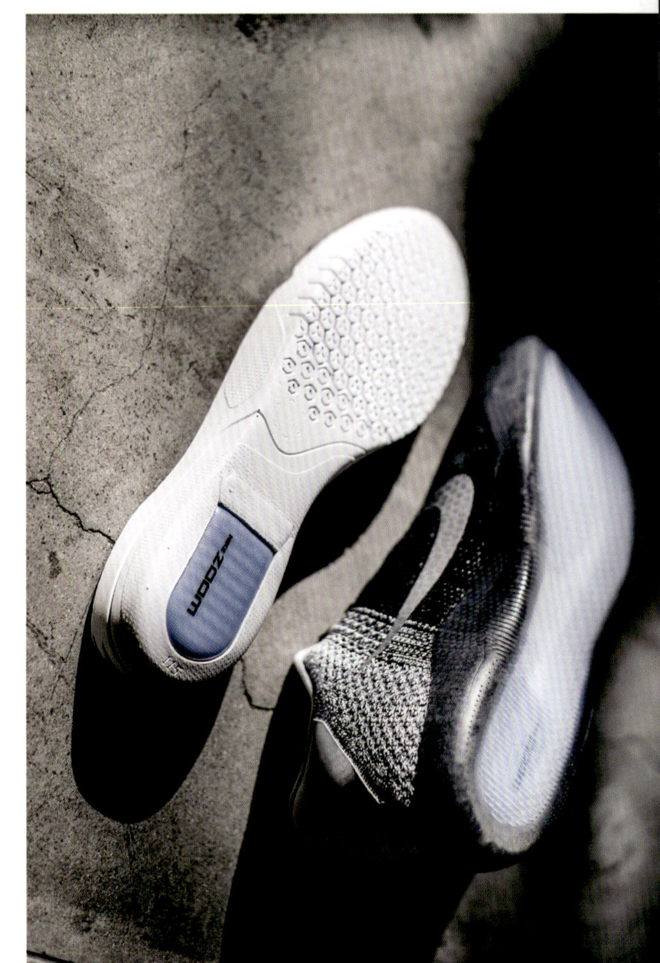

Details

The Last Emperor features a drop-in midsole, a Zoom Air bag in the heel, and flex grooves in the forefoot of the Lunarlon foam. The outsole is made of translucent gum rubber.

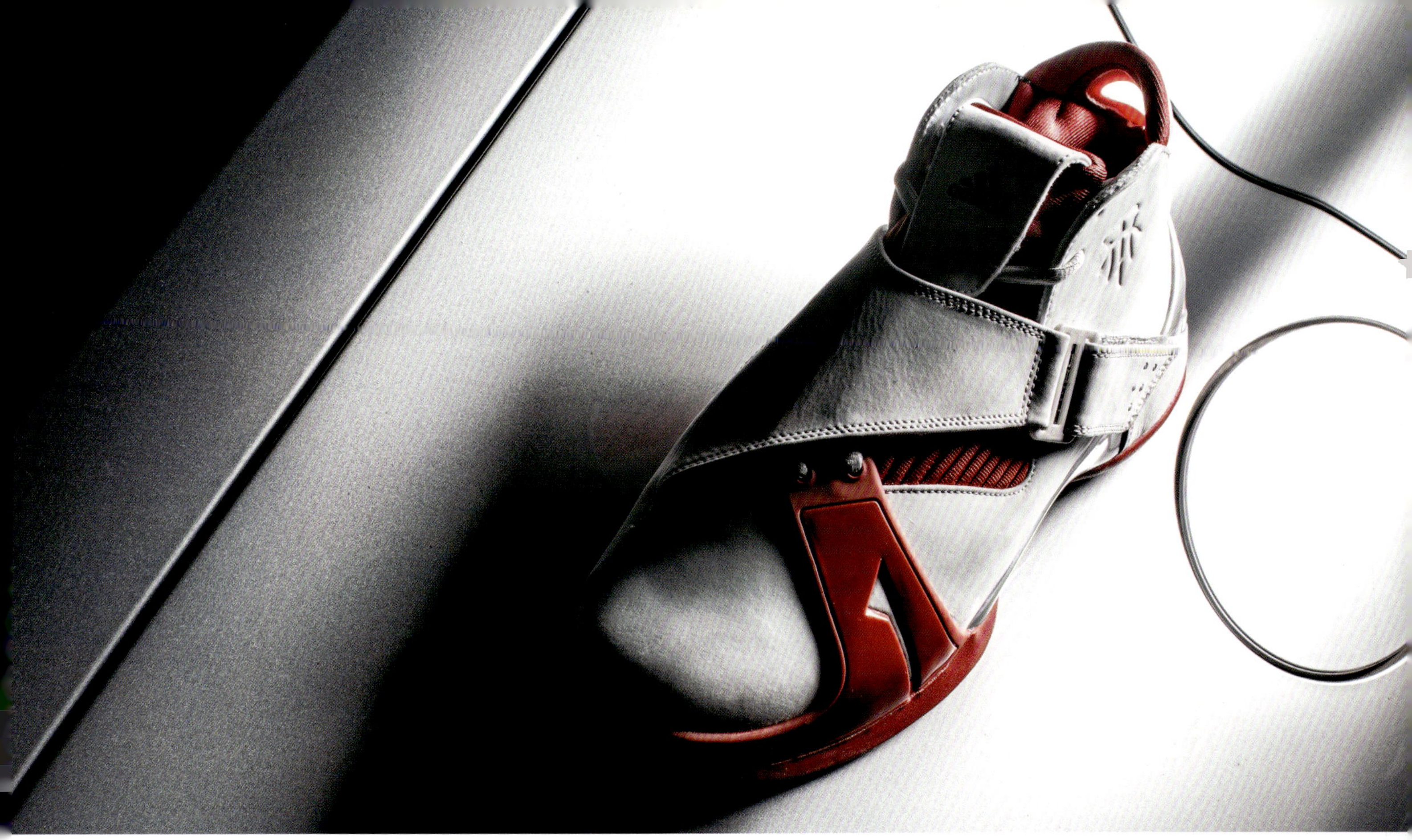

ADIDAS T-MAC 5 [ASG2006]

Released in 2006, it is the All-Star edition for Tracy McGrady's fifth signature sneaker.

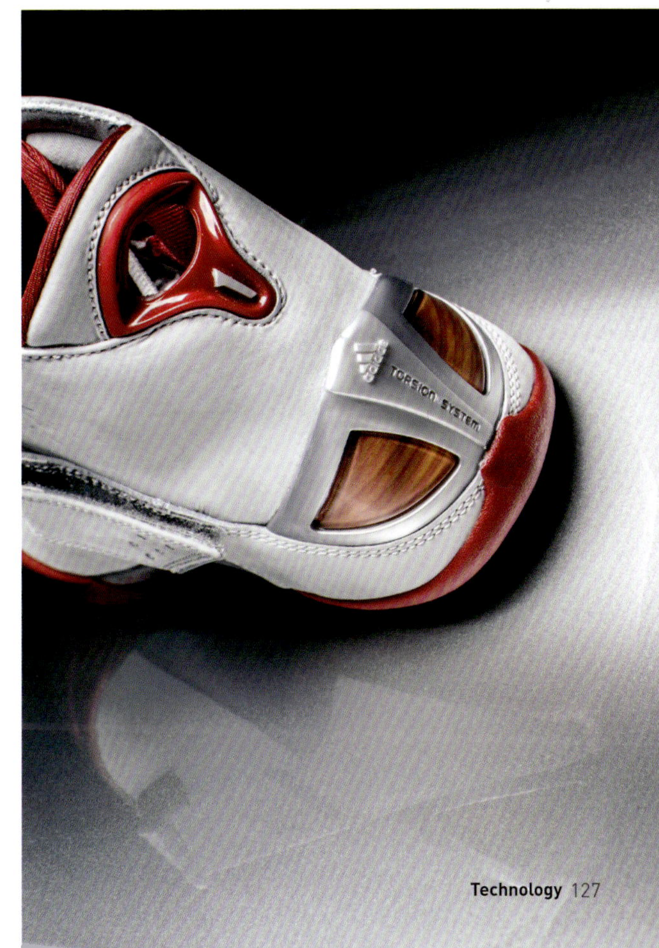

Details

The heel and the midfoot feature a Torsion System with hardwood built into the sole. The original version boasts an adiPRENE cushioning technology in the forefoot and heel, while its retros have lowered the configuration.

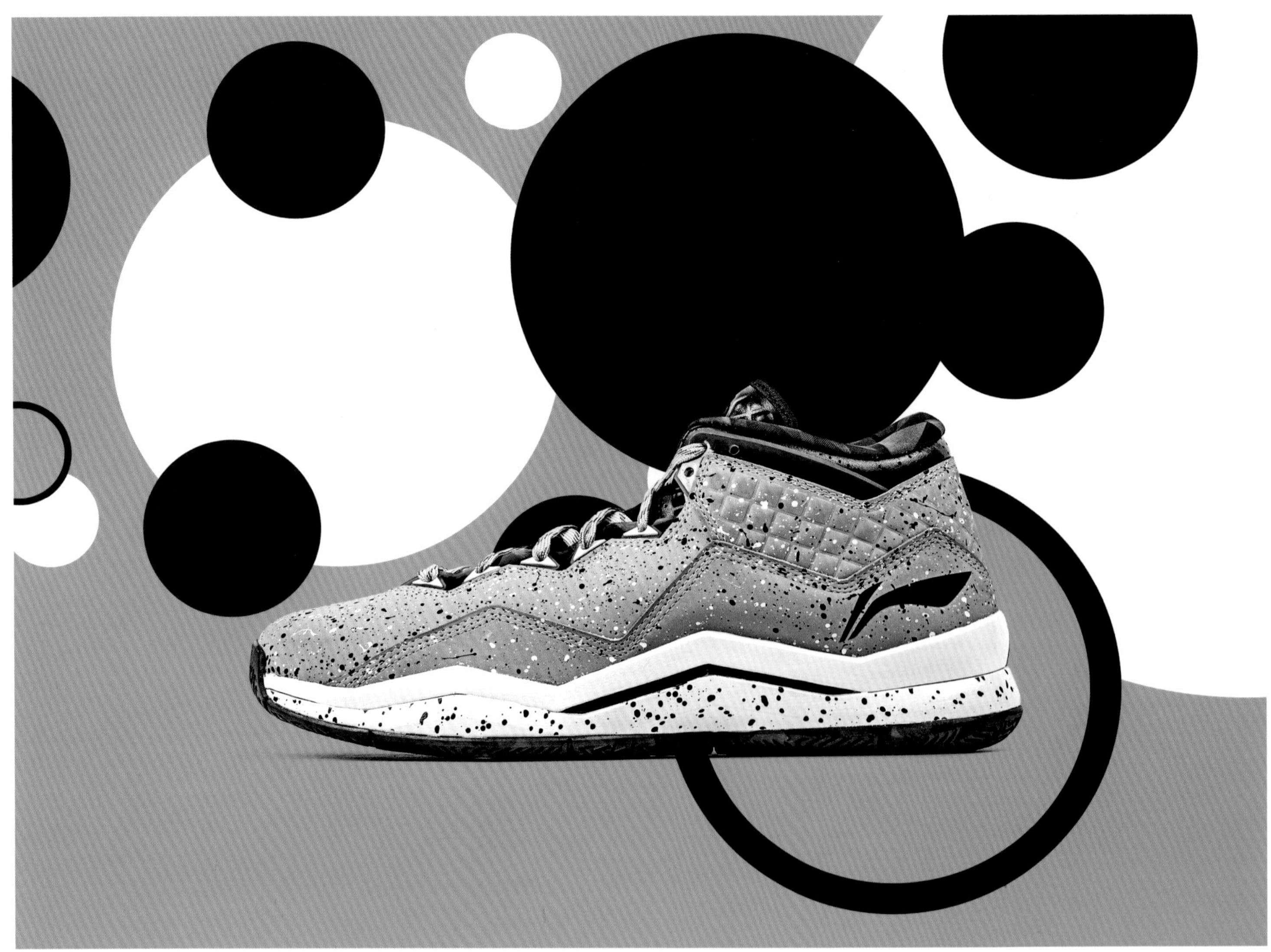

LI-NING WAY OF WADE III [GREY BOYS]

Launched in 2015, Grey Boys, by designer Eric Miller, is Dwyane Wade's third signature sneaker in Li-Ning. The colorway is inspired by Wade's gray high-school uniform.

Details

The midsole has for the first time adopted a double-layer design. The top layer is composed of EVA material, with Bounse technology applied to the front and Cushion to the heel. The bottom layer boasts Li-Ning Cloud technology, with large carbon fiber unit placed at the midfoot.

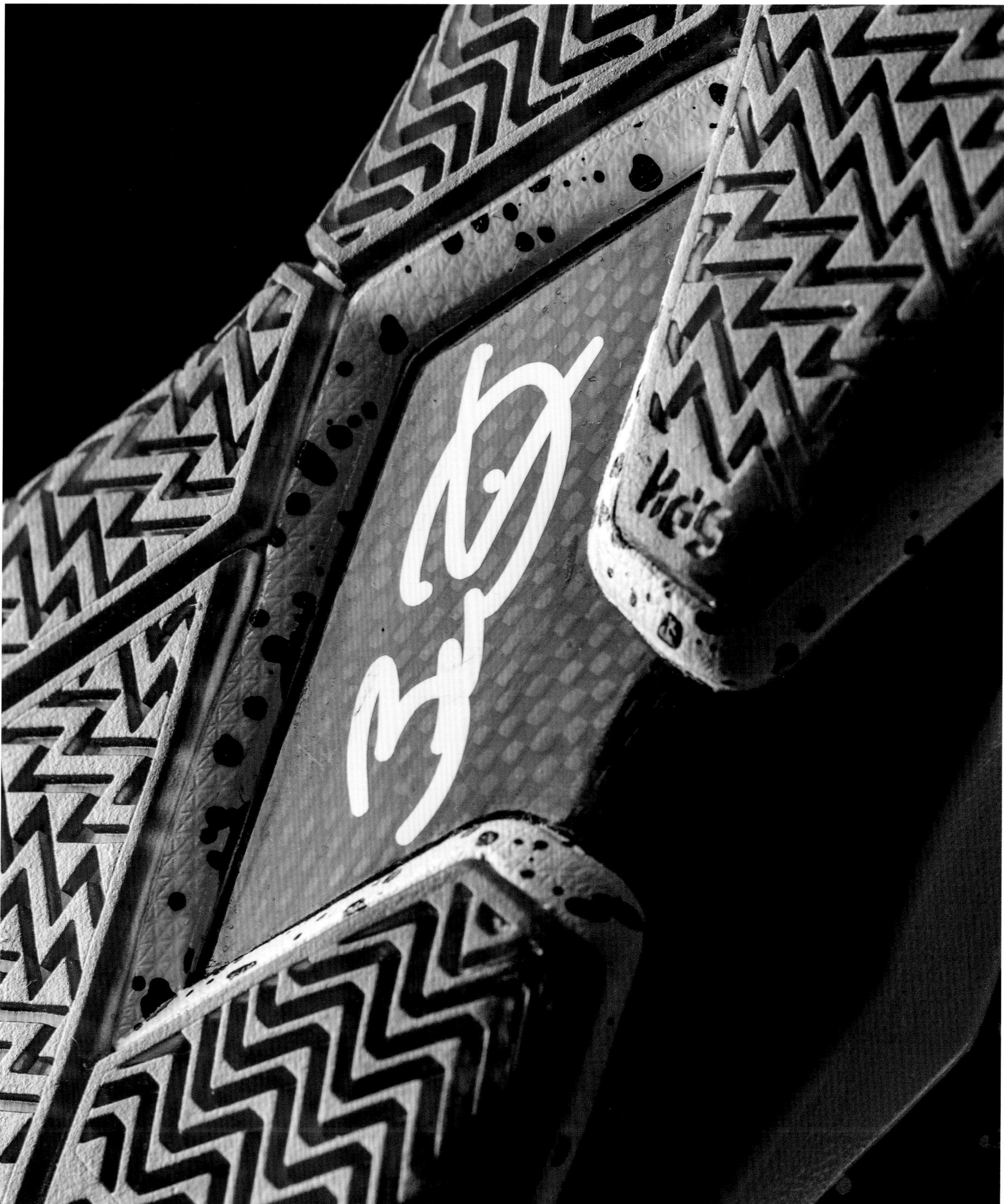

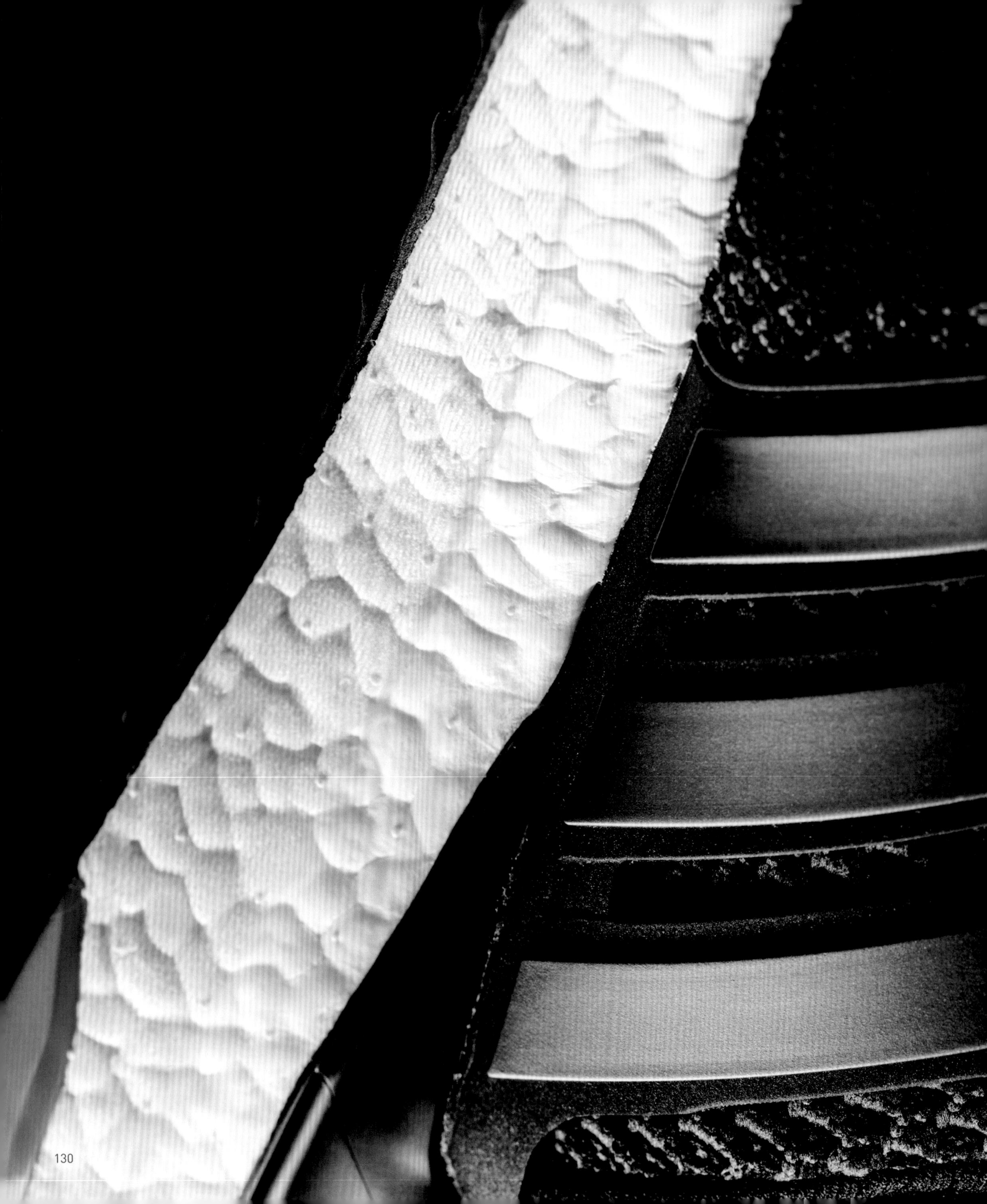

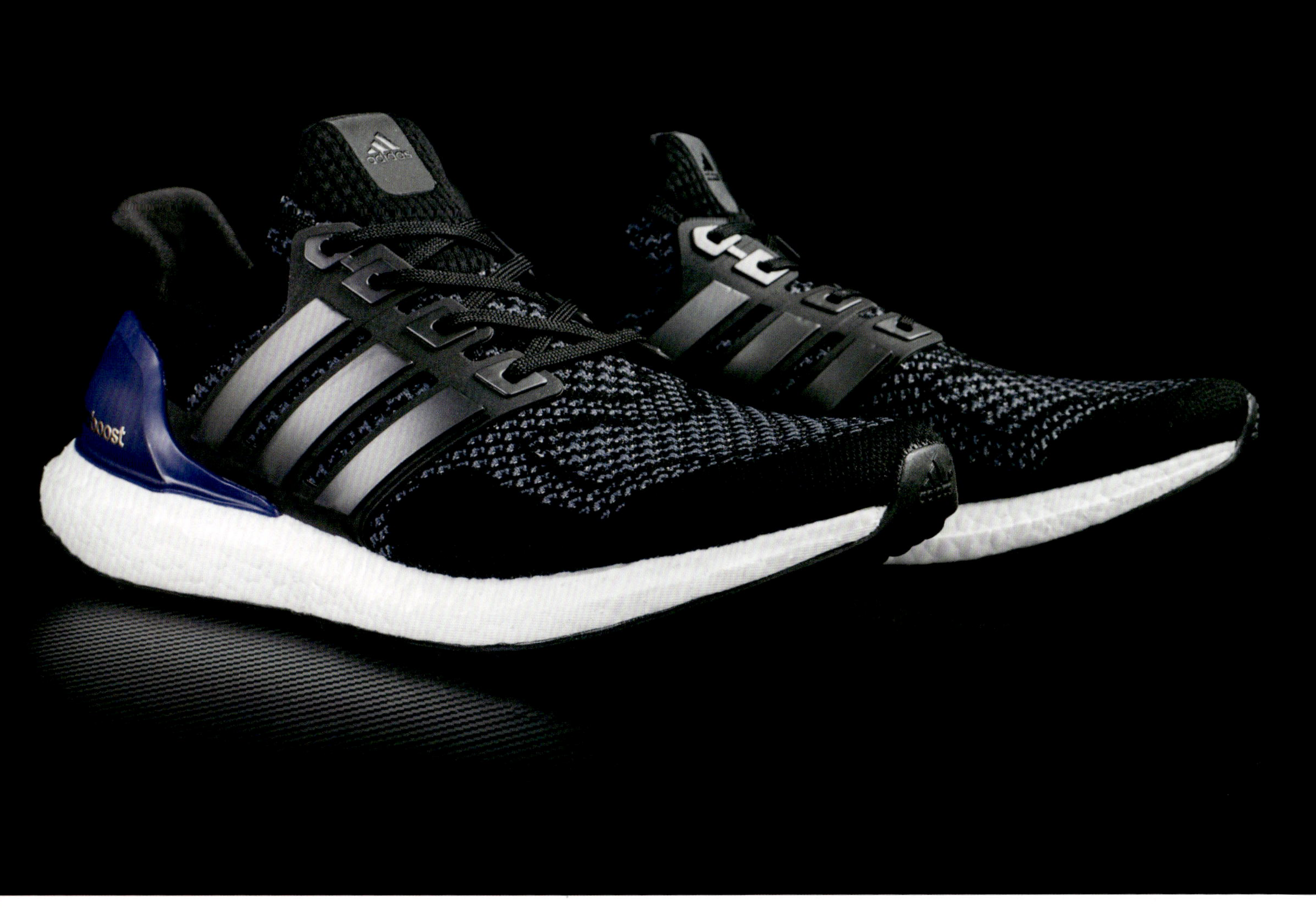

ADIDAS ULTRA BOOST

In 2015, adidas unveiled its new flagship running shoe Ultra Boost, which features a Primeknit upper.

Details

The midsole is comprised of Boost Cushioning capsules, with a Torsion System embedded into the shoe's base. A Stretch Web rubber outsole is presented with a perforated and elastic design.

Details

The one in the picture is the limited edition colorway launched by Nike and Fragment Design. A lightweight outsole equipped with Nike Free technology constitutes a highlight of Natural Motion (NM).

FRAGMENT DESIGN × NIKELAB ROSHE DAYBREAK NM

Mixing the silhouettes of two classic models, Daybreak and Roshe One, the Swoosh redesigned and released the new hybrid Roshe Daybreak NM in 2016.

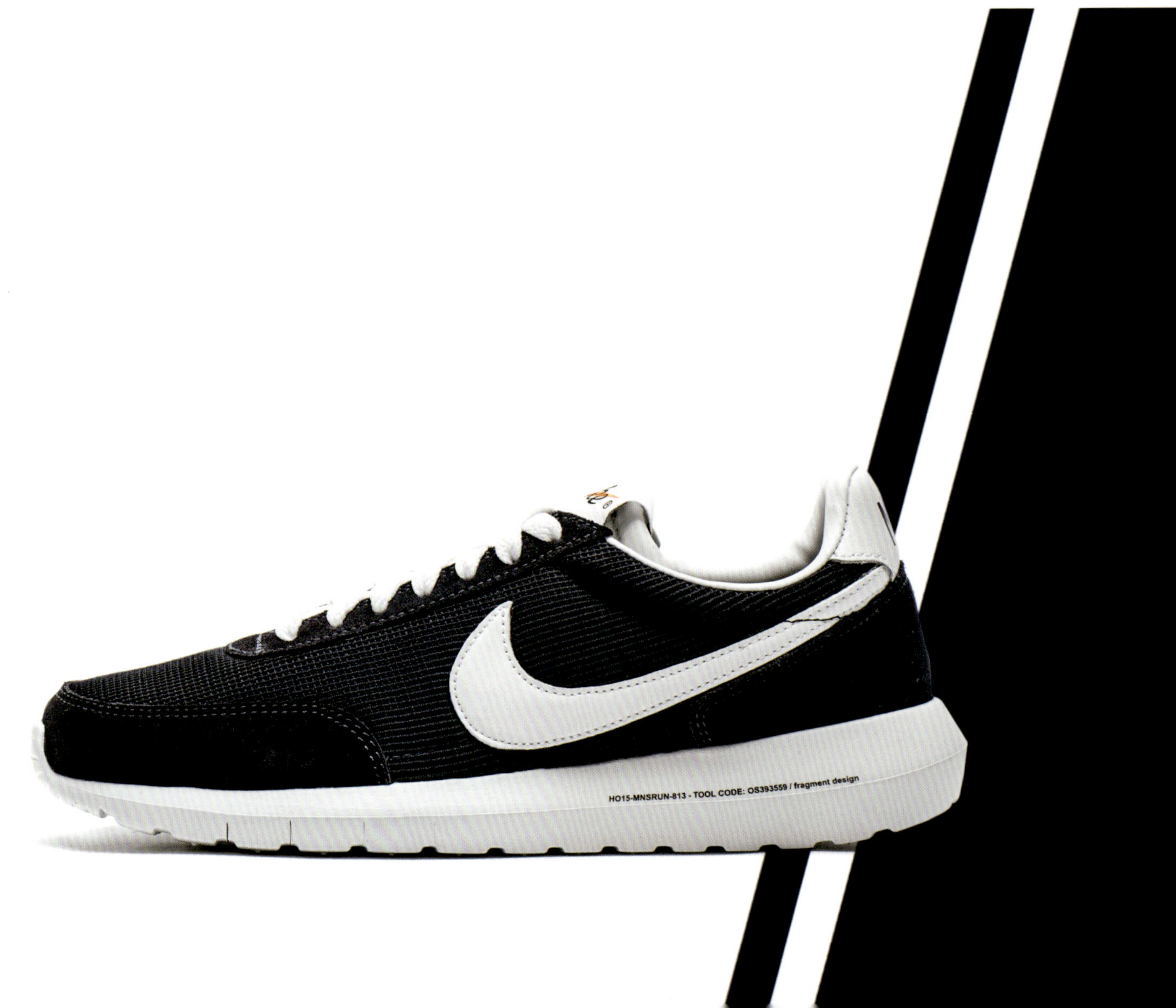

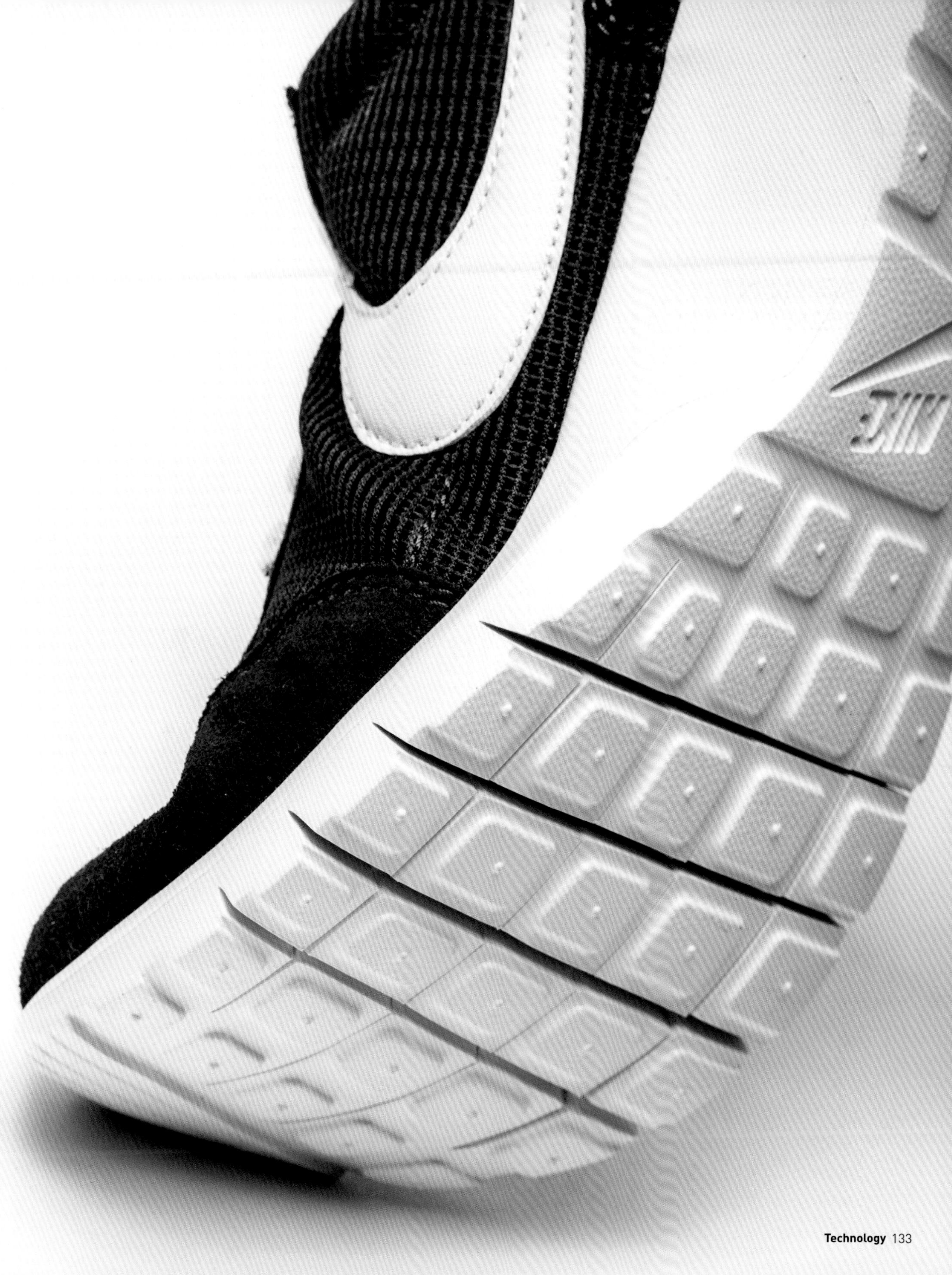

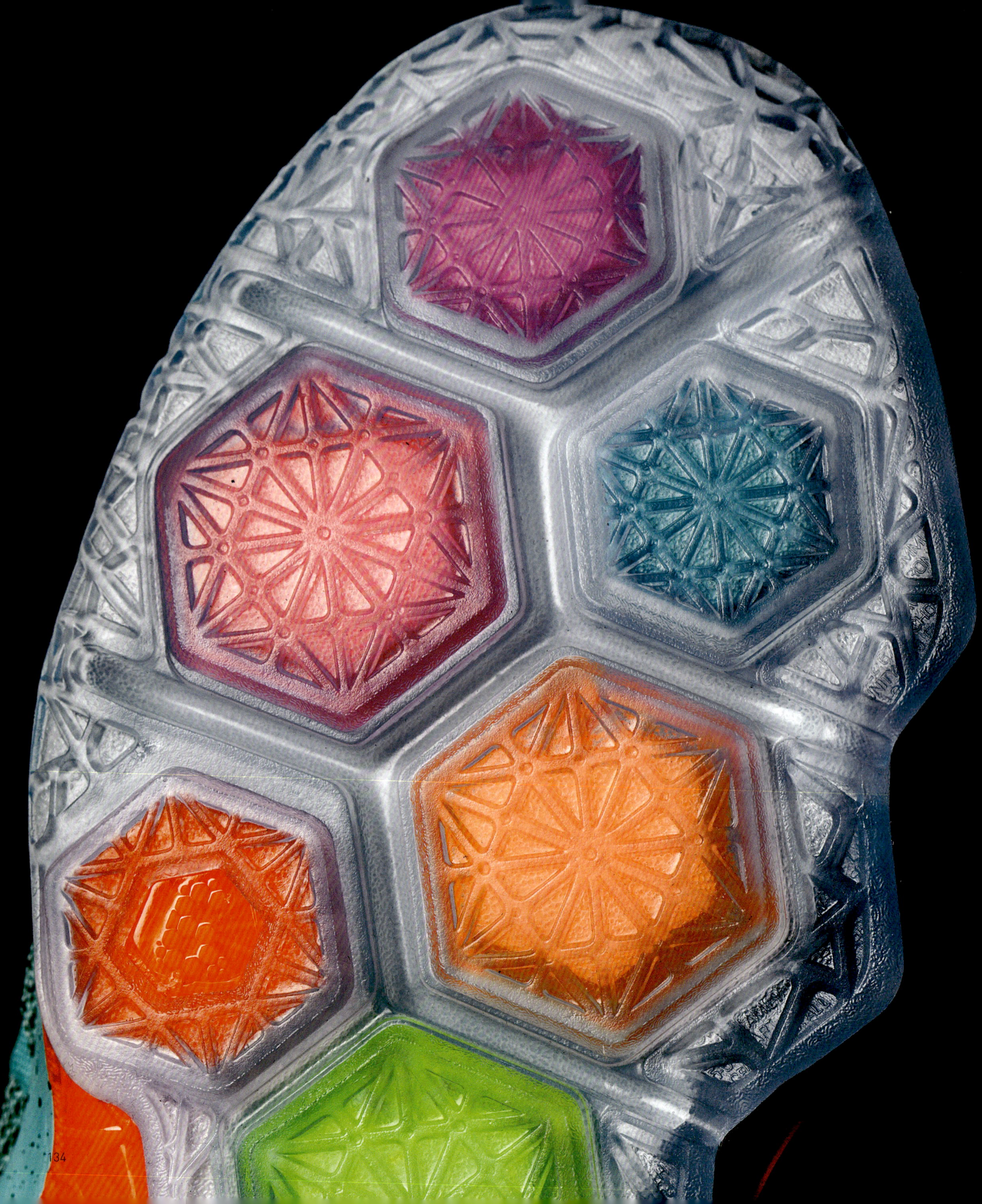

Details

The colorway is inspired by the new shoe's genesis in the Nike Sports Research Lab. The previous Nike Zoom Air bag is divided into five visible, hexagonally-shaped pods. Each pod works individually, rendering enhanced agility and more accurate cushioning.

NIKE LEBRON XII [NSRL]

Unveiled in 2014, NSRL is the 12th signature sneaker of LeBron James. Jason Petrie designed the model.

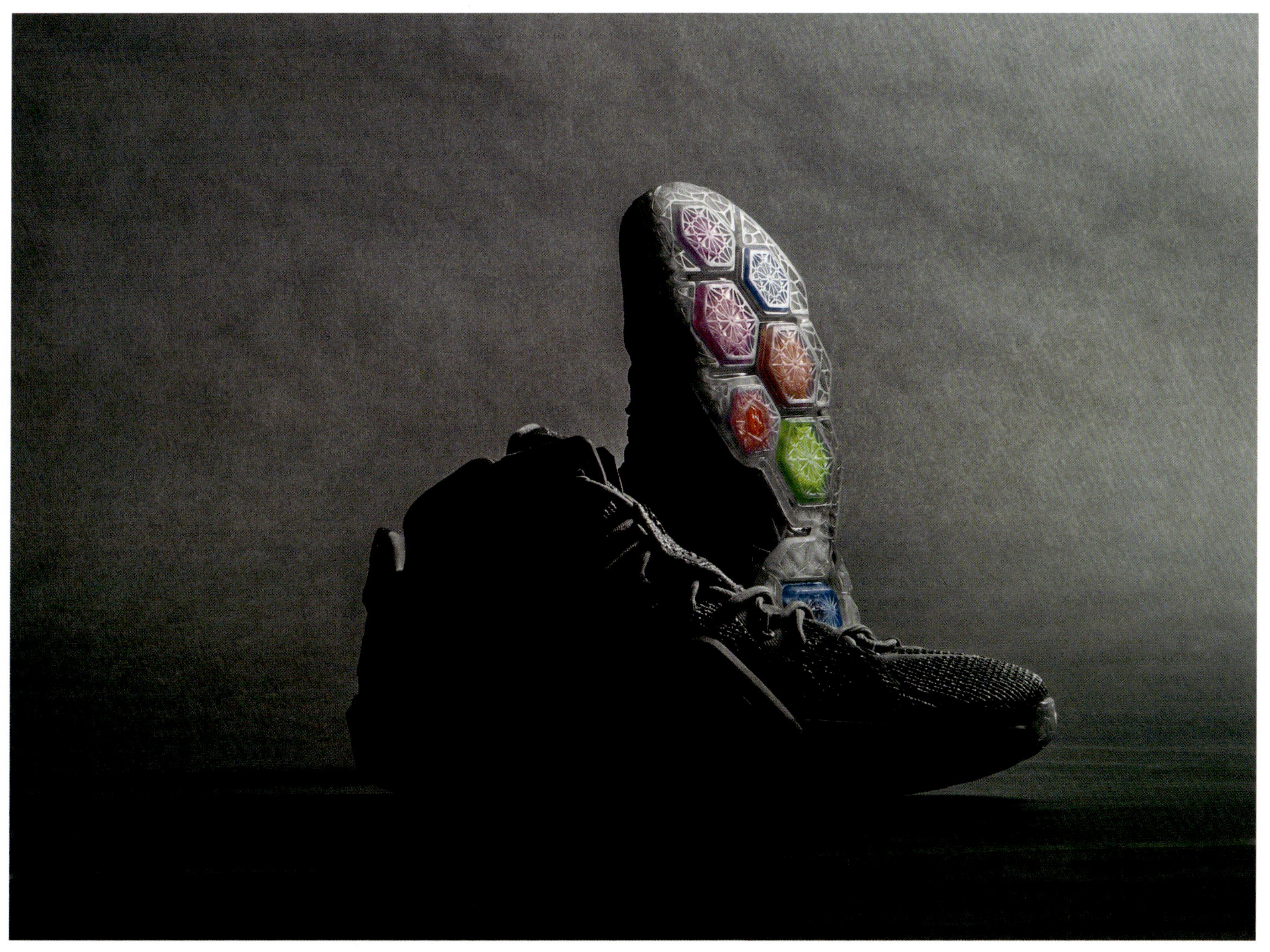

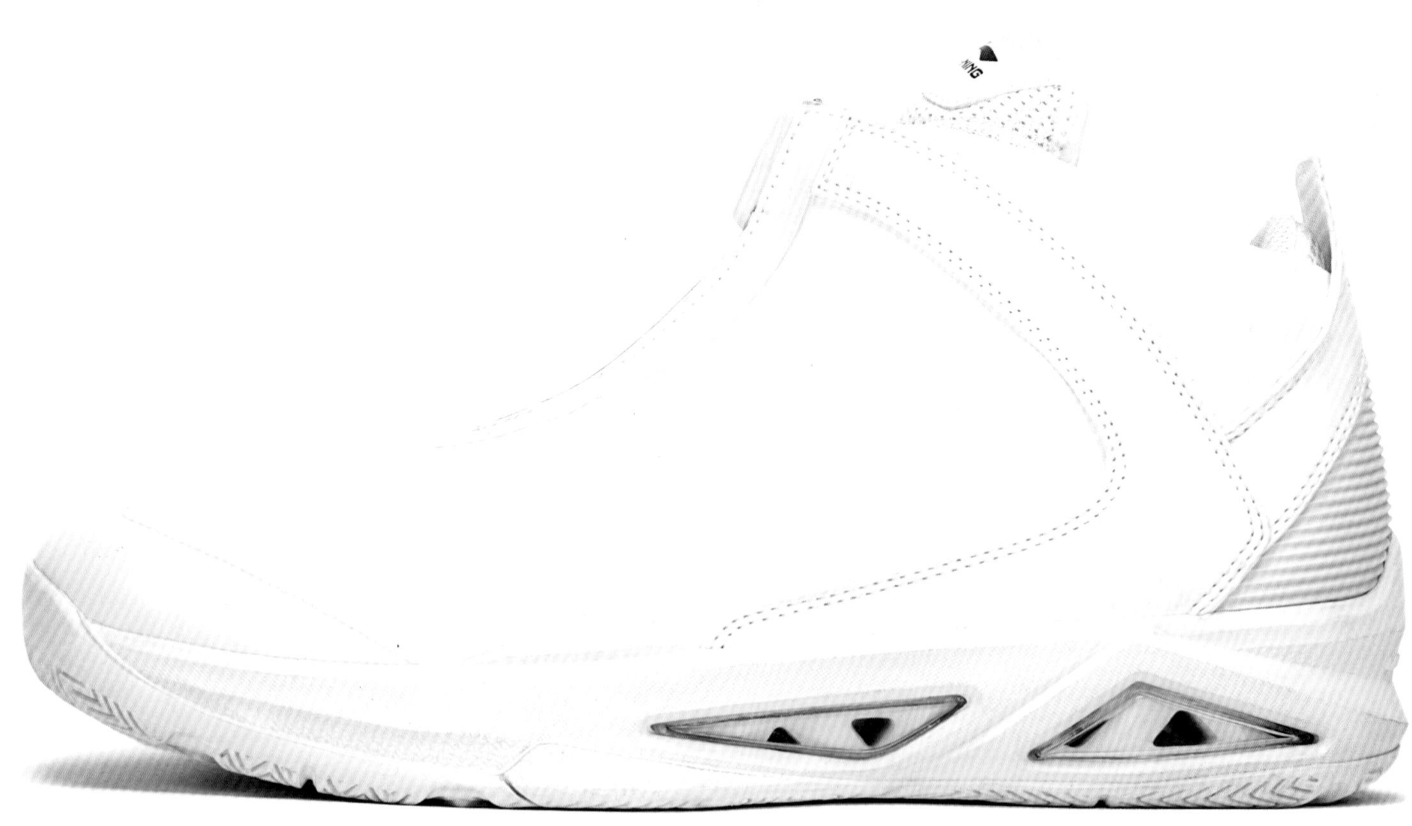

LI-NING ASSASSIN

Released in 2014, the shoe features a brand new Flex Shell upper. The outer layer is composed of elastic material with a zipper design.

Details

The outsole boasts the Li-Ning Arc 4.0 cushioning technology. Piggybacking on this technology, shock-absorbing material is processed into arc-shaped units. When bent, it will provide protection for harmful impact. In addition, a transparent shell is also designed to protect these units while delivering more support.

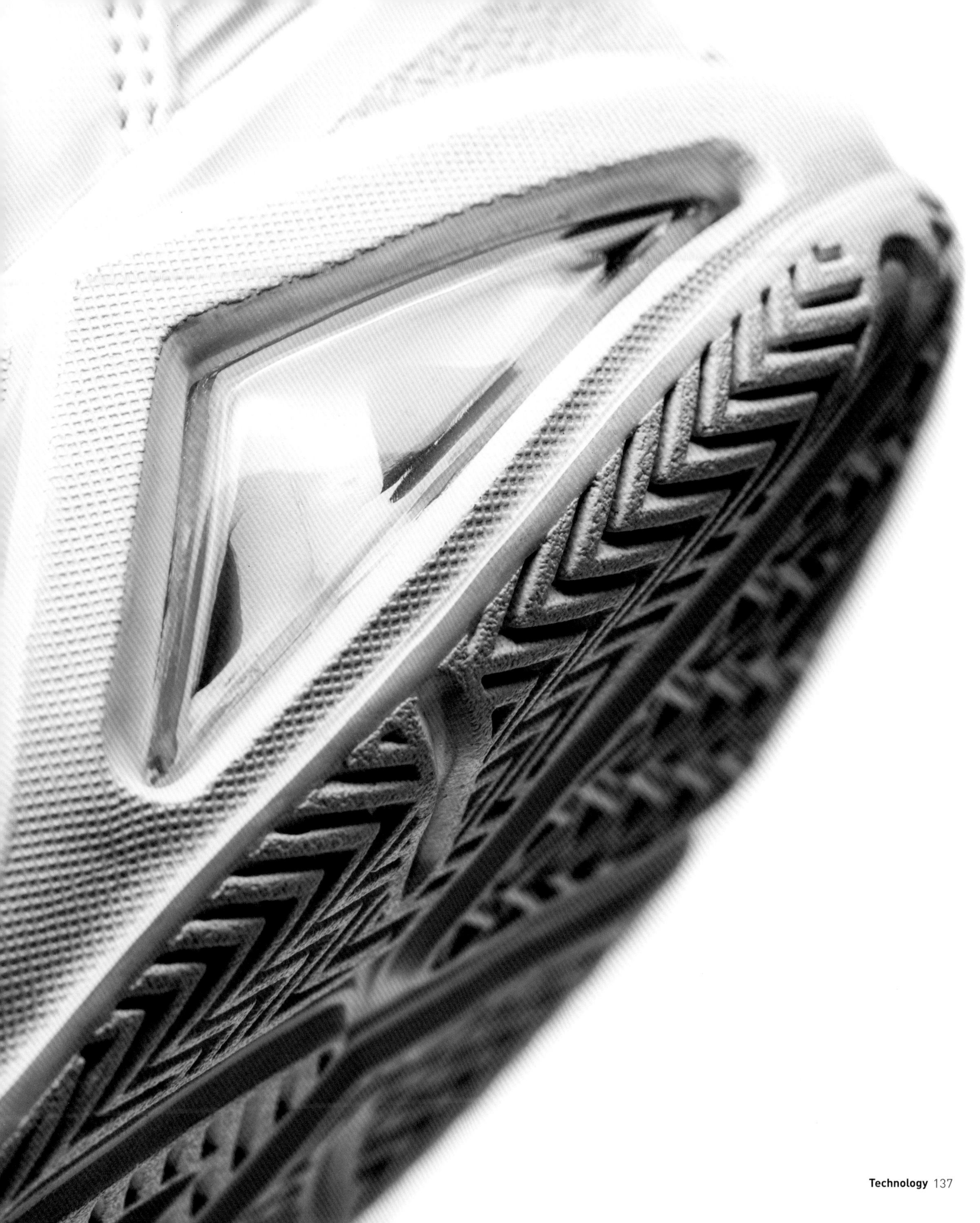

Details

The shoe features a full-length IP cushion midsole with a Cushion unit in the heel. Equipped with the SAS (Synchronization Adjustment System), the hollowed-out midsole and a TPU plate help deliver supportive cushioning in every step, while ensuring unmatched breathability and stability.

LI-NING YU SHUAI VII [YEAR OF THE SNAKE] SAMPLE

Yu Shuai VII came out in 2012. It was designed by Ma Xun, a former Li-Ning designer. The pair in the picture is not available on the market; it boasts a seamless upper.

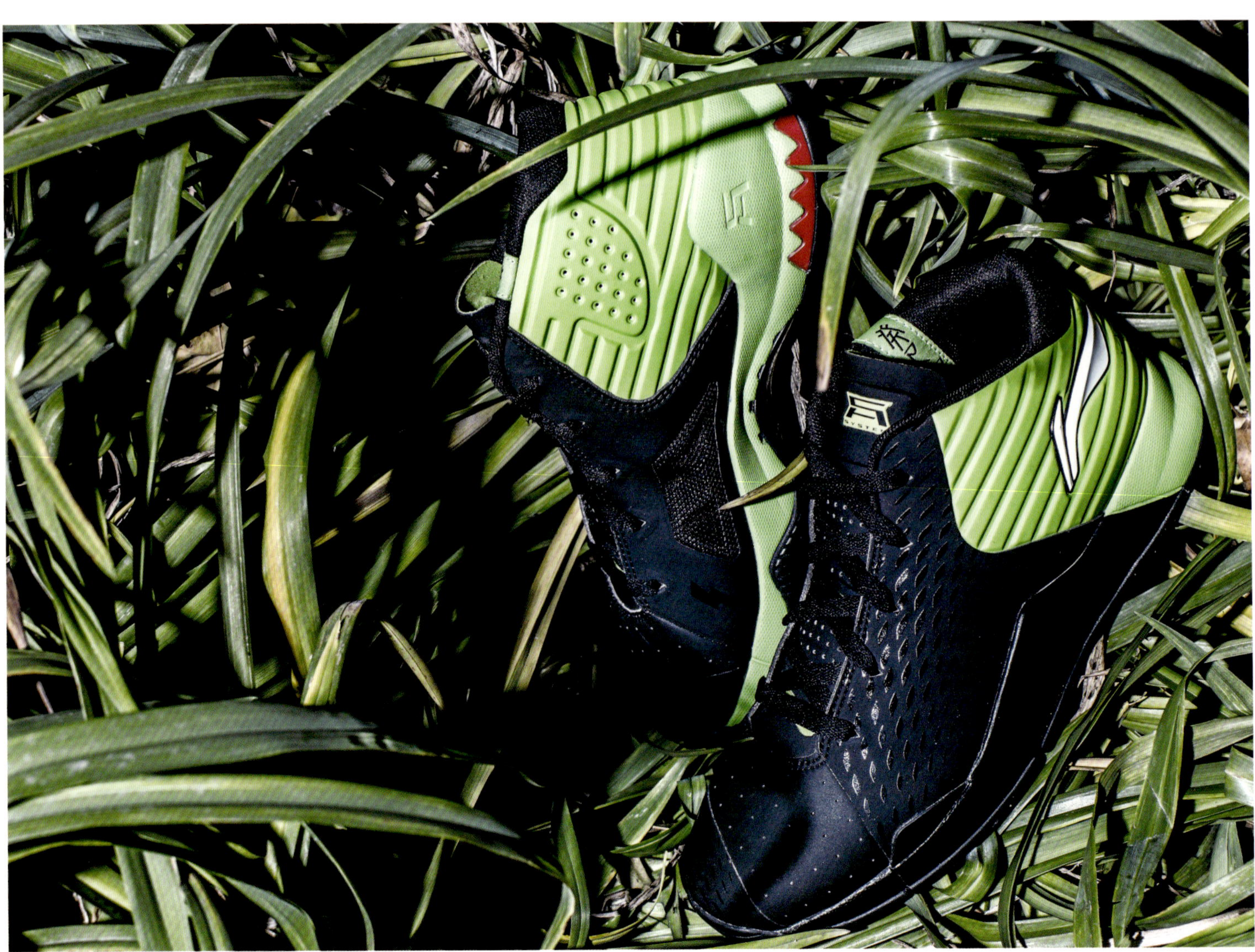

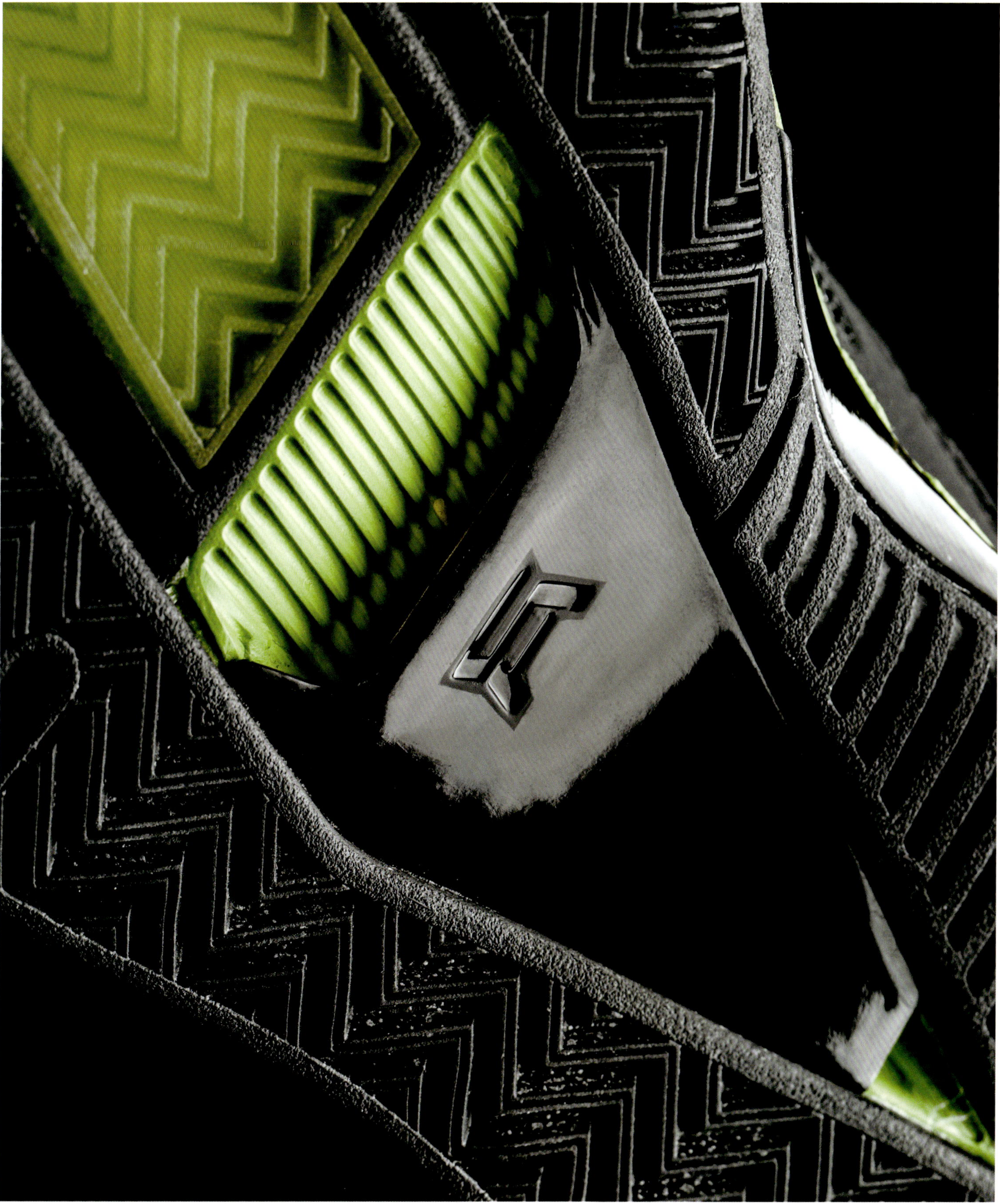

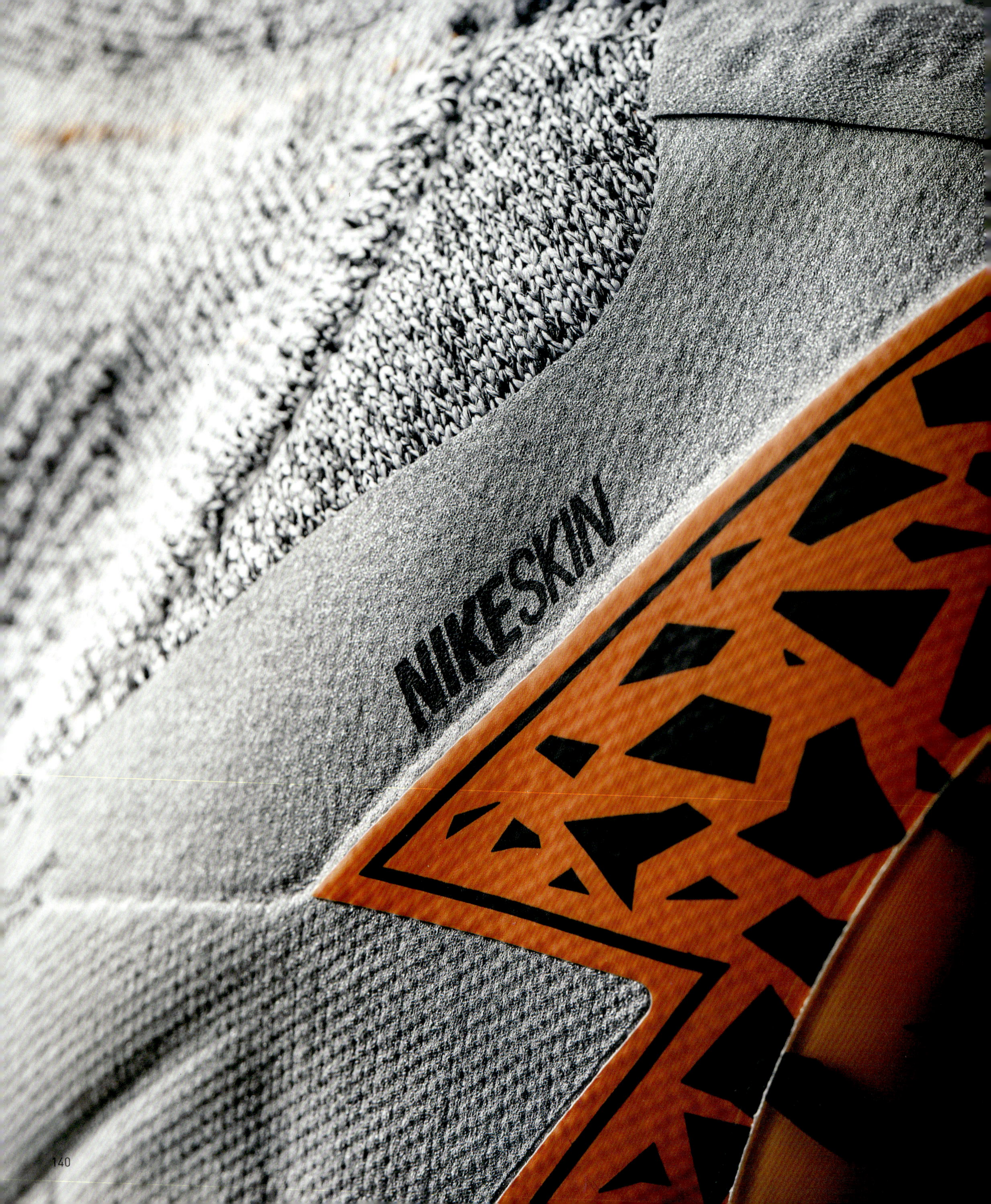
NIKESKIN

Details

The upper is completed with both NikeSkin and ACC (All Condition Control) technologies. A hypershield outer layer helps the boot to absorb less water, remove more dirt and dry faster, without sacrificing its unmatched ball touch and feel.

NIKE HYPERVENOM II

Released in 2015, Hypervenom II is the first Nike cleats that have combined Flyknit collar with an enhanced mesh upper.

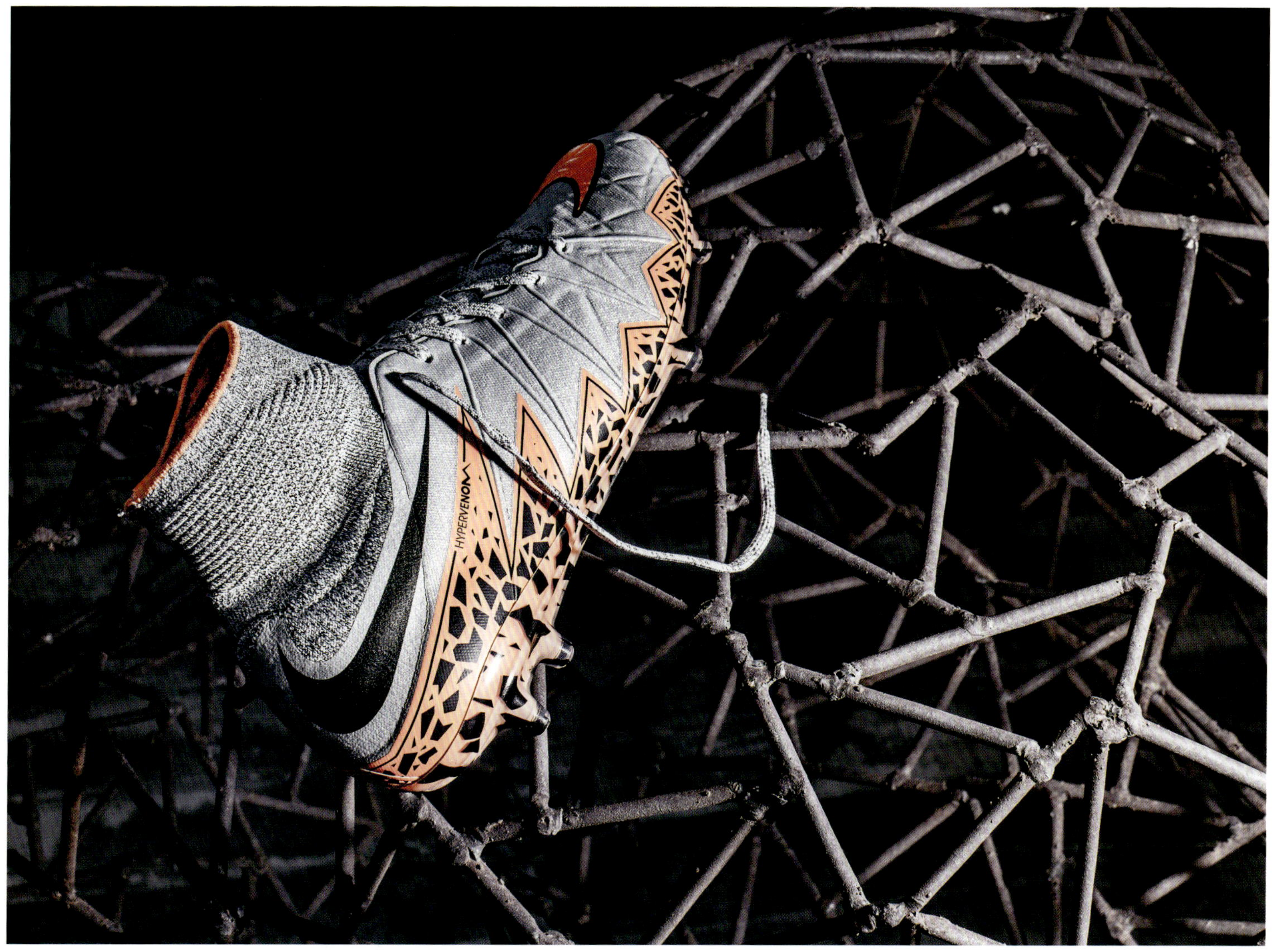

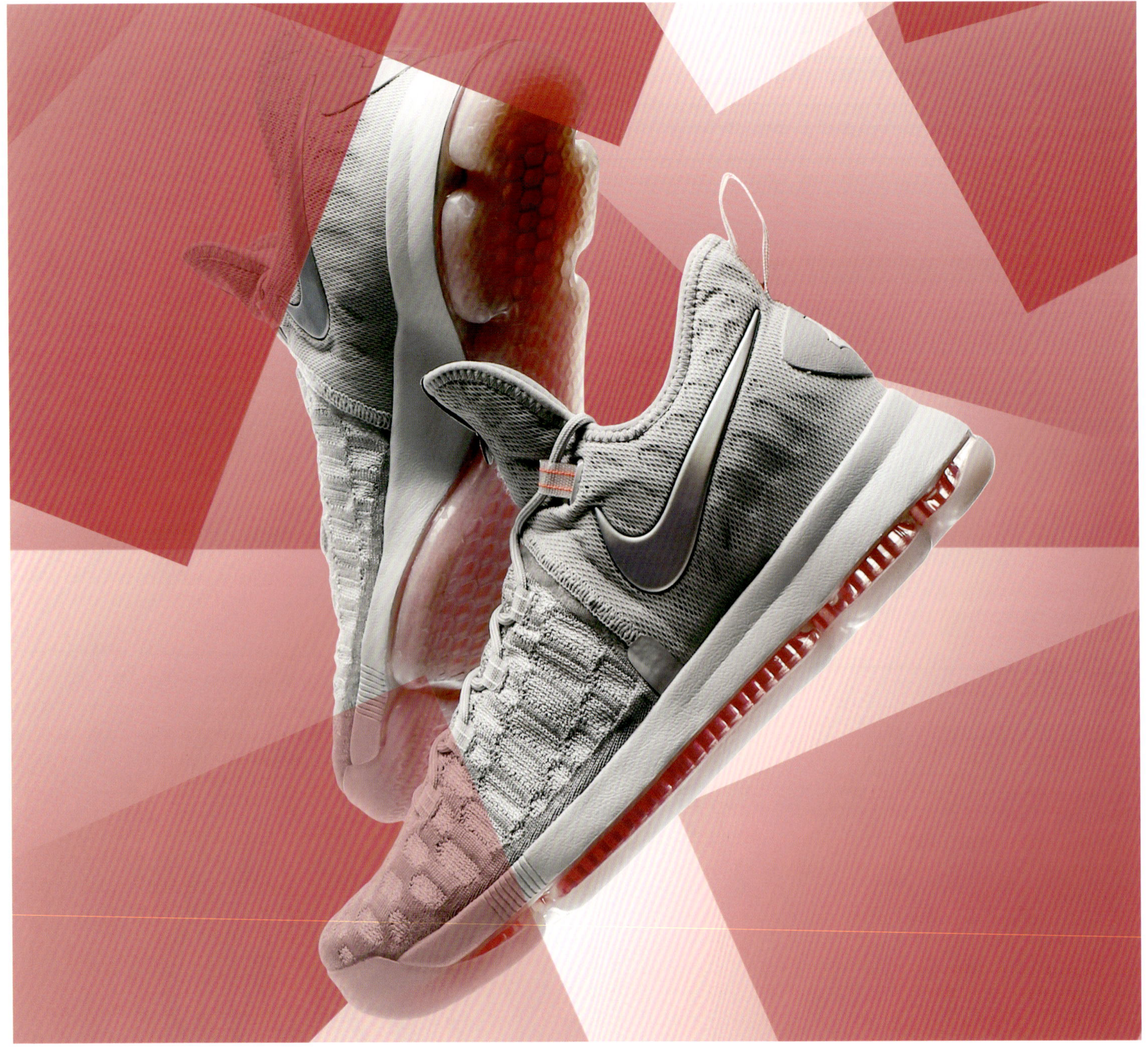

NIKE ZOOM KD 9 [ZERO]

Released in 2016, Nike KD 9, by designer Leo Chang, is the ninth iteration in Kevin Durant's signature line.

Details

In a groundbreaking manner, the sneaker has introduced Flyknit technology to the KD line. The upper, which foregoes the traditional tongue design, is made in a one-piece fashion for better stretch and support. And for responsive cushioning, the midsole highlights a full-length visible Zoom Air unit, which is thick at the heel and progressively gets thin to the forefoot. The flex grooves at the front are designed to enhance flexibility.

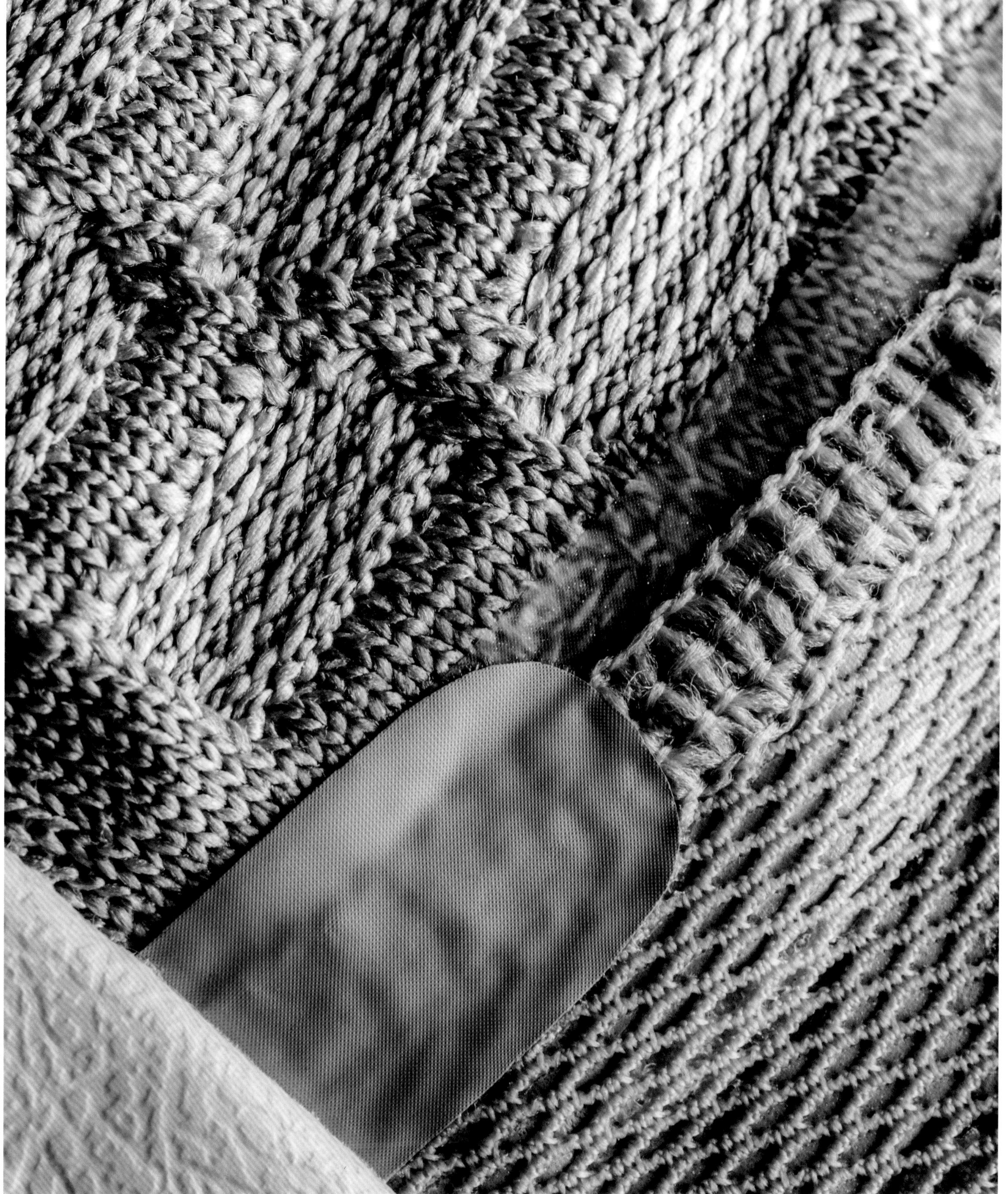

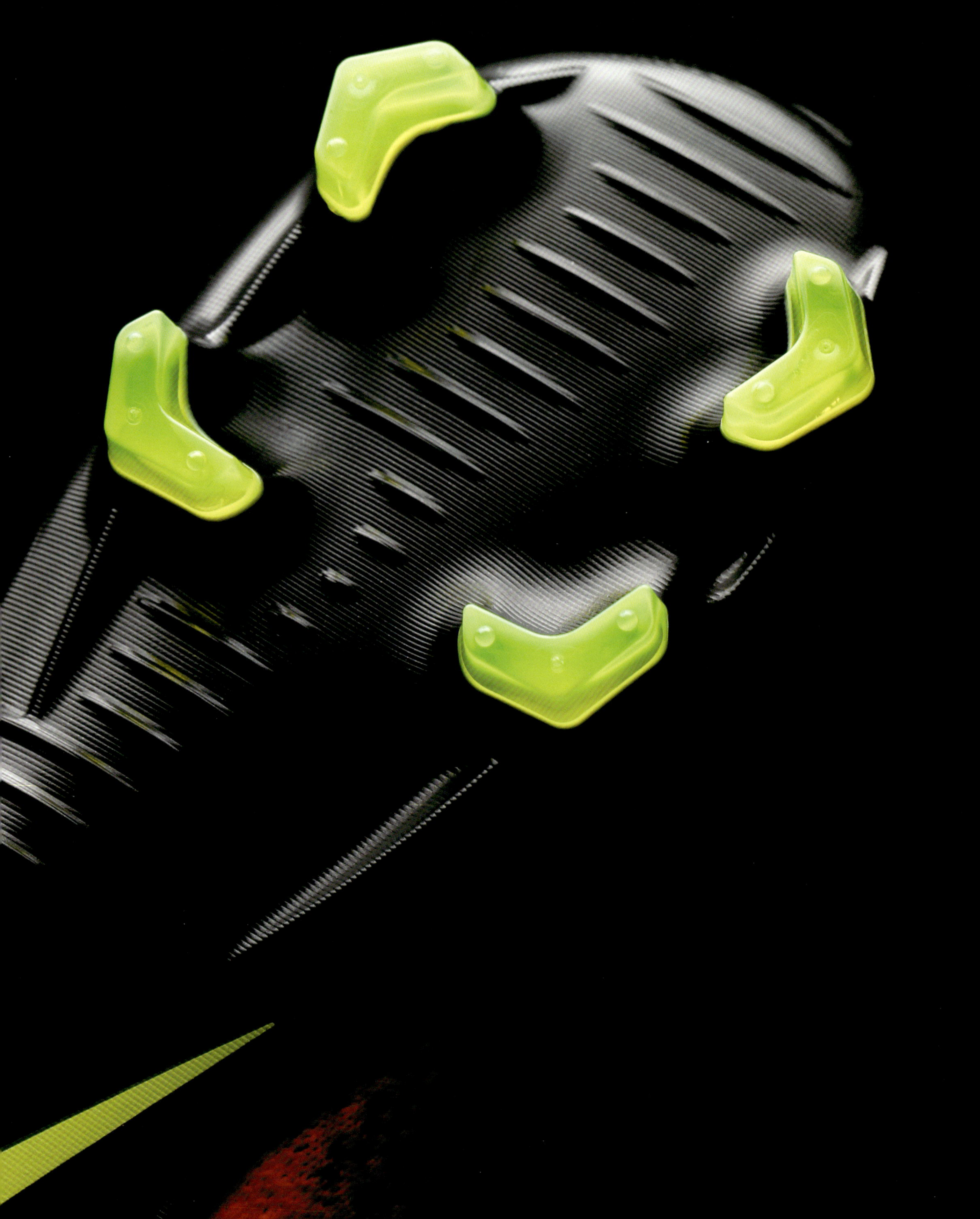

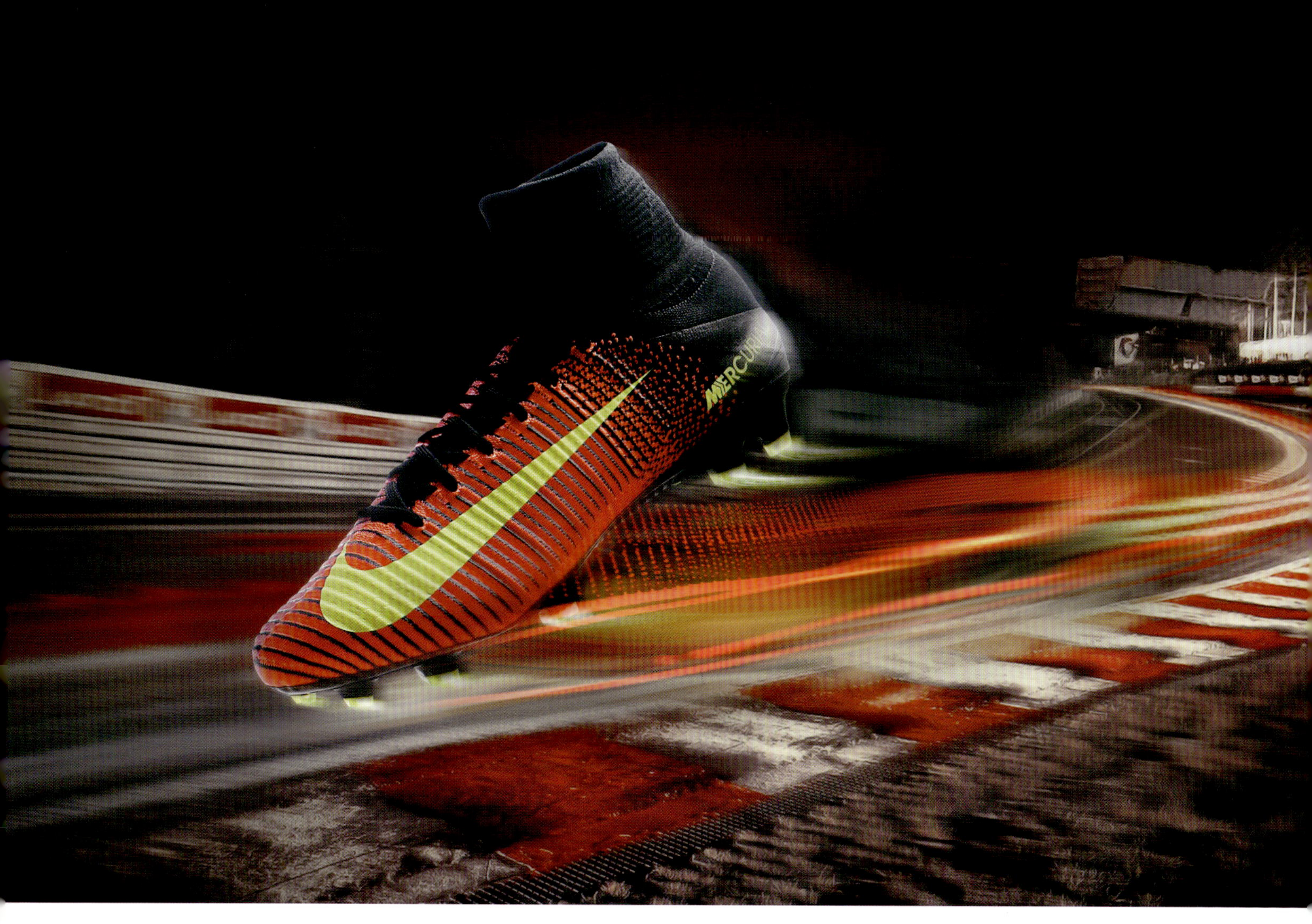

NIKE MERCURIAL SUPERFLY V

Released in 2016, the Nike Mercurial Superfly V features a one-piece Flyknit upper with NikeSkin and ACC (All Condition Control) technology for an all-weather ball control.

Details

The outsole is upgraded by Nike Anti-Clog Traction. The new technology prevents mud from clogging the sole plate, which will promote a player's performance on wet fields. The entire outsole weighs about 40 percent less than the previous carbon fiber one, and boasts a brand new stud pattern for great explosiveness.

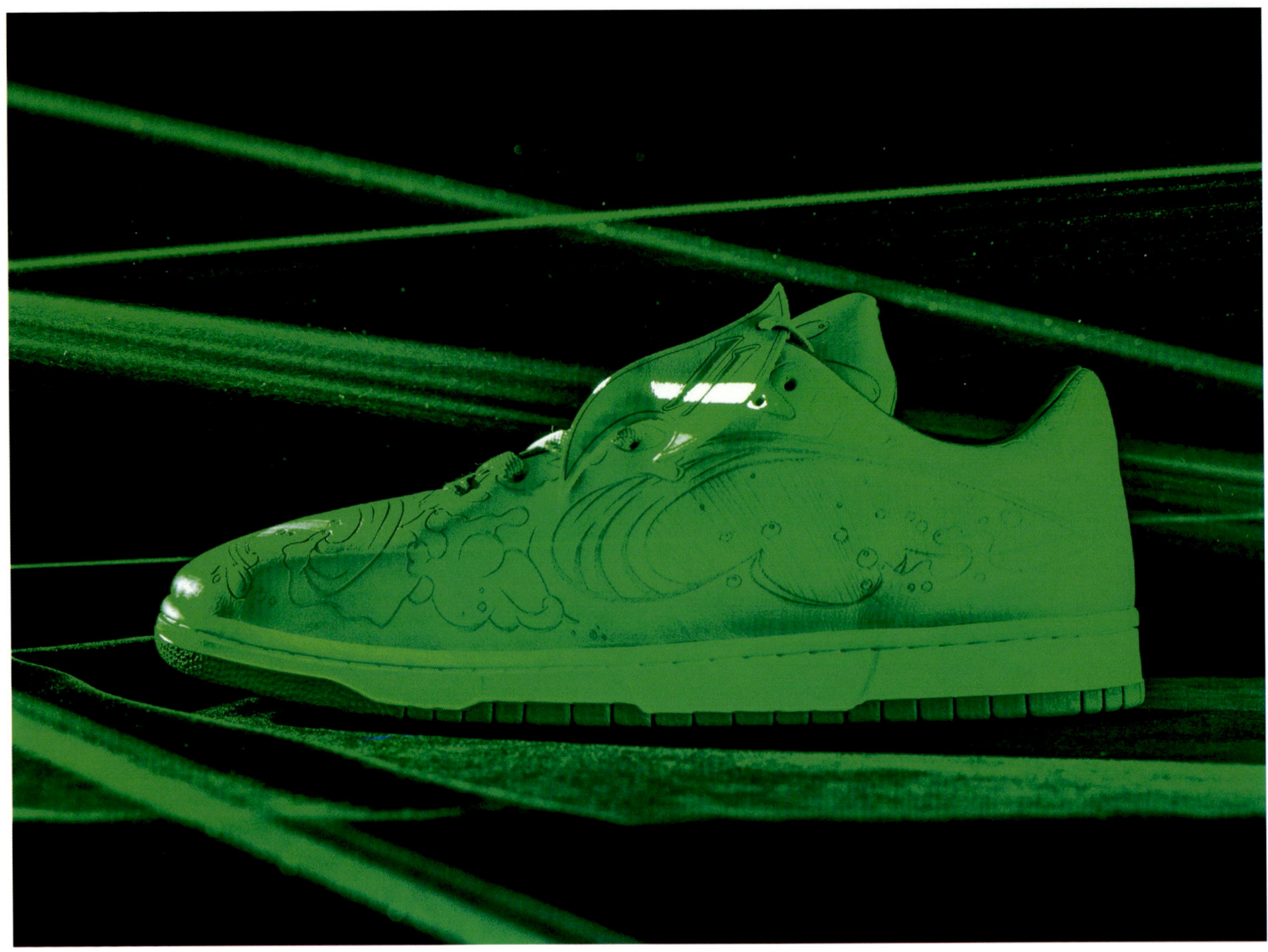

NIKE DUNK LOW

This model, which debuted in 2003, was designed by Mark Smith together with pro surfer and artist Chris Lundy. Only 200 pairs were released to the public.

Details

The upper is made of an entire piece of leather. A crashing ocean wave pattern is marked on the surface using lasering techniques. Each pair also has a laser-made size tag.

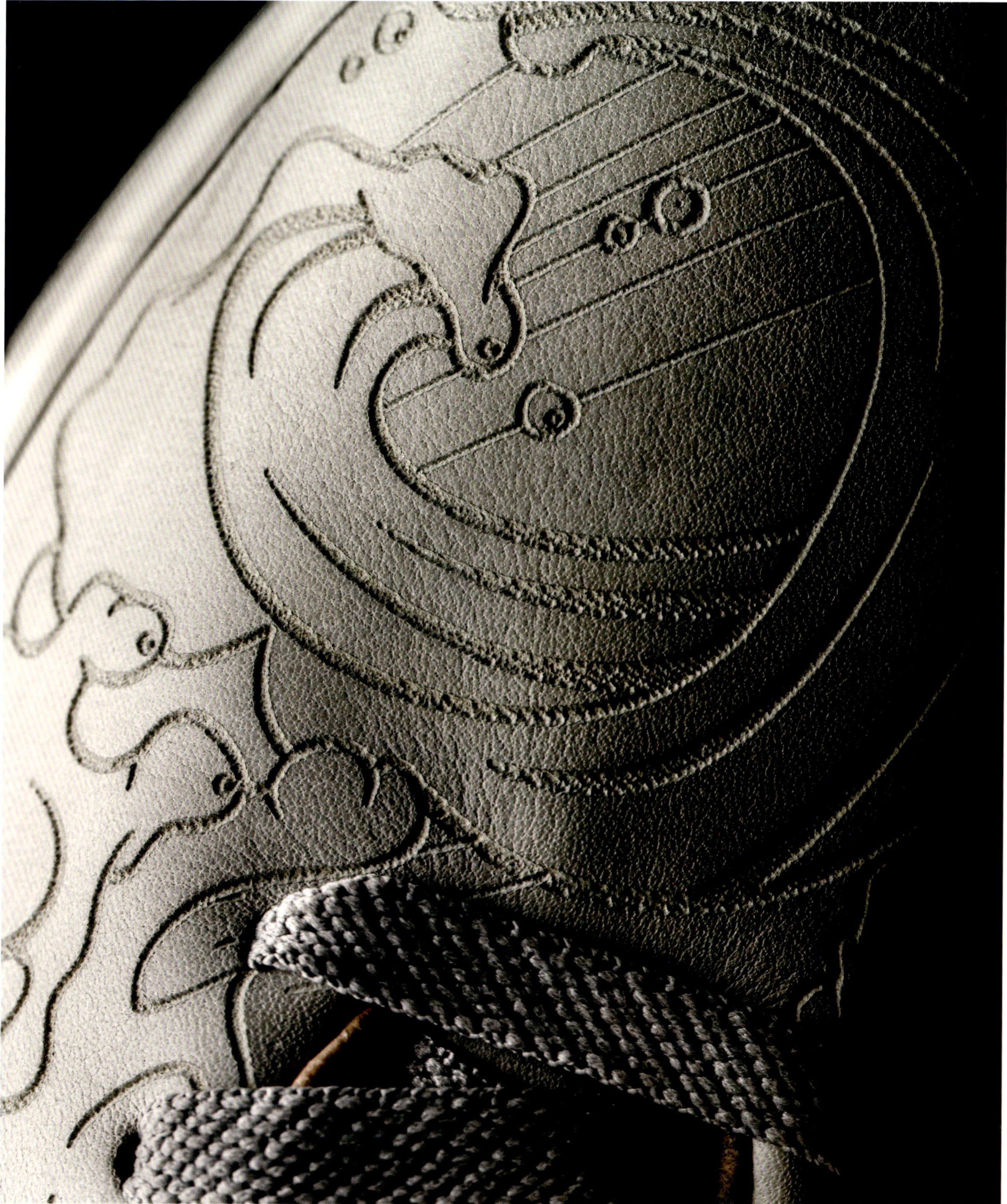

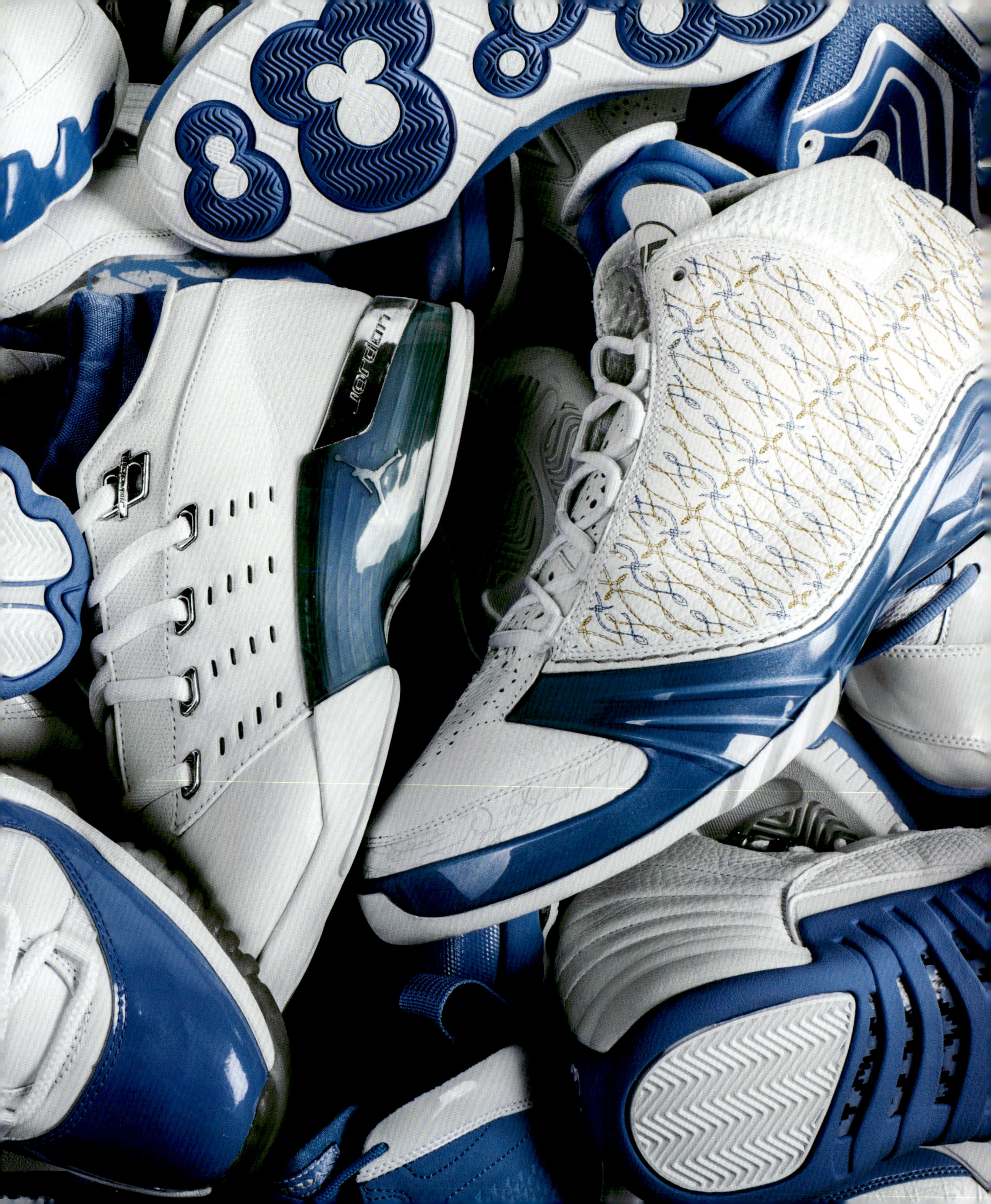
Jordan

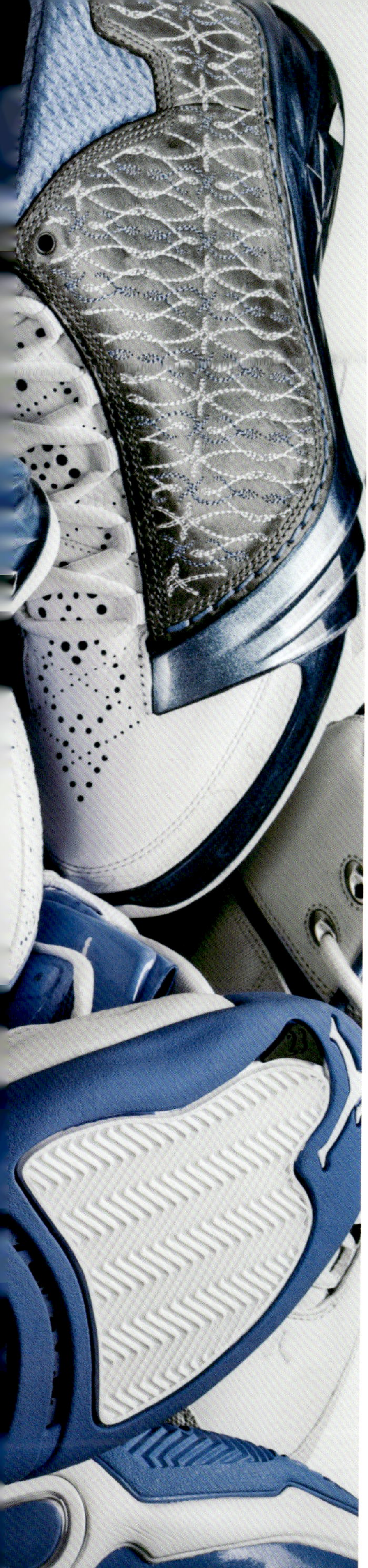

Continuity and legacy are reasons why people find sneakers fascinating. As time goes by, the first pair expands to a whole series. The changes in sneaker design also mirror the progress of craftsmanship and shifts in people's aesthetics.

SERIES

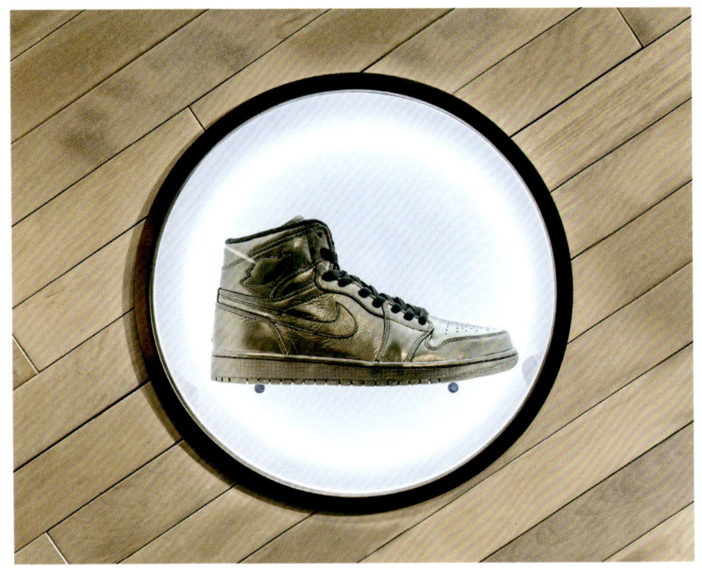

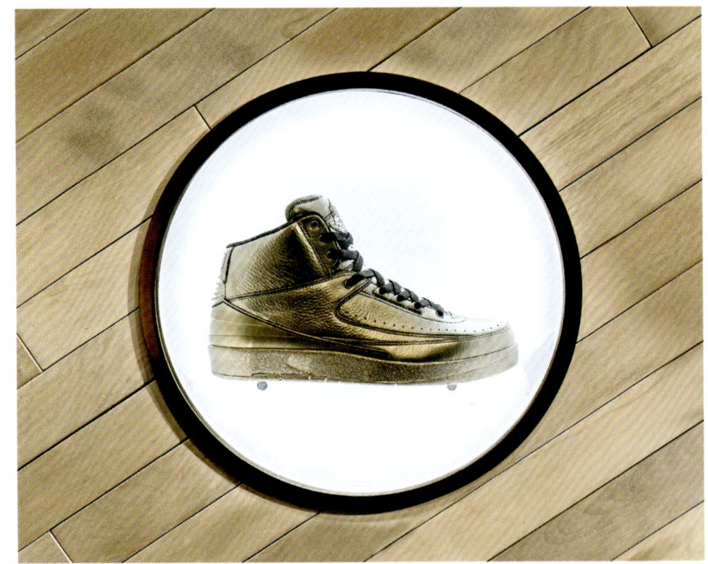

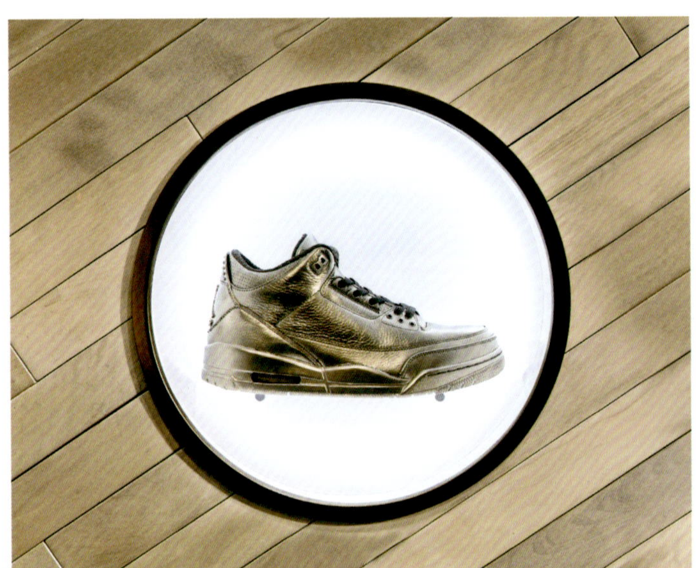

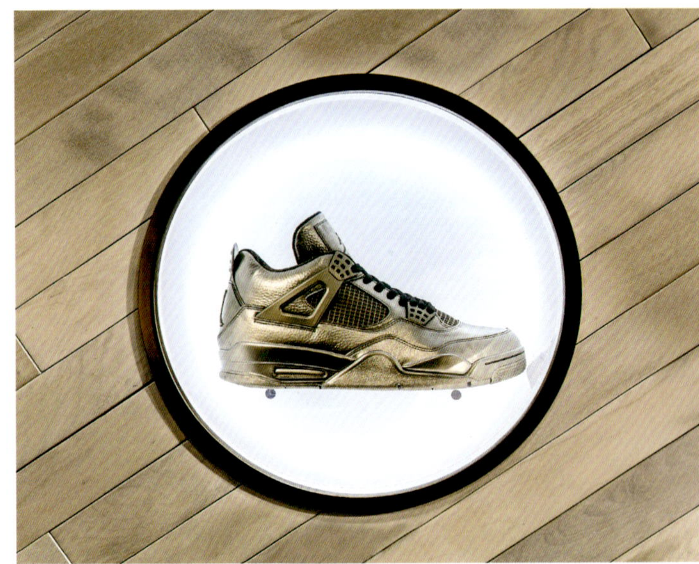

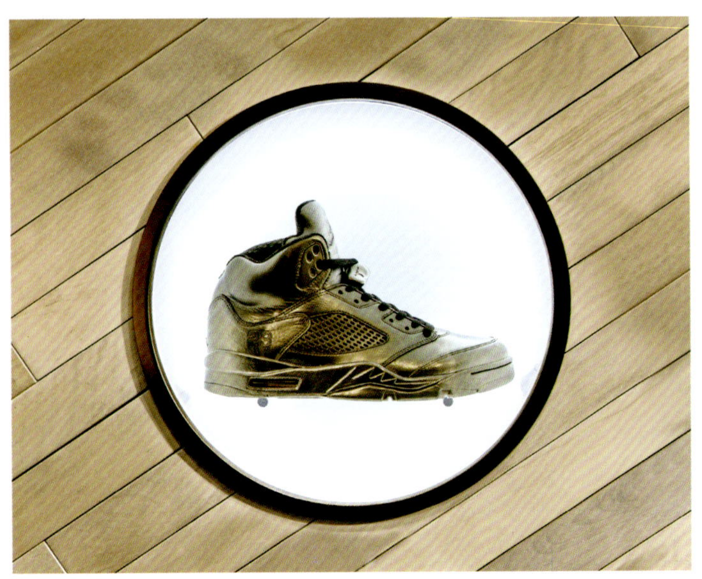

AIR JORDAN GOLD SERIES

On Feb. 20, 2016, Jordan 8 Wellington, Asia's largest Jordan-only store in Hong Kong officially opened. This latest location boasts a wall of all 30 Air Jordan sneakers, the highlight of which is a series of metallic gold Jordans ranging from 1 to XX9.

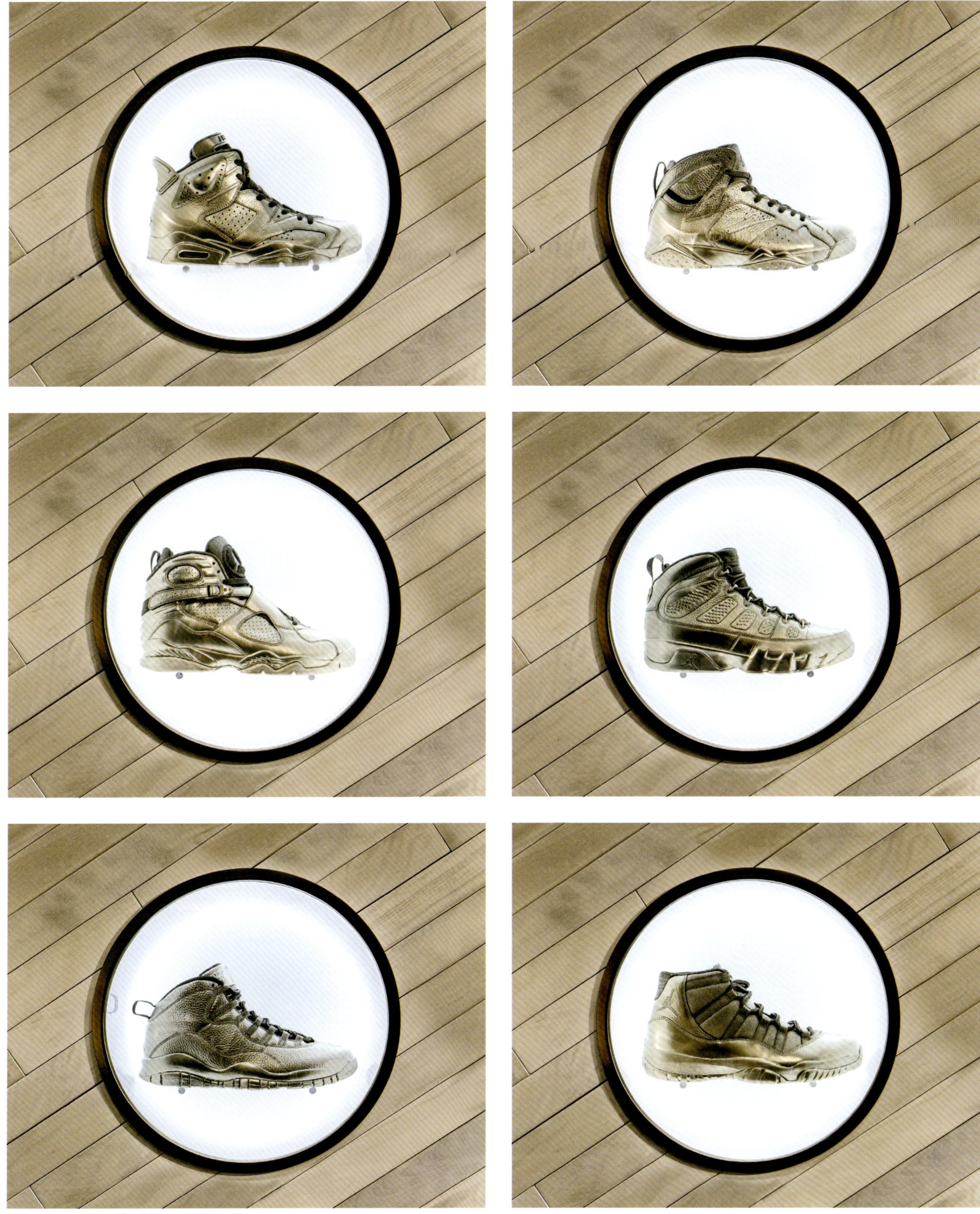

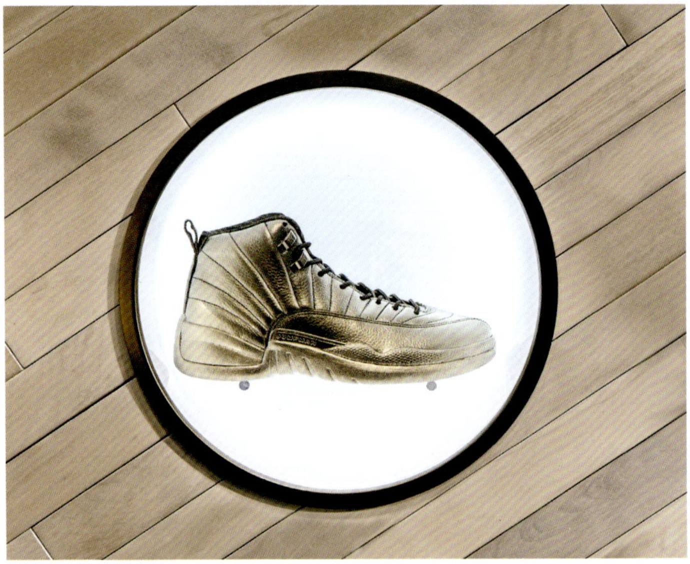

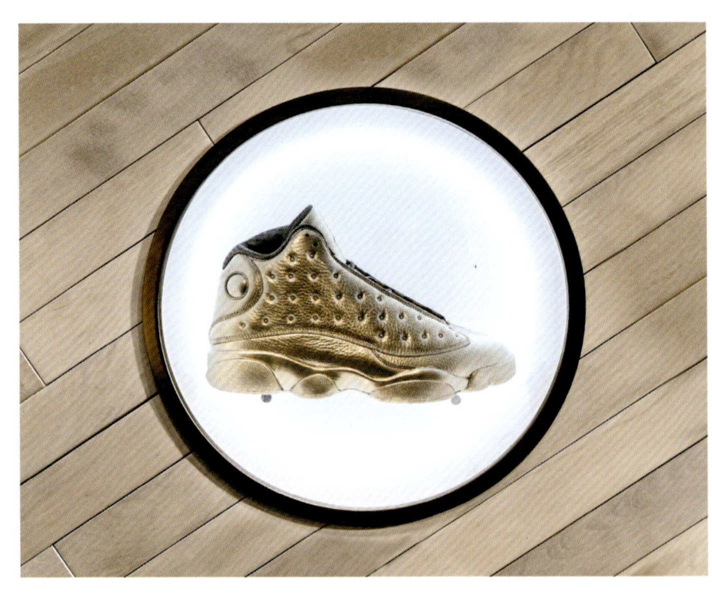

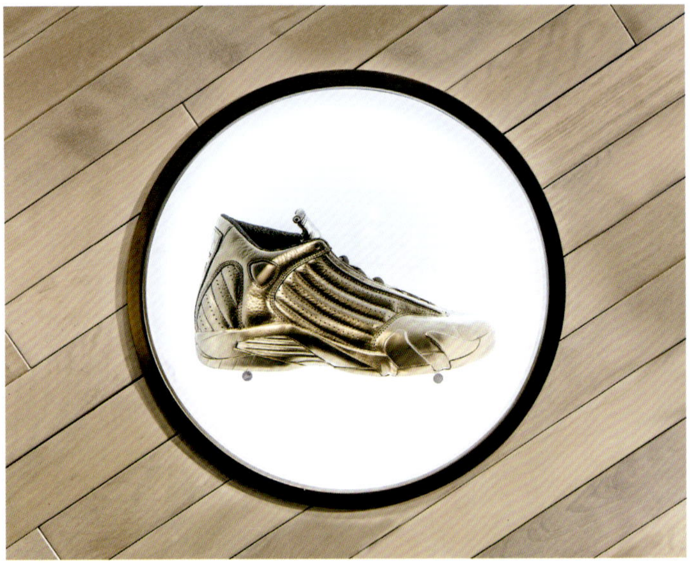

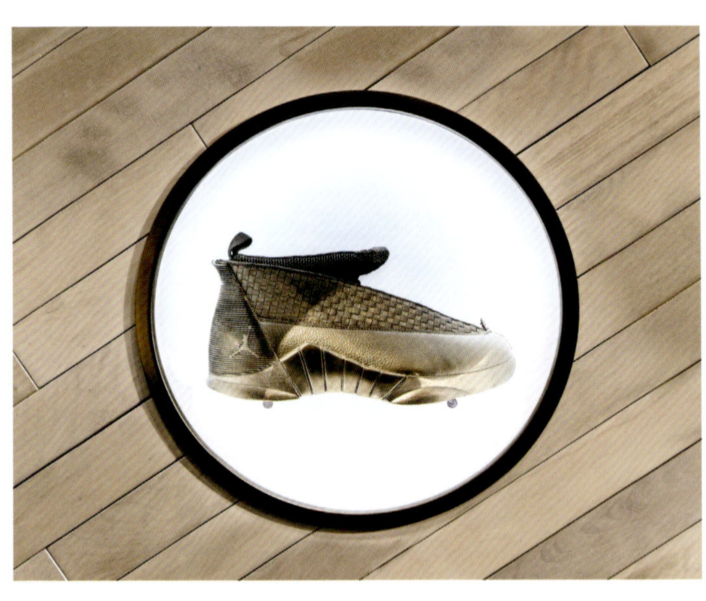

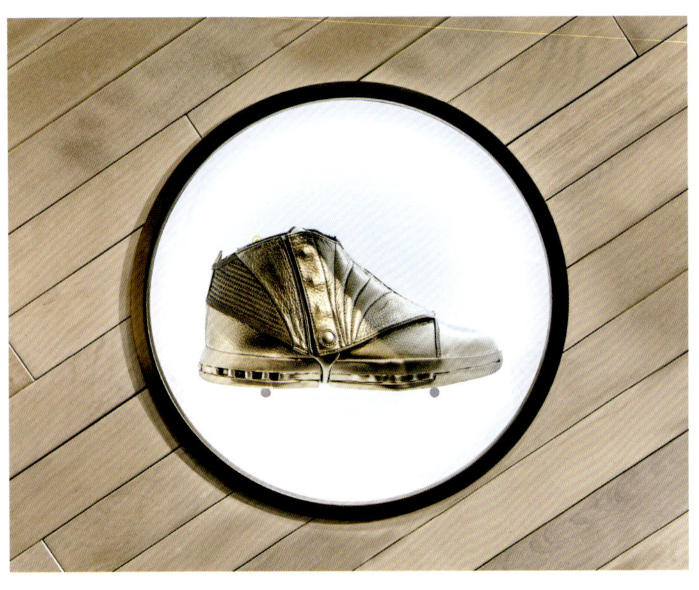

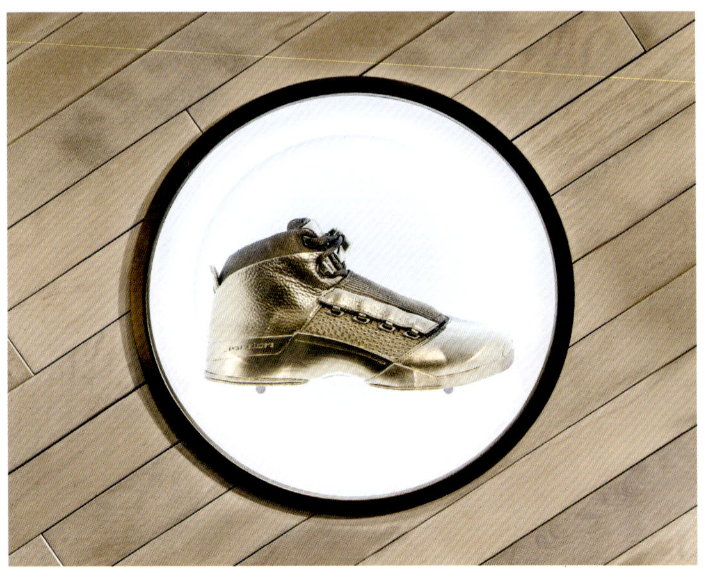

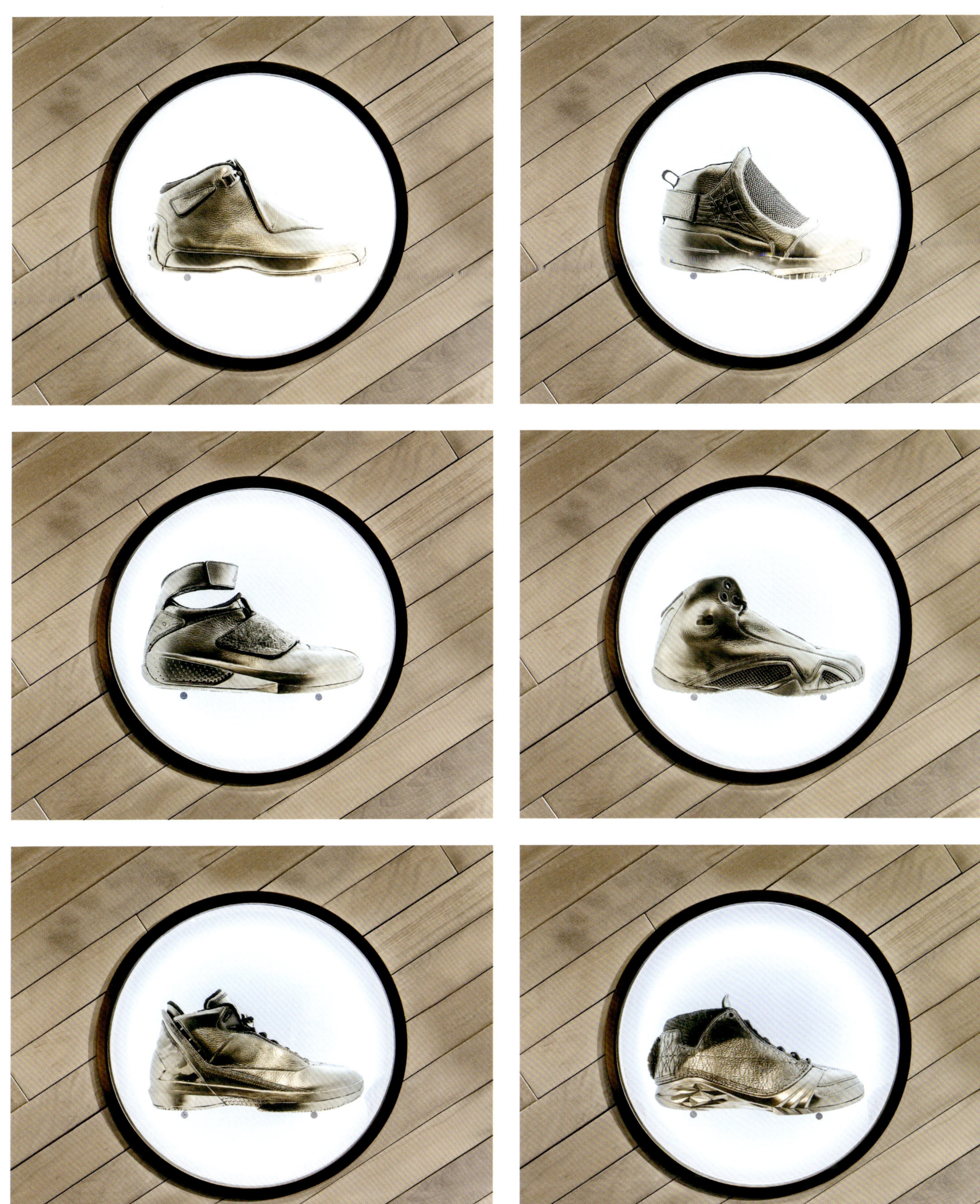

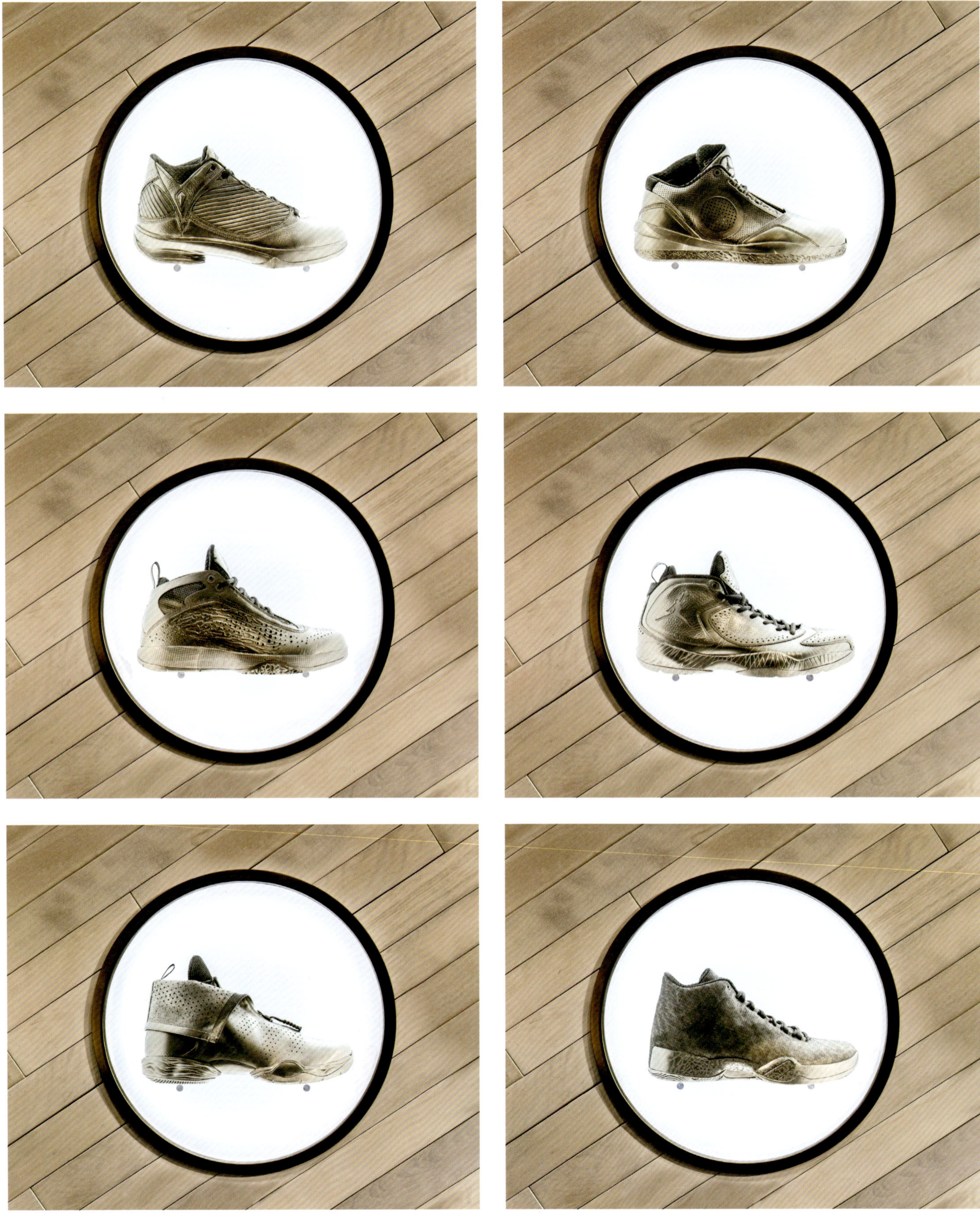

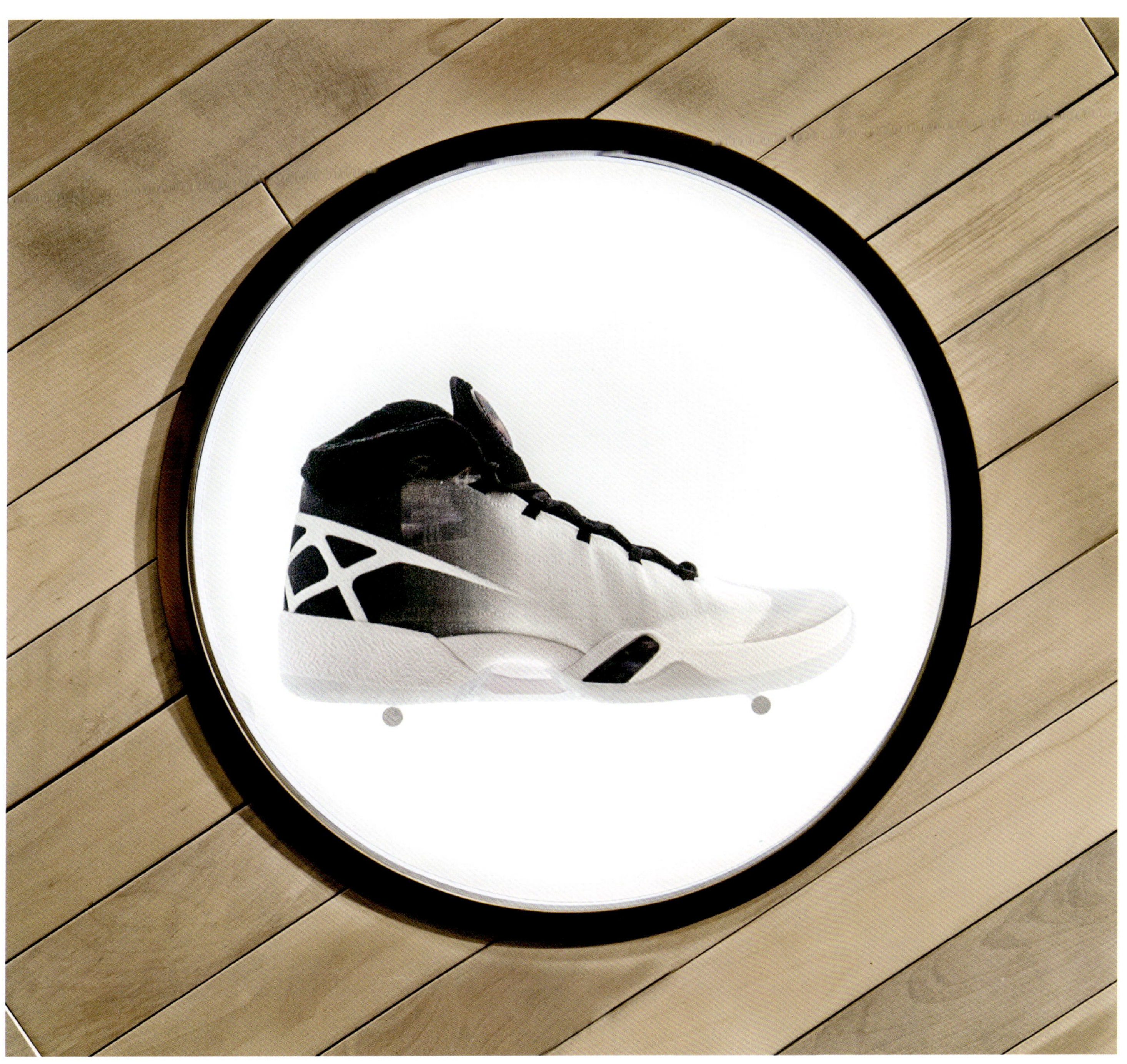

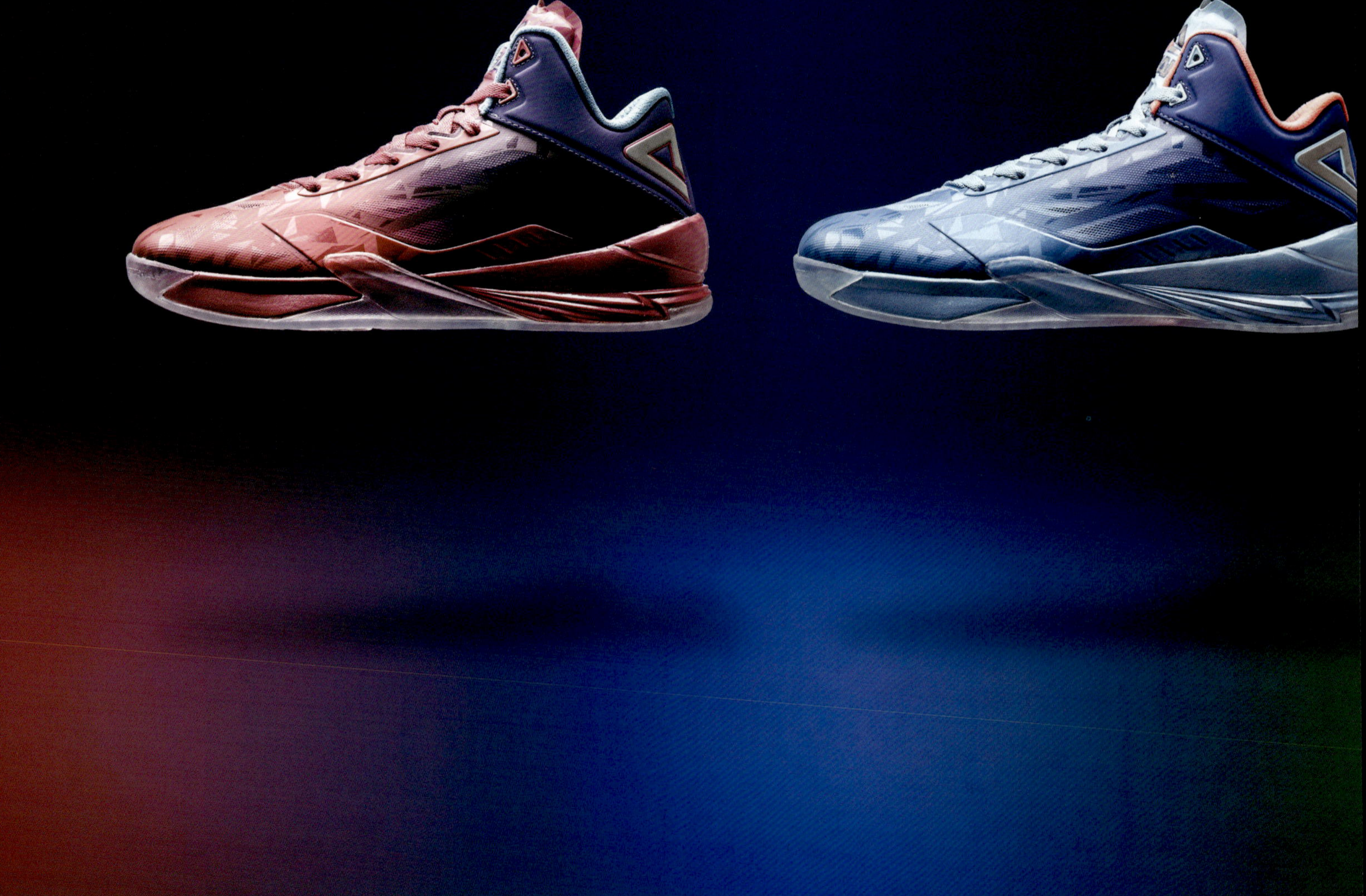

PEAK LIGHTNING IV × ICE FACTORY

In 2016 Peak teamed up with cold drink brand Ice Factory and designed four special colorways for the Lightning IV. They were inspired by four ice cream flavors.

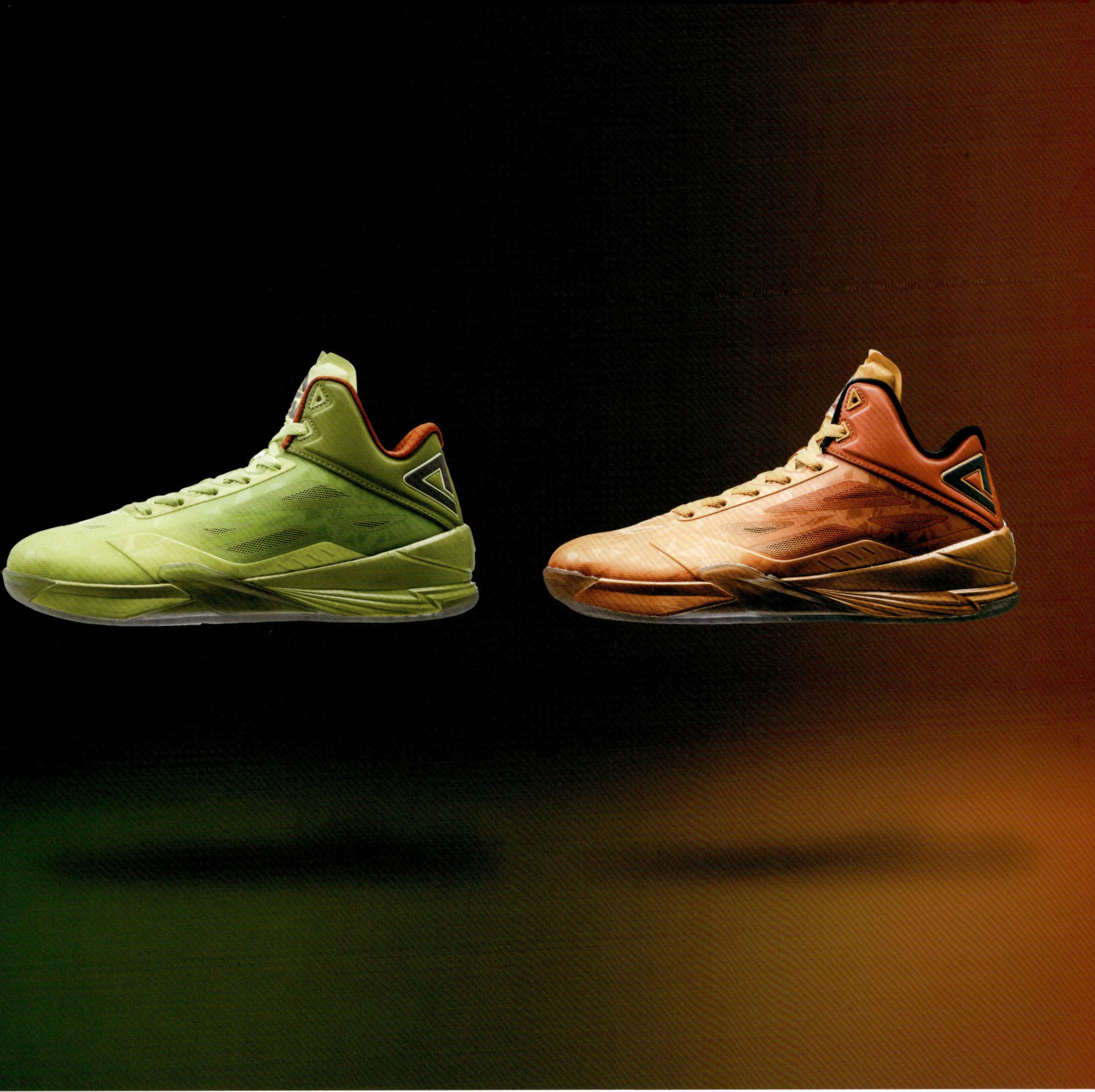

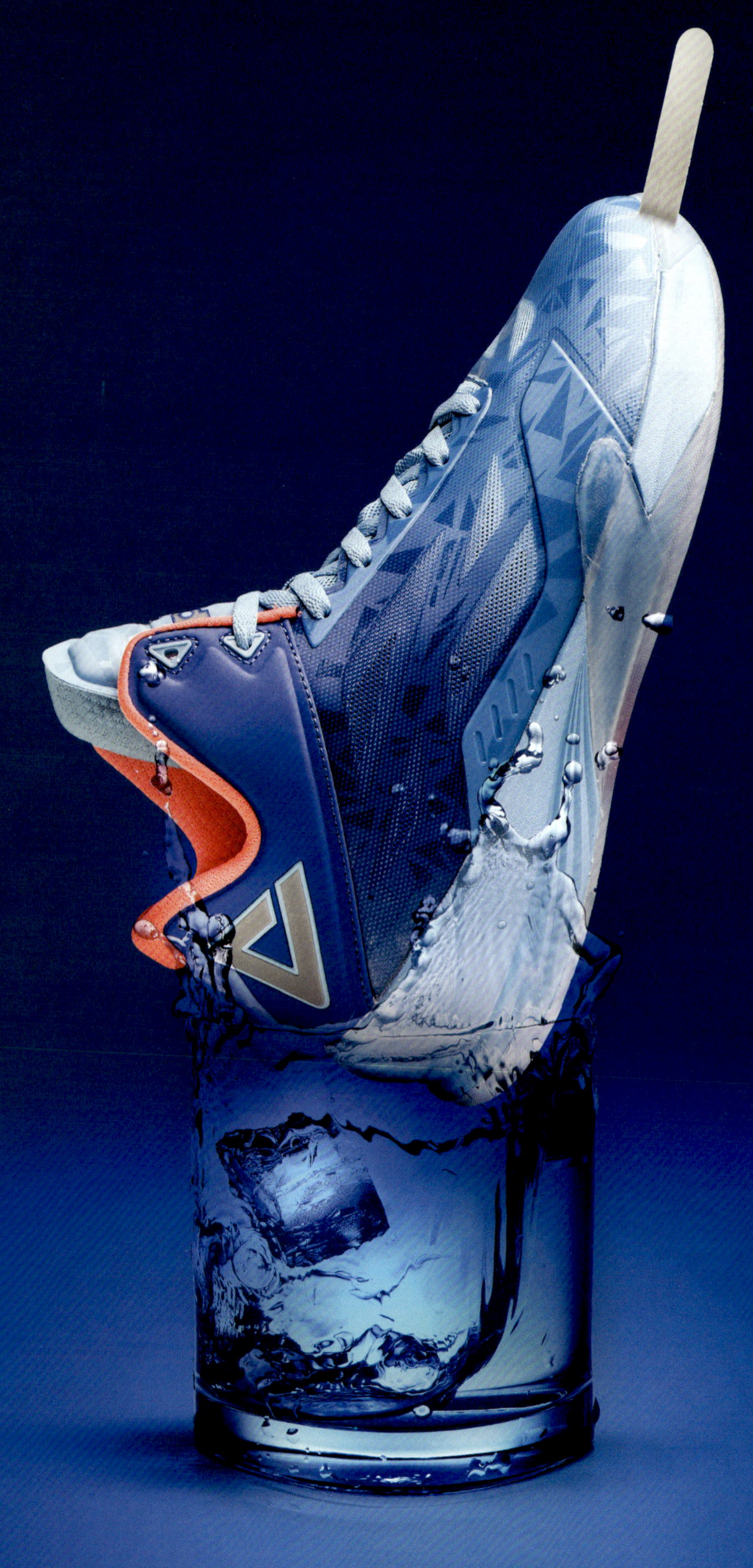

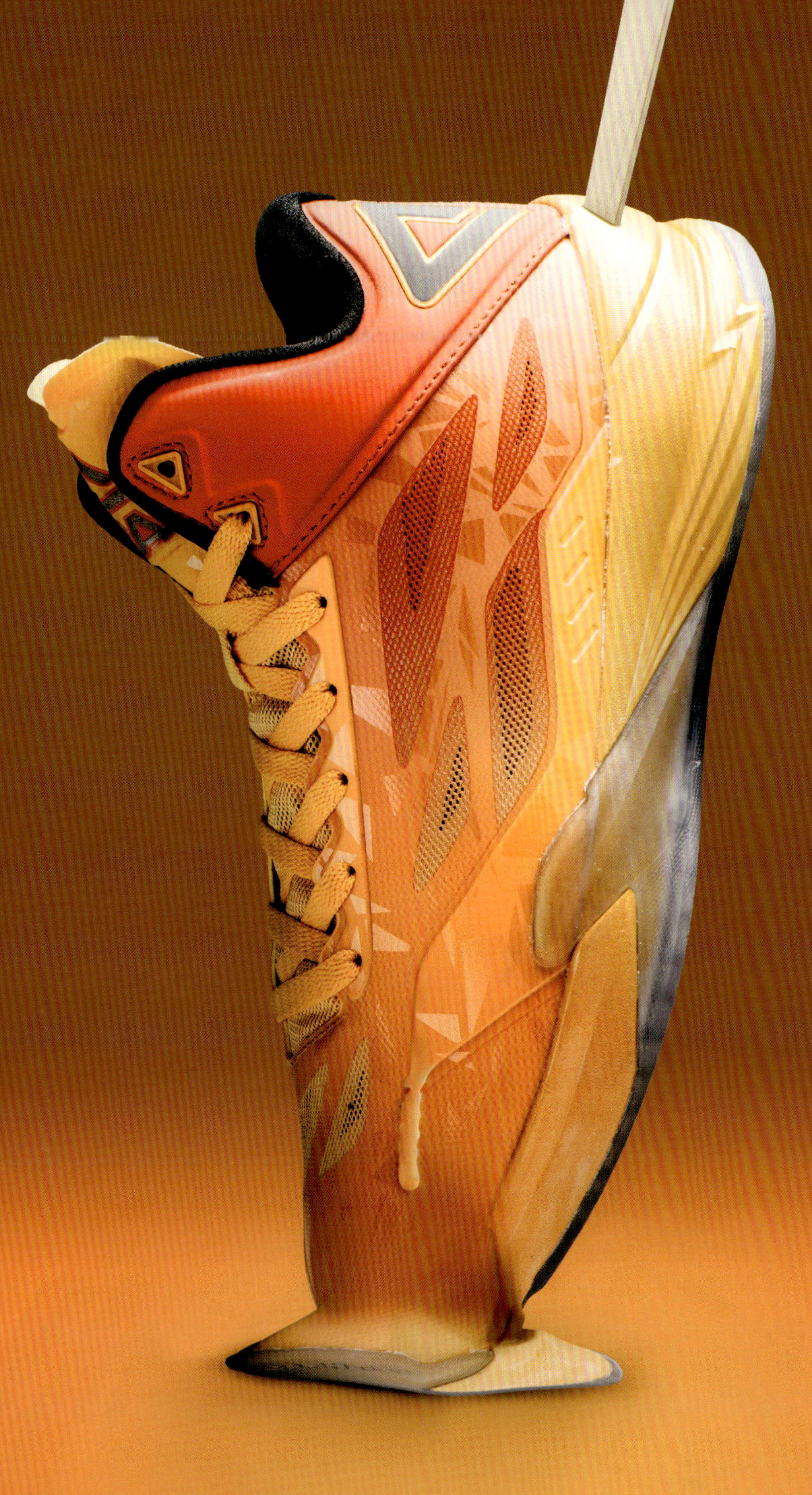

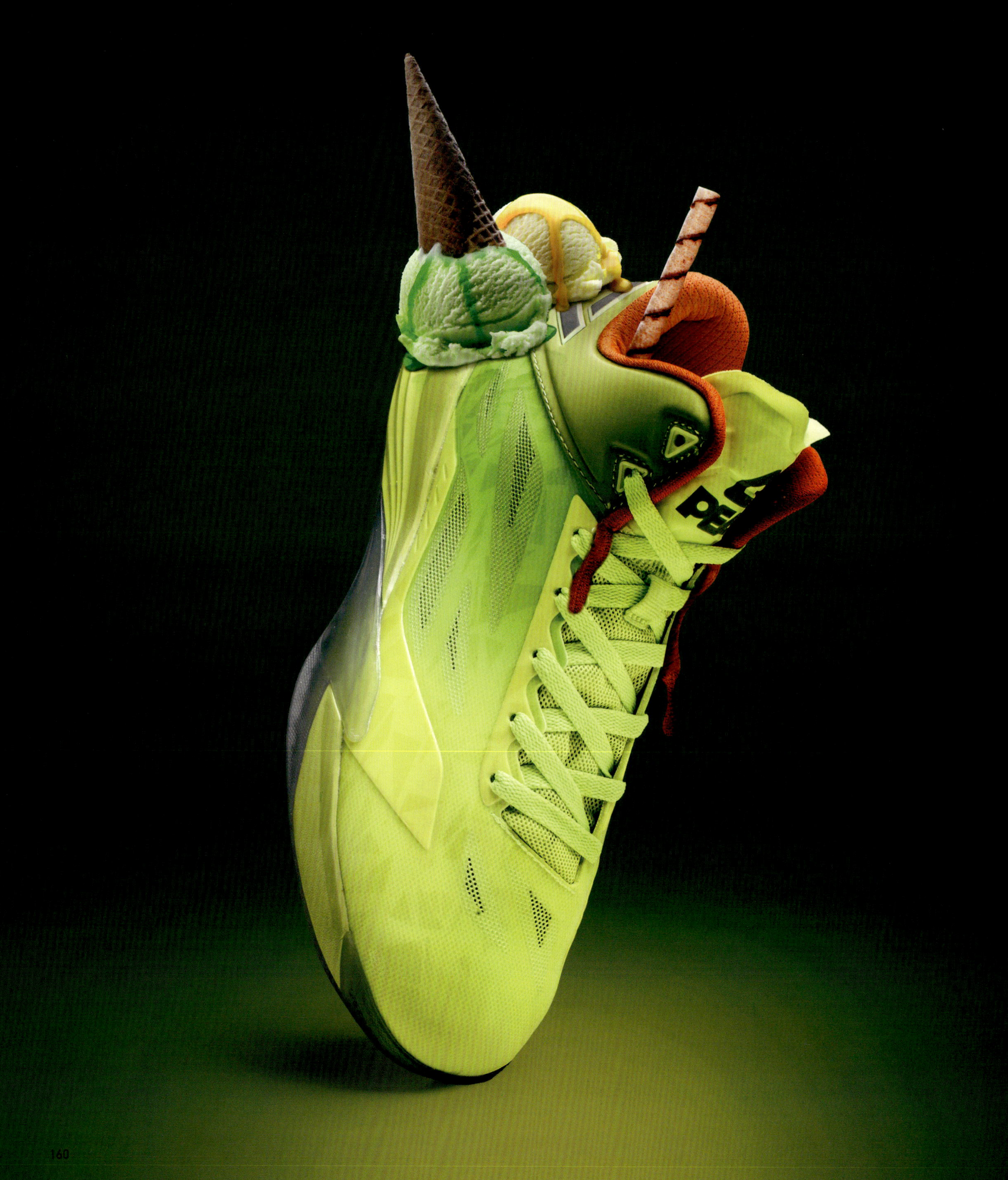

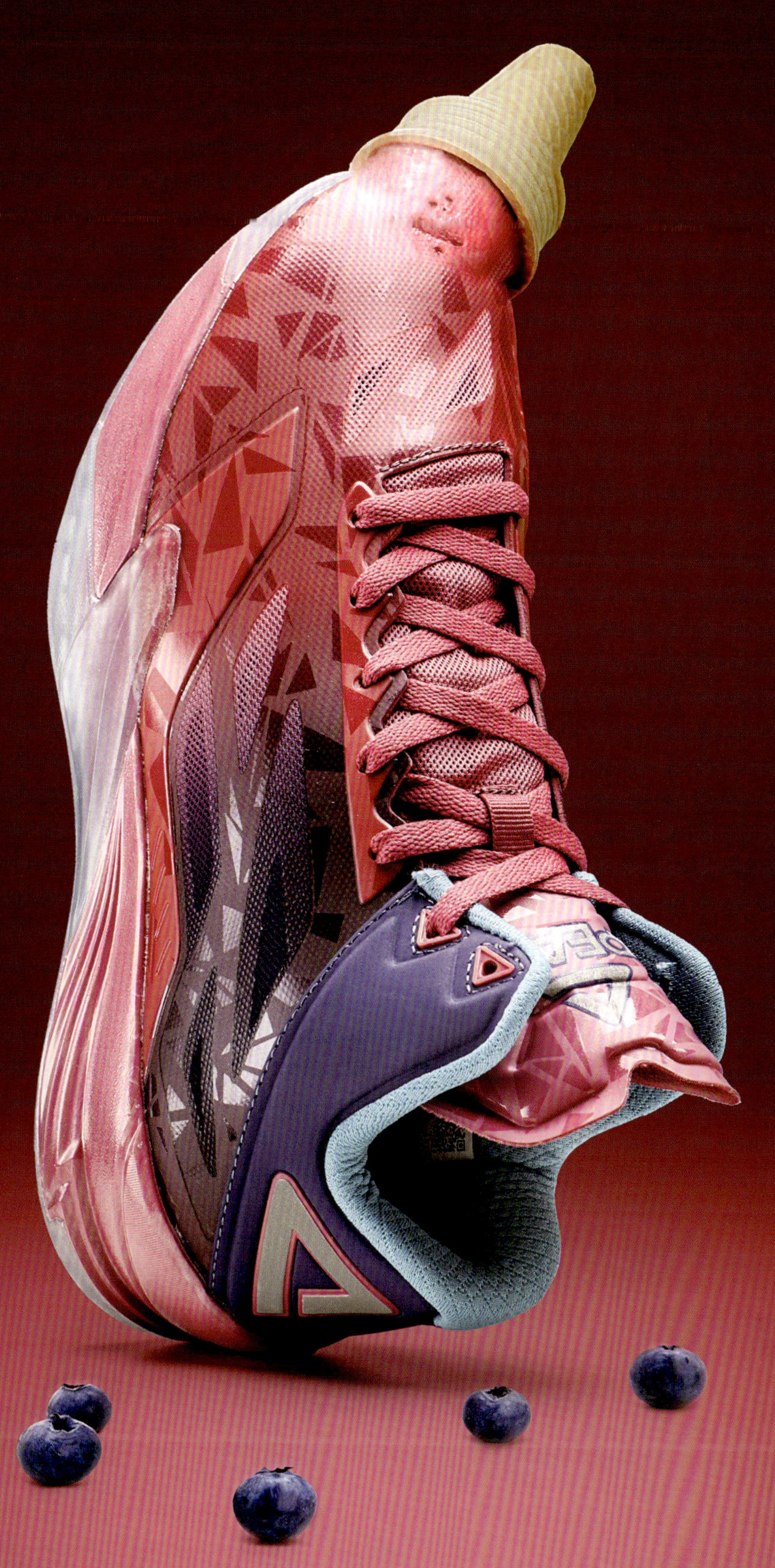

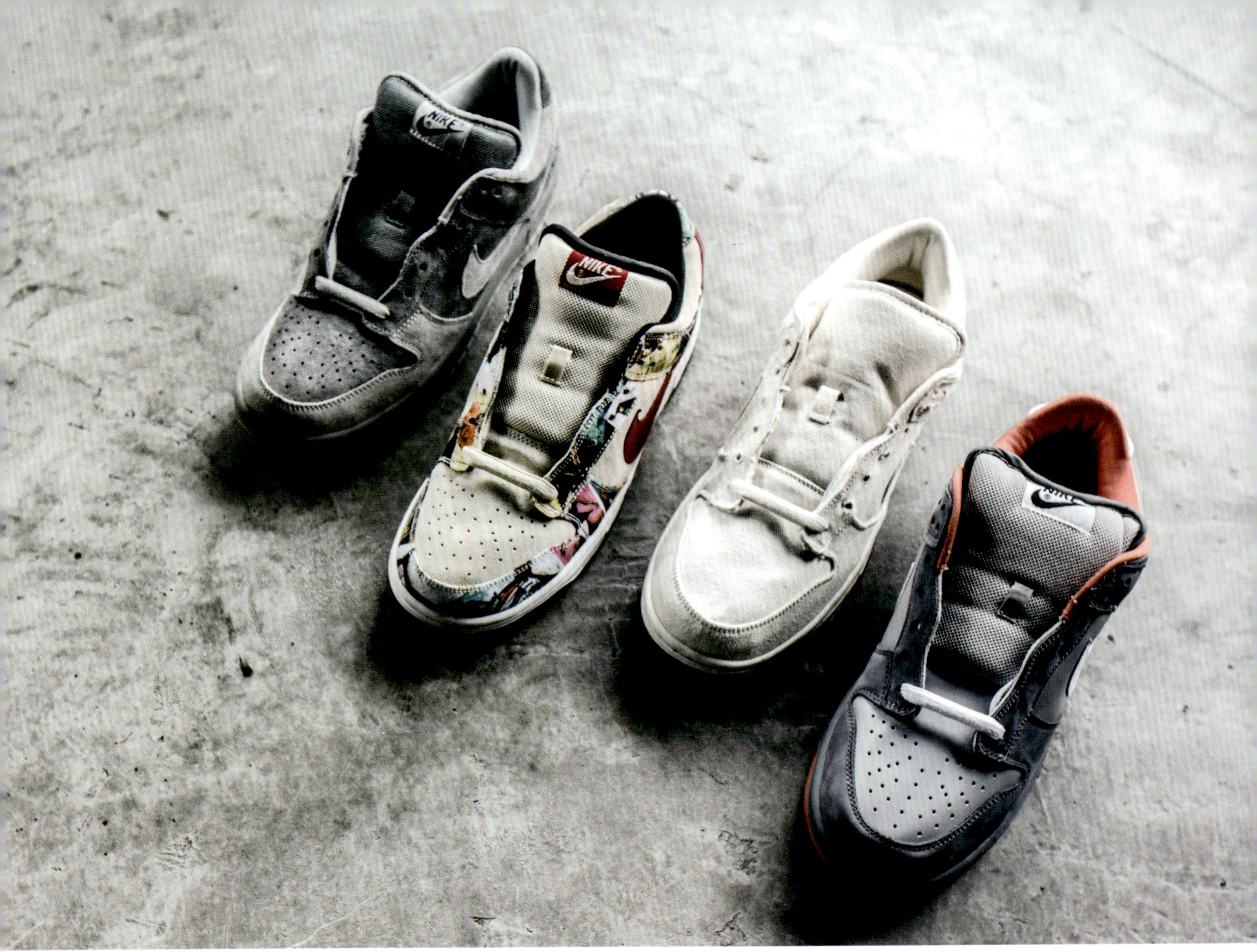

NIKE DUNK LOW PRO SB [CITY PACK]

STAPLE DESIGN NYC (upper right): In 2005, Nike, working in conjunction with Staple Design, released the City Pack to represent New York. Only 202 pairs were available on the market, among which 30 pairs were sold in Staple stores.

TOKYO (lower right): The Tokyo Dunk came out in 2004 with a limited supply of 202 pairs. The upper is made of canvas.

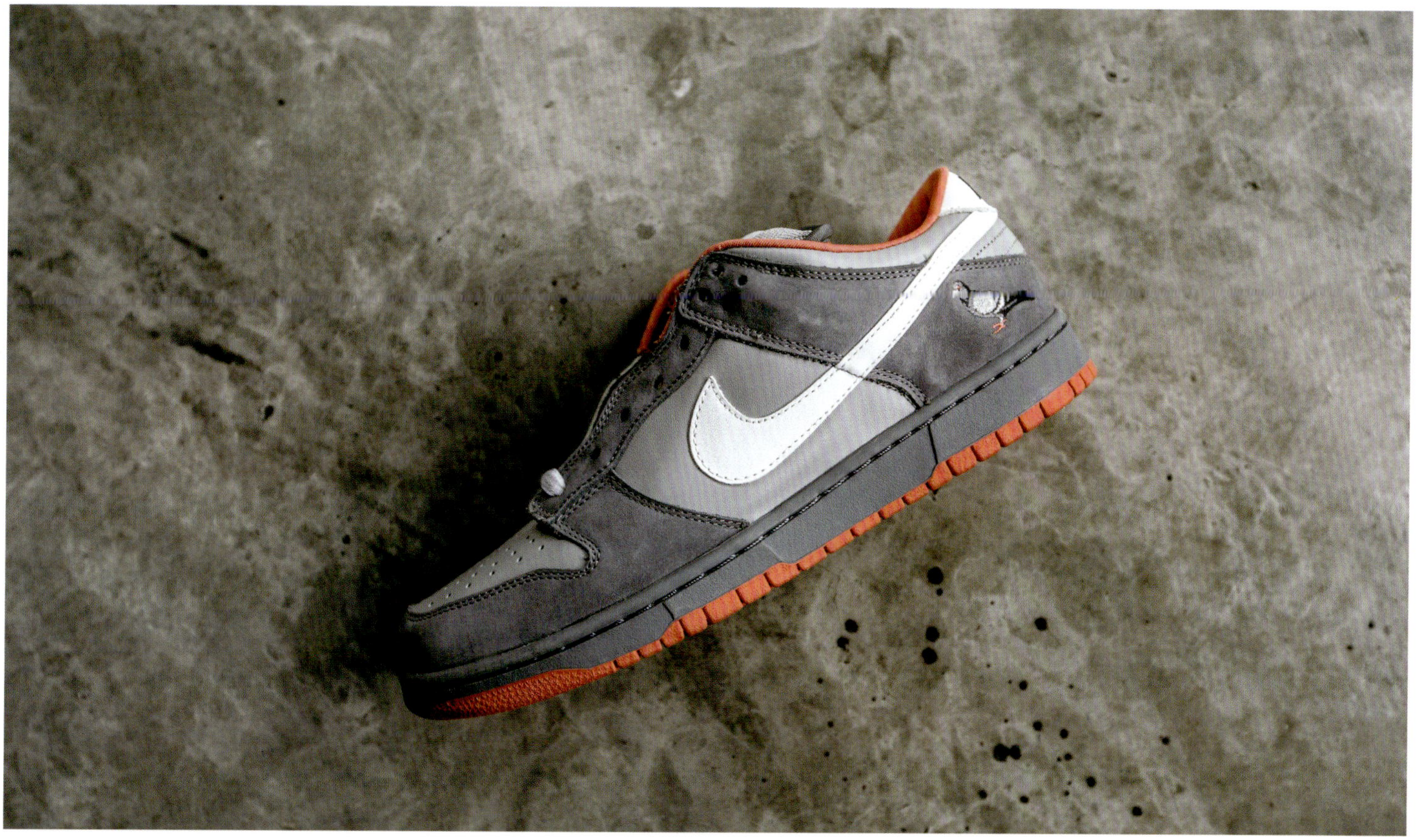

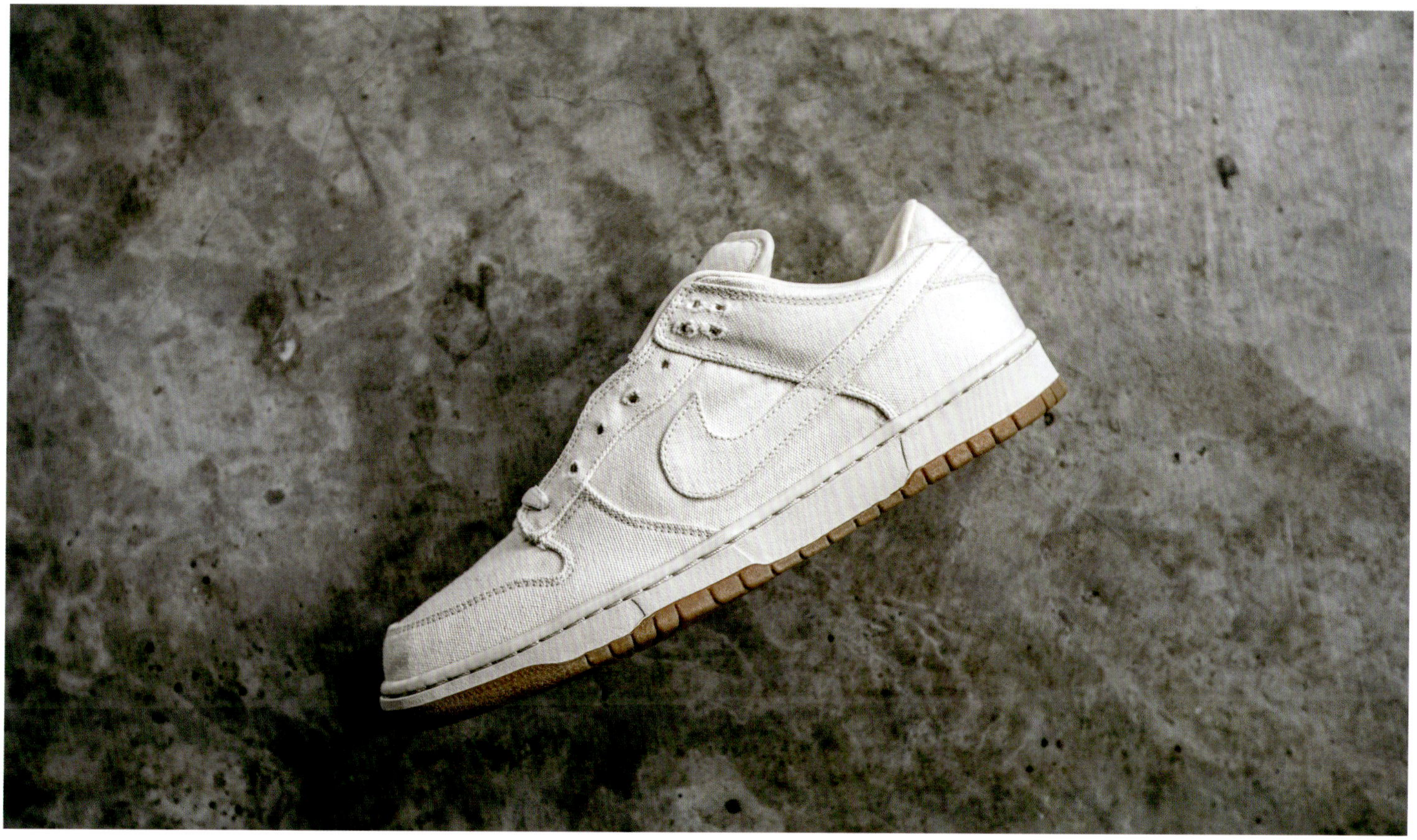

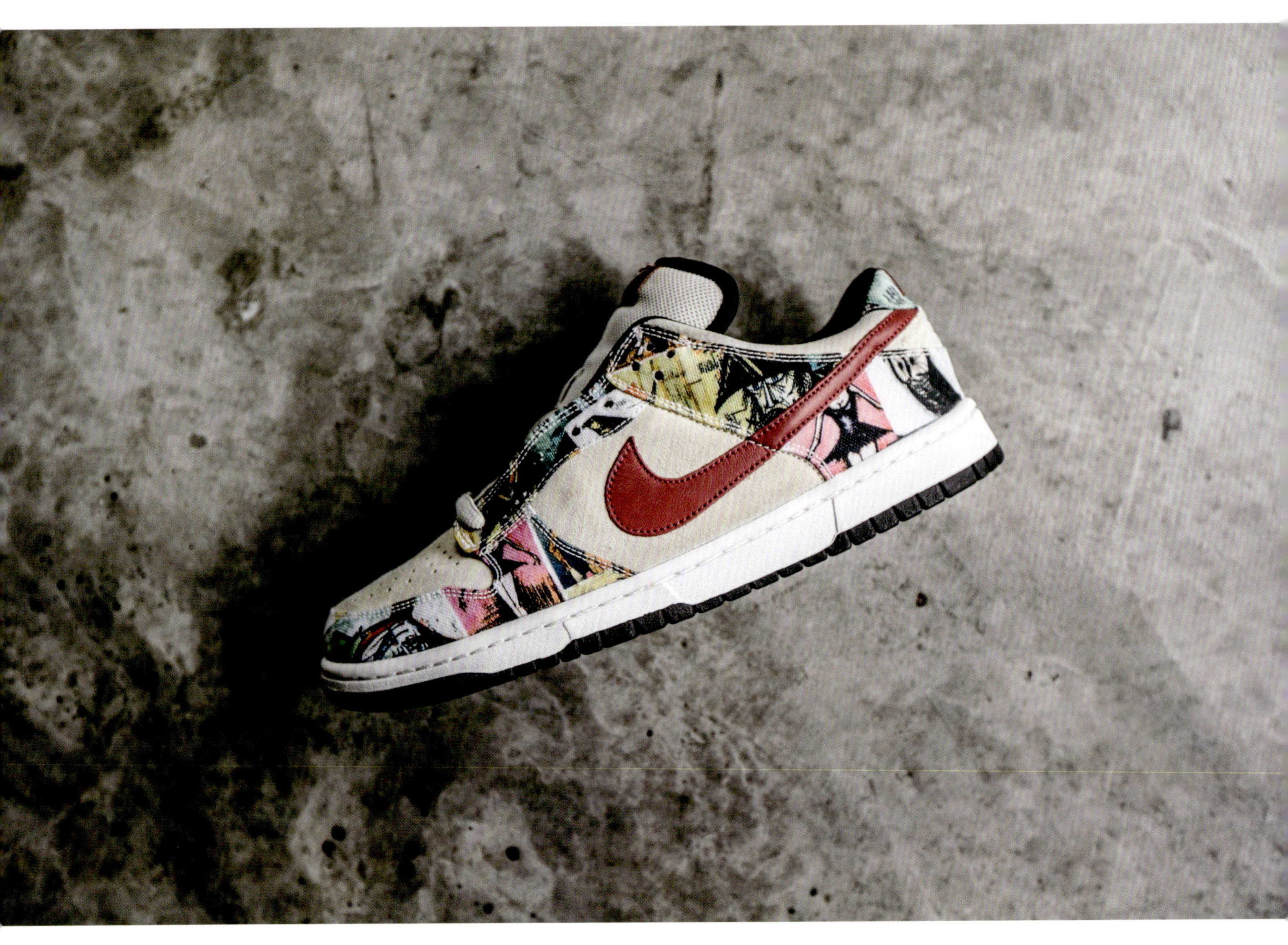

PARIS: The Paris Dunk was released in 2003 with only 202 pairs on the market. The pattern design is inspired by the artwork of Bernard Buffet, a modern French expressionist. No two pairs are alike.

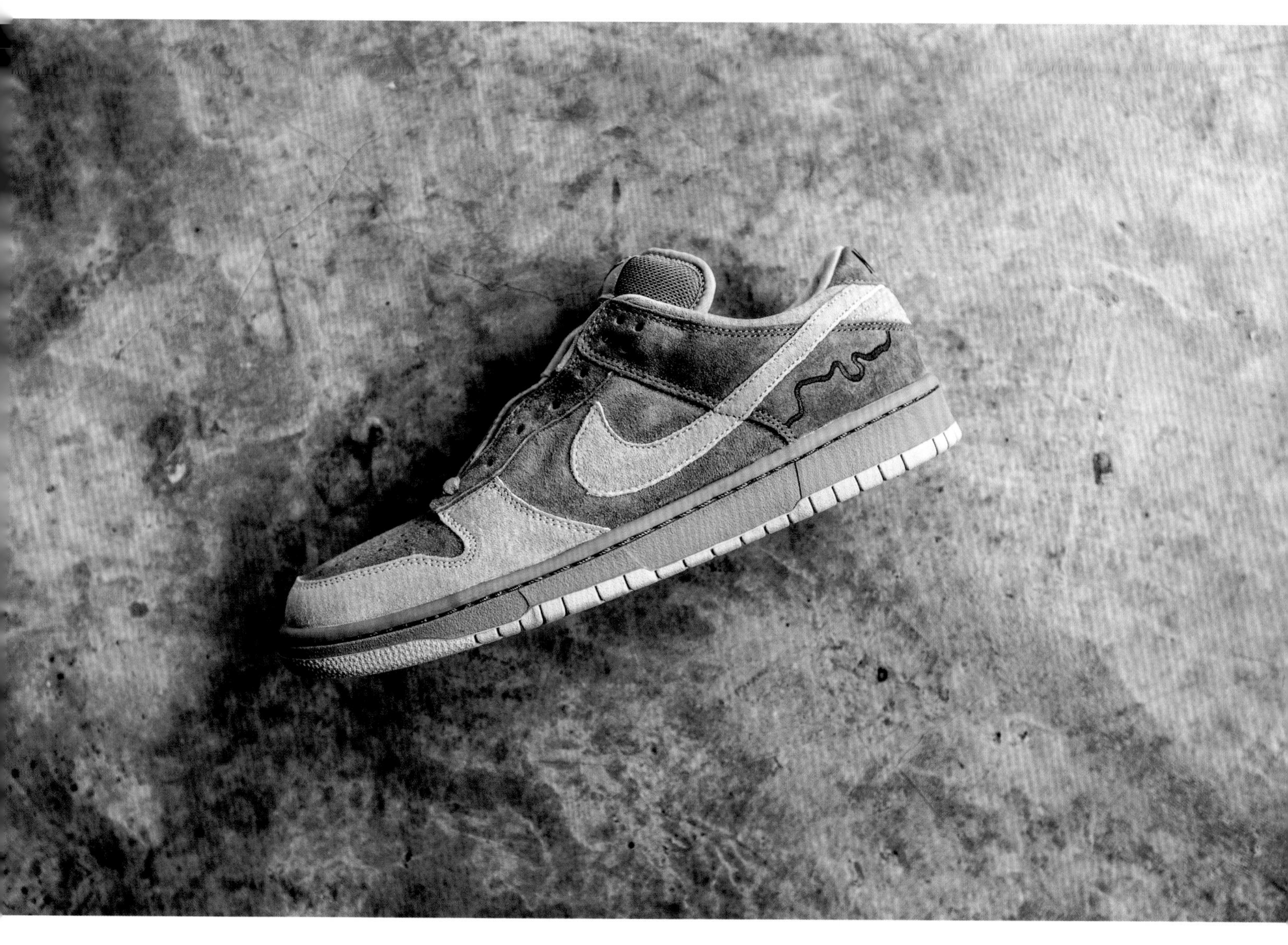

LONDON: The London Dunk debuted in 2004 with only 202 limited edition pairs. The gray suede upper is a metaphor for the gloomy weather in London. And the River Thames is embroidered on the outside of the heel.

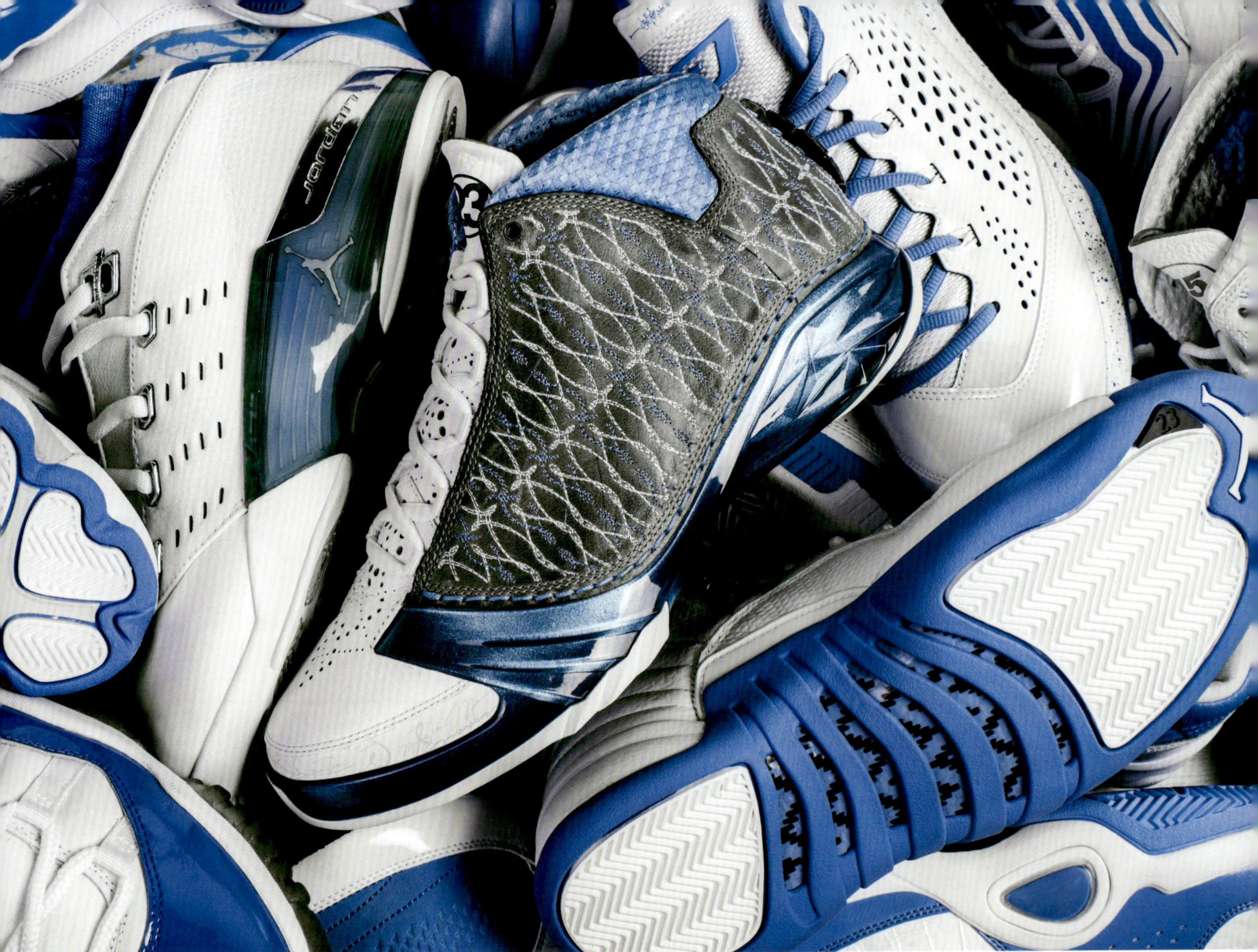

UNIVERSITY BLUE SERIES

As Michael Jordan's alma mater and Jordan Brand's sponsor the University of North Carolina has a position in Nike & Jordan Brand's exclusive colorway every year.

NIKE ZOOM BRAVE IV INOUE TAKEHIKO (lower right): Released in 2011, it is tailor-made for the Asian market. In 2011, when a 9.0-magnitude earthquake and tsunami hit Japan, the caricaturist Inoue Takehiko teamed up with Nike and created this colorway. It aims to inspire people to regain their faith in life.

AIR JORDAN XVII LOW: Launched in 2002, this shoe is the low-top edition of Michael Jordan's 17th signature sneaker. Wilson Smith III designed it with inspiration from Aston Martin and jazz music.

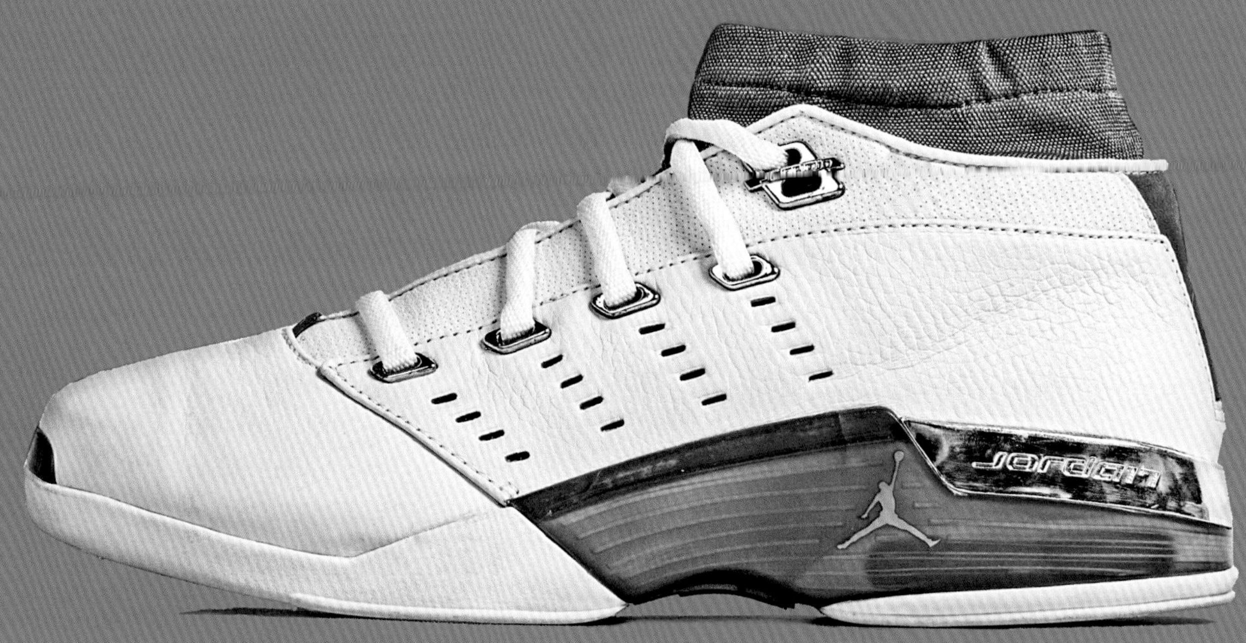

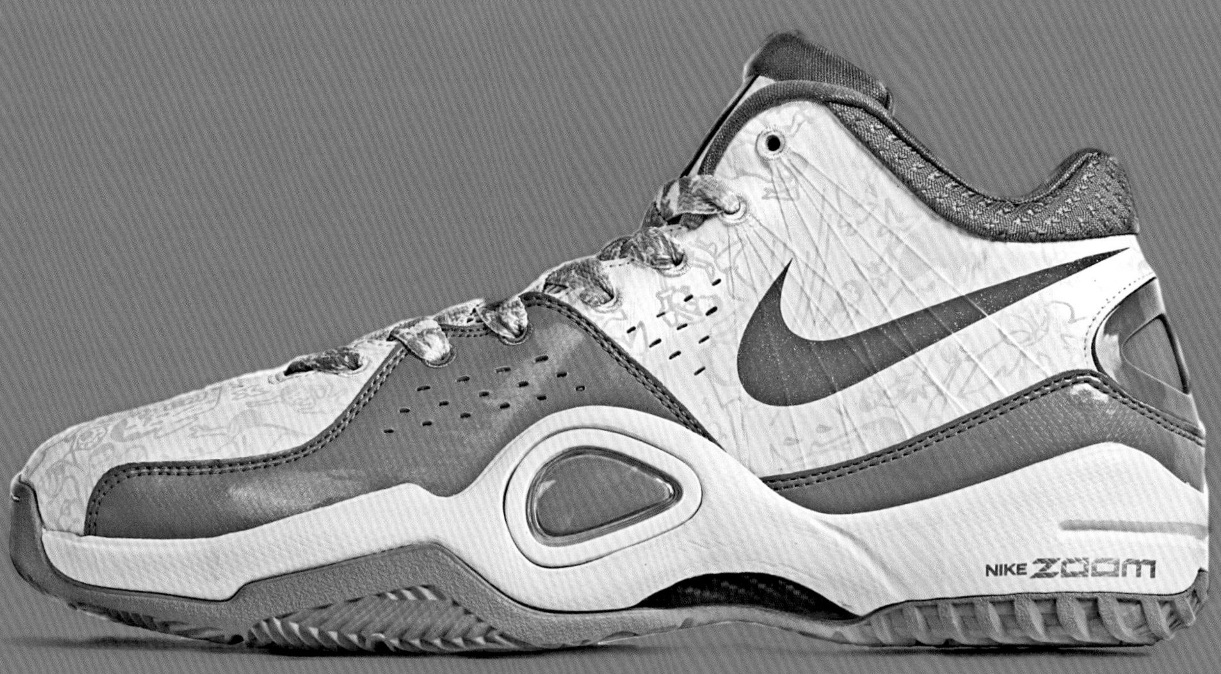

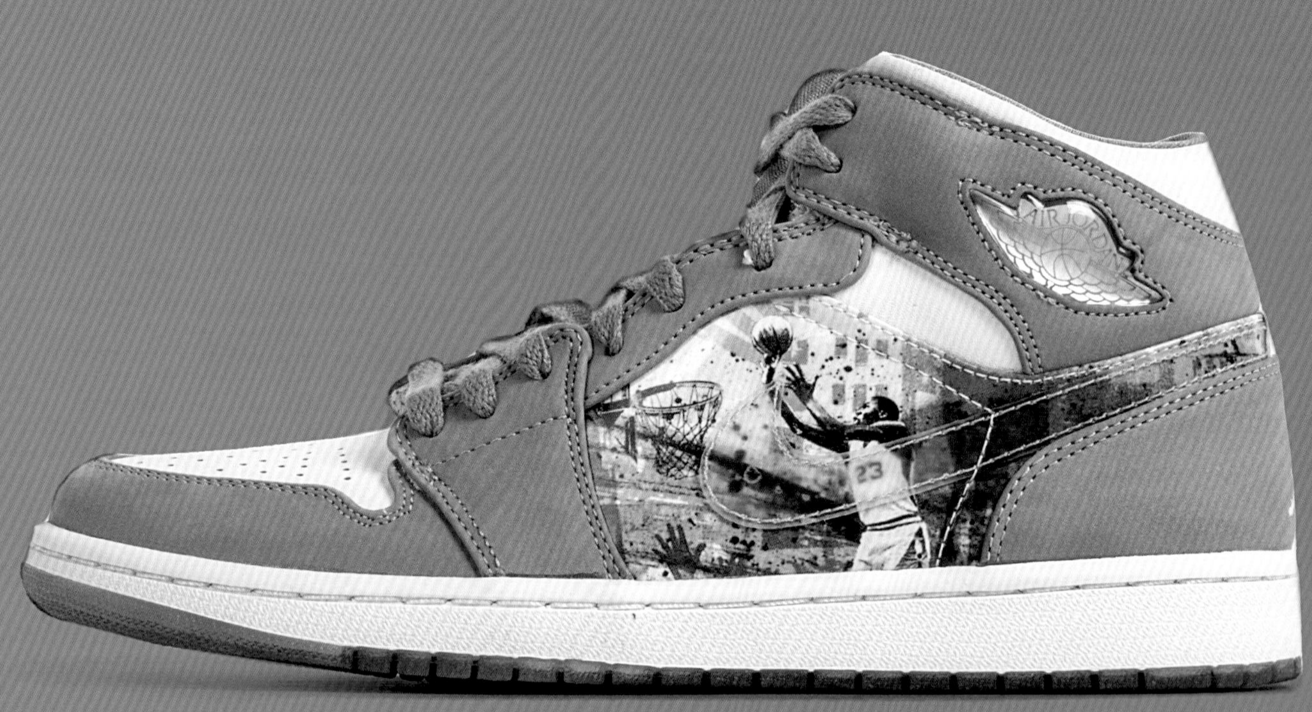

AIR JORDAN 1 RETRO [ALPHA]: The model was released in 2007. You can see an illustration at the quarter panel showing Michael Jordan's game-winning jumpshot against Georgetown University.

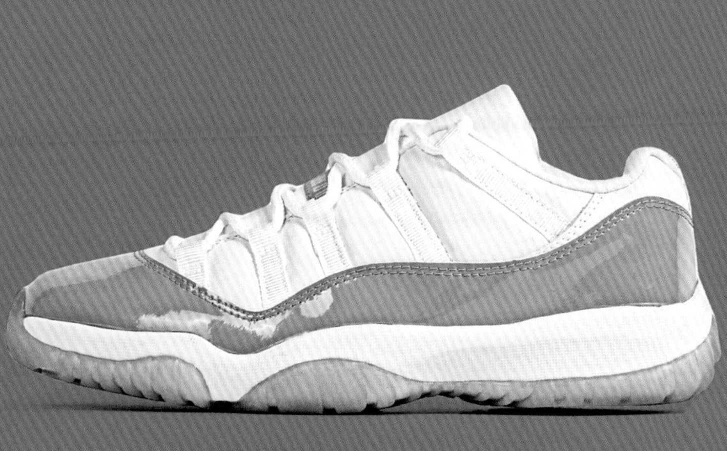

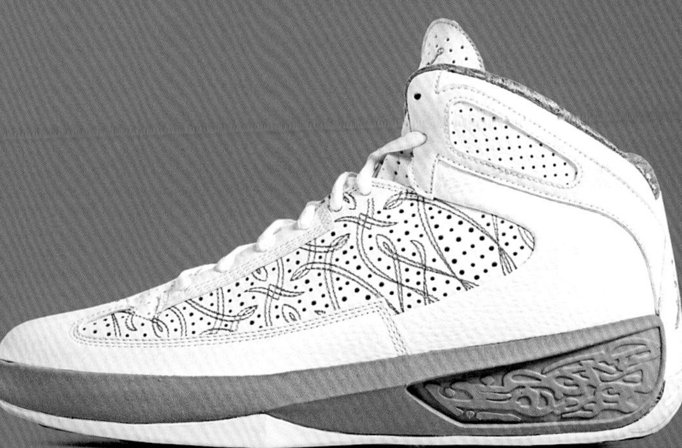

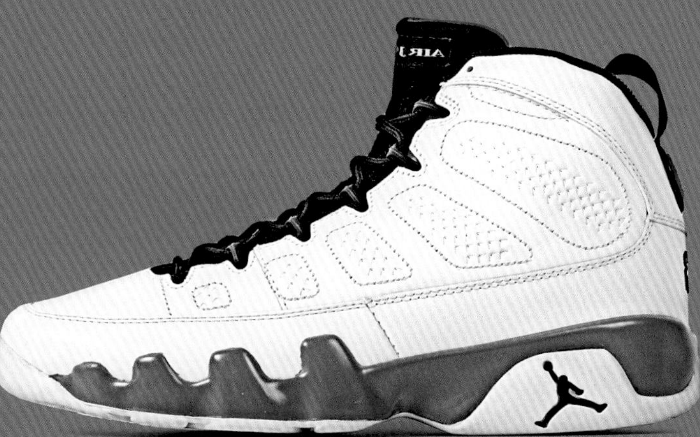

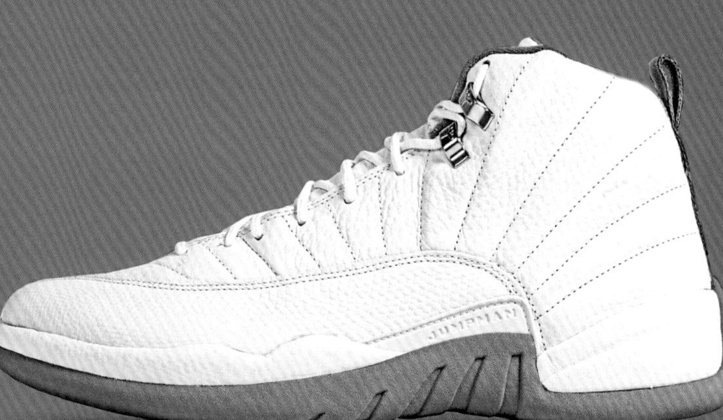

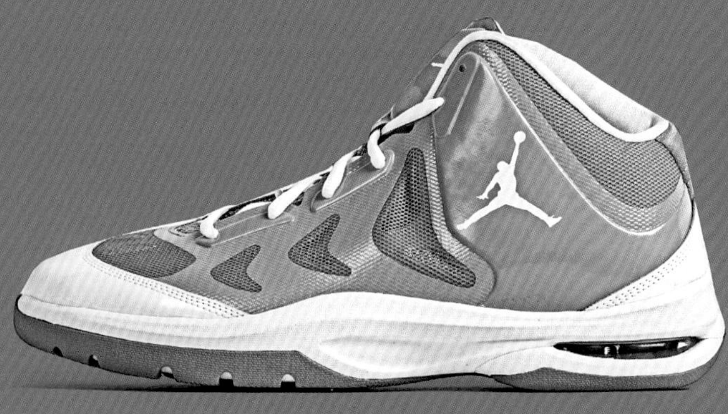

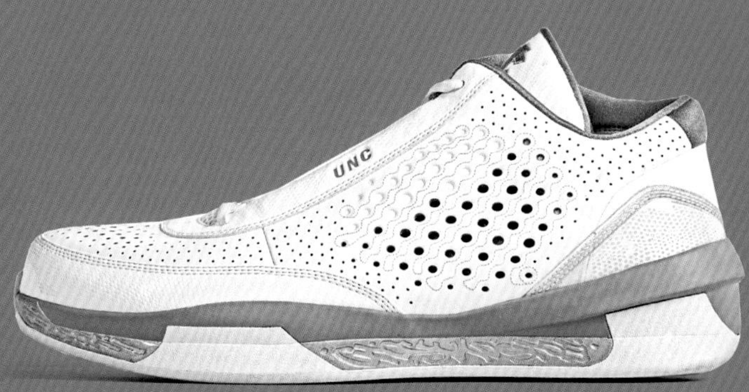
UNC

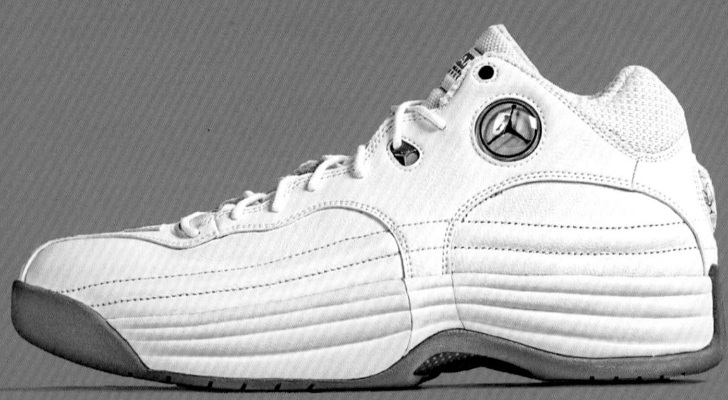

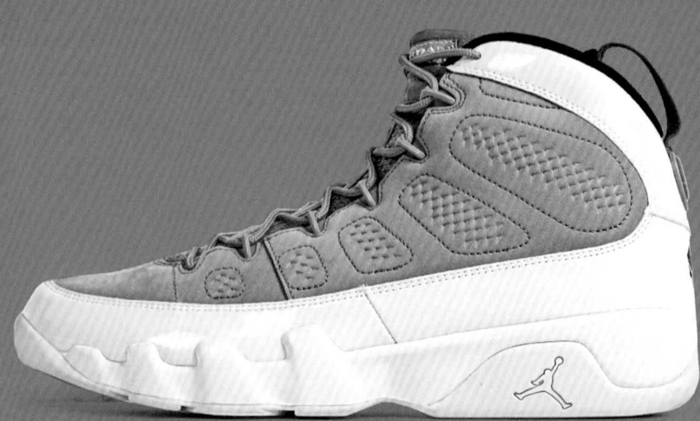

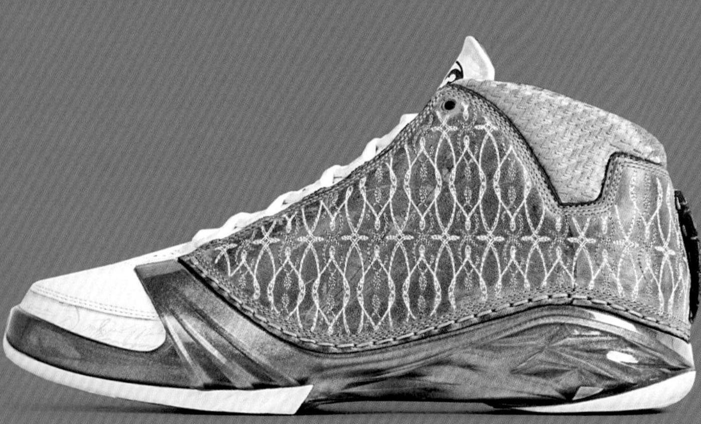

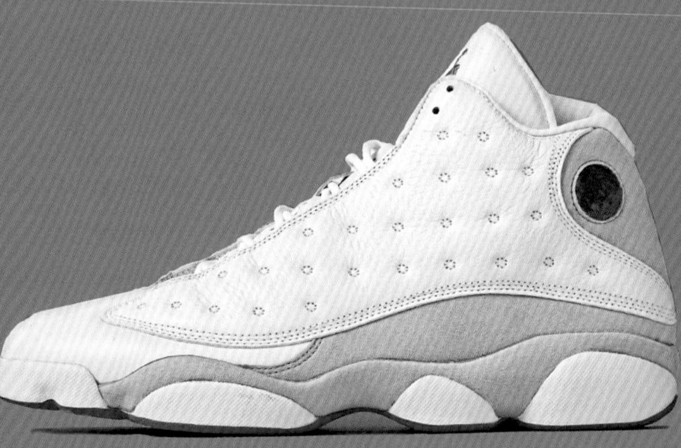

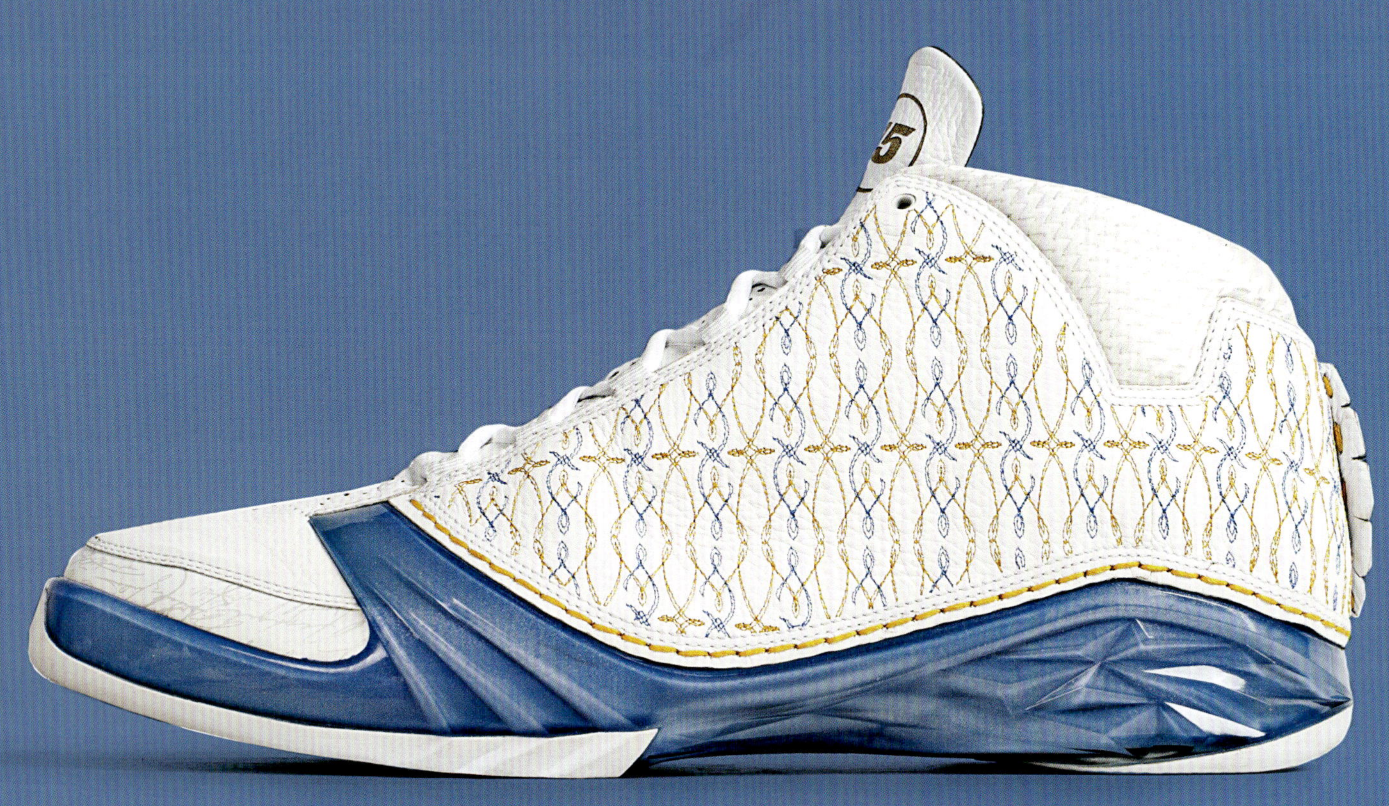

AIR JORDAN XX3 [MELO] PE: The pack, not sold in public, is a player exclusive to Carmelo Anthony. The colorway resembles the home jersey for Denver Nuggets, with a palette of white, yellow and "university blue." Melo's squad number "15" is marked on the left foot's tongue.

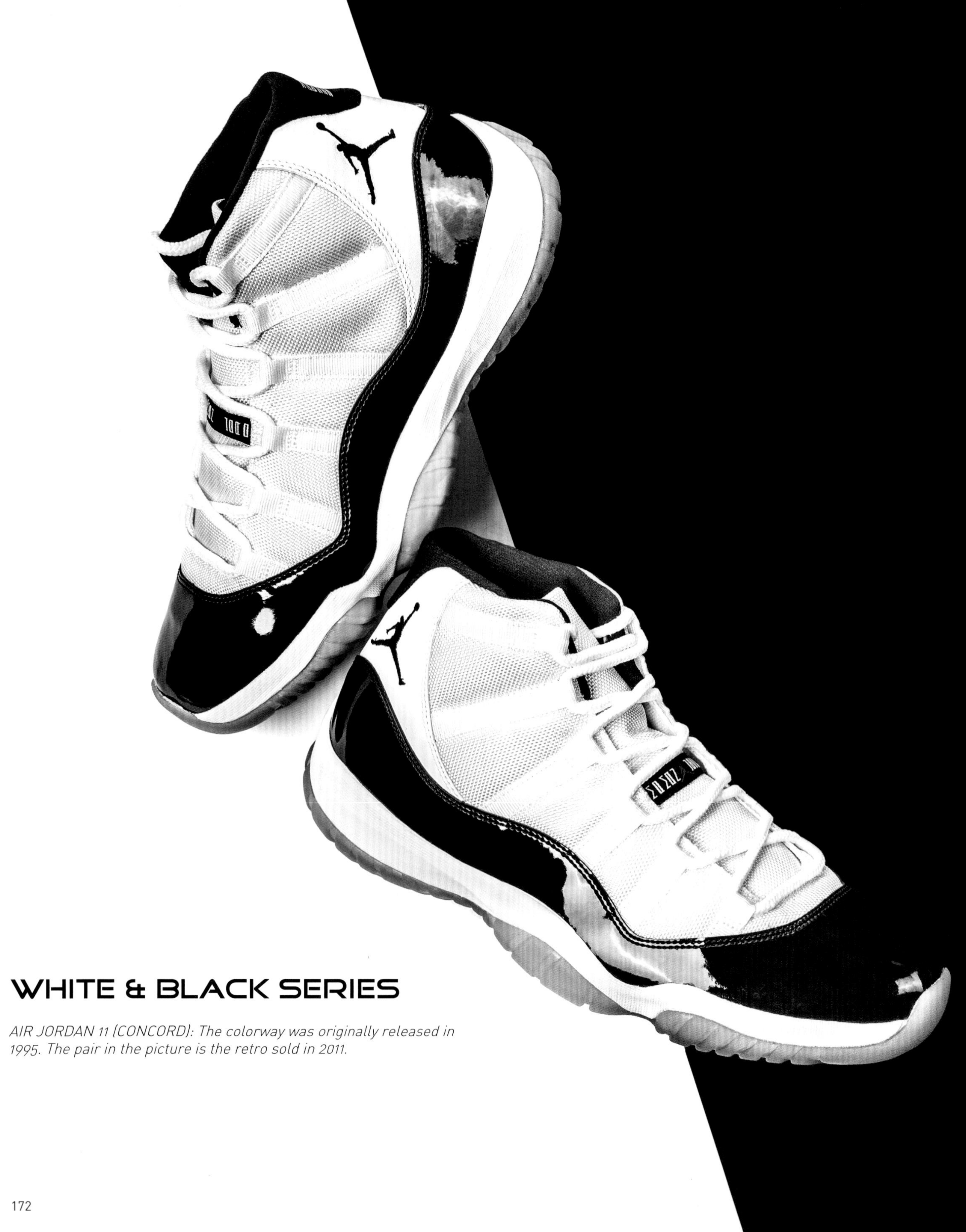

WHITE & BLACK SERIES

AIR JORDAN 11 (CONCORD): The colorway was originally released in 1995. The pair in the picture is the retro sold in 2011.

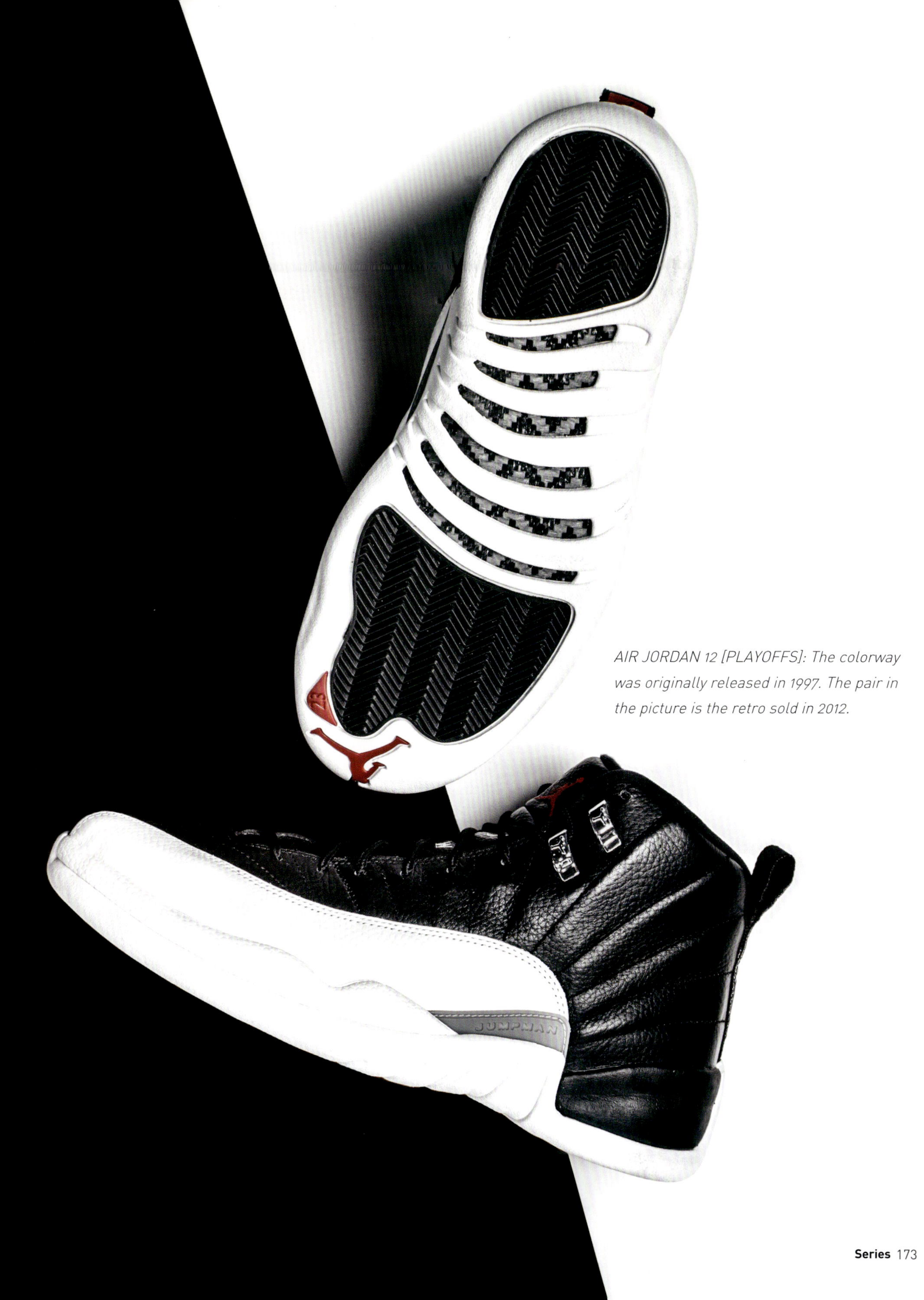

AIR JORDAN 12 [PLAYOFFS]: The colorway was originally released in 1997. The pair in the picture is the retro sold in 2012.

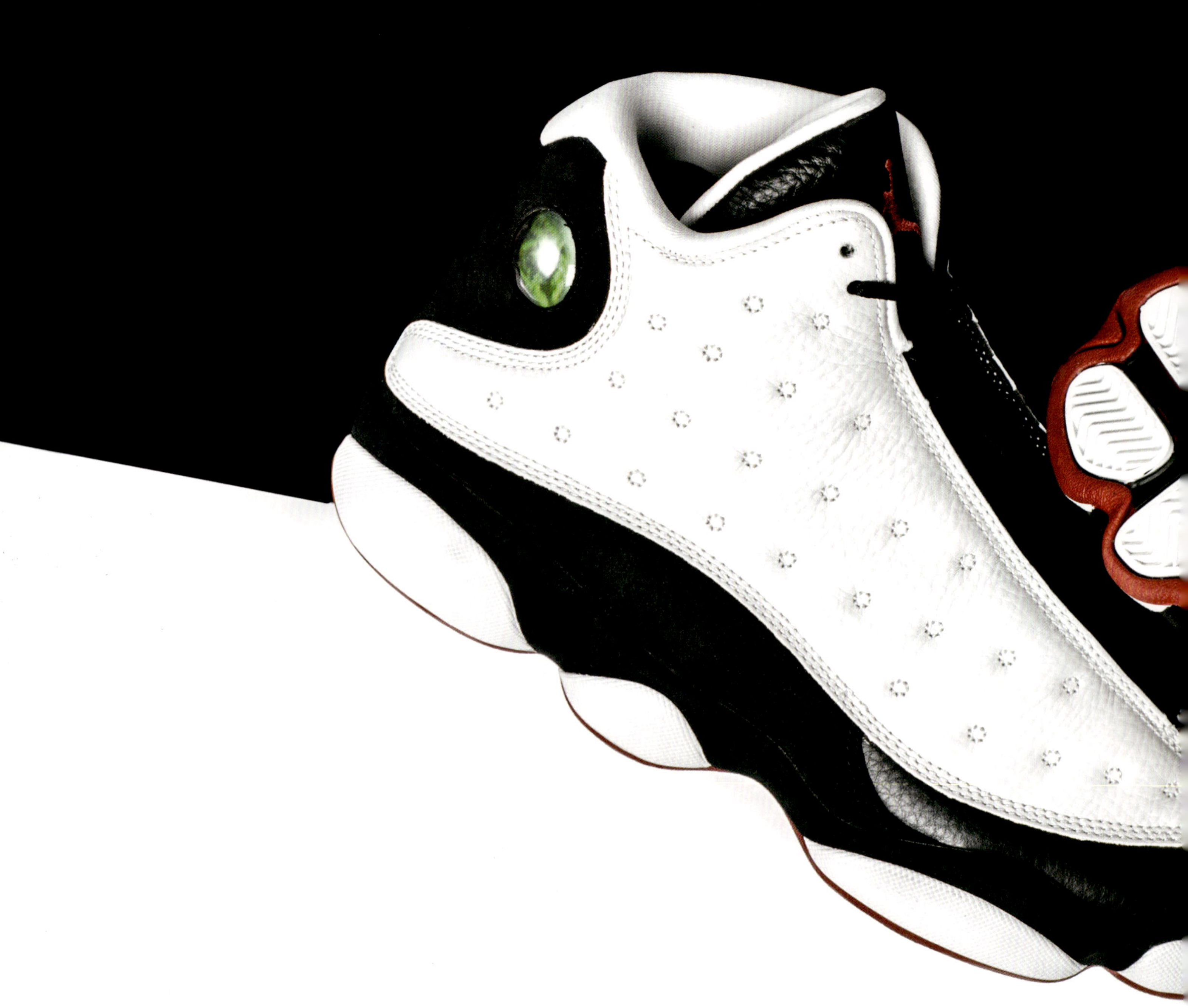

AIR JORDAN 13 [HE GOT GAME]: The colorway was originally released in 1997. The pair in the picture is the retro sold in 2013.

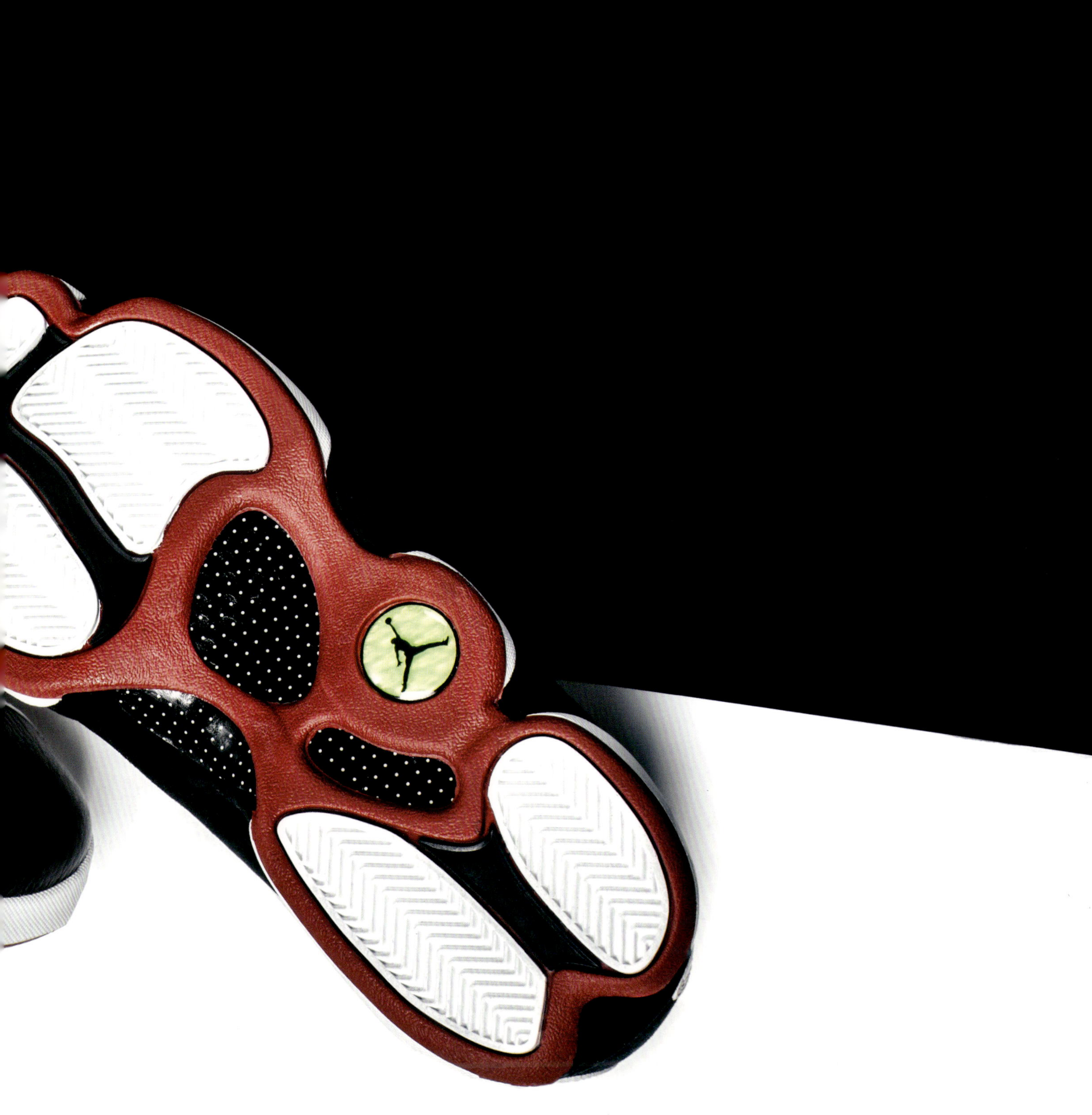

AIR JORDAN 14 [BLACK TOE]: The colorway was originally released in 1998. The pair in the picture is the retro sold in 2014.

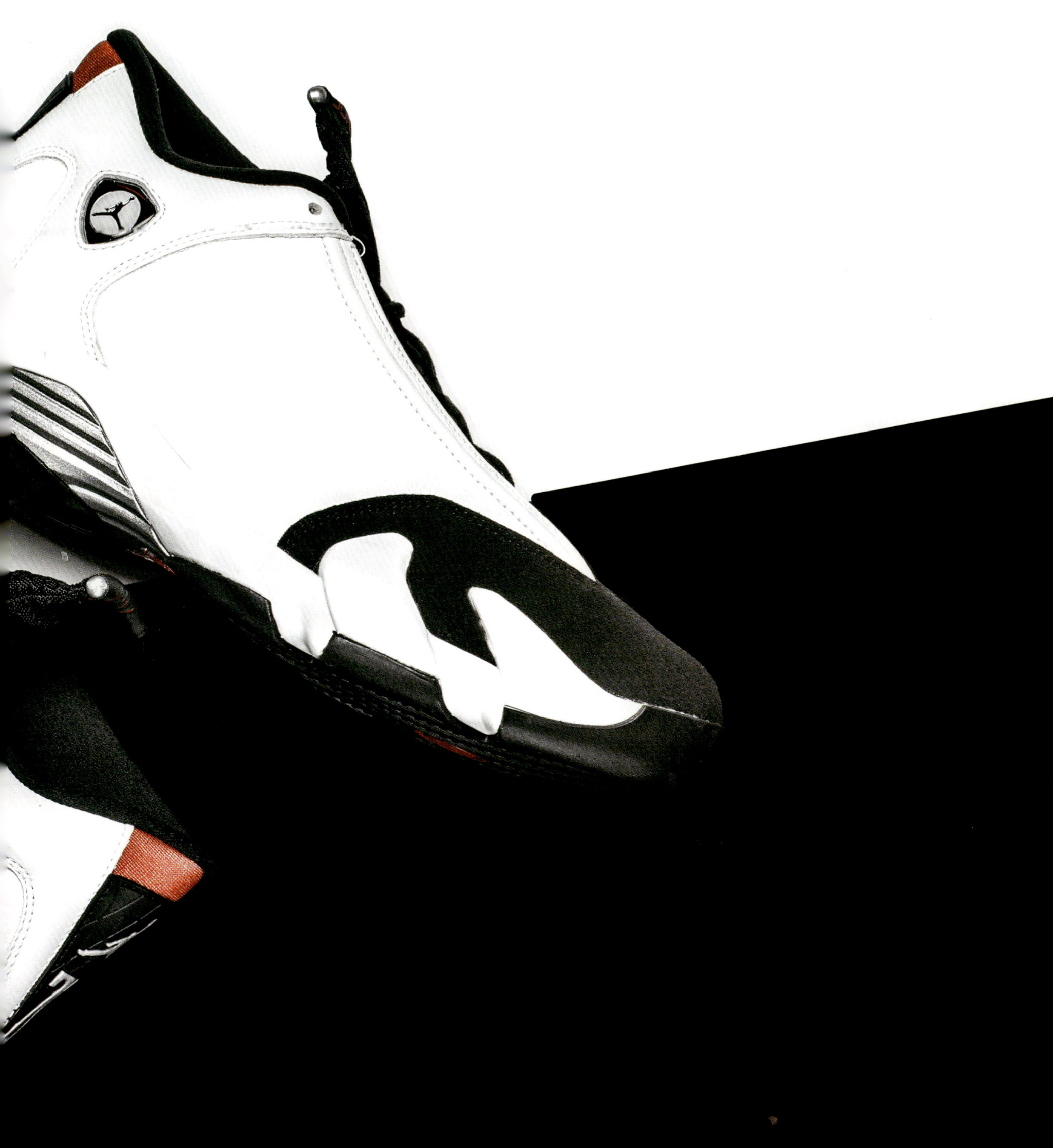

ADIDAS BASKETBALL [BALLIN'DEAD] 2015

In 2015 adidas unveiled its Halloween-themed collection, "Ballin's Dead." The pack, including D Rose 6 Boost, J Wall 2, D Lillard 1 and Crazy 8, features each model with a cartoon brain print and glow-in-the-dark outsoles.

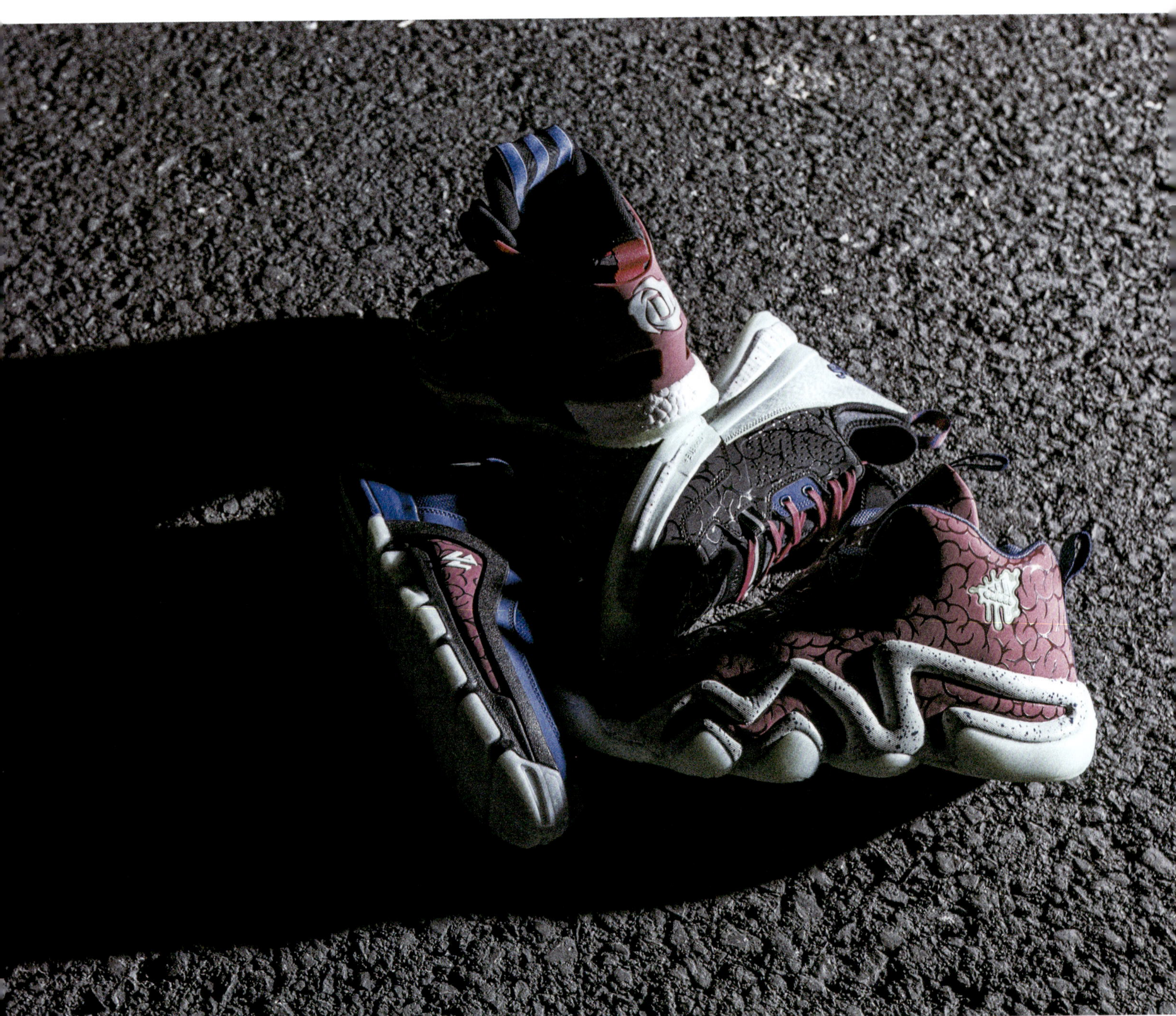

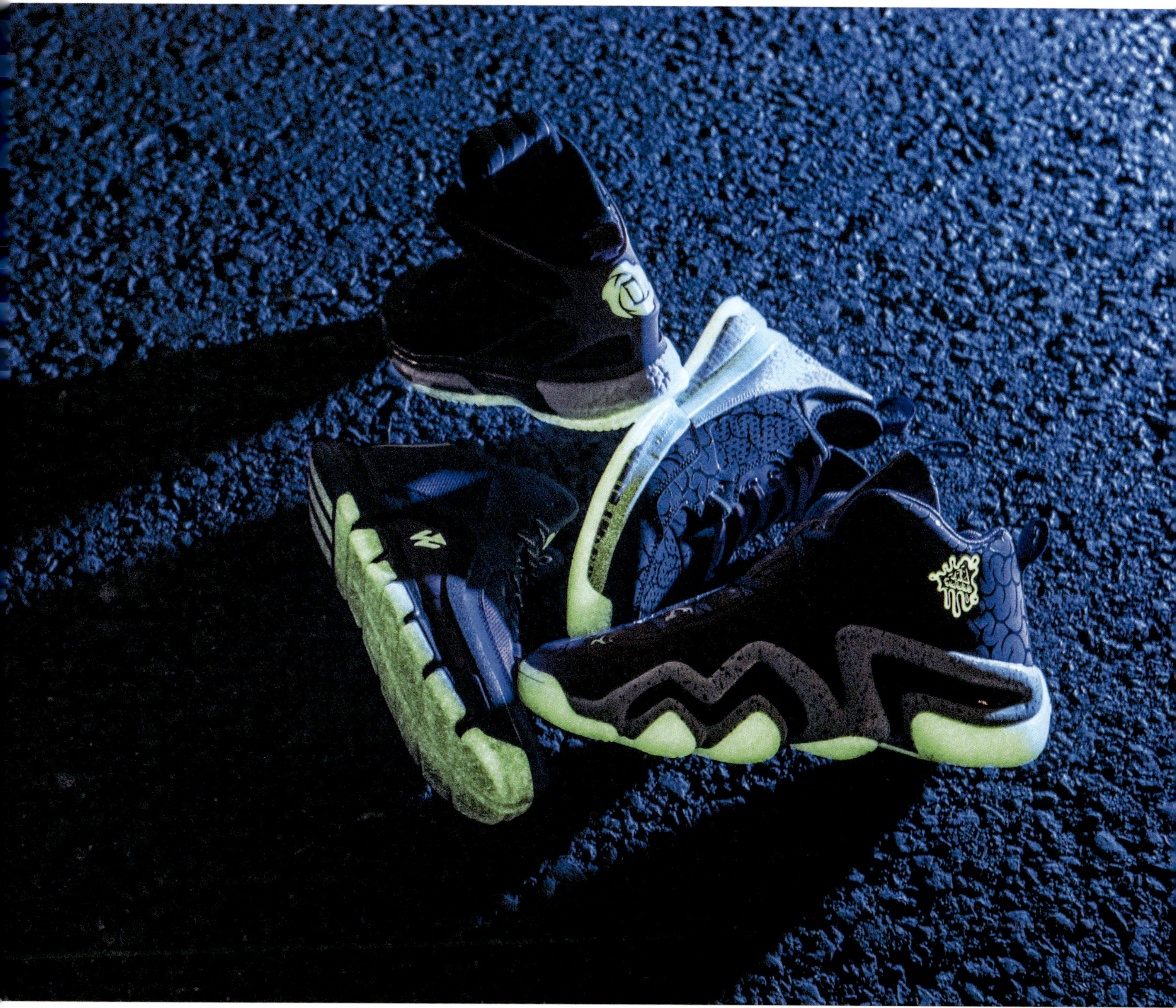

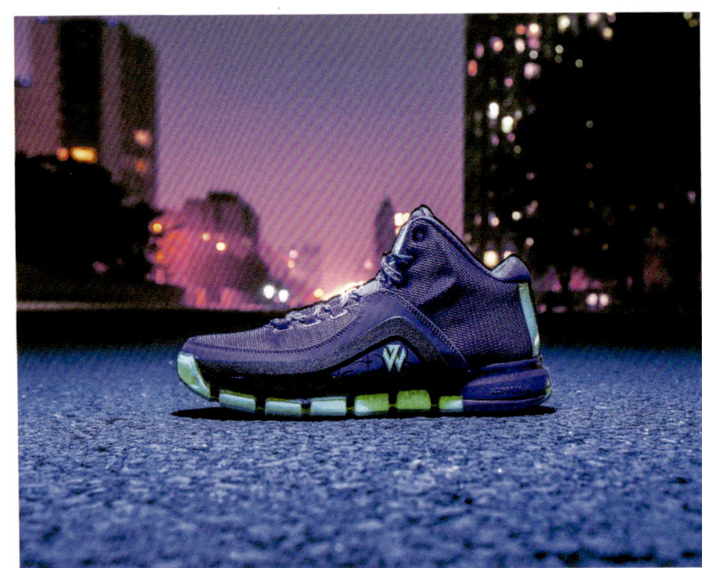

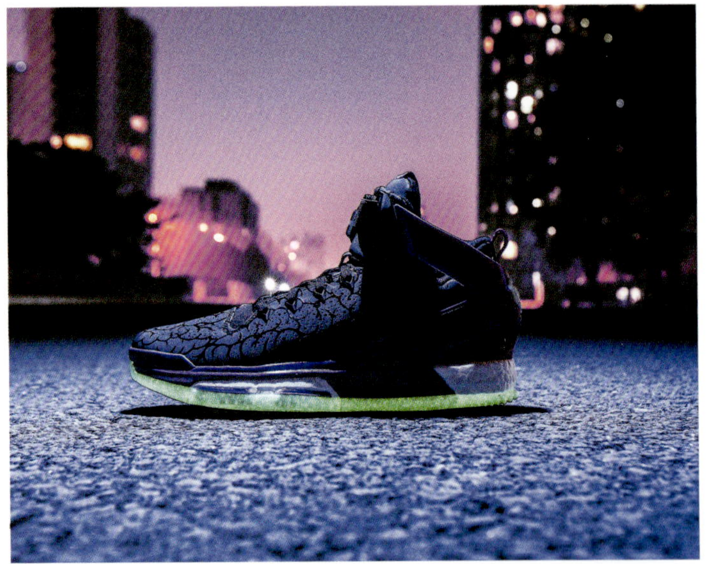

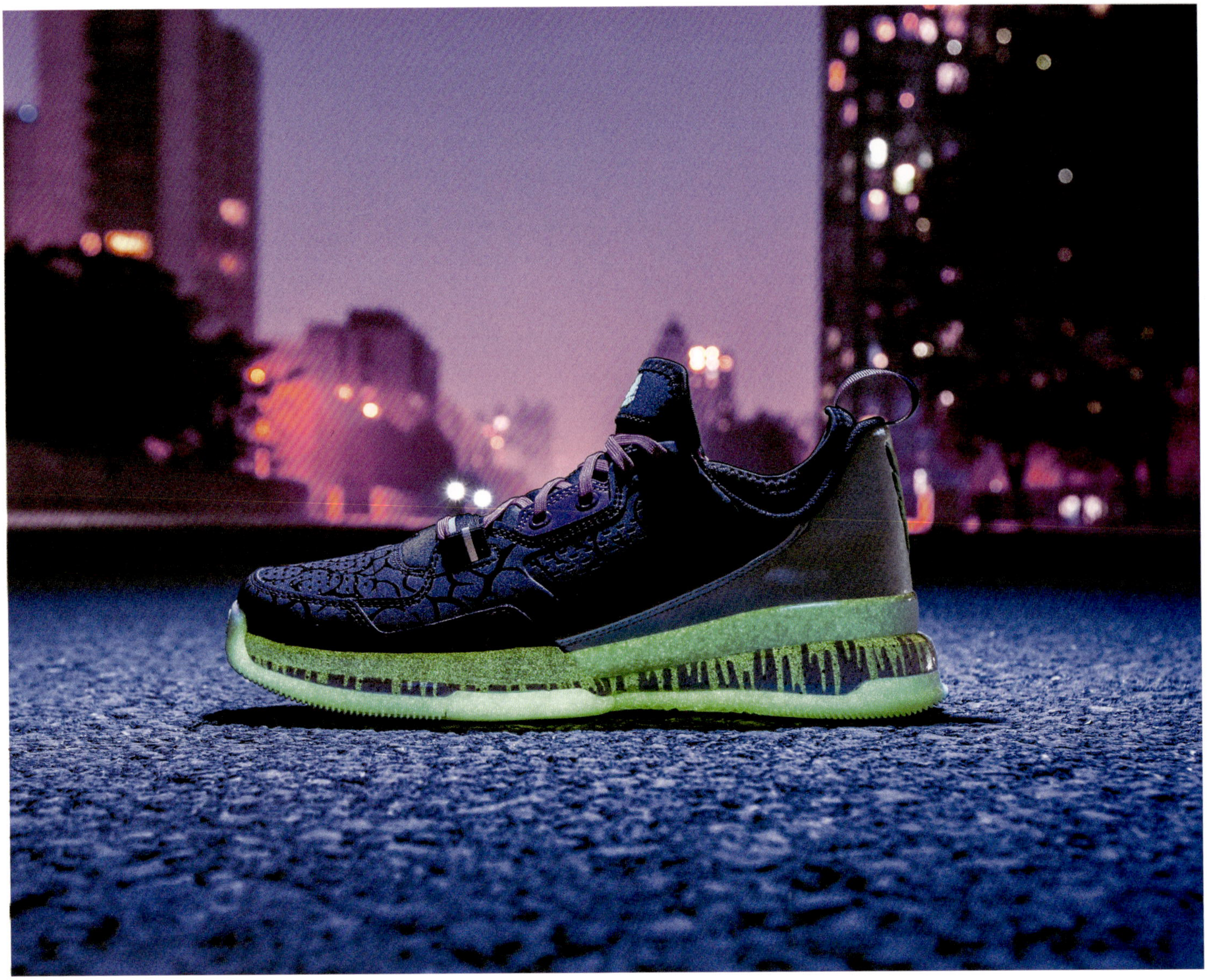

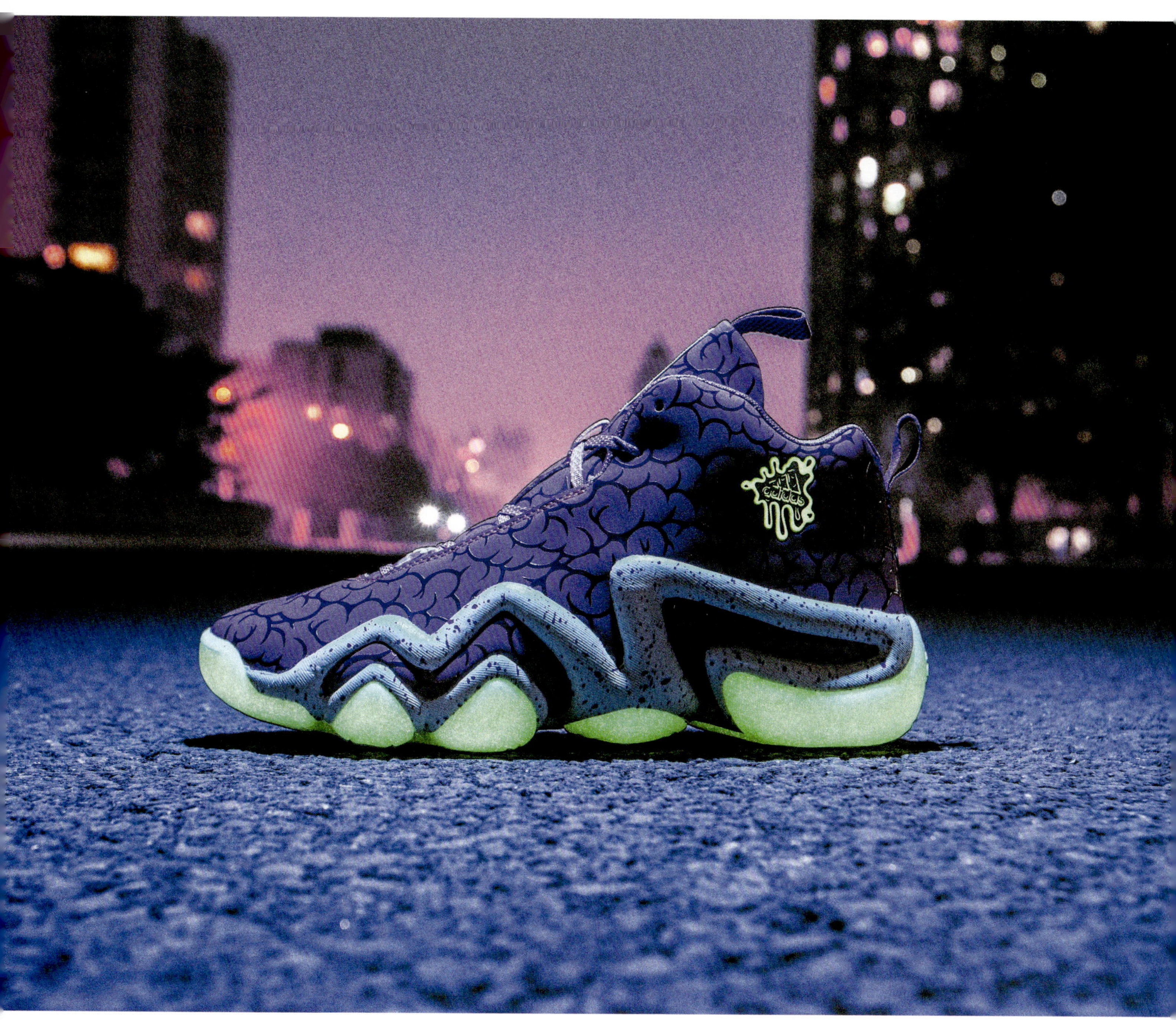
adidas

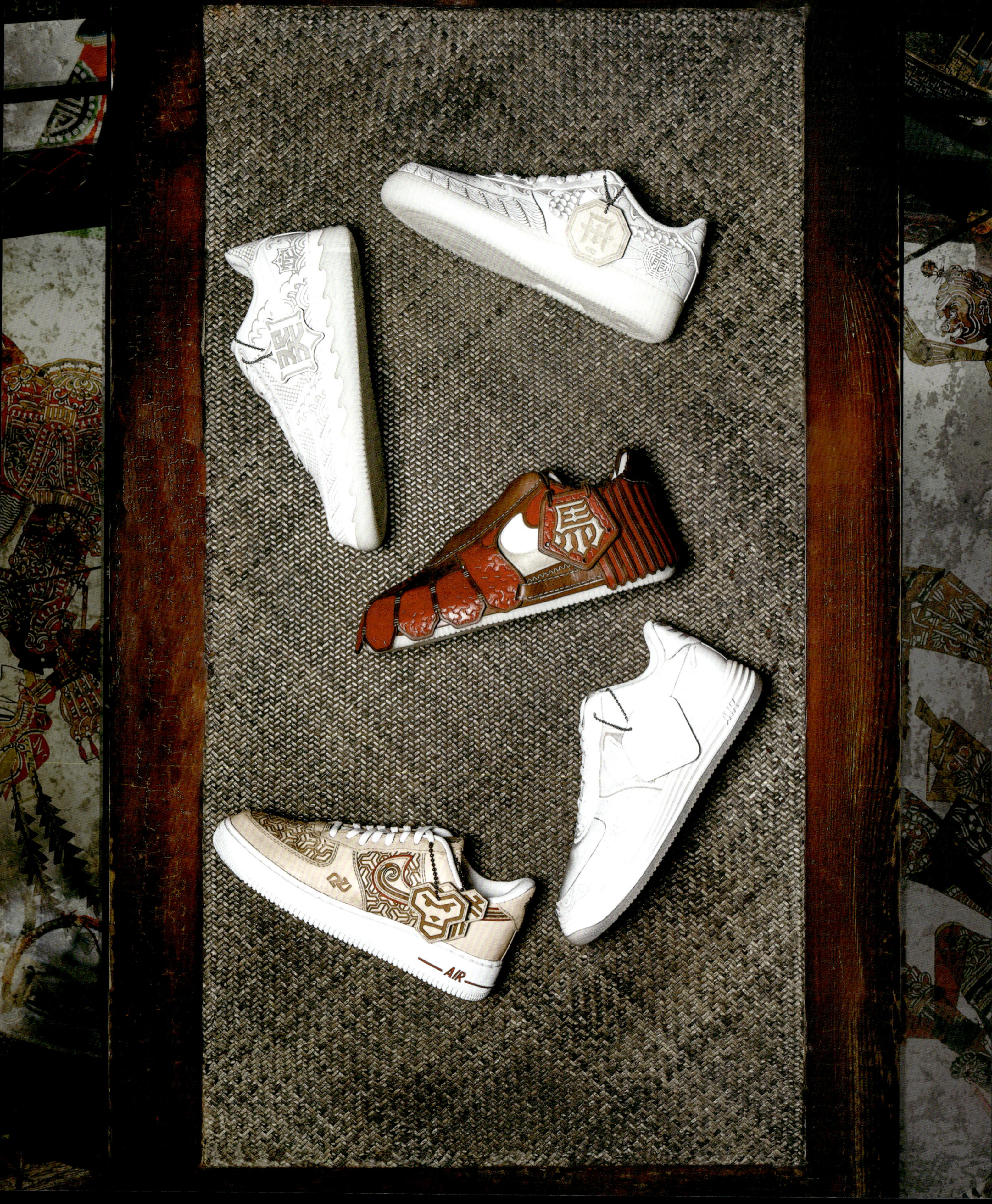
AIR

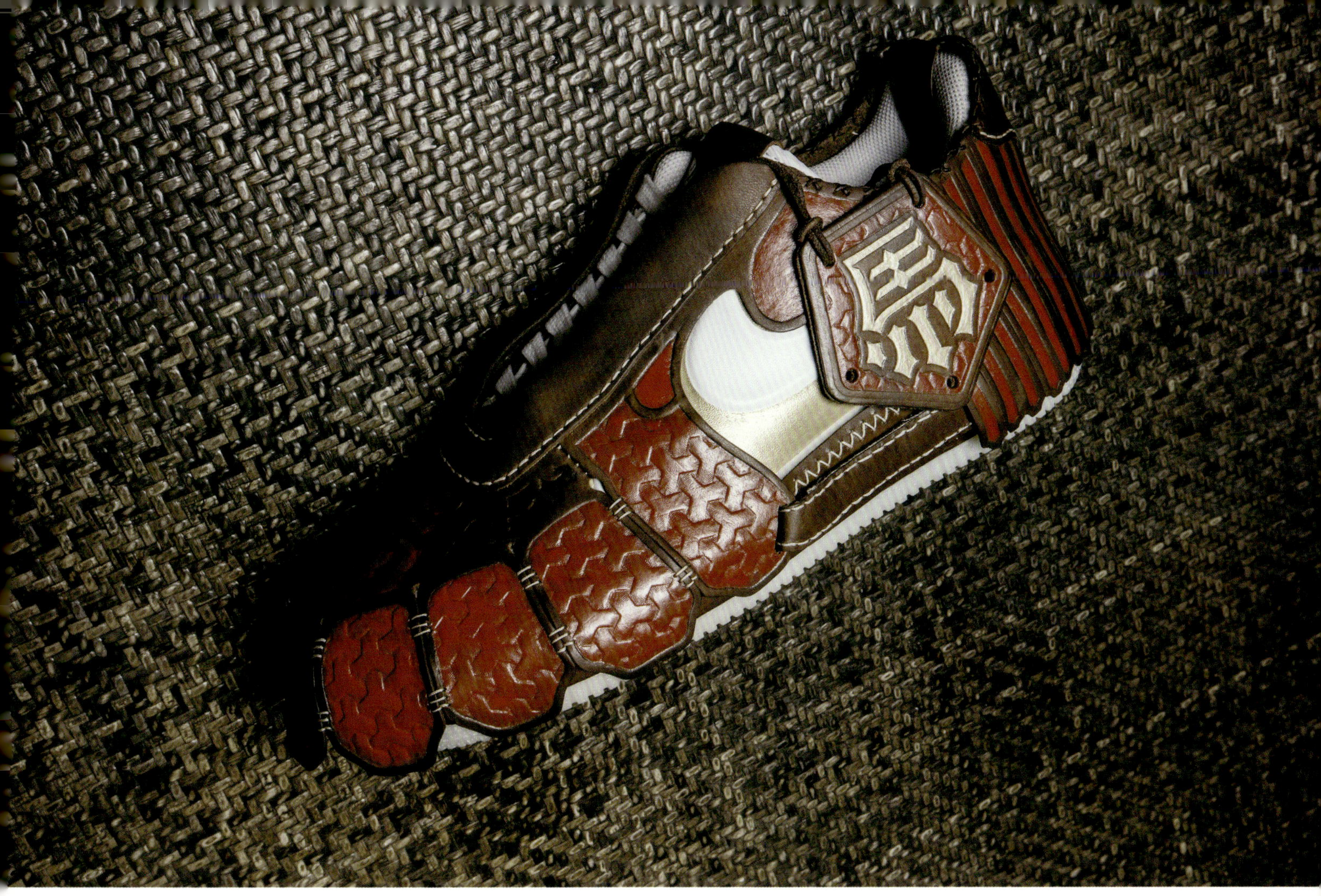

NIKE AIR FORCE 1

Based on different editions of Nike Air Force 1 and mingled with zodiac elements, the zodiac custom sneakers series (2012-2016) was brought alive by Chinese designer Zhijun Wang.

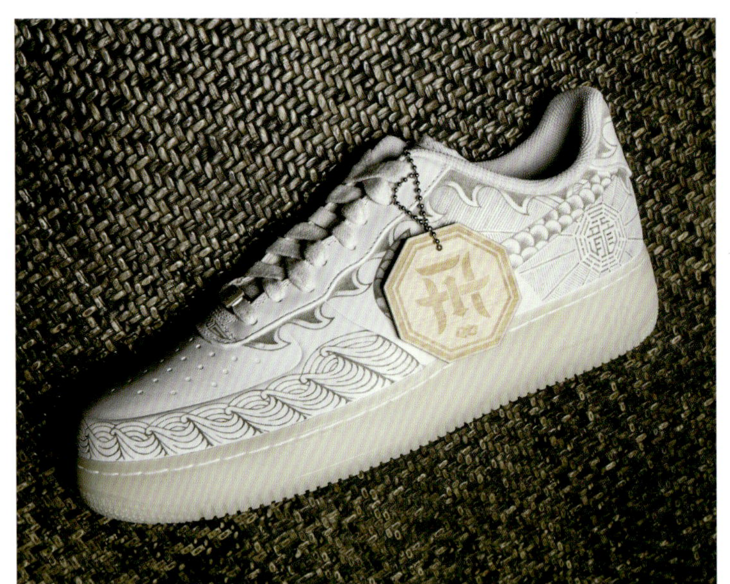

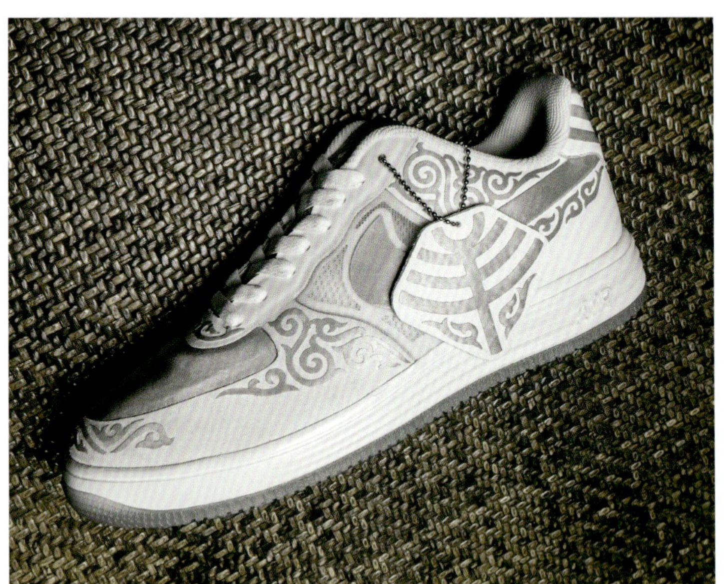

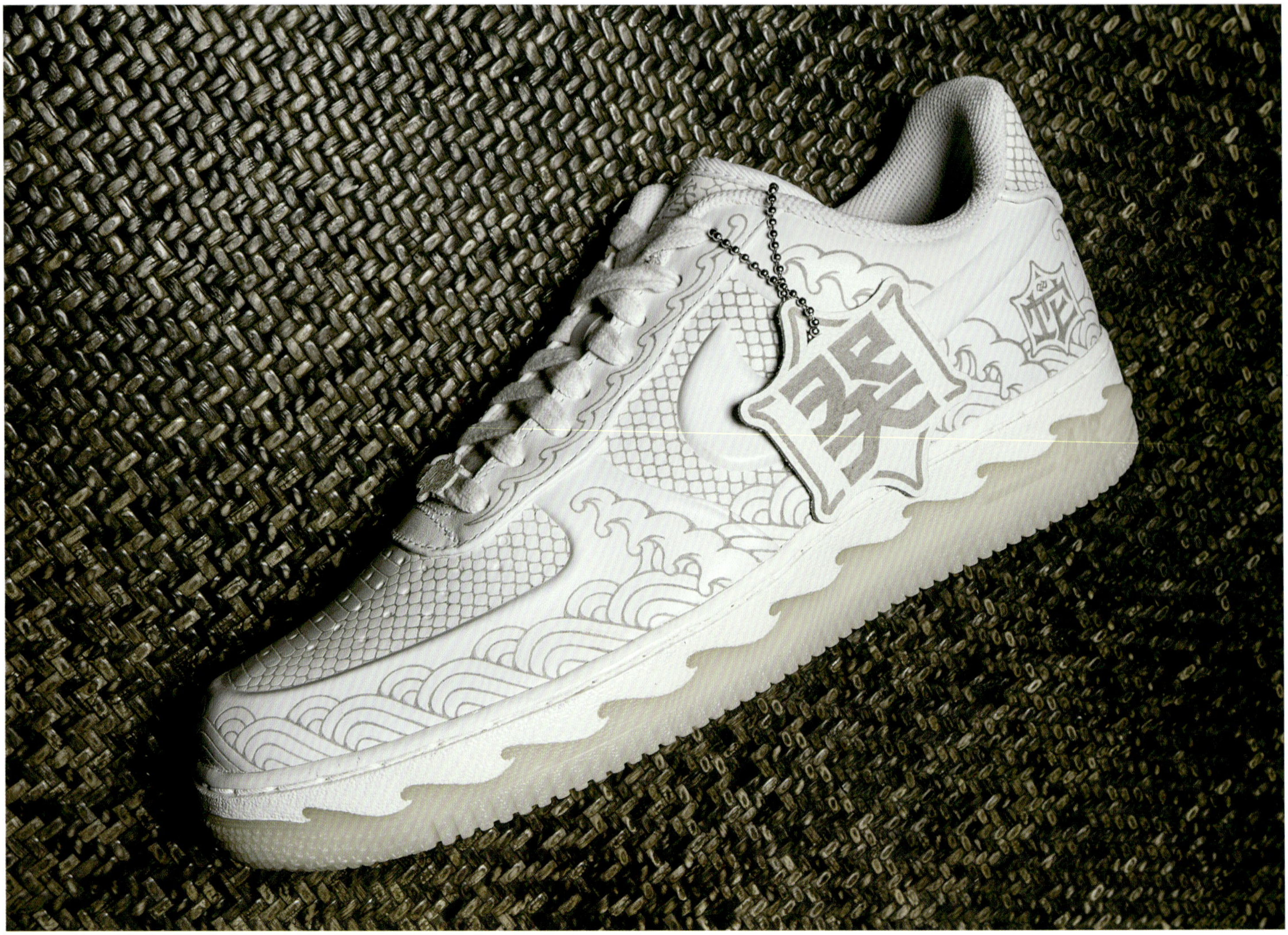

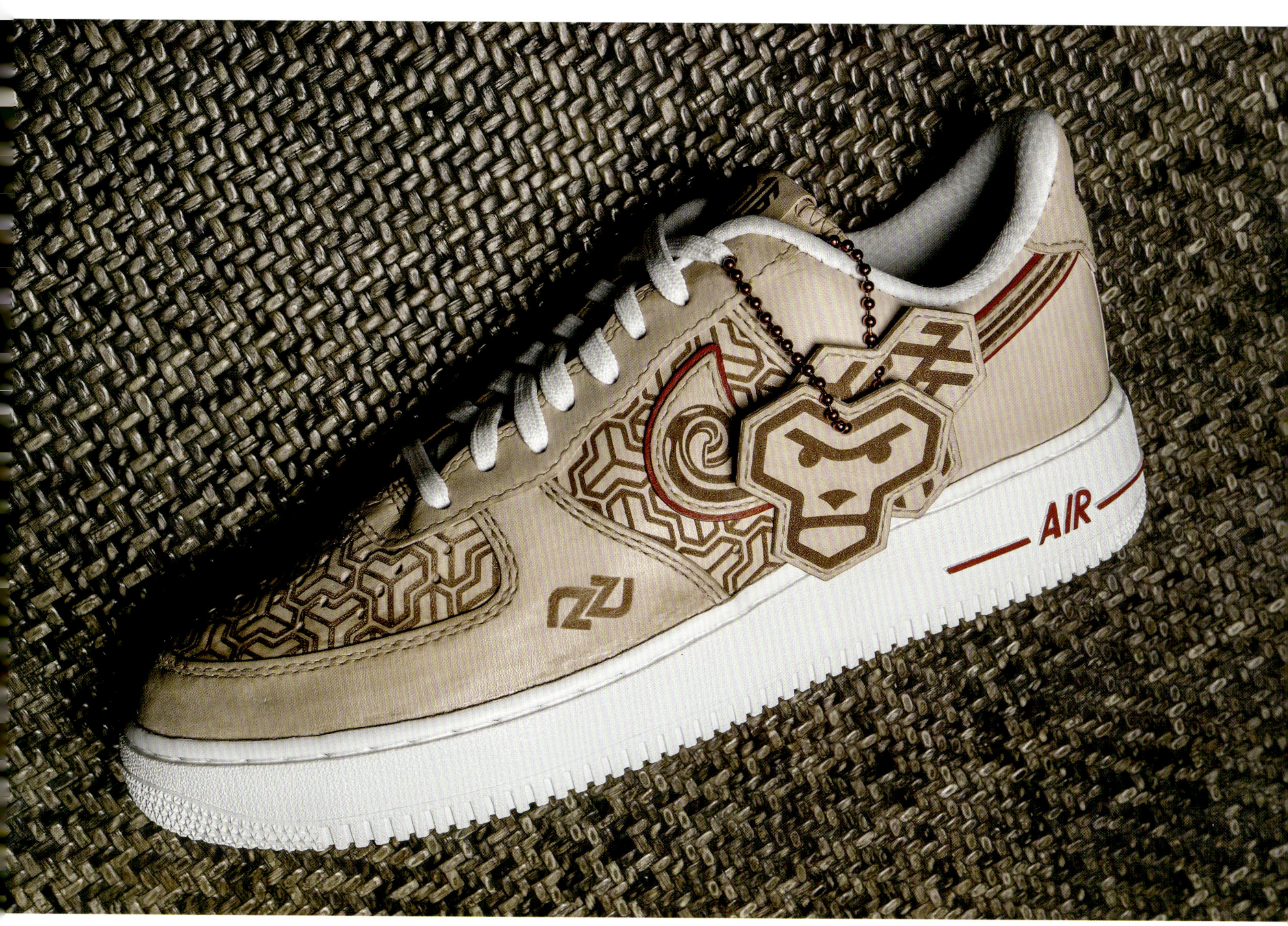
AIR

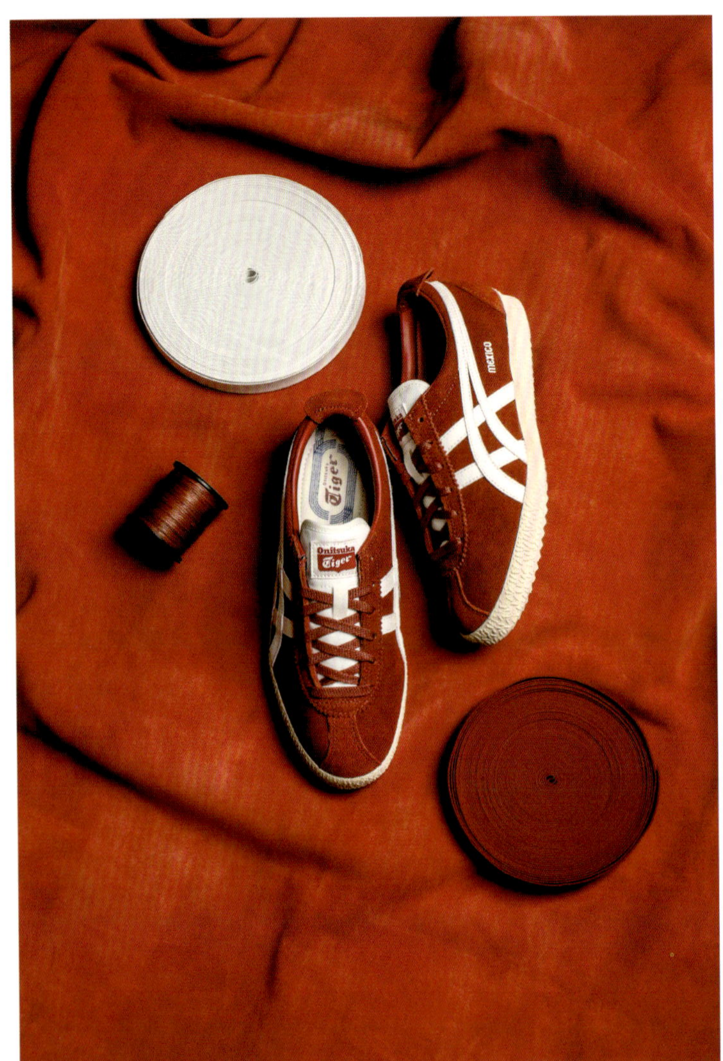

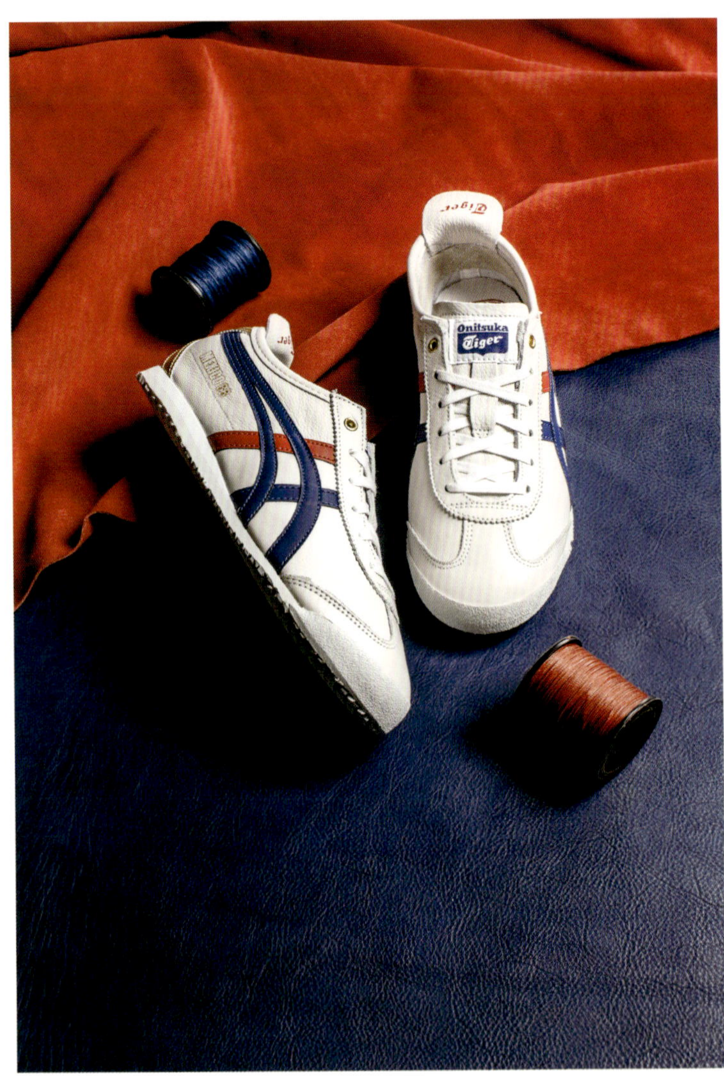

ONITSUKA TIGER [50TH ANNIVERSARY]

To mark the 50th anniversary of its iconic stripes logo, Onitsuka Tiger released a commemorative collection, including Mexico 66, Mexico Delegation and Mexico 66 Saeculi.

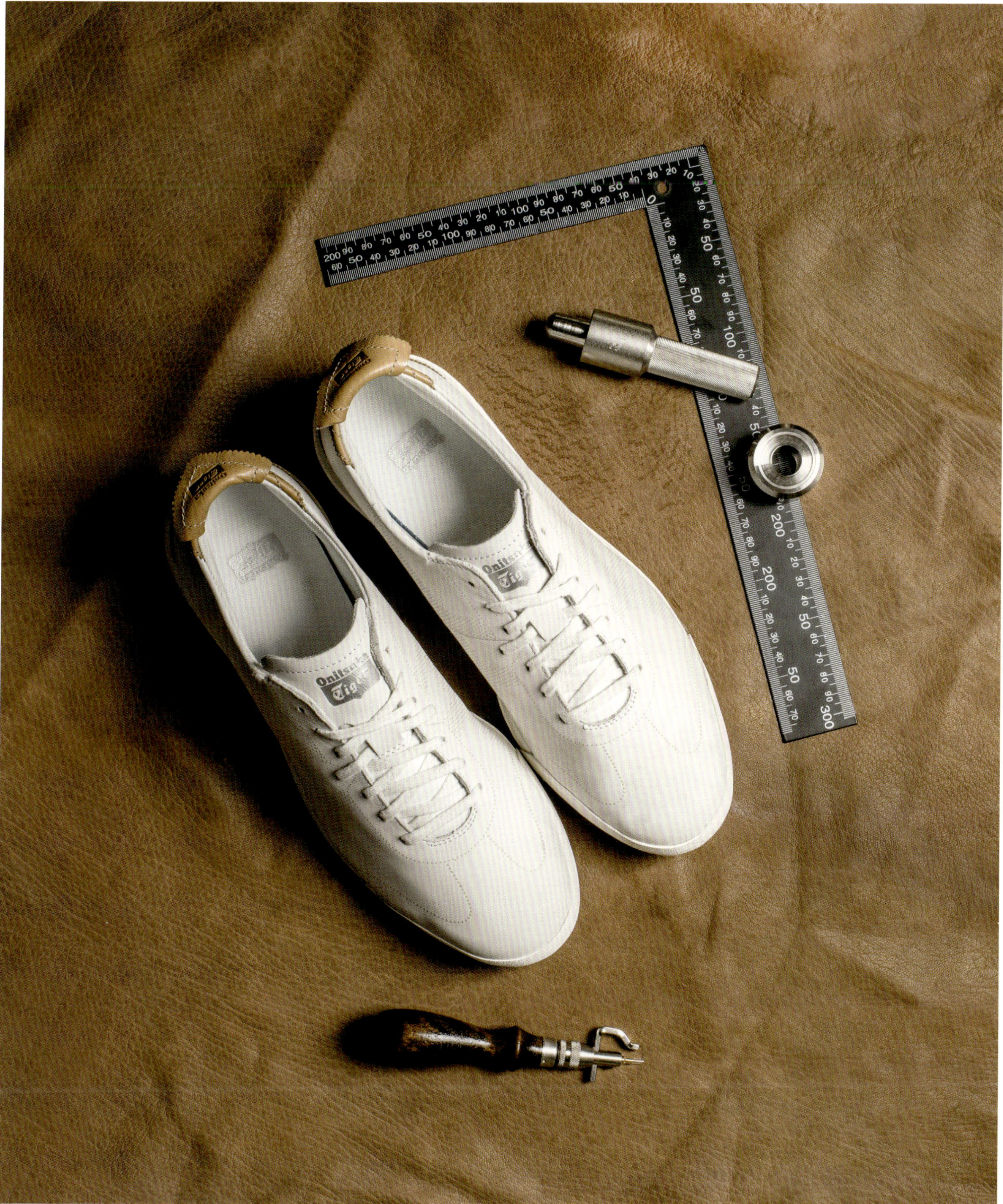
Onitsuka

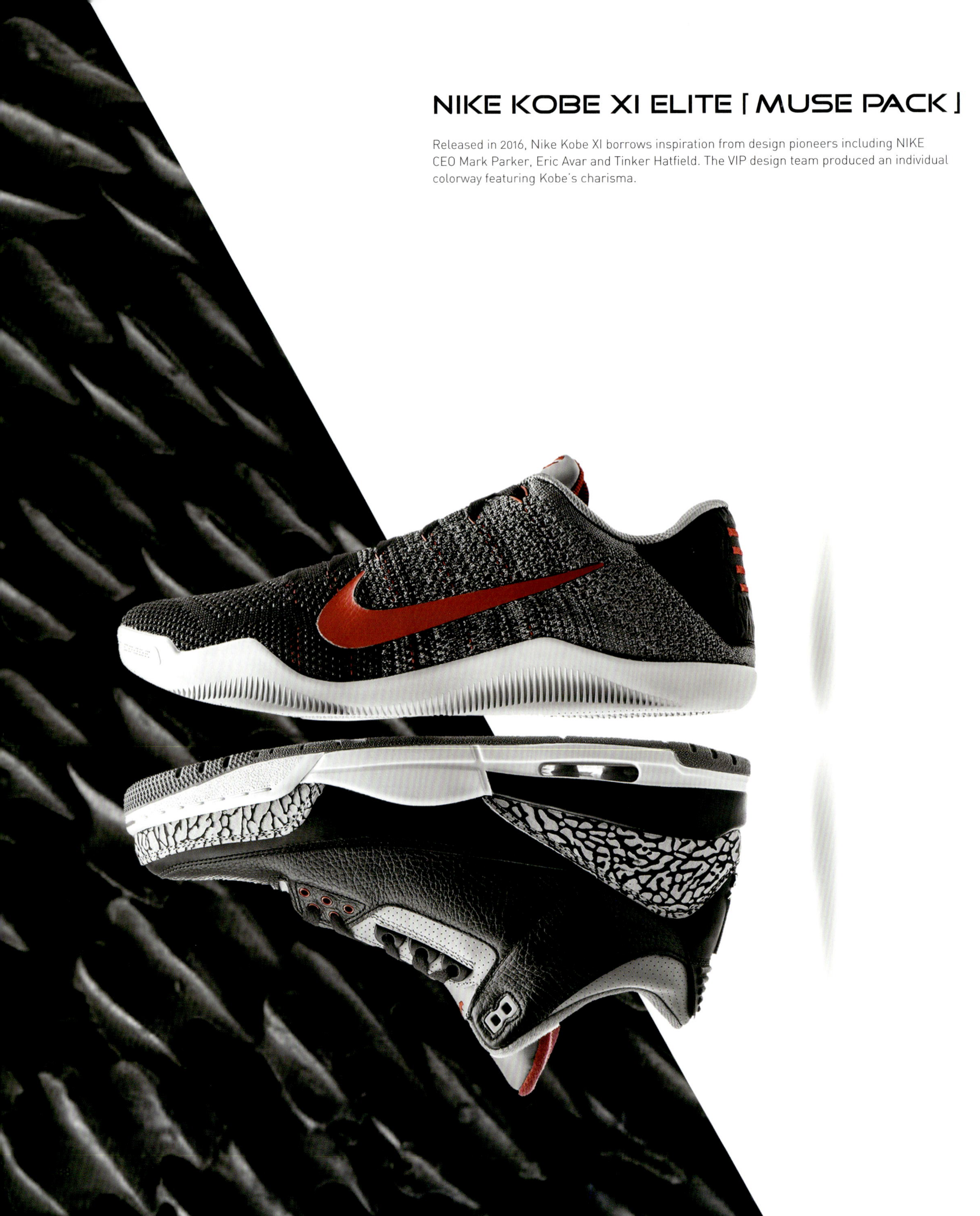

NIKE KOBE XI ELITE [MUSE PACK]

Released in 2016, Nike Kobe XI borrows inspiration from design pioneers including NIKE CEO Mark Parker, Eric Avar and Tinker Hatfield. The VIP design team produced an individual colorway featuring Kobe's charisma.

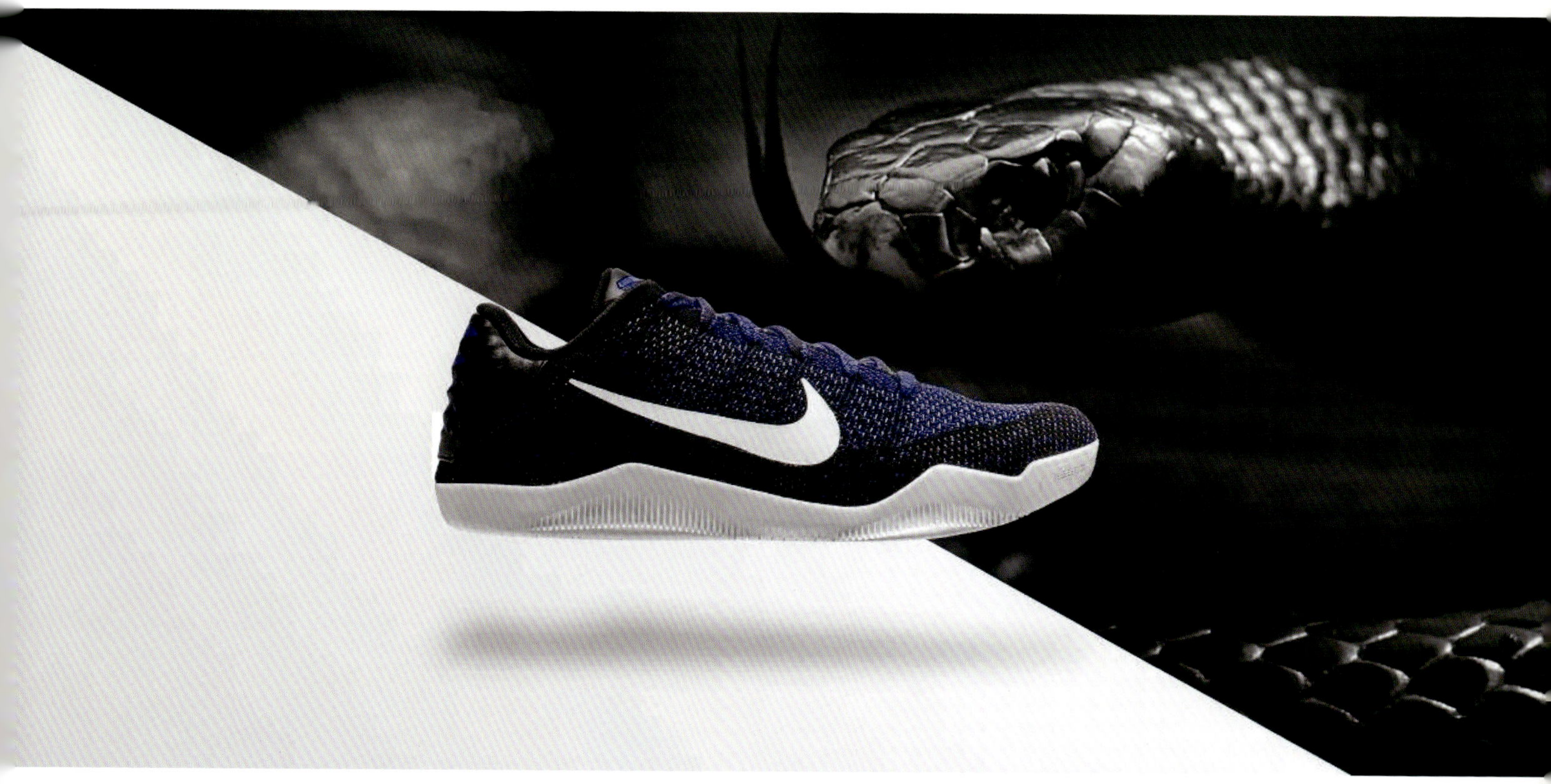

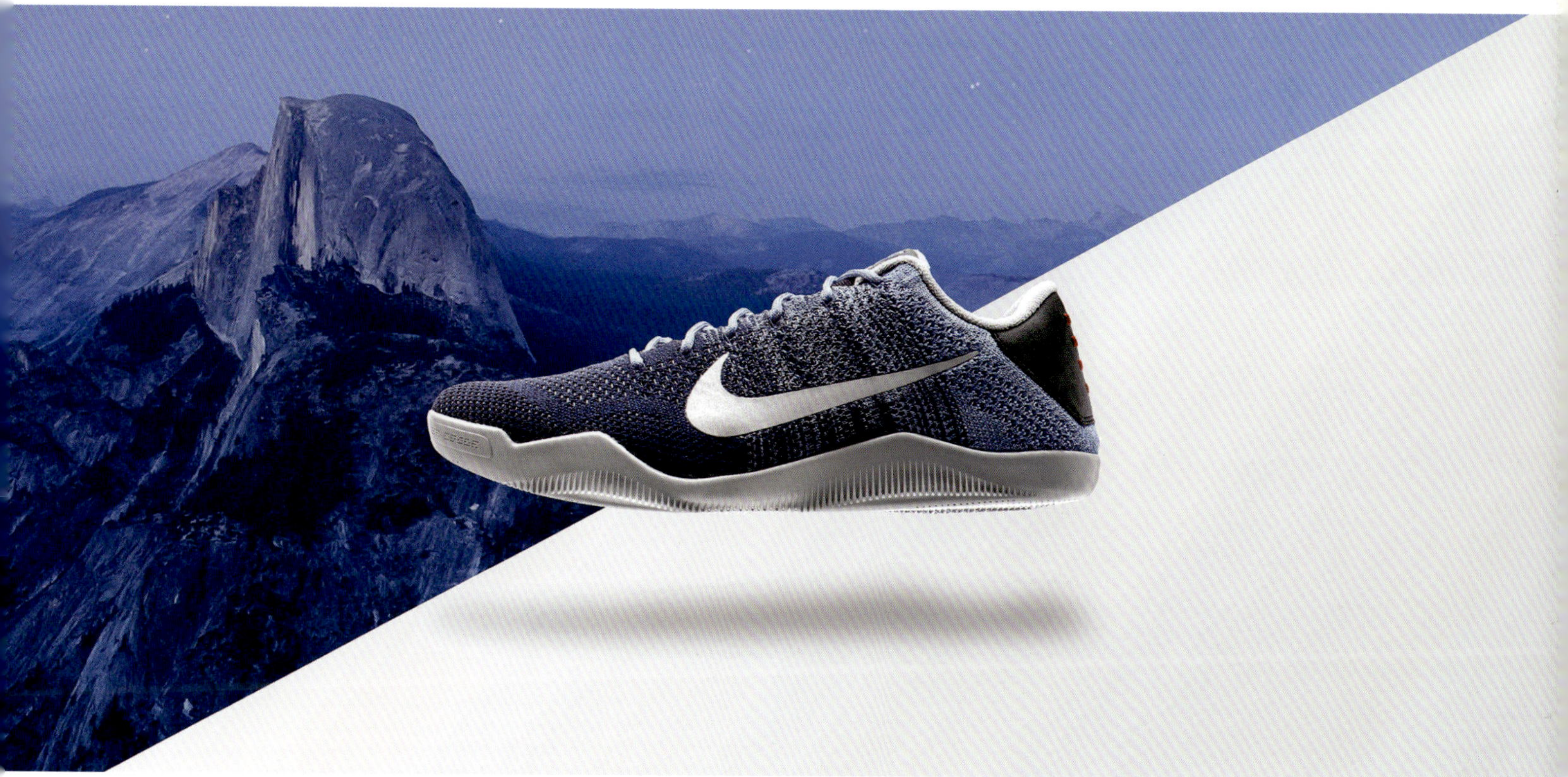

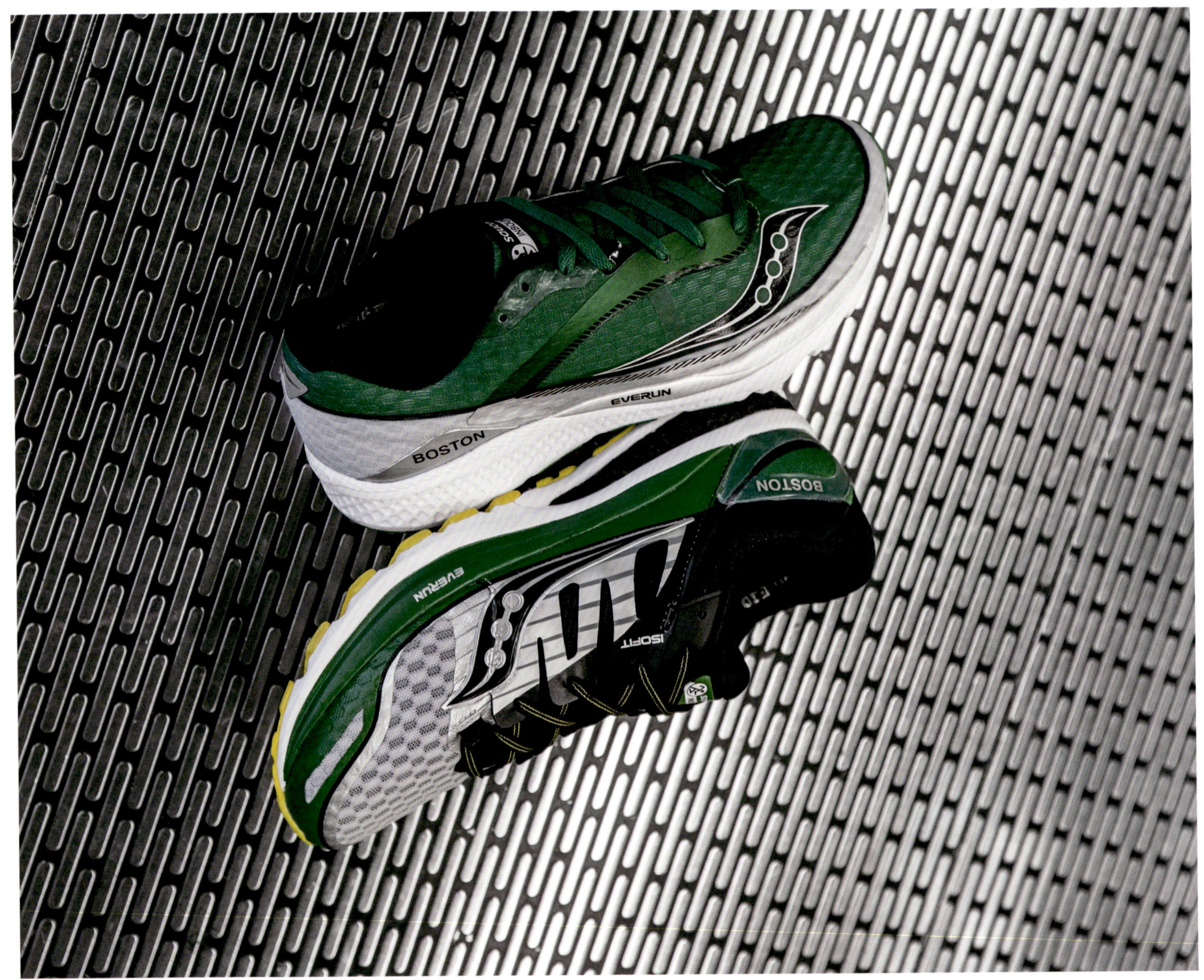

SAUCONY [BOSTON PACK]

To celebrate the 120th Boston Marathon in 2016, Saucony unveiled its special edition of two running shoes, TRIUMPH ISO 2 and KINVARA 7. Only 36 pairs were released in China.

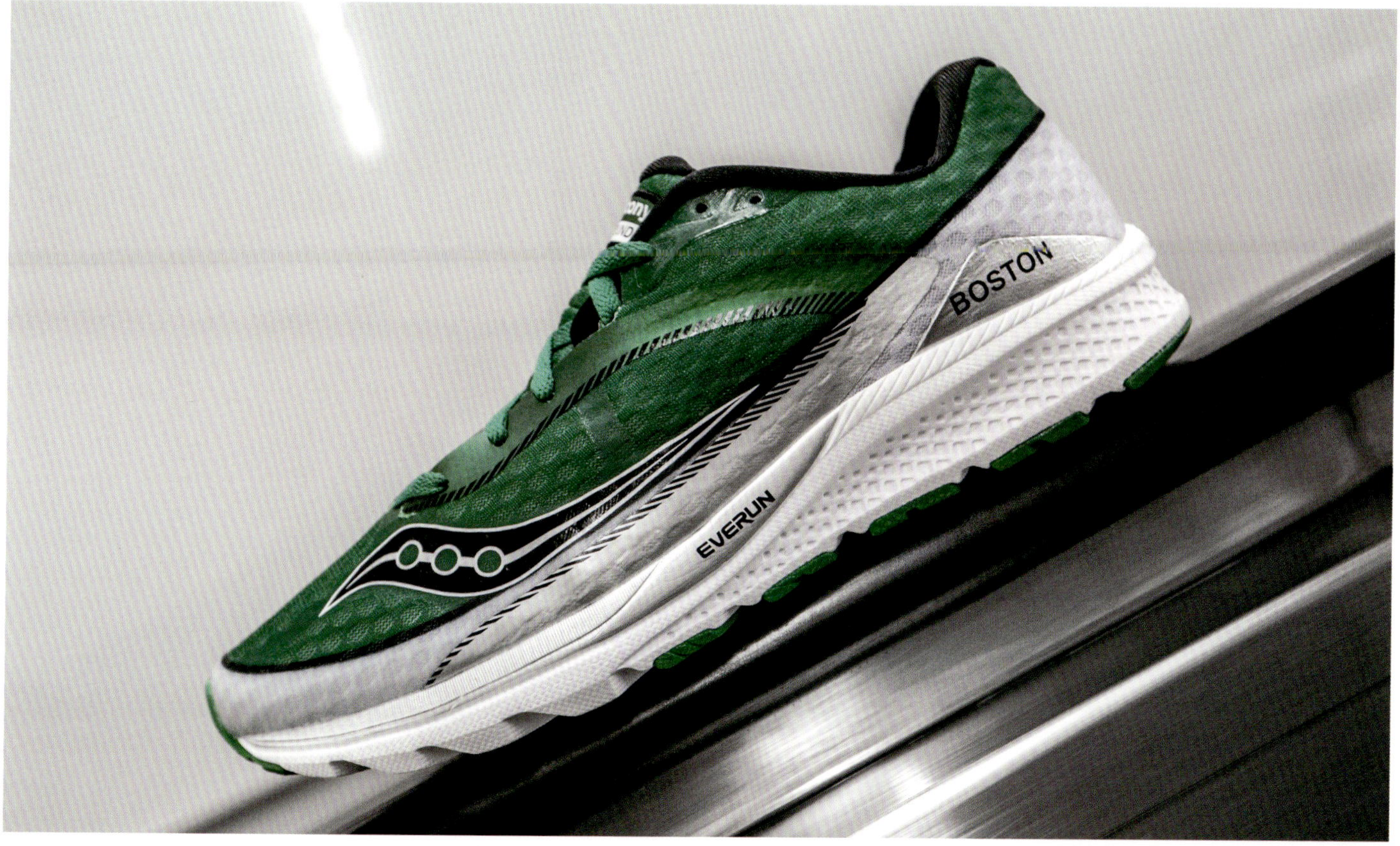
BOSTON
EVERUN

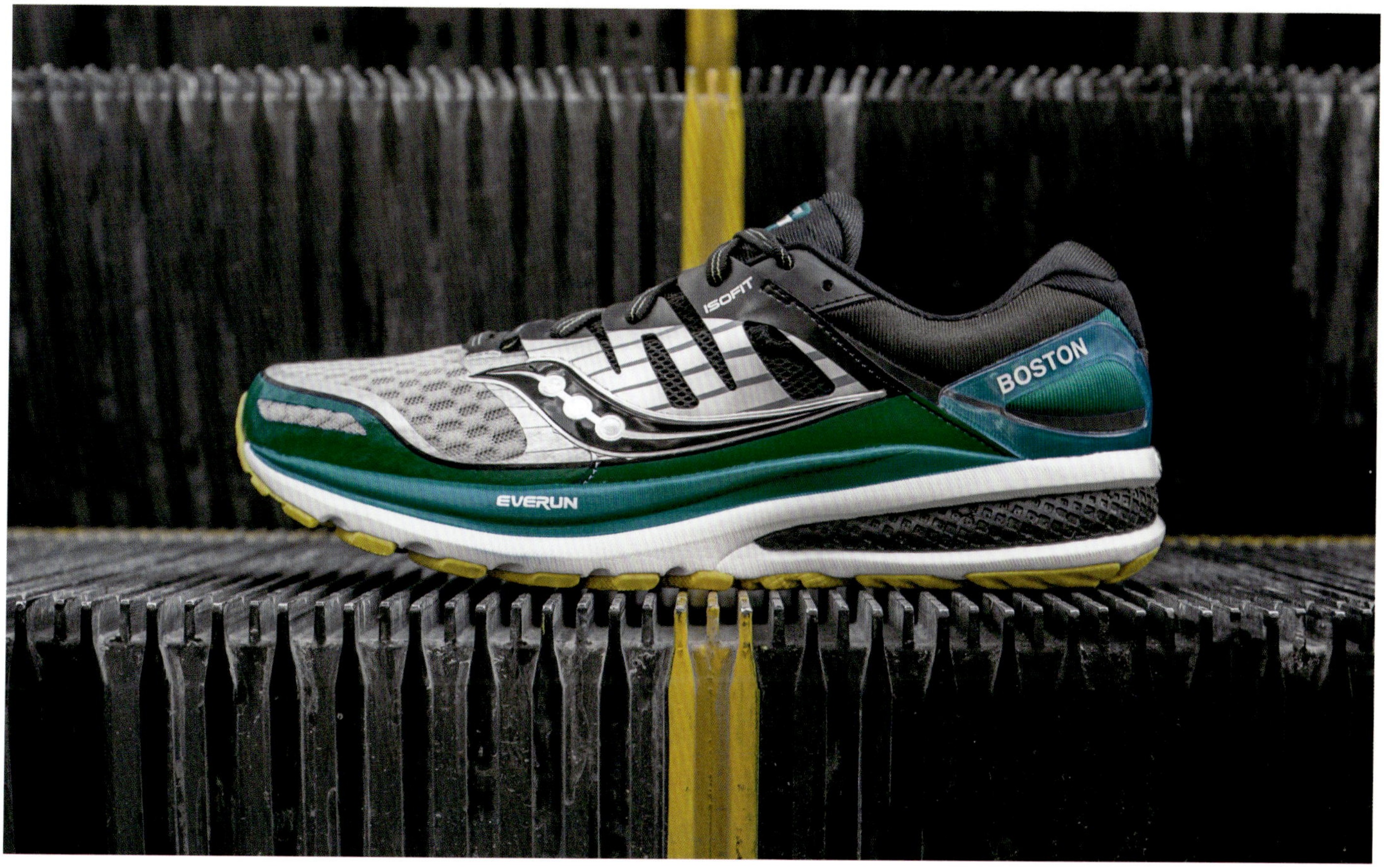
ISOFIT
BOSTON
EVERUN

REMARKABLE SNEAKERS: SHOTS, STORIES AND DETAILS

Author: Ammo Dong
Commissioning Editors: Guo Guang, Mang Yu, Chen Hao
English Editor: Jenny Qiu
Copy Editor: Jimmy Nesbitt
Book Designer: Wu Yanfeng
Translator: Hou Sheng

First published in the United Kingdom in 2017 by CYPI PRESS

Add: 79 College Road, Harrow Middlesex, HA1 1BD, UK
Tel: +44 (0) 20 3178 7279
E-mail: sales@cypi.net editor@cypi.net
Website: www.cypi.net
ISBN: 978-1-908175-34-2
Printed in China